OUR KNOWLEDGE OF THE LAW

In the long-standing debate between positivism and non-positivism, legal validity has always been a subject of controversy. While positivists deny that moral values play any role in the determination of legal validity, non-positivists affirm the opposite thesis.

In departing from this narrow point of view, the book focusses on the notion of legal knowledge. Apart from what one takes to constitute the grounds of legal validity, there is a more fundamental issue about cognitive validity: how do we acquire knowledge of whatever is assumed to constitute the elements of legal validity? When the question is posed in this form, a fundamental shift takes place. Given that knowledge is a philosophical concept, for anything to constitute an adequate ground for legal validity, it must satisfy the standards set by knowledge. In exploring those standards, the author argues that knowledge is the outcome of an activity of judging, which is constrained by reasons (reflexive). While these reasons may vary with the domain of judging, the reflexive structure of the practice of judging imposes certain constraints on what can constitute a reason for judging. Amongst these constraints are found not only general metaphysical limitations but also the fundamental principle that one with the capacity to judge is autonomous or, in other words, capable of determining the reasons that form the basis of action. One sees, as soon as autonomy has been introduced into the parameters of knowledge, that law is necessarily connected with every other practical domain.

It is demonstrated, in the end, that the issue of knowledge is orthogonal to questions about the inclusion or exclusion of morality, for what really matters is whether the putative grounds of legal validity are appropriate to the generation of knowledge. The outcome is far more integral than much work in current theory: neither an absolute deference to either universal moral standards or practice-independent values nor a complete adherence to conventionality and institutional arrangements will do. In suggesting that the current positivism versus non-positivism debate, when it comes to determining law's nature, misses the crux of the matter, the book aims to provoke a fertile new debate in legal theory.

Our Knowledge of the Law

Objectivity and Practice in Legal Theory

George Pavlakos

·HART·
PUBLISHING

OXFORD AND PORTLAND, OREGON
2007

Published in North America (US and Canada) by
Hart Publishing
c/o International Specialized Book Services
920 NE 58th Avenue, Suite 300
Portland, OR 97213-3786
USA
Tel: +1 503 287 3093 or toll-free: (1) 800 944 6190
Fax: +1 503 280 8832
E-mail: orders@isbs.com
Website: www.isbs.com

Hart Publishing, 16C Worcester Place, OX1 2JW
Telephone: +44 (0)1865 517530 Fax: +44 (0)1865 510710
E-mail: mail@hartpub.co.uk
Website: http://www.hartpub.co.uk

British Library Cataloguing in Publication Data
Data Available

ISBN-13: 978-1-84113-503-8 (hardback)

Typeset by Columns Design Limited, Caversham
Printed and bound in Great Britain by
Lightning Source UK Ltd

Στους γονείς μου Ιωάννη και Ανδρονίκη

Acknowledgements

This book started as an improved version of my PhD thesis. There is little of the original thesis, however, that has found its way into the final outcome. The decision to write what is, more or less, a different book has been a slow process, and took shape during the comforting 18 months of a generous Alexander von Humboldt Foundation fellowship, which was spent at the Christian-Albrechts-Universität zu Kiel. During this time, Robert Alexy has been a wonderful host in every aspect but, above anything else, as a most thought-provoking discussant of many of the ideas of the book. I can only hope that I have done justice to the quality of his suggestions and criticisms.

During the long time it took to complete the book I was fortunate to benefit from a number of thoughtful remarks. Neil MacCormick read the whole book for Hart Publishing and commented on many points. Without his insightful comments and wise advice the writing of the book as well as its contents would have been a much poorer endeavour. Amongst those who read parts of the manuscript are Carsten Heidemann, Sean Coyle, Stefano Bertea, Dimitrios Kyritsis, Veronica Rodriguez-Blanco, Bartosz Brożek, Emilios Christodoulidis, Nicos Stavropoulos and Timothy Williamson. I thank them all for their comments, while undertaking full responsibility for any remaining errors. A number of other friends and colleagues helped through discussions and exchange on many of the topics of the book, either in public events, or private conversations, or both: I am indebted to Andreas Takis, Philippos Vassiloyannis, Emmanuel Melissaris, Robin Hickey, Rory O'Connell, Jonathan Gorman, Stanley Paulson, Siobhán Mullaly, Gordon Anthony, Giovanni Sartor, Koen de Feyter, Nino Rotolo, Corrado Roversi and Carsten Bäcker. Also I would like to extend my gratitude to audiences in Granada, Bologna, the Cornell Law School, Kiel, Leicester, Aberystwyth, Belfast, Prague and Ripatransone, where different parts of the book were presented over the past few years.

A few other people and institutions have decisively supported the project in a number of ways: the Queen's Law School has put a lot of faith in me by generously extending my sabbatical leave; Richard Hart has continued believing in me even when I had violated every deadline we had agreed on; the Heidemanns (Carsten, Susanne (Bracker) and Jacob), through their selfless and warm hospitality in Kiel during the difficult final months of the writing; the Zinsstags (Evelyne and Georges), by putting up with sudden disappearances from family tables, when I absolutely had to make note of some argument; Panos Koutrakos, Alexandra Xanthaki and Aristotle Kallis for their love and support over all those years. My wife, Estelle Zinsstag has, through her love and generosity, adorned my life in so many ways that it would take much more than words to thank her. The completion of this book is only a very tiny proof of the benefits of her presence in my life. Finally, I would like to dedicate this book to my parents Ioannis and Androniki without whom not.

An earlier version of Chapter 5 has appeared as G Pavlakos, 'Law as Recognition: H L A Hart and Analytical Positivism' in T Murphy (ed), *Western Jurisprudence* (Dublin, Round Hall, 2004). I wish to acknowledge the kind permission of the publisher to reprint the relevant portions.

Contents

Introduction

If the formation of concepts can be explained by facts of nature, should we be interested, not in grammar, but rather in that in nature which is the basis of grammar? . . . But our interest does not fall back upon these possible causes of the formation of concepts; we are not doing natural science, nor yet natural history—since we can also invent fictitious natural history for our purposes.[1]

It makes no sense to try to observe the world to discover whether or not it obeys some given logical law. Reality cannot be said to obey a law of logic.[2]

The Problem

THIS IS A book about our knowledge of the law. To deny such knowledge one need not reject all knowledge. Instead, one could assert that it is possible to know a great deal about a lot of things, as for instance the fact that one has five fingers in each hand or that (s)he had had eggs for breakfast or that Kiel is the capital of Schleswig-Holstein, and yet fail to know anything that is specifically legal. Indeed, of those who think and write philosophically about the law, there is hardly anyone who would quarrel over our general ability for knowledge. What some question is that there is anything that is *specifically* legal to be known. Such sceptics about the law usually claim that there exist no such things as legal standards which determine our behaviour, but only certain fictions or mental constructs that are caused by an array of social, economic, psychological or even biological factors, which actually are at work. The rest is all ideology and, perhaps, the cunning of lawyers who strive to bestow a certain allure on their profession. Of course, such critics would be happy to concede, it is possible to study those factors and explain the genesis of legal fictions: the type of knowledge, however, one would obtain through their study, far from being legal, would concern facts about the non-normative phenomena that legal language covers up, phenomena that would better be studied by the appropriate social or natural science they fall under. Contrapositively, legal knowledge would require that there exist the kinds of entities ordinary legal discourse refers to: rules, principles, rights, contracts, claimants, treaties and so on.

[1] L Wittgenstein, *Philosophical Investigations*, 3rd edn (Oxford, Blackwell, 2001) 195.

[2] M Dummett, *The Logical Basis of Metaphysics* (London, Duckworth, 1991) 1–2.

What would it take, then, to argue against the sceptical assumption in order to uphold the idea of legal knowledge? Fortunately, considering the restricted ambit of legal scepticism, no general proof of existence of the external world is needed! Be that as it may, arguing for the existence of a distinct realm of legal facts may turn out to be equally hard. Standardly, accounts of knowledge presuppose some notion of *objectivity* as a minimum requirement for knowledge. Objectivity with respect to a domain of facts requires that there be facts which exist independently of what we happen to think on any particular occasion. This makes room for the idea that what we believe to be the case might turn out to be false or be otherwise. On the face of it, arguing for the idea of objectivity involves an argument for the existence of some kind of distance between our thoughts and that which is depicted by them. It follows that the foremost task of a complete account of knowledge is to explain the nature of that distance. In the case of law, as in other domains that purport to regulate action, there is the additional issue of normativity that needs to be accommodated: legal facts need to account for the obligatory character of law, which manifests itself in the complex network of rights and duties that pertain to legal subjects within an institutional legal order. Somewhat simplifying, normativity or the obligating character of legal facts consists in their ability to function as motivating reasons for action,[3] as opposed to mere causes that prompt physical movement. This distinct normative quality, which sets apart normative from non-normative facts, is a salient characteristic of the legal realm, which needs to inform the account of objectivity and knowledge in the legal realm.

The Practice Theory of Law

In this book I argue for an account of legal knowledge I call the Practice Theory of Law (for short PTL). Succinctly put, PTL argues that legal facts can be known objectively, if we conceive of legal practice as a normative activity of making assertions (judging). On one hand, the property of normativity generates standards which 'guide' practice. The ability to judge, on the other, makes it possible to refer to legal facts through well-formed sentences. Combine the two conditions and what you get is the possibility to make reference to legal facts through sentences whose truth can be grounded by adducing objective standards. In advancing the Practice Theory of Law, the book is putting forward only indirectly a defence of the possibility of legal knowledge. A direct defence of that possibility would require that one engage in detail with the various sceptical or reductive[4]

[3] H L A Hart has shown the function of legal standards as reasons for action in his combined discussion of what distinguishes legal rules from habits *and* orders backed by a threat. See his *Concept of Law* 2nd edn (Oxford, Clarendon Press, 1994) chs 2 and 4.

[4] I undertake a thorough discussion of the issue of reduction in legal theory in ch II of my *Rechtsontologie und praktische Vernunft* (Baden-Baden, Nomos, 2007).

accounts of law, which have been proposed over the years, and attempt to rebut their arguments to the full. Conversely, the indirect defence purports to buttress the possibility of legal knowledge by engaging in dialogue with other existing cognitivist legal theories. Despite having identified the ingredients for legal knowledge correctly, such theories have failed, or so I argue, to defend its possibility fully. Thus, although cognitivist legal theories agree on the central role of practice for legal knowledge, the accounts of practice those have tendered are inappropriate for arriving at knowledge. This would explain perhaps why legal scepticism has, in recent years, regained its momentum with some versions of socio-legal or other reductive accounts claiming exclusivity in the area of legal theory.[5] In this light the purpose of PTL is to assess the possibility of legal knowledge by offering a fresh account of objectivity and practice. If the account of PTL is sound, then the book will have also defended legal knowledge against sceptical accounts. However that defence will merely be indirect; for it will have emerged from a contrapuntal dialogue with other cognitivist views, rather than a direct rebuttal of the sceptical premises.

In engaging in dialogue with other cognitivist legal theories I distinguish between two different types of such theory: conventionalist ones and essentialist ones. While the former comprise most versions of contemporary analytical positivism, the latter include any such views that conceive of conditions of objectivity in a practice-independent manner. Here I include interpretivism as well as natural law theories. Both accounts are accused of failing to reconstruct legal practice so as to offer the possibility to depict objective legal facts.

First, legal conventionalism: according to it normative standards, including legal, are constituted by a social practice under the supposition that what constitutes a valid normative standard is exhausted by what the community decrees to be a standard. To the threat of relativism, arising from the absence of any distance between what is the case and what the community takes it to be the case, analytical positivism responds by reverting to an 'objective' external point of view, one that allows an observer to describe the legal standards of a community by referring to the facts of the practice that generate those standards. Standardly such facts are conceived of as pertaining to the various instances of use of legal expressions by legal practitioners. Instances of use function as a compass for locating non-normative, neutral facts which effect the *recognition* of legal standards, without requiring the observer to appreciate the content of the standards themselves. Subtle as it may be, this manoeuvre ends up blurring the boundaries between the analytical and some other reductive account, for non-normative

[5] The reader should be made aware that the present work does not reject socio-legal or reductive accounts *tout court*. Those accounts are, as I note in the conclusion, extremely valuable for what they actually offer: a causal analysis of the empirical aspects of legal phenomena. However, they almost become imperialistic, when they claim that there is nothing to say about the law, other than what they do. For a representative version of this kind of claim, see P Leith and J Morison, 'Can Jurisprudence without Empiricism ever be a Science?' in S Coyle and G Pavlakos (eds), *Jurisprudence or Legal Science?* (Oxford and Portland, Hart Publishing, 2005) 147.

facts of recognition, identifiable through the use of legal language, cannot account for the substantive beliefs of a community in respect of what is and is not normatively required. However, according to analytical positivism, it should be beliefs of the latter sort that bring about law's normativity.[6]

Second, legal essentialism: any theory that takes the truth of legal propositions to rest on grounds that are conceptually prior to and independent of legal practice, may be classified under the essentialist strand.[7] Essentialist accounts attempt to account for objectivity by trading on the idea of a realm of value that exists independently of our thoughts or practices. This realm is supposed to comprise evaluative entities which are *sui generis* in that they have some kind of to-be-doneness inscribed in them.[8] In this context, legal properties are alleged to derive their normative authority from moral and ethical properties in virtue of being sub-species thereof. Granted the existence of a special realm of value, legal concepts acquire their meaning not through practices of use but, instead, from a one-to-one correspondence with the properties they depict. This rigid or inflexible relation between concept and property renders practice secondary in importance, in that it serves merely the purpose of 'discovering' what legal concepts mean anyway, that is, irrespective of their employment in communication. Despite cutting the Gordian knot in a spectacular way this view is extremely problematic, for it requires that one buy into a metaphysical package which is rather extravagant, not the least so because it suggests that we be equipped with some sort of special sixth sense which is suitable in registering normative properties.[9]

The Philosophy of Pragmatic Rationalism

In order to avoid the pitfalls of those two theories, ultimately with an eye to offering a firm underpinning of legal knowledge, the book looks into their philosophical presuppositions and replaces them with a fresh philosophical account of practice as a source of objectivity, which I label *pragmatic rationalism*.[10] The road to pragmatic rationalism passes through a detailed critique of the philosophical assumptions behind conventionalism and essentialism. It is argued that both views, in resting on a flawed understanding of our cognitive practices, conceive of objectivity in a manner that effects a gap between criteria of knowledge and the domain knowledge purports to be about. No sooner has the gap arisen, than indeterminacy and scepticism threaten to undermine knowledge.

[6] See Chapter 5.
[7] See Chapter 6.
[8] This is the accusation that Mackie levels against realist theories of value and morality. See J Mackie, *Ethics: Inventing Right and Wrong* (Harmondsworth, Penguin Books, 1990) ch 1, 38–42.
[9] *Ibid.*
[10] See Chapter 4.

Conventionalism, in its wider philosophical outlook, is the view that meaning and conceptual content depend on the mere fact of convergence of the behaviour of those who partake of the practice.[11] Typical for this conception is the construction of formulas of validity, which are assumed to collect conditions for the obtaining of the required convergence. Such formulas cannot explain practice as a constrained activity, comprising actions that are performed for a reason but, instead, leave it open to an array of conflicting interpretations, which fail to identify what the practice is about. As a result, any assertion of truth or existence of the propositions uttered in the practice falls prey to a regress of interpretations and remains indeterminate. Insofar as the existence of any fact is asserted through true propositions, it is here impossible to ground in an objective manner the existence of those facts the practice purports to be about. Conversely, in essentialism, the gap between conditions of knowledge and practice arises from the existence of a distant realm, which can be accessed independently of the practice of cognition[12] itself. The strong requirement of objectivity as the radical distance between what is performed in the practice and what is really the case in the realm of essences, amounts anew to an inability to determine grounds of truth for the propositions put forward in the practice. Such inability implies indeterminacy by sparking the deep worry that our thought and action might consistently fail to track the realm of reality.

Contrapositively, the philosophy of pragmatic rationalism effects a cognitivist account of legal facts by reconstructing practice as a normative activity that can supply objective grounds for the truth of propositions. The line of argument leading to this conclusion is rather long and will occupy the first half of the book. The first step is to undercut the crude conception of objectivity as *distance* between thought and environment, for such a view undermines knowledge at the grass-roots level. In its place a more level-headed explication of objectivity will be advanced, by taking stock with recent discussions in the philosophies of mind and language. This will result in the thesis that the issue of distance between thoughts and their object, considered by many a prerequisite of objectivity and knowledge, is less basic than an issue of intelligibility arising with respect to what entities exist and can potentially be known.[13] Intelligibility is antecedent to distance in that it is not possible to even ask which entities exist, unless we already know what *kinds* of entities our thoughts are capable of connecting to.

[11] See section 3.3.2.

[12] A clarification must be added here: essentialism's epistemic component is intuitionism, or the view that we can 'grasp' essences independently of any practice of reasoning. In this sense, intuitionism can also be thought of as a practice of cognition that is alternative to practices involving inferential reasoning, defeating thus my claim for a gap between practice and cognitive domain. There are good grounds for rejecting this view, however: Intuitionism, as a method for achieving knowledge, rests on the assumption that the standards of knowledge are practice-independent. As such it can only trivially be called a 'practice'. See also the more detailed discussions in Chapters 1 and 6. Many thanks to Neil MacCormick who raised this point.

[13] See Chapter 1.

Failure to address the latter question would deny the correlation between mind and world, a correlation that is essential in bringing about knowledge by bridging the distance between our thoughts and their referents. To put it bluntly, anything whose existence is conceived of independently of the boundaries of thought will remain radically elusive, thus escaping for ever our capacity to acquire knowledge of it.

Turning to what determines intelligibility we need to consider the structure of the linguistic units (sentences) that express our thoughts (*structure of thought*). The structure of thought may be represented by a network of rules, a grammar,[14] which, in specifying the conditions of a well-formed sentence, facilitates our arranging our thoughts in a manner that makes them assertoric, in other words suitable for tracking the world. In this way thought becomes conducive to knowledge by demarcating existence and reference through a grammar that indicates which kinds of entities can possibly exist and be 'discovered'. That said, grammar does not exhaust the issue of knowledge. Despite the a priori character of rules of syntax and semantics, both of which are essential components of grammar, what may *intelligibly* exist does not yet exhaust what *actually* exists (and, hence, can be known), for the latter requires to be 'discovered' through our transactions with concrete situations, albeit ones that stand a serious chance of connecting to our thoughts rather than being elusive. Insofar as this is the case, it is possible, by resting on the idea of grammar, to uphold the valuable idea of intelligibility which supports the link between mind and world, without giving up the initial intuition of objectivity as regards the relative distance between what we think and what actually is the case.

The ability of grammar to preserve, alongside intelligibility, knowledge is guaranteed by a move that is distinctive of the project of pragmatic rationalism. This move purports to link grammar to the various cognitive domains in a manner that ensures the amount of flexibility necessary for accommodating error, correction and improvement (all three being essential for knowledge). This is guaranteed when rules of grammar are looked at in the perspective of a practice.[15] On a static conception, rules of grammar serve the narrow purpose of specifying conditions under which a sentence would count as one that is well-formed. Conversely, when viewed as a practice, rules of grammar become responsive to the facts of a particular domain, which function as grounds/reasons

[14] I use 'grammar' more or less along the lines of the tradition Wittgenstein's work has established. Despite associating grammar with logic in the early stages of his work, Wittgenstein came over the years to regard grammar as a more flexible and elusive network of rules that determine what move is allowed as making sense, and what is not, within a cognitive practice that is linguistically structured. For a more detailed discussion of the content of grammar see Chapters 1 and 2. For a succinct exposition of the place grammar occupies in Wittgenstein's work, as well as its relation with other philosophical traditions, see A Biletzki and A Matar, 'Ludwig Wittgenstein' in E Zalta (ed), *The Stanford Encyclopaedia of Philosophy*, Summer 2005 edn, available at http://plato.stanford.edu/archives/sum2005/entries/wittgenstein/.

[15] See Chapters 3 and 4.

for the truth of sentences. Here, forming a sentence, far from being a static conceptual exercise, becomes a reflexive activity that can accommodate error, correction and improvement in the light of the reasons adduced in the domain. Within such a practice of judging, a sentence may count as well-formed, not just by complying with the structural-logical rules of grammar, but also with such pragmatic rules as reflecting the special purposes of the practice and, through them, drawing attention to those facts that may function as grounds for knowledge. (That said, such facts, lest they become unintelligible, need to comply with the general ontological categories specified by the static elements of grammar.)

For the completion of this move it is necessary to extend grammar to include a class of pragmatic rules, namely rules that reflect the particular context within which sentences are employed. Such rules refer to the specific purposes enshrined in particular contexts of use corresponding to the various cognitive domains (law, physics, morality, ethics, history and so on). In this regard, there are two levels of pragmatic rules to be taken into account: on the one hand, there are general rules of *judging simpliciter*,[16] whose purpose consists in ensuring knowledge and justification *in abstracto*. Such rules ensure that a fundamental interest in knowledge through a practice of judging be inscribed in grammar.[17] Pragmatic rules of such degree of abstraction may sit well alongside the a priori rules of syntax and semantics, which constitute grammar on a more traditional understanding. On the other hand, there are rules of *judging in a domain*.[18] Such rules have a more particular outlook which connects to the purposes ascribed to specific cognitive domains; as a result, it is likely that pragmatic rules vary strongly between the various domains (law, morality, politics, physics and so on). Such rules, far from enjoying a priori status, are intertwined with the facts of the relevant domain and may be disclosed in the particular context of judging.

An understanding of grammar in terms of a cognitive practice that is answerable to domain specific reasons makes grammar normative in a sense that is of special significance for law. In being capable of handling reasons in an abstract manner, agents who partake of the activity of grammar may be deemed rational. The capacity to be rational bestows on those agents autonomy, consisting in the freedom to exercise discretion in the application of rules.[19] The issue of autonomy can be tackled from many a direction. Here, of particular importance is the *moral* meaning of autonomy. This amounts from the ability of rational (judging) agents to handle evaluative reasons. Resting on a well-known argument by Christine Korsgaard, I shall argue that the ability to handle evaluative reasons renders judging subjects the source of all value.[20] This entails that judging

[16] See section 4.3.1.

[17] Such rules have been deemed by Apel and Habermas to constitute the transcendental-pragmatic conditions of communication, see section 7.5.1.

[18] See section 4.3.2.

[19] See section 4.4; also section 7.6.3.

[20] See section 4.4.3.

subjects are bestowed with inherent value or, to use the Kantian jargon, they become ends-in-themselves. This inherent value ranges over and above the particular evaluative reasons that may be found in the various discrete normative domains (law, ethics and morality). Although such reasons may be tied down to particular contexts (cultural, political and so on) and also may stand in conflict with one another (legal versus moral and ethical values), the reflexive capacity to appreciate and handle such reasons is elevated to a distinct and self-standing value which may claim universal validity, at least to the extent that the activity of judging is universal in its own right. Owing to its overarching character the value of autonomy compels for a coherent account of value within the various normative domains. Coherence is postulated with an eye to guaranteeing the unity of judgement and agency of judging subjects, one that is further linked to their identity as persons. As a by-product of the postulate for unity, legal reasons become necessarily connected with moral and other practical reasons, to the extent that all of them purport to demarcate the autonomy of rational agents or, what is to say the same, their status as persons. In this respect, I shall subscribe to a modified version of Robert Alexy's special case thesis.[21]

Before turning to lay out the structure of the book, it should be clearly pointed out that this is a book about foundations of legal knowledge and as such it goes little into more special debates on the nature of law such as occupy most of analytical legal theory writing today. As a consequence, a lot of what may seem important when it comes to evaluate the contribution of different scholars and their theories within the narrower field of jurisprudence is here of secondary concern. If, that is, certain positivists insist that their view is fundamentally different from the conventionalism of classical positivism (its most prominent expression being to this day the work of H L A Hart), their objection would be almost too fine-grained to target the present project. Far from being interested in the refinement of conventionalist views—in which case the objection would be valid—the present work aims at a clarification of the conditions of legal knowledge. In this light, the various versions and refinements of conventionalism, otherwise of considerable weight in any debate on legal conventions, make little or no difference concerning the relationship of conventions to the possibility of knowledge. In this respect Hart's conventionalism will be used instead of any of the many sophisticated versions of contemporary positivism[22] with an eye to illustrating the problems of conventionalism.

The same is the case with all essentialisms as regards legal normativity. There, what is of importance with respect to the discussion of knowledge is the fact that

[21] See section 7.6.2.

[22] Lest the impression arise that every positivist theory is an instance of conventionalism, the reader should be reminded of the existence of other versions of positivism. Most prominent amongst them in the modern history of ideas has been the normative positivism of Hans Kelsen. His theory is cordoned off from the present project, for its failure to amount to legal knowledge derives from idiosyncratic reasons which need to be taken up separately.

grounds of knowledge are conceived independently of legal practice. As far as this constitutes the main feature of essentialism, it justifies a wholesale treatment of the various forms this may take. However, in this work, I have chosen to take Ronald Dworkin's interpretive theory of law or interpretivism[23] as a study case of essentialism. The reason for this choice is that interpretivism is that amongst essentialist theories which fails in the most interesting way. While standard essentialist views, those that are usually associated with natural law, fail at an early stage, as a result of their disregard for the importance of practice, interpretivism still recognises the importance of practice for a cognitivist account of law. Things become more complicated when, despite having acknowledged the centrality of practice, interpretivism turns to specify practice-independent grounds of knowledge. The *lapsus* is committed in a more subtle manner: in spite of proclaiming the importance of legal practice for the cognition of standards of truth for legal propositions, interpretivism takes those standards to be conceptually prior and independent with respect to practice[24]; almost as if practice were merely a medium for getting hold of some profound, practice-independent notion of truth and knowledge. This seems to me to be the position that is forced on Ronald Dworkin, when he opts for a realist explication of grounds of truth for legal propositions,[25] notwithstanding his recent denials[26] that his is an essentialist jurisprudence. Of course this is not a problem for Dworkin only. There are a few other distinguished philosophers calling themselves realists who share the view about the importance of practice but who, before the fear of being accused of some form of practice-relativism, rush in at the last moment to supplement their account with the one or the other essentialist tenor.[27]

I shall say a final word about the general philosophical background of the work. As regards the views on knowledge propounded in it, it comes extremely close to being a form of transcendental idealism. I choose this cautious formulation, because there is obviously a lot in it that diverges from Kant's original philosophy, not the least so with regard to the extensive references to ideas that are typical of the linguistic turn, the philosophical movement that followed Kant almost by two centuries. What, however, remains Kantian is a firm interest in conditions of knowledge which extend beyond contingent or random occurrences, such as habitual or conventional facts. Such conditions focus on a notion of validity of (normative) propositions which aims to transcend what just

[23] See N Stavropoulos, 'Interpretivist Theories of Law' in N Zalta (ed), *The Stanford Encyclopedia of Philosophy* Winter 2003 edn, available at http://plato.stanford.edu/archives/win2003/entries/law-interpretivist/.

[24] For the relation of conceptual priority and dependence between standards of knowledge and a cognitive domain see section 3.6.1. And in the context of interpretivism, see section 6.4.

[25] See his classic defence of realism in legal theory in R Dworkin, 'Objectivity and Truth: You'd Better Believe It' in (1996) 25 *Philosophy and Public Affairs* 87.

[26] See his 'Introduction' and 'The Concepts of Law' in R Dworkin, *Justice in Robes* (Cambridge Mass, Harvard University Press, 2006).

[27] Such prominent philosophers include Donald Davidson and Susan Hurley, see section 3.6.1.

happened to be the case. In contrast to Kant, this notion of validity is not cast in terms of a transcendental philosophy of consciousness but by reference to a conceptual scheme that constrains our practices of judging in a variety of contexts (law being just one of them). The conceptual scheme can be stated within the semantic structures of language (grammar). While grammar incorporates certain a priori, logical elements that present the idea of validity and knowledge as non-contingent, it still leaves a lot of room for refinement and discovery, for there are still infinite ways to cast the conceptual scheme depending on the practices we engage in. Even then, however, every particular practice and the reasons it supplies must stand under the general constraints of the most general practice our conceptual scheme demarcates: the practice of regarding something as an object or, what is to say the same, the practice of judging. Insofar as those views constitute the philosophical background of the book, PTL can be conceived of as an instance of legal idealism![28]

Plan of the Book

Part One of the book attempts to develop a general philosophical framework for an account of law's knowledge. Chapter 1 undertakes some major clarifications of the relationship between objectivity and knowledge. Most agree that objectivity, as a condition of knowledge, requires a distance between what we believe and what we can know. The chapter warns against an exaggeration of this distance and suggests that knowledge be subjected to a constraint of *intelligibility*. Chapter 2 undertakes to develop the idea of intelligibility. Intelligibility is linked to a conceptual scheme (grammar) which ensures that anything that can be known may be reported within the semantic structure of language (the 'semantics exhausts ontology' thesis). Chapter 3 deals with problems arising from a too-rigid conception of grammar. Such a conception of grammar would reduce knowledge to a static state, one that does not allow for the possibility of error. To avoid this, it needs to be supplemented with a dynamic aspect. In introducing the latter the chapter follows a pragmatic reading of Ludwig Wittgenstein's *Philosophical*

[28] With all due respect to a very good friend and colleague (who, incidentally, has contributed a lot to the refinement of many of the ideas exposed in the course of this work), I profoundly disagree with the way Sean Coyle coins idealism in a series of recent papers and talks (most prominent amongst them S Coyle, 'Positivism, Idealism and the Rule of Law' in (2006) 26 *Oxford Journal of Legal Studies* 257). Coyle uses 'idealism' to denote the dedication or attachment some legal theories demonstrate vis-à-vis some central moral ideal. I think the term idealism is orthogonal to the distinction he introduces between idealist and non-idealist legal theory, in that it refers to a metaphysical view of modesty that may be applied to moral ideals as much as to tables, conventions and anything else that can be the object of intentional activity. To that extent, it seems to me, one can be an idealist without subscribing to any single ideal or ultimate point of view and vice versa. After all, we should not forget that Kant used idealism precisely in order to move away from a centralist conception of knowledge, which uncritically assumed the existence of a given essence (the so-called *Ding an sich*), and, instead, to subject all knowledge to critical scrutiny.

Investigations and proposes that grammar be conceived of as a *practice* of judgement formation. Chapter 4 is aimed at a fresh explication of practice as a condition of knowledge, in the light of the discussion in chapters 2 and 3. This explication, dubbed *pragmatic rationalism*, argues that, for them to deliver knowledge, cognitive practices must be constrained by the appropriate kind of reasons. In unpacking the notion of reasons, pragmatic rationalism takes cognitive practices to comprise two levels: on the one hand general conditions of judging, such as indicating the need to refer to reasons within the domain we judge. On the other, domain-specific conditions enshrined in such reasons as arising within each and every particular context of cognition. While the general need to refer to reasons gives rise, as it were, to a formal constraint of knowledge, domain-specific reasons prescribe substantive constraints, with respect to particular cognitive practices. Besides circumscribing general formal constraints, however, the need to refer to reasons—as an inherent characteristic of judging—points, further, to a notion of autonomy with regard to subjects of judging. It will be argued that anyone who is capable of partaking of a practice of judging that is responsive to reasons (reflexive) is autonomous in a minimal sense. To that extent, the ability to partake of a reflexive practice is the most basic characteristic of persons.

Part Two transfers the results of the discussion of part one to the domain of law. Chapter 5 deals with the problems of conventionalism. The focus of the chapter is Hart's theory of law. Against the background of that theory the chapter argues that conventionalist legal theory is incapable of underpinning legal knowledge, for it fails to conceive legal practice as being subjected to such constraints as are required for arriving at knowledge of the law. Chapter 6 deals with essentialism and its eventual failure to account for legal knowledge. The case study here is interpretivism. Interpretivism is shown to reduce the importance of practice for legal knowledge, by reducing truth and knowledge of propositions of law to grounds/reasons that are conceptually independent of and prior to legal practice. By contrast to conventionalist and interpretivist accounts, Chapter 7 proposes the Practice Theory of Law. This implements the lessons of pragmatic rationalism in the area of legal theory. It argues that legal practice, in order to fulfil its cognitive requirements, in other words to generate knowledge about the law, must be conceived of as one that is constrained by reasons. Such reasons are domain-specific with respect to law, but need also to be in agreement with the minimal amount of autonomy, which the general capacity to judge bestows on persons. Subjecting reasons or grounds for legal knowledge to the scrutiny of the minimalist notion of autonomy, the one enshrined in the capacity of persons to judge, gives effect to a communication between the various domains of practical reason (ie morality, ethics and law). As a result, instead of being disjoined from one another, moral, ethical and legal reasons must stand in a coherent relation which ensures that the capacity of persons to judge in any practical domain be upheld. To that extent law is upgraded to one amongst other cases of practical reason.

Part One

The Grounds of Knowledge

1

Knowledge and Objectivity

1.1 Introduction

THE CHAPTER DEMONSTRATES the relation between objectivity and knowledge and then warns against a misconception with respect to objectivity. The misconception threatens to undermine knowledge by fanning scepticism. In an attempt to disable the misconception, an alternative understanding of objectivity is advanced, one that safeguards knowledge. The rest of the book is more or less an effort to make this idea of objectivity work.

The relation between objectivity and knowledge is explored in the first part. Knowledge requires that we do not always get things right; for if we were infallible there would be no distinction between knowing and merely believing something. Conversely, knowledge presupposes that things be what they are irrespective of what we think of them. This, in turn, assumes that things are the way they are irrespective of our ability to grasp them. To put it differently, knowledge rests on the possibility that there are objective facts which, on occasion, might elude us. This idea of objectivity can be illustrated as the asymmetry or the distance between believing that X and knowing that X. It is in this sense that knowledge requires objectivity. Yet, objectivity so conceived may give rise to a misunderstanding: namely that, for knowledge to be possible, a radical separation between thought and environment (the world)[1] is required. On this view, objectivity can materialise only if what is in the head can be conceived of independently of what the environment contains, and vice versa. It is only then, the story goes, that it is possible to distinguish between mere belief and knowledge. In the history of Western philosophy this misunderstanding has survived in the two main philosophical traditions which have attempted to explain knowledge.

[1] I take an expansive view on what can constitute part of the environment. In particular, I consider anything that can be depicted by the referential structure of the assertive sentence as being potentially a constituent of the environment. Thus, not only concrete objects, such as trees, bottles and other living organisms, but also numbers, norms and facts belong to the class of entities constituting the environment. Such an expansive understanding of constituents of the environment is facilitated by the semantic explication of ontology I put forward in Chapter 2.

The first is *mentalism* or *representationalism*, which is taken up in section 1.3.1 This is the idea that the environment is conveyed to our minds through mental representations: our thoughts correspond to certain mental images which, depending on a number of factors, may be good or bad representations of the environment. Good representations are those that manage to bridge the mind-world gap, thus amounting to knowledge; while those that fail to do so are flawed and fail to amount to knowledge. By retaining the mind-world gap representationalism manages to illustrate the possibility of error as a key ingredient of objectivity. Alas, the same gap that purports to illustrate the possibility of knowledge is bound to undermine it, for once the gap has been put in place nothing guarantees that we can bridge it. Yet, failure to do so gives rise to indeterminacy of thought and, ultimately, scepticism (which lies in the antipodes of knowledge).

Things are not much different with respect to the rival account put forward by the other philosophical tradition, *referential realism*. As section 1.3.2 argues, referential realism fails to shake off the mind-world dualism and the suspicion of scepticism lurking in it. Notably, some contemporary versions of referential realism have directed a devastating critique at mental representations, only to end up widening the gap between thought and environment. In an attempt to ground objectivity firmly, such views have argued that the contents of our thoughts are directly shaped by the environment. Insofar as the latter constitutes an objective (mind-independent) realm it is possible, the argument goes, that we are unaware of the contents of our thoughts! Despite an ability to demonstrate the meaning of objectivity in an emphatic manner, such views offer a new impetus to sceptical speculation. If knowledge is construed independently of our ability to contemplate it, then it becomes unattainable. What is more, if our thoughts are individuated by an environment which systematically fails to be known, we end up losing hold not only of that environment but also of our minds, as Donald Davidson has very eloquently pointed out.[2]

In contradistinction to elusiveness and scepticism, I suggest that objectivity (and knowledge) be subjected to a condition of *intelligibility*: any account of error and correction, as essential elements of knowledge, needs to safeguard first-person authority, ie the ability of persons to know the contents of their minds at any given time. We need, as a result, a device which combines the following two tasks: on the one hand, it accounts for the possibility of error; on the other, it guarantees that such error can be clarified and corrected without resorting to an unknowable reality. In alluding to such a device, I argue that it has to be understood as a conceptual substratum or scheme outside of which it is not possible to have thoughts about anything. This substratum I shall call grammar (section 1.4).

[2] D Davidson, 'Knowing One's Own Mind' in D Davidson *Subjective, Intersubjective, Objective* (Oxford, Clarendon Press, 2001) 22.

Grammar[3] guarantees that all human linguistic communication and all human thought that uses the medium of a language remain intelligible. Only sentences which are syntactically well-formed and use words in accordance with some understood scheme of semantics achieve intelligibility (not that every single grammatical lapse is always fatal for intelligibility). Syntax and semantics together make up grammar,[4] and every natural language used by humans contains these. Without them, there would be utterances perhaps, but not meaningful ones. Without grammar there is no possibility of intelligible and coherent human thought. Understood normatively, grammar sets constraints on how we can think anything, though not constraining what we can think within the domain of the intelligible. To that extent, a fundamental thesis of the present work is that human knowledge, in any domain in which people may seriously claim to have knowledge, and to be able to distinguish knowledge from error (mistaken beliefs), is wholly dependent on grammar in this sense. Grammar delivers knowledge because, in underwriting both mind and environment, it does not let the gap between those two take shape. Yet, in avoiding the gap it still confines thoughts within the province of minds, as opposed to locating them in a remote reality that is as impervious as to be unfathomable by minds.

This has important implications for the character of knowledge in and of law, as well as in other similar normative domains. In law, as much as in morality and ethics, there is a strong assumption that normative facts and states of affairs are intellectual constructs, hence that they are doomed to be subjective and circumstantial. However, grammar offers us the possibility to place such facts on the same footing with all other types of fact, for anything that can be inserted within the structure of grammar is as good a fact as anything else. Legal norms, considered as the paradigmatic case of a legal fact,[5] become in such a scheme perfect candidates for knowledge. In that respect, grammar provides the broadening of the ontological inventory of things that can be known that is necessary for legal knowledge. At the same time, it shows that there is a real distinction between true and false answers, which is of key importance for knowledge. Within grammar, legal norms can be depicted in the same way as any other fact without need to locate them in either of the ends of a dualist spectrum: the (subjective) corner of our minds—or the (objective) materiality of the natural environment.

[3] I am indebted to Neil MacCormick for having prompted me to introduce the idea of grammar in clearer terms, in this and the next paragraph. I am also grateful to him for some of the more successful formulations in those two paragraphs.

[4] As remarked in the Introduction, the notion of grammar I employ in this work follows, by and large, the tradition established by Ludwig Wittgenstein. For a concise discussion of Wittgenstein's idea of grammar see A Biletzki and A Matar, 'Ludwig Wittgenstein' in E Zalta (ed), *The Stanford Encyclopaedia of Philosophy*, Summer 2005 edn, available at http://plato.stanford.edu/archives/sum2005/entries/wittgenstein/; also section 1.4.

[5] The plausibility of this statement will not transpire until an analysis of legal precepts as normative facts in section 7.5.2.

1.2 Objectivity as Asymmetry

Objectivity can be understood in terms of the asymmetry between, on the one hand, beliefs about the facts of a domain and, on the other, knowledge of those facts. The asymmetry may be conceived of as the distance or the space that separates our thoughts from the domain in question. Such distance allows for the possibility of error: what we believe to be the case and what actually turns out to be the case may part company with one another.

In the domain of law, the asymmetry can be represented as one between what we believe the law to be in some case and what it actually is. Notwithstanding differences in accent, advocates of the possibility of legal knowledge often depart from an asymmetry with respect to the amount of information that different accounts of law contain (ie an asymmetry between accounts of law that are complete and others that are partial or incomplete). An early attempt to make this distinction is to be found in the opening pages of *The Concept of Law*. There, Herbert Hart pointed to the pressing need to offer a fresh account of the nature of law (or the concept of law) for earlier and contemporary legal theories had merely amounted to an incomplete or partial account of law's nature, upon which remark he set out to offer a full account of 'the concept of law'.[6] In pinpointing this asymmetry, Hart focussed on a foundational convention which could fully account for the validity (or existence) of legal norms.[7] Legal knowledge would then arise from the most complete possible description of this convention. The more detailed the description of the master convention of a legal system the more successful the amounting knowledge with respect to the valid rules of the legal system in question.

Not too long after that Ronald Dworkin advanced the view that the master convention behind a legal system cannot fully explain the difference in cognitive content between an account that amounts to legal knowledge and one that fails to identify the true grounds of propositions of law. A central argument in his reasoning builds around the fact of disagreement between lawyers. Dworkin argued that disagreement about the law survives the most complete description of the master convention of a legal system. Hence, he concluded, conventional grounds may not exhaust the issue of legal knowledge but, instead, there must be a deeper, more subtle source thereof, which is in need of identification. In

[6] See H L A Hart, *The Concept of Law*, 2nd edn (Oxford, Clarendon Press, 1994) 2.

[7] The view that norms are valid, rather than existent, has found in legal theory a more or less universal acceptance, especially in connection with the work of the Austrian legal philosopher Hans Kelsen. In developing his views on validity Kelsen draws on the so-called 'two-worlds' theory (*Zwei-Welten-Lehre*) proposed by his fellow neo-Kantian philosophers and in particular Heinrich Rickert: while world one comprises all physical and psychological entities, world two is the world of senses or meanings. For a more detailed discussion see S L Paulson, 'Der Normativismus Hans Kelsens' (2006) 11 *Juristenzeitung* 529. Also *idem*, 'Faktum/Wert-Distinktion, Zwei-Welten-Lehre und immanenter Sinn. Hans Kelsen als Neukantianer' in R Alexy *et al* (eds), *Neukantianismus und Rechtsphilosophie* (Baden-Baden, Nomos, 2002) 223–52.

elaborating on this point, some more years down the line, he explained the grounds of legal propositions as comprising principles of political morality in whose light the conventional arrangements in a legal system can be reconstructed in the best possible moral sense.[8]

More recently, in a powerful restatement of his Institutional Theory of Law,[9] Neil MacCormick, has argued that the grounds of legal knowledge are to be found in the existence of institutional facts. The existence of such facts is a complex event, comprising conventional as well as evaluative elements, which must carefully be weighed against each other before one can affirm the existence of a rule of law. While rejecting Hart's shallow account of the centrality of a master convention for legal knowledge, MacCormick also warns against the existence of an obligation to seek the best moral meaning of a legal system, as a condition of legal knowledge.

Despite such controversies, or perhaps precisely because of them, the concept of asymmetry seems to retain its momentum in an account of legal knowledge. For even philosophers with little in common other than a belief in the possibility of legal knowledge, appeal to standards that purport to distinguish between full and partial accounts of law. Let me try to demonstrate the meaning of asymmetry with a little more precision. Examples of asymmetry present the following sets of (true) judgements[10]: J1: 'homosexual masochistic activity Φ is *yuk*' and J2: 'homosexual masochistic activity Φ injured Y', to use a familiar example from the UK jurisdiction.[11] Or, to take the topical, albeit controversial subject of lesbian parenting, between J3: 'X is a militant lesbian' and J4: 'X has repeatedly mistreated the child' (the issue here is parental responsibility for lesbian parents). It is important to reiterate that all four judgements are assumed to be true. Be that as it may, the amount of information each of them conveys is not the same. Differences in information amount to some of them generating legal knowledge while others fail to do so.

The standard demonstration of the difference between true propositions that amount to knowledge and those which fail to do so is to be found in Edmund

[8] Dworkin's views are discussed in detail in Chapter 6.

[9] See N MacCormick, *Institutions of Law* (Oxford, Oxford University Press, 2007) ch 16.

[10] The term 'judgement' refers in this context to a sentence that is used assertively. I prefer it to Dworkin's term 'proposition' for it is less loaded, metaphysically speaking. Propositions are usually associated with Platonic entities that reside in a mind-independent realm, which exists outside any particular language (in Russell, for instance, the constituents of a proposition are the actual entities the proposition refers to). Despite being metaphysically loaded, however, the talk of propositions is a good way to illustrate the fact that meaning can be objective across a variety of languages and formulations. This valuable aspect can be retained, if one stipulates propositions to exist within the limits of sentences, hence to be language-dependent. Such a semantic explication of propositions dovetails with the broader semantic explication of ontological categories which I put forward in Chapter 2, and must be assumed whenever the term is employed in the book to report the views of the author.

[11] Here I allude to the infamous *R v Brown* case which decided that sadomasochistic homosexual activities between consenting adults constitute a criminal offence. For the facts and the ratio decidendi of the case see *R v Brown* [1994] 1 AC 212.

Gettier[12]: even if one has reasons to believe that p and p turns out to be true, one might still fail to know p. Jim works in the same office as John. It is the time of the year for promotions and the boss asks John to come and see her in her office. On his way out John takes £5 in pound coins to buy coffee and scones for Jim and himself. Given his evidence, Jim is perfectly justified in believing that 'the man who works in this office and has five £1 coins in his pocket will be promoted'. However, it turns out that the promotion goes not to John but to Jim who, unbeknown to him, had also five £1 coins in his pocket (suppose his pocket had a hole from which all other coins he thought he had slipped out). Jim's original belief still holds true. However its truth is not grounded on the facts that constitute his evidence but on a different fact that he ignores. Hence his belief is only randomly true and random truth is insufficient for knowledge.

Things are, of course, more complicated in the domain of law. Be that as it may, the main point holds *mutatis mutandis*: a legal theory that fails to pick the appropriate evidence falls short of generating knowledge regarding its subject matter (law's nature). This is not hard to imagine: a theory might take a proposition of law to be true on grounds that do not relate properly to the truth of the proposition, thus failing to generate legal knowledge (eg by arguing that proposition p is legal on the grounds that it is stated in a work by Shakespeare). Ordinary cases of failure of legal knowledge tend to be far less extravagant than the one just mentioned. Setting aside the details of an exact typology, such cases are generally associated with legal theories that capture truth-conditions of legal propositions through the formula 'P is legal if and only if contained in a statute or decided case'. The resulting failure of legal knowledge, sooner or later, amounts to erroneous statements regarding various aspects of the law: the existence or non-existence of gaps in the law, the correctness of an interpretation or the question which norms should be included in the legal system. In contrast, the chances of legal knowledge increase when a theory expands its understanding of the grounds of legal propositions by including into them practical reasons for action: 'P is legal only if it is justified in the light of reason F'.

Along these lines, a judgement such as 'homosexual masochistic activities are *yuk*' is only randomly true, hence does not amount to (normative) knowledge with respect to prohibition of homosexual masochist activities. It may be compared to the judgement 'the man who has three coins in his pocket will be promoted' which fails to amount to knowledge. In both cases the true judgement might amount to knowledge about something else: eg about which things are *yuk* etc. Let me press this analogy a bit further:

In the case of Jim's promotion, an account in terms of 'coins in the pocket' does not convey knowledge with respect to the subject of promotion precisely for the reason that such an account refers 'neutrally' across multiple individuals and/or events. In fact there could be a number of male subjects in the same office

12 The *locus classicus* is E Gettier, 'Is Justified True Belief Knowledge?' in (1963) 23 *Analysis* 121.

who share the property having five £1 coins in their pockets (*cf* with 'anyone who has two £1 coins in their pocket has £2 in their pockets' or '1+1=2' which is analytically true). What actually conveys knowledge *promotionwise* is reference to the actual individual Jim. Along these lines: a description *yuk*-wise or *facts-of-recognition*-wise may refer 'neutrally' across a variety of facts, situations or individuals. However, in order to convey knowledge *normative*-wise one would need, also in this case, to focus on the appropriate facts. That said, there is an asymmetry between law and the promotion example. In the promotion example it was sufficient to switch our reference from facts about coins to individuals (ie to switch between different segments of the environment). This will not suffice in the case of a legal norm: changing our description from a concrete set of facts to another (perhaps more pertinent to the case the norm purports to regulate) won't do the job. What is required here is a change of the mode of presentation of the relevant set of facts. Changes of the mode of presentation are trivially part of our everyday lives: think of a book my father bought me as a present. I can refer to it as 'a book'; 'dad's present'; or 'a work in metaphysics' (suppose it is Kant's first critique); or even as 'a body that occupies space X in my bag'.

The case of normative knowledge requires a somewhat similar shift in the mode of presentation, albeit a slightly more complex one. When I want to depict something as *normatively significant* (or if you prefer *action-guiding*) I need to switch into the modality of 'ought'.[13] In taking this leap I view the world through a different lens, one that is constituted by entities that can not be accounted for through descriptions of the environment, however many segments of the environment I may take into account (and in however many ways/combinations I may do it). Insofar as this is true, the modality of the 'ought' blocks reductive accounts of normative concepts. Other than in the case of descriptive concepts, normative concepts cannot be reduced to concepts such as to describe aspects of the physical environment. In the book example above, most of the modes of presentation ('dad's present', 'work in metaphysics', etc) can be reduced to the physical characteristics of the object (shape, weight and other primary properties). Such a reduction would not be fruitful in the normative/legal case (*cf* would it make sense to reduce proposition '1+1=2' to 'accounts of coins'?). This is a further proof that amongst the evidence for normative knowledge there are to be found aspects of the world, which cannot be accounted for descriptively but, instead, need to be addressed separately, through a normative account.

In order to avoid any complications arising from switching between modalities, we can capture the modality of ought through the idea of the normative fact. With a more detailed explication of the ontology of such facts waiting for later,[14] it may be already anticipated that normative facts have the advantage of conveying the much needed switch of modality, while they can still be depicted as any

[13] For the differences between the two modalities see the classic discussion of Hans Kelsen in his *Reine Rechtslehre*, 2nd edn (Vienna, Franz Deuticke, 1960) 1–25 and 204–9.

[14] See section 7.5.

other type of fact. In fact the idea of the normative fact can even contribute a more precise demonstration of the meaning of the asymmetry that is required for legal knowledge: accounts of law, which fail to depict[15] normative facts, would fall within the gap of the asymmetry and, for that reason, fail to amount to normative knowledge about the law.

Finally, the idea of a normative fact introduces a new theme: namely the question of mind-independence (or –dependence) reality must possess in order for the notion of asymmetry and knowledge to be able to work; in other words: is it necessary that we presuppose that knowledge can materialise only with respect to an environment that could in principle elude us all the way along? Or, to borrow Kant's terminology, do we really need to say that knowledge presupposes that there are things-in-them-selves (*Dinge an sich*)[16] which we may or may not succeed to fathom? Those who would assent to this view, would also adduce to its support the proposition that, were we to conceive of objects as being constituted through an intellectual activity (as Kant suggested), there would be no way of constructing the asymmetry between what we might erroneously believe and that which is actually and really there; for in the end, when operating under any of the available mind-dependent explications of objects, what we believe must also be deemed true. As I shall proceed to explore in the next section this view is hopelessly naïve, despite its intuitive appeal. Before turning to do so, however, I shall offer a comment with an eye to taking out some of the steam from that argument.

Normative facts, if indeed they are a good way for representing objectivity in law, are a rather tangible proof that the legal realm is in some fundamental way mind-dependent. For it would be absurd to argue that such things as 'insolvency' or 'the contract between X and Y' or even the norm 'thieves ought to be prosecuted' could occupy any actual time-space in the physical environment (or impinge in some manner upon our senses).[17] Now it is most notable that those

[15] Kelsen made the purpose of his Pure Theory to purge law from any psychological or other naturalistic accounts of normativity (this is what Stanley Paulson has coined Kelsen's 'objectification programme'; see Paulson, above n 7). Surprisingly, Kelsen pursued this task merely with respect to law, while leaving the normativity of morality outside the scope of his Pure Theory. As a result, Kelsen argued that law should never be mixed up with morals, not because the former must remain morally neutral, but because morality fails to live up to the standards of objectivity law incorporates. For Kelsen's efforts to rebut psychologism in legal theory see Paulson, above n 7.

[16] Kant uses the term '*Ding an sich*' to refer to entities that exist independently of our sensory and conceptual capacities. Notably in his *Critique of Pure Reason* he goes in great lengths to reject the availability of such entities, and to argue that knowledge of any entity is dependent upon a conceptual scheme comprising our sensory and conceptual capacities. For an illuminating introduction to Kant's theoretical philosophy, see P Guyer, *Kant* (London and New York, Routledge, 2006) ch 2, where also the main ideas of transcendental idealism are explained.

[17] With the exception of the normative sentence 'thieves ought to be prosecuted' none of the other expressions refers yet to a fact. For that it would be required to insert them in sentences of the form 'it is a fact that…' (eg 'it is a fact that Mary became insolvent'; or 'it is a fact that the contract between John and Gordon is valid'). For a detailed discussion of this strategy, see section 2.5.2.2 and section 7.5.2.

people who adduce the above argument to support a strong notion of objectivity in law are very fond of the language of normative facts—however this will constitute an embarrassment for their views, unless there were a way to reconcile the obvious mind-dependent aspect of normative facts with the strong view of objectivity as radical mind-independence (of the rank of a *Ding an sich*) they solicit. Succinctly put, such reconciliation has two (known to me at least) paths: the first is reduction (ism). This is a way that has been followed in legal theory time and again. When it has not led to explicit denial of the possibility of legal knowledge it has failed to capture the normative dimension of the 'ought' along the lines explained earlier (see more or less the discussion of conventionalism later in Chapter 5); the second path is that of essentialism—this is a rather candid path, for it does address head on the condition for strong objectivity: it furnishes the environment with normative entities which can, somehow, be felt. In line with a prominent supporter of this view, G E Moore, normative essentialists would argue that we possess something like a sixth sense, through which we may 'intuit' normative, including legal, facts. (This is more or less the view that may be ascribed to the metaphysics of interpretivism, see Chapter 6.) Both alternatives will be discussed and rejected in the course of the book

To conclude this section, it is the asymmetry at the level of the evidence that causes the asymmetry at the level of knowledge. What is more, this asymmetry must be explained if we want to arrive at normative knowledge. (We need in other words to explore the source of the asymmetry for it to be possible to locate the source or the requirements for normative knowledge.) This is the task of a metaphysical inquiry which all legal philosophers undertake, sooner or later (even those who abhor the idea of metaphysics). Depending on the results of this enquiry we can discriminate between accounts that successfully generate normative knowledge and those that fail to do so (or do so only in a partial and incomplete manner). In this type of enquiry metaphysical abstinence, shyness or abhorrence will not lead too far.

1.3 Conceptions of Objectivity

An understanding of objectivity in terms of distance calls for an elucidation of the latter and is confronted with the problem of how thought tackles the environment. To that extent, the nature and extent of objectivity available with respect to any domain depends on our more general understanding of the relation between the mind and the environment.

Two philosophical traditions will be looked at in an attempt to arrive at an understanding of the relation between mind and environment. The two traditions are reflected succinctly in a distinction from Frege's philosophy of meaning. Roughly speaking, Frege argued for two determinants of the meaning of words, sense and reference.[18] The sense of a word consists in a mental image that can be stated independently of what the word is about (ie the entity in the environment the word purports to depict). Far from being peculiar to any one speaker, this mental image can be communicated between speakers and serves the purpose of a mental compass (or blueprint) in relating the word it is an image of to the entities it stands for in the environment. On the other hand, the reference of a word is the entity in the environment it stands for. For instance, the word 'Venus' has at least two senses ('morning star' and 'evening star'), depending on one's standpoint vis-à-vis the environment, whereas it has only one reference in virtue of its standing in a one-to-one relationship with just one object in the environment (the planet Venus).

1.3.1 Representationalism

Mental representations, a species of which Frege's senses are, stand in the centre of the more traditional understanding of the way mind and environment mesh with one another; to that extent, the term 'philosophy of representation' or simply 'representationalism' may be reserved for the numerous variants of this view. Notwithstanding differences in detail, philosophies of representation submit that in order to gain access to the environment and its constituents we need to delve in our minds and study some special mental objects that are capable of representing to the mind what lies outside it. A lot of different entities have been held to constitute mental representations in the long and prominent history of representationalism (amongst them: images, ideas, senses and so on[19]). Since the shift to the philosophy of language, a shift located by many in the work of Frege, one may safely conclude that the only interesting representations are those that have propositional structure.[20] Propositional representations combine the following two advantages: on the one hand, they retain what is prominent with representationalism, namely the idea of the priority of thought over the environment, which is indispensable for explaining first-person authority over one's own thoughts[21]; on the other, they avoid the obscure metaphysics pertinent to the idea of mental objects capable of reflecting the environment in virtue of some mysterious mirror-like properties they possess. With the shift to propositions, the

[18] The most representative work of Frege regarding this distinction is G Frege, 'Über Sinn und Bedeutung' in *idem, Kleine Schriften*, I Angelelli (ed) (Hildesheim, Georg Olms, 1967) 143–62.

[19] See for a more detailed discussion section 2.2.2 and section 3.2.1.

[20] For an almost exclusive concern with propositional representations amongst contemporary discussions, see instead of others Donald Davidson, 'Knowing One's Own Mind' in *idem, Subjective, Intersubjective, Objective* (Oxford, Clarendon Press, 2001) 15–38 (at 35).

[21] For an insistence on first person authority, albeit without representationalism, see Davidson, above n 2.

philosophy of representations becomes part of the philosophy of language and the study of thought is delegated to the philosophy of language. To speak with Michael Dummett[22]:

> It has until recently been a basic tenet of analytical philosophy ... that the philosophy of thought can be approached only through the philosophy of language. That is to say, there can be no account of what thought is, independently of its means of expression; but the purpose of the philosophy of thought can be achieved by an explanation of what it is for the words and sentences of a language to have the meanings that they bear, an explanation making no appeal to an antecedent conception of the thoughts those sentences express.[23]

Linguistic representations are beset by two significant problems (what is argued with respect to linguistic representations may apply *mutatis mutandis* to all types of representations). The first arises with respect to the *stability of reference of linguistic signs*. In the representational model, signs refer to the environment in accordance with mental images that possess a propositional structure. Those can be thought of as definitions which specify exhaustive conditions or criteria for the application of signs and which, in virtue of being mental constructs, are immediately available to the mind. The deficiency of mental representations *qua* definitions has been illustrated through cases of failure of signs individuated on the basis of definitions to represent the environment. Saul Kripke and Hilary Putnam, in a series of writings that have come to be regarded as classics of twentieth-century philosophy,[24] have demonstrated the failure of mental definitions to determine the reference of proper names and kind names (for instance, 'Aristotle' and 'gold' respectively). On their view, definitions are not suitable for individuating the meaning of signs for they do not exhaust the nature of the entities or events (in the environment) signs refer to. Accordingly, if our world had been slightly different (or new historical evidence came to light) and Aristotle, having failed to respond to an invitation by Philip of Macedonia, had never actually taught Alexander, the definition 'the Stagirite philosopher who taught Alexander' would fail to pick the individual Aristotle. Instead, those authors argue, what actually confers to proper names and kind names their ability to consistently (or rigidly) refer to the same entity is a direct link between the linguistic sign and its referent. Thus the name 'Aristotle' would still be referring to the individual Aristotle even if certain of the properties we identify with him had been otherwise. Problems of reference arising for particular sentential components can be generalised to apply to whole sentences (thoughts). Thoughts that are individuated by definitions functioning as mental blueprints

[22] See M Dummett, *Truth and Other Enigmas* (London, Duckworth, 1978) 458.

[23] M Dummett, *The Logical Basis of Metaphysics* (London, Duckworth, 1991) 3.

[24] See S Kripke, 'Naming and Necessity' in D Davidson and G Harman (eds), *Semantics of Natural Language*, 2nd edn (Dordrecht and Boston, D Reidel, 1972) 253; H Putnam, 'The Meaning of 'Meaning'' in *idem*, *Philosophical Papers*, vol 2, softcover edn (Cambridge, Cambridge University Press, 1979) 215; see also the discussion in section 6.4.1.1.

would fail to distinguish between what is the case and what one believes to be the case. Then, the bad case of referring to illusory or non-existing objects, and more generally of being in error, could not be distinguished from the good case of genuine knowledge. Covering the ground between the bad and good case would require one to break out from the 'prison-house' of language.[25] Yet, as long as one's thoughts are individuated by representations that reside in the mind, no break-out will be possible.

Bad cases of thought-reference point to the more general problem of scepticism. Representationalism cannot guarantee that we can ever know anything about the world. This predicament comes in two versions: weak and strong. The weak version locates the problem of scepticism in the difficulty of bridging the gap between mental representations and the world. If mental definitions are conceived as being independent of the environment, there is no guarantee they say anything about the world; what is more, there is no way of checking them against the world, since they themselves are the vehicle of our thought, of what we know (or can know) and what not. On the other hand, the strong version of scepticism argues that representations cannot even get off the ground if the autonomy of the mental is upheld, for representations are, from their nature, supposed to be representations of something. Accordingly, if they are conceived as being independent of what they represent, representations are prevented from being representations of anything, hence they fail to materialise in the first place.[26] In that case the darkness of the prison-house is overwhelming, for there is nothing there to be presented to the mind, with the result that the ensuing scepticism becomes devastating.

It would not be an overstatement to say that the shortcomings of representationalism arise from a desire for too much certainty. This desire yields the belief that, unless what individuates our thoughts is situated in the mind's immediate vicinity, one is not able to know what one's thoughts are thoughts of. However, in conceiving the determinants of thought independently of the environment, representationalism achieves a rather fragile certainty for there is no guarantee that what we are thinking is really the case.

1.3.2 Referential Realism

In the antipodes of representationalism stands a different conception of objectivity, one that calls for modesty as regards what minds have access to, with an eye to broadening the range of the things at which we can potentially direct our

[25] The expression is borrowed from P Hanna and B Harrison, *Word and World: Practice and the Foundations of Language* (Cambridge, Cambridge University Press, 2004) 17 *ff*.

[26] For the two forms of scepticism see D Davidson, 'On the Very Idea of a Conceptual Scheme' in *idem*, *Inquiries into Truth and Interpretation* (Oxford, Clarendon Press, 1984); *idem*, 'The Structure and Content of Truth' (1990) 87 *Journal of Philosophy* 279; also N Stavropoulos, *Objectivity in Law* (Oxford, Clarendon Press, 1996) 40–41.

thoughts. On this conception, thoughts are not individuated by self-standing, environment-independent mental constructs (definitions, representations) but, instead, by what they stand for in the environment. What we think is not constrained by mental constructs but by an environment which exists independently of our minds. This view, *referential realism* (for short *realism*), has recently received a fresh impetus through a number of thought experiments by Kripke and Putnam who demonstrated that certain constituents of thoughts (names such as 'Aristotle' or 'gold') acquire their meaning through a direct causal link with their referents in the environment.[27] Conceived of in this way, the name-bearer relationship offers a highly plausible account of the failures of reference which appear puzzling from the standpoint of representationalism.

Referential realism is usually linked with a physicalist picture of the mind. According to such a picture, mental states stand in a line with the physical environment and, as a result, acquire their contents through causal transactions with the latter, transactions that can feature in nomological explanations of the natural sciences. To put it figuratively, the mind becomes a vehicle for thought which is steered by the environment. An important implication of this picture is that often we do not know what precisely our minds interact with, for we are not always in a position to discriminate the precise nature of the environmental factors that individuate our thoughts, whether because of the complexity of the context of conversation[28] or in virtue of our ignorance of the hidden microstructure of the referents of our words.[29]

Notwithstanding its important insights with respect to the individuation of thought, referential realism is not free of problems itself. Most of its shortcomings arise from the zeal with which referential realism attempts to buttress the notion of objectivity, by removing thoughts from the heads and placing them in the environment. The problems faced by such a move can be distinguished, on the one hand, in problems of a more technical nature, those illustrating the inability of the theory to account for meaning, and, on the other, in problems with more far-reaching philosophical consequences, which threaten realism in a more decisive manner.

1.3.2.1 Problems of Realism

Despite purporting to resolve a series of paradoxes of meaning and reference, arising from the adherence to mental representations, referential realism has itself

[27] For an accurate summary of the views of Kripke and Putnam on the matter, see Hanna and Harrison, above n 25, chs 7 and 11; and for an application of those theories in legal semantics, see Stavropoulos, above n 26, ch 2, who also coins the term K-P semantics.

[28] Imagine a west coast American who utters 'mezzanine' in conversation with an east coast American in a cafe in London; here it is not readily clear whether the word refers to the first floor or a separate floor between the ground floor and the first floor.

[29] Although no one in ancient Athens knew the chemical composition of water, people's thoughts involving the concept 'water' would still be about the stuff water, for their contents, then as now, would be individuated by the physical microstructure of the stuff, ie H_2O.

been criticised for generating a number of puzzles as regards the meaning of terms.[30] These include cases of non-referring names; problems from the change of reference; and problems of discrepancy between speakers' intent and meaning.

A first category of problems arises with respect to non-referring names, such as 'unicorn': in this case, there is nothing in the environment to causally determine the meaning of the name. However, the name continues to make perfect sense to any speaker who employs it; indeed it may feature in sophisticated conversations regarding art or mythology. In fact, some type of mental entity is better equipped to account for the meaning of non-referring names. Assuming there is a mental component fixing the reference of names, explains why 'unicorn' continues to make sense even in the absence of a certain type of creature. In addition, unless this mental component were to share certain features with the mental components that fix the meaning of concepts such as 'horse', 'foal' or 'colt', an adequate explanation of the meaning of 'unicorn' may remain elusive.

Another family of problems concerns cases of change of reference. Not infrequently, it so happens that the meaning of a term occurs as a result of an error, the question arising then being whether or not the error should be discounted. To take an example, it is reported that the name 'Madagascar' Marco Polo used to denote that island, resulted from a misunderstanding with respect to the use of the name by the indigenous population for denoting a part of the mainland. On the realist view, the name should still continue denoting the same part of the mainland it originally did, irrespective of the intent of Marco Polo and his companions, a result which obviously would be absurd.[31]

Finally, it is worth mentioning cases of discrepancy between the intent of the speaker and the actual meaning of a name: suppose I employ 'Paul' in order to refer to a friend of mine in a conversation in the pub. If what determines the meaning of 'Paul' is its causal connection with Paul my friend, it becomes problematic to determine what, on a later occasion, causes my use of 'Paul' to shift from denoting my friend to meaning another person (say one of the 12 apostles). Any representationalist theory which accepts the importance of the mental realm in fixing meanings could easily account for the shift by saying that what determines the shift is the intent of the speaker. But this explanation is not

[30] For a thorough criticism of referential realism (in both its versions as casual theory of names and direct reference) see Hanna and Harrison, above n 25, chs 7, 11, 12.

[31] If the realist objects that what determines, in the environment, the meaning of 'Madagascar' is not a geographical location but the actual conditions under which the name was really employed by Marco Polo, then an explanation is owed as to the criterion that determines which part of the environment is relevant, in each case, for determining meaning. In other words, if what determines meaning in the last instance is not some unadulterated bit of the world but instead one that has already been interpreted, then the environment ceases to be the final arbiter of meaning and an account of the criteria of interpretation is called for.

available to referential realism, for the causal link with the environment outweighs any internal states of the speaker. The paradox, then, is that I may end up meaning things I do not intend to.[32]

Such technical problems of meaning and reference may, roughly, be attributed to two causes: essentialism and first-person authority.

1.3.2.2 Essentialism[33]

First the issue of essentialism: in removing meanings from the head, referential realism propounds that what fixes meaning lies in the intrinsic nature (essence) of the entities denoted by words. In the context of a physicalist understanding of the world, which takes the environment to be exhausted by a full description in the vocabulary of physics, essences are identified with the molecular microstructure of the substances or kinds the environment consists of. A problem with collapsing essence with microstructure is one of indeterminacy: microstructures are no more certain or determinate as guides of thought-content than are mental representations. In fact the idea of microstructure might turn out to be unattainable for, as Mellor has demonstrated[34] there are more microstructures to be associated with the same natural kind or, worse, there are kinds that do not have any microstructure at all but can be perfectly thought of and depicted by using concepts. To demonstrate the first of the two cases, suppose we have different samples of some natural kind (water) all of which share 10 properties when considered conjointly, however no one sample has all 10 of them. The question that arises here concerns the crucial properties for determining the microstructure of the kind (water). Supposing that any combination of any nine of these properties suffices for a sample to be water, shall we say that the microstructure of water consists in the disjunction of all conjunctions of nine of the above properties? And if yes, does this sound more determinate than the definitions realists purport to attack? Hardly! The second, more devastating, case comprises cases of kinds (elements) to be found high in the periodic table that do not occur in nature, nor have they ever been manufactured. We do have names for them, but there may be no microstructure that may constrain our use of those names, at least not in the manner realism purports.[35]

In that respect, and in the absence of further precision, the concept of the microstructure exudes a certain air of magic, for we never know what the microstructure of a kind actually is, given that all properties we associate with the meaning of a name are never final or even determinate. Granted indeterminacy, the reference (and, consequently, the meaning) of names seems to be always

[32] This argument can be found in Evans, 'The Causal Theory of Names' (1973) 47 *Aristotelian Society Supplementary Volume* 187.

[33] See also the detailed discussion with respect to interpretivism in Chapter 6.

[34] D H Mellor, 'Natural Kinds' (1977) 28 *British Journal for the Philosophy of Science* 219.

[35] For both examples cp Mellor, above n 34, 219 (at 306).

forthcoming, along with the elusive microstructure of essences. What is forthcoming or elusive, however, can only be a bad advisor for knowledge. It seems, therefore, that microstructure rather emerges like a gratuitous concession to essentialism, or a clever trick for producing the rabbit of essentialism out of the hat of philosophy.

With respect to law essentialist strategies are even less likely to succeed. For in that domain microstructures are likely to strike us as even more counterintuitive. As already stated,[36] it is absurd to suppose that there are normative essences which furnish the environment (or a special realm, analogous to the natural environment) and to which we could hook on with our senses (or with a special sixth sense, apt to receiving normative signals!). The alternative to essentialism would be to align with reductionist strategies and attempt to reduce legal facts (objects, properties and so on) to physical entities. This is also unsatisfactory in light of its inability to account for the obligating dimension of the law.[37] In view of the flaws of the proposed alternatives, and keeping in mind essentialism's abhorrence of definitional, or any other mind-dependent understandings of meaning, how are the inconsistencies of essentialism to be accounted for?

In law as well as in science, essentialists have tried to circumvent the problems of a microstructural analysis of essences, by alluding to an intermediate level of analysis, one that can determine content in a more fluctuant way, such as can anticipate the vagueness (or even absence) of microstructures. With this in mind proponents of essentialism talk about archetypes or stereotypes, as the determinants of thought-content.[38] Stereotypes are something like provisional definitions of content that remain revisable in the light of further discoveries about the essence of the kind in question. They are constructed by taking paradigmatic cases of the kind in question, while keeping an eye on not making final definitions out of them. In that respect stereotypes work as environment-responsive definitions but are not totally unlike Fregean senses or any other kind of definition. It is contestable, whether stereotypes can carry the full weight of realist accounts even in the philosophy of science, for, as many critics have argued,[39] the problems of indeterminacy that beset the idea of the microstructure may be carried over to bear on stereotypical definitions. Leaving the debate in the philosophy of science aside I shall focus, for present purposes, merely on the legal case.

Stereotypes in law seem to build a central component of the interpretivist account of law.[40] They are to be encountered in what Dworkin calls the

[36] See section 1.2.

[37] A second reason for rejecting this solution is that any reduction to natural kinds will have to face anew the indeterminacy arising from the microstructural analysis of any natural kind, as already indicated.

[38] See Putnam, above n 24, 247 *ff*.

[39] For a summary of such criticisms, see Hanna and Harrison, above n 25, 237 *ff*.

[40] I take interpretivism to constitute the essentialist account par excellence in the field of legal theory, despite Dworkin's recent objections to this characterisation (*cf* R Dworkin, *Justice in Robes*

'pre-interpretive stage' of an account of the law. Here, Dworkin argues, the lawyer is forming a rough idea about her subject matter: the legal material which she will be called to fully interpret in the next, the so-called interpretive, stage with an eye to arriving at a full account of the valid law. Suppose I am checking whether English tort requires causation as a necessary condition for liability. Dworkin argues that this judgement can follow only after the interpretive stage; however, it is possible to roughly identify the relevant legal materials (rules, precepts, judgments, opinions etc) already in the pre-interpretive stage. In doing so we may point at such paradigmatic cases of tortious liability which prima facie give a first idea as to the role of causation in English tort. This indication may not be final by any means. In fact, Dworkin would probably argue that in this particular example, the pre-interpretive stage is likely to produce different results from the interpretive stage: for prima facie it seems that causation should indeed be included in those conditions that are necessary for liability. Conversely, the interpretive stage, in asking us to make the best moral reading of any legal system, is more likely to deny that prima facie conclusion and conclude, in the light of considerations of corrective justice, that causation is, at the most, a sufficient, albeit not necessary condition for tortious liability (see his examples of Mrs Soerensen).

This understanding of the pre-interpretive stage has been attacked by many critics as assuming the possibility of capturing law through criteria or definitions which can be formulated irrespective of anything that would count as an essential legal property. Such criteria, far from assuming that there are essential legal properties, rather affirm the domain of law as mind-dependent, one that is susceptible to definitions of the kind conventionalist (or other definitional) accounts suggest. It is easy to see why: legal stereotypes can only be of a definitional nature for there is nothing of the type of a legal microstructure or essence to underpin them, the way essentialism calls for. Of course, it is a different matter whether those definitions should rest on conventions, as positivism insists, or some alternative basis. Saving the answer for later in the book, it suffices for now to affirm the difficulty of building a sensible or workable account of legal knowledge that is based on legal essences, whether they be captured in microstructures or stereotypes.

A last move that purports to retain the basic essentialist intuition of interpretivism is the appeal to the concept of interpretive or substantive theory.[41] Reference to theory is intended to steer clear of problems of indeterminacy of a microstructural explanation of essences, without at the same time giving in to

(Cambridge Mass, Harvard University Press, 2006), Introduction and ch 8). For the details of the pre-interpretive stage and the idea of paradigms in law see R Dworkin, *Law's Empire* (London, Fontana Press, 1986) 65–68 and 90–96; see also Stavropoulos, above n 26, 137–38.

[41] The origin of this argument is to be found in Dworkin's idea of theoretical disagreement (Dworkin, *Law's Empire*, above n 40, 4–5 and 31–43; it is further developed by Stavropoulos, above n 26, 73–76.

claims of mind-dependence and the attendant definitional explications of law. Substantive theory possesses an even higher level of flexibility than microstructure or stereotypes, without being completely disconnected from them, at least to the extent that it purports to be sensitive to the essence of law. This claim may accommodate the intuition for an essence or true nature of law without needing to point at any particular 'legal microstructure' (which would succumb to the problems iterated earlier). At the same time substantive theory can account for objectivity and knowledge in a strong mind-independent manner, one that is not available to definitional accounts akin to the ones contemporary positivists employ. Substantive theory gains its key role through the fact that the truth of any proposition of law, whether in the interpretive or the pre-interpretive stage, is proclaimed theory sensitive. This entails that, far from taking some abstract formulation to be definitive of the nature of law, the grounds for the truth of legal propositions are subjected to constant theoretical scrutiny: the theory is checking provisional understandings of the legal materials against what is taken to be fundamental or essential values and principles of the practice at hand. Here it is often the case that what we took prima facie to constitute a rule of law turns out, after careful reflection involving salient principles and values, not to be one, as the case of Mrs Sorensen has shown earlier.[42]

Again the idea of theory is not likely to bring us too far. Either theory serves the role of the magic wand for gratuitously delivering essentialism or it is merely a truncated form of a conceptual account. In the first case, theory just covers up for the fact that there is no pure or unadulterated essence of law. However, in promising to deliver an account of essentialist truth-conditions it makes itself vulnerable to sceptical moves. For, given that there is no set of theory-independent properties, which can be definitively linked to the referents of legal terms, reference must, anew, be fixed mysteriously by hooking on to a strange, forthcoming microstructure. Or, in the second case, it is actually theory itself that fixes the reality of law. Hence, to the extent theories are intellectual constructs, law's nature is mind-dependent in some basic sense. Of course being mind- or thought-dependent and being of the kind representationalism assumes are two very different things. I suppose interpretivists would want to distance themselves from any representationalist explication of the role theory plays in their account, especially one that would involve fixed definitions or criteria, along the lines positivism suggests. There is definitely a second possibility of interpreting a theory-sensitive account of law, one that takes theoretical reasoning to constitute itself a reflexive practice of judging, which obeys internal criteria of rationality and consistency. This is more or less the path that will be followed in this book. However, in taking this path, I shall set aside 'theory' as a term of any use, with an

[42] Compare with the classic example in Putnam where look-alike pencils turn out, on more careful investigation, to be living organisms. See Putnam, above n 24, 242–45.

eye to avoiding unnecessary associations with the bad effects of interpretivism. Whether my account is compatible with interpretivism or not, must remain open at this stage.[43]

1.3.2.3 First Person Authority and Elusiveness

But even if all those objections were to fail and the existence of essences, manifested in microstructures, were to hold good, a deeper problem would still remain for realism. This is the problem concerning first person authority. First person authority refers to the ability of thinkers to have access to their own thoughts. In fact realism, in arguing for a strong connection between thought-content and the environment, puts that authority in question. For, if the content of one's thoughts, and consequently the meaning of the words one uses to formulate them, is fully individuated by the environment—without any 'input' on behalf of thinkers—then the absurd conclusion would follow, that they do not know what they are thinking of. Expelling content from the heads leads to ignorance of the standards that guide content and meaning, hence thoughts become elusive. Most notably, they become the more elusive, the stronger the version of essentialism to which one adheres. Strong essences tend to determine more decisively the content of our thoughts, while weaker ones may do so less. Along these lines, the argument from elusiveness may be delivered in two degrees: a weak and a strong one. While the weak version might still serve a healthy notion of objectivity, strong elusiveness (what I shall dub ontological elusiveness) stands in a straight line with scepticism and ignorance.

In its weak version elusiveness merely requires that our thoughts are about things and events which exist outside our heads. This view requires us merely to assume that there is a distinction between what is internal to minds and what is external to them, as part of the environment. The distinction makes it possible to conceive of what individuates thought as being external to it in such a manner that our thoughts might occasionally fail to depict it. In that respect we may account for the possibility of error and correction which is essential to knowledge as argued before. All of this is possible without subscribing to any strong ontology of essences. All we need is to exploit the natural idea that minds are not hopelessly self-referential. However, the possibility of error should *not* become the rule. If it becomes the rule then the question arises: is it ever possible to know anything at all, or are we constantly sunk in an illusion?

Strong elusiveness entails consistent failure to track truth. This gives rise to a different, more intense form of scepticism, one that builds on a stark notion of

[43] Judging from the metaphysics of interpretivism (which I discuss in Chapter 6), rather not. However those metaphysics do not always feature consistently or even fully in the various interpretivist accounts. What is more, the general lack of overview of the philosophical basis of interpretivism often leads to contradictory remarks and conflicting views. To the extent that reasons of coherence and consistency would call for a 'correction' or restatement of the metaphysics of interpretivism, a chance may arise for an approach between the two accounts.

externality, which assumes that what individuates our thoughts are (natural or other) kinds that might remain, in principle, inaccessible to our thinking. The motivation behind this version derives from a desire to oppose the view that confines the limits of the world to the limits of our thought. Noble as it may be, this desire leads to ontological elusiveness, as the state in which we end up forming, unbeknown to us, thoughts about things we can never know about—in this absurd state not only do the objects of our thoughts remain elusive, but also our thoughts of them become unintelligible. Ontological elusiveness is much more than mere revisability or correction of thoughts on the basis of new evidence. Ontological elusiveness implies that the kinds of things we purport to track remain unintelligible to us.

Assuming that ontological elusiveness (and anything that presupposes it) is an invitation to deep scepticism, this view will not be pursued here. Elusive objects are of no interest to the project at hand for two reasons: first, because a minimum relevance of ontology to thought is indispensable.[44] Even if our mental states are directly world-involving it should be still possible to form intelligible thoughts of all the things we encounter in the environment. Thoughts are still located in heads and therefore their contents must be known to those who think them. Secondly, even if there were such things as elusive entities, which, in principle, cannot be thought of, they could not be obligation-generating entities (eg norms, values and so on). Obligating or action-guiding entities, for reasons submitted earlier, cannot remain in principle unfathomable to agents, for such entities need to be determinate in order to be able to regulate agency. A succinct manner to capture this requirement is Joseph Raz's postulate of the determinacy of law.[45] This argues that before subjecting legal materials to any interpretation, those must have been identified in a determinate manner, through a rule of recognition. The proviso of recognition aside, this condition can be generalised as requiring that no normative (legal) proposition may be based on grounds that are elusive (along the lines interpretivism or any other essentialist theory of law might require).

1.3.2.4 Companions in Failure

Should one be surprised that scepticism besets both realism and representationalism? Prima facie it may seem rather odd that two diametrically opposed views suffer from the same predicament. After all, since the two views are antithetic, one of them should at least escape what is a predicament of the other. That this is not the case might lie in the fact that both views share a desire for a strong epistemic foundation for knowledge. It seems that both representationalism and realism require a strong link between thoughts and whatever they take to

[44] This point will be developed in the following section of the chapter.

[45] To be found in J Raz, 'Dworkin: A New Link in the Chain' (1986) 74 *California Law Review* 1103 at 1119.

determine thought-content, be it representations in the former or essences of things in the latter. It is this fundamentalism that causes one-sidedness of the account of objectivity or the relation between thought and the environment, by placing the entire weight of the account on the two ends of an otherwise continuous activity. Viewing the two extreme moments in isolation obscures the fact that thoughts acquire their content as a result of a more complex and continuous practice, where minds interact with the environment under certain constraints or conditions of intelligibility. These conditions are dynamic and static at the same time: dynamic in that they always allow for new information to make its way into our thoughts and concepts; static in the sense that they provide for a normative structure which constrains the practice of content formation, making out of it a regulated or normative activity, as opposed to one that happens randomly, or for no reason. Disregarding the practice of thought-formation and the normative scheme or matrix that underlies it invites indeterminacy and scepticism with regard to all (including legal) content. Far from being endemic of mental representations only, as Donald Davidson argues in his exemplary discussion of representationalism,[46] such disregard extends to most (if not all) versions of referential realism.

1.4 Wittgenstein's Idea of Grammar

Clearly, when compared to mental representations realism is more apt in fleshing out a notion of distance as a condition of objectivity for knowledge. Referential realism, however, was deemed not to be free of problems either, as the discussion of essentialism and ontological elusiveness has revealed. To put it in a nutshell, the main difficulty of referential realism is that, in addressing the 'how' of thought-individuation, it neglects the more fundamental question of *why* we care about thought-individuation in the first place (call this the 'why' question). The why question is about what makes thought in the first place assertoric or truth-tracking, in the sense of attempting to match the world.

Wittgenstein, already in the years before the *Tractatus*, addressed this issue as part of his overall dissatisfaction with Russell's early realist philosophy. This, in a nutshell, is the problem: Russell argued that in order to know that a sentence expresses an assertoric content capable of being characterised as true or false (ie a proposition), we must know that there exist facts of a certain type.[47] Wittgenstein's objection to this was that it is not possible to even raise the question about

[46] See Davidson, above n 2.

[47] See Hanna and Harrison, above n 25, ch 4; J Skorupski, 'Meaning, Use, Verification' in B Hale and C Wright (eds), *A Companion to the Philosophy of Language* (Oxford, Blackwell, 1999) 29-60. In legal theory the general argument can be cast as a special argument for the intelligibility of legal reasoning. For the importance of intelligibility in law see J Raz, 'The Truth in Particularism' in B Hooker and M Little (eds), *Moral Particularism* (Oxford, Clarendon Press, 2000) 48; also G Pavlakos,

what facts exist unless we already know what type of fact our sentence does sketch out. The latter knowledge, Wittgenstein suggested, cannot come from the world but has to come from the sentence we are employing. To that extent our thoughts, expressed in sentences, were assumed by Wittgenstein to constrain existence: if something cannot be thought of consistently, because thinking it would give rise to a contradictory sentence (eg 'X is red and green all over'), we do not even need to ask whether that type of fact exists in the world. If, on the other hand, something can be thought of consistently then we can know merely from the constitution of the sentence that expresses our thought, how things would have to stand in the environment for it to be true or false. The criterion for what is consistent and what not has to do with the rules that determine the structure of our sentences. Such rules, according to Wittgenstein, belong to logic and are a priori, hence capable of being stated independently of experience. Conceived in this way, logic acquires priority over questions of reference and ontology and becomes a preliminary issue regarding judgements about what kinds of entities or facts exist in the environment. This is more or less the idea behind the slogan-like statement in the *Tractatus*: 'Die Logik muß für sich selber sorgen' ('logic must take care of itself') .[48]

So conceived, Wittgenstein's idea of logic establishes the relative priority of thought over questions of reference and ontology, for the simple reason that the latter cannot be even conceived of outside the former. If Wittgenstein was right this priority should be neutral vis-à-vis the controversy between representationalism and realism for it touches upon an issue that is preliminary to the individuation of thought: the issue of *intelligibility*. Whether it is in fact, depends on what one takes the rules of logic to consist of. Over the span of his philosophical career Wittgenstein himself, although he never abandoned the belief in the primacy of logic, changed considerably his views on what its rules comprise. Despite a close adherence to the idea of logic in his *logisch-philosophische Abhandlung* (better known as *Tractatus Logico-Philosophicus*), later writings contain a number of modifications where the components of logic are modified, shifted or supplemented. The most striking change was perhaps, his dissatisfaction with the a priori character of logic, as a result of which he opted for a more flexible scheme of rules. Those shifts are clearly illustrated in Wittgenstein's modifications of terminology: as early as in a set of notes that were later published as *Philosophical Grammar*, he replaces 'logic' with 'grammar'. Later again, in his *Philosophical Investigations*, grammar is used along with such concepts as 'language-game', 'practice' and 'form of life'. Such shifts notwithstanding, the idea of a core conceptual scheme that connects thought with its objects

'Two Conceptions of Universalisation' in Z Bankowski and J Maclean (eds), *The Universal and the Particular in Legal Reasoning* (Aldershot, Ashgate, 2006).

[48] L Wittgenstein, *Tractatus Logico-Philosophicus*, D F Pears and B F McGuinness (trans) (London, Routledge and Kegan Paul, 1961), para 5.473. For a very illuminating discussion of Wittgenstein's slogan as well as the coinage of the term, see Hanna and Harrison, above n 25, 77–94.

remains present throughout Wittgenstein's work. This is no better illustrated than in his late notes *On Certainty*[49] where he makes repeated references to such a scheme in order to combat scepticism, or any other attempt to undermine knowledge by separating thought from the environment.

In this book I shall use *grammar* in order to refer to the conceptual scheme that guarantees the intelligibility of thought, through a network of rules which determine what linguistic move is allowed in making sense and which is not. An obvious reason to be adduced for this choice is the propositional structure exhibited by the conceptual scheme. Of course to assert this, one would have to determine whether language exhausts thought, a task whose Herculean dimensions lie well beyond either the scope of this work or the philosophical capabilities of its author.[50] To that extent, I am happy to concede that, in abiding by the thesis that language exhausts thought, I am doing no more than helping myself to what has been a constant throughout Wittgenstein's thinking. Indeed, even in what is his most radical modification of his early idea of logic, ie the notion of the language-game, the importance of the primacy of language remains obvious.[51] Even when the details and the strong a priori character of logic recedes into the background, the idea of a conceptual scheme that is interwoven with language and purports to guarantee the intelligibility of thought *tout court* remains in place. Its elements or ingredients are neither as well-defined nor so clearly stated as in the early days of the *Tractatus* for, in the meantime, Wittgenstein had discovered that logical perspicuity may lead to rigidity and this to an array of new failures for meaning and knowledge.[52] Despite such particularities and turns in Wittgenstein's thinking, the term 'grammar' will be employed throughout with an eye to capturing ideally the linguistic structure of thought.

There are certain items which are compulsory for any conceptual scheme that is linguistically conceived of. Thus, grammar comprises rules of syntax and semantics, such as to prescribe when a sentence is capable of tracking truth. Sentences that are well-formed in the above sense, guarantee for intelligibility and are capable of effecting communication. This is not to say that any grammatical lapse leads to unintelligibility or loss of meaning, only that, by and large, rules of grammar form the background against which error and correction can be accounted for. In the course of the book a further type of rule will be added, namely rules that relate sentences to particular purposes. Such rules, also known

[49] L Wittgenstein, *On Certainty* (Oxford, Blackwell, 1975) paras 96–102, where he compares the conceptual scheme to the bank of a river in which the 'water' of experience flows.

[50] Neil MacCormick has most insightfully suggested that instead of subscribing to the stronger thesis that all thought be exhausted by language, one may simply say that the domains of thought in relation to which humans are capable of discriminating knowledge from error seem to be all instances of thought formulated or capable of being formulated linguistically. So even if thought is conceptually wider than thought-in-language, only the latter remains the proper concern of this book. This line of argument is actually carried out in section 2.3.

[51] See Hanna and Harrison, above n 25, ch 4.

[52] See Chapter 3.

as pragmatic, besides enjoying the benefit of being grounded in Wittgenstein's later thought, are valuable for avoiding certain pitfalls, which arise from a purely formal-logical conception of grammar (akin to the one Wittgenstein put forward in the *Tractatus*). Far from undermining grammar, pragmatic rules will be used in order to advance an understanding of grammar as a practice of judgement formation.[53]

Under the condition that a grammar can be worked out, such as can deliver the task of intelligibility, any controversies arising about content individuation would materialise on a different level. What is meant here is that intelligibility must be found to cut across issues of content individuation, in the sense that any viable conception of individuation will have to presuppose it. In other words one can reject representationalism without discarding intelligibility and the idea of a grammar that underpins it. In this context, the criticisms referential realism directs at the priority of thought over the world, amount to a sensible and valuable critique only if they are interpreted as problems of content individuation, hence compatible with the idea of grammar. Conversely, for the part they purport to offer a rival view of intelligibility they will be rejected swiftly as evoking elusiveness and radical scepticism, along the lines suggested earlier. When it respects intelligibility the realist critique becomes a powerful tool for distinguishing between, on the one hand, defective versions of grammar, those that rely on mental constructions that can be individuated independently of the environment, on the other, healthy versions that comprise rules for the application of sentences in a manner that is world-involving. In this light the condition of intelligibility, far from granting gratuitously the notion of grammar, allows all voices in the debate on objectivity and knowledge to be heard, with a view to arriving at a rounded view on the matter.

That grammar is capable of underpinning claims of knowledge will be demonstrated incrementally in Chapters 2 through to 4. Chapter 2 focuses on the intelligibility grammar generates, by conceiving of it as a rational structure prescribing that all thoughts are propositional. Chapter 3, on the other hand, purports to combat dualism and the sceptical results the latter connotes. Here grammar is linked up with the activity of forming thoughts (judging). As a result of this linkage grammar is explicated as a practice of judging. Notably, as Chapter 4 argues, judging is not a random practice, but instead is subjected to reasons. In the light of those reasons, judging is rendered a 'deep' activity, one that enables thinkers to refer to complex reasons for grounding their judgements. Given complexity, the possibility of error and correction is grounded in the factual inability of thinkers to have a complete overview of the reasons that constrain their judgements: thus the asymmetry between belief and knowledge is grounded on the possibility that we are missing out on some of our reasons, rather than on any substances in the environment.

[53] For the details of this move see Chapter 3.

2

Objectivity and Grammar

2.1 Introduction

In this and the next chapter I shall outline the main tenets of a philosophical theory which purports to underpin a grammar-based account of objectivity. Such an account reverses the traditional order as regards the relation between language and environment: instead of requiring that a grasp of content-bearing units (concepts and propositions[1]) be antecedent to our understanding of language, a language-dependent explication suggests that concepts and propositions be individuated according to how we employ signs within judgements (assertoric sentences). Connectedly, our grasping of concepts and propositions follows the semantic rules which regulate the structure of judgements.[2] To put it in a succinct and somewhat provocative way, a grammar-based account of content abides by the slogan: *semantics exhausts ontology*. This slogan is taken to guarantee intelligibility of content and, hence, knowledge.

The chapter opens with a restatement of the requirement of the intelligibility of thought through the idea of intentional realism. Intentional realism argues, roughly, that thoughts are real, for otherwise it is impossible to account coherently for the behaviour of thinking beings. Intentional realism purports to block scepticism without falling back into the problems of traditional representationalism. In discussing this tenet, a re-evaluation of representations is offered. Not all representations are bad, but only those which succumb to mind-world dualism. Conversely, intentional states can be thought of as having a representing function, albeit without slipping back to the type of mind-world dualism that saddles

[1] Concepts and propositions are traditionally taken to represent non-linguistic counterparts of names and sentences respectively. Such counterparts guarantee communication (and translation) beyond the linguistic forms of particular languages. The main matter of controversy in respect of concepts and propositions is whether they are individuated independently of language or not. See the discussion in section 3.5.2.

[2] On the face of it, all other ontological categories are constructed within this framework. Properties are identified through concepts (and can be represented as unsaturated functions for instance); objects are identified through their structural link with concepts within the structure of the sentence; and facts are individuated via propositions. The semantic framework will be supplemented by pragmatic rules in the context of a reconstruction of grammar as a practice of judging in the next chapter.

traditional representations. This is rendered possible by endorsing a non-reductionist conception of intentional states while maintaining that they are linked to the environment.

Sections 2.3 to 2.5 attempt to tackle the issue of individuation of intentional states in a non-dualist manner with an eye to blocking undesirable sceptical conclusions. The line of reasoning is broadly Fregean in that it endorses the key idea about language posing limits to thought. An important consequence of this tenet is the belief that the logical-semantic structure of language circumscribes the very possibility of thinking. Faithful to the rationalist tradition[3] he himself belonged to, Frege thought of the semantic structure of judgement as constituting the conceptual scheme which enables us to grasp the various ontological partitions of the environment. As a result, dualism is undermined at the grass-roots level, for it is not possible to even articulate the *distance* between thought and its objects outside this conceptual scheme. This priority of language over thought is cast as the *semantics exhausts ontology thesis* (section 2.3). In working out the various details of this position, the discussion takes up a number of important issues which were touched upon in Chapter 1: the problem of scepticism connected to the individuation of thought within language and the possible loss of objectivity that is linked to it (section 2.4); the demonstration of the ability to individuate ontological categories (objects, properties) within the structure of judgement (section 2.4); finally, the main tenets of a semantic theory of truth, which completes the claim of the semantics exhausts ontology thesis for the priority of thought over ontology and reference (section 2.5). In the end, grammar emerges as the set of conditions which govern judgement formation and can exhaustively account for the truth of judgements.

The final, sixth, section of the chapter addresses a concern as regards the ability of the Fregean framework to escape scepticism in the form of the prison-house of language and the radical indeterminacy of content resulting from it. This is the worry that, while the semantics exhausts ontology thesis is successful at the level of reconstructing thought-content intelligibly, it may fall short of grounding knowledge in the sense explained in the previous chapter.[4] This possibility arises from an ambiguity that is in-built in the Fregean reconstruction of grammar. Notably, this ambiguity allows for at least one reconstruction of grammar which renders it a sort of intermediary between mind and environment (not unlike representations), one that is hard to connect with either of those. Notably, the problem arises when grammar is conceived of as a static structure which, in order

[3] For the rationalist roots of Frege's thought, see T Burge, 'Frege on Sense and Linguistic Meaning' reprinted in *idem, Truth, Thought, Reason* (Oxford, Clarendon Press, 2005) 242–69. In the same vain, see A Coffa, *The Semantic Tradition from Kant to Carnap* (Cambridge, Cambridge University Press, 1991) who considers Kant to belong to the same semantic tradition as Frege.

[4] *Cf* Chapter 1. See also the discussion in D Davidson, *Truth and Predication* (Cambridge Mass, Harvard University Press, 2005), who identifies as the main shortcoming in Frege's theory his desire to connect predicative constituents of sentences to some extra-sentential (hence grammar-independent) entities (at 145).

to generate content, must comply with criteria that are external to it. A well-known variant of this conception is the one put forward by logical positivism during the opening decades of the twentieth century. In this context criteria are taken to refer to elementary experiential items (sense-data) which are fed into grammar in order to generate content. The principal problem with this understanding is that, in assuming that individuation of content takes place externally to grammar, it inverses the order between semantics and ontology. No sooner, however, has ontology taken over from semantics than the precious, for knowledge, intelligibility withers away.

Chapter 4 advances a remedy to problems arising from the criterial understanding of grammar. While linking judging (and broadly thinking) to criteria reopens the mind-world dualism and invites anew sceptical conclusions, it is argued that reference to the idea of practice can escape the sceptical *impasse.* Wittgenstein came to see the problem of criteria as part of the broader criticism he directed at superlative facts or ultra-determinants of content. Eventually this criticism led him to repudiate the semantics he had developed in his early work, when he was still under the influence of Frege's philosophy. Along these lines any reference to grammar-independent criteria is accused of confining one to scepticism, for such criteria fall short of bridging the gap between thought and the environment, upon which indeterminacy of content breaks out. Conversely, Wittgenstein arrived at the conclusion that judging can generate sustainable knowledge only if it is conceived of as a normative activity, namely the activity (or practice) of rule-following.

The normative element introduced by practice is juxtaposed to an idea of objectivity that is linked to grammar-independent criteria. While the desire for objectivity invites a criterial reading of grammar, one that opens up a gap between thought and environment, the notion of practice manages to close the gap by rendering practices constitutive of content. Thus the normativity of practice can replace objectivity without losing hold of intelligibility: once we are within the realm of practice, intelligibility and objectivity are delivered *uno actu* via the reality of the practice. Along these lines, Chapter 4 carries out the transition from objectivity to normativity which has been implicitly alluded to since the opening pages of this work. With this transition in place a more comprehensive understanding of grammar is called for. Grammar needs to be expanded to include, aside from a priori rules of logic and syntax, also a posteriori rules that pertain to the various domains of judging. The expanded notion of grammar is discussed in Chapter 4, as well as in Chapters 5 and 6 with respect to law. Finally Chapter 7 will attempt to explore the relation between the two levels of grammar, while advancing a fresh account of legal phenomena.

2.2 Intentional Realism

The fact that we possess mental content enables us to acquire knowledge of the environment, to draw conclusions about the past, plan our behaviour for the future and, generally, appreciate the patterns that underwrite the environment and the behaviour of other content-possessing beings. In other words, content gives us both knowledge and intentionality. For this reason, any discussion of content is required to elucidate the connections between the mind and the environment, in a manner that can best align the thoughts of thinking subjects with their behaviour. In what follows, I shall take the philosophy of content to occupy a central position or, even, to be prior to the other domains of the philosophy of mind, ontology and metaphysics. Following many philosophies after the linguistic turn, I take priority of content to show that the query into the patterns of world and mind is only meaningful through (or mediated by) the explication of the patterns of thought and content. On a first glance the priority of thought and content follows from the trivial fact of the existence of human intentional behaviour. Any attempt to comprehend this behaviour as being intelligible (or rational) will lead to the endorsement of some sort of *intentional realism*,[5] or the idea that intentional states (eg beliefs) are real. In a further stage, it will be shown that those real intentional states are mainly embedded within linguistic structures. To that extent the discussion of content will turn into a discussion of the patterns of propositional content. The latter will, further, reveal something like an a priori (logical) grammar. I will take grammar to indicate more than the formal-syntactic grammar that linguistics deals with. 'Grammar', in the context of the present discussion, will stand for the *normative patterns* that regulate thinking and whose existence can be demonstrated transcendentally.

Now, because of the assumption of the priority of content, this grammar is not going to be merely a grammar of thought, but, what is more, it is going to map the whole domain both of metaphysics (ontology) and the philosophy of mind. Questions and answers about what categories of entities exist, or about which types of brain states and events are brought about, are all answerable to the normativity of the grammar of thought. This is not to say that what exists in the mind/brain[6] and the world, exists in virtue of the grammar of thought (idealist presumption); the claim is, rather, that the patterns of grammar are (transcendentally) necessary in order to map the mind and the environment.

[5] The term comes from M Luntley, *Contemporary Philosophy of Thought and Language* (Oxford, Blackwell, 1998) 4. The use of the concept 'realism' in this context serves merely the purpose of stating that intentional or mental states or phenomena exist as distinct from brain states.

[6] The physical aspect of the mind (brain) can readily be taken to be part of the physical world. The non-physical part of the mind apparently contains the principles that put together the a priori grammar of thought.

The ensuing discussion is going to tackle the issue of the priority of intentional content and its underlying grammar by tacitly endorsing the structure of a two-stage transcendental argument:

P1: intentional behaviour is a fact

P1': for intentional behaviour to be possible, one has to assume the existence of intentional states

C1: there are intentional states (intentional realism)

P2: there are intentional states (C1)

P2': for intentional states to exist, they have to exhibit certain patterns of logical structure (grammar)

C2: there is a logical grammar of thought

Alternatively, one could take the fact of the existence of intentional behaviour as already containing the claim of intentional realism about beliefs and other states, thus simplifying the structure of the transcendental argument. This would probably be relatively uncontroversial in the face of a widespread agreement on the issue amongst philosophers.[7] In either case, the discussion will have to clarify two issues: first, the 'self-evident' reality of intentional states; and second the nature of the underlying grammar.

2.2.1 The Shift from the Philosophy of Mind to the Philosophy of Content

Intentional realism is the view that there is such a thing as intentional content.[8] This claim enjoys the status of a necessary presupposition 'projected' upon the trivial fact of the existence of human behaviour that interrupts, as it were, the causal flow of the physical universe (see the given premiss P1). It is this necessity to account for human behaviour coherently or meaningfully, as an intervening-in-the-world factor, that forces on one some version of realism about thoughts, beliefs and other intentional states. If, in other words, one wants to account for human behaviour then concepts like 'believing that…', 'hoping that…' or 'wishing that…' cannot be eliminated from one's explanation.

Put in those terms, the claim of intentional realism, robust as it may be, does not proceed to say how content is individuated; that is, it does not prejudge the way one is going to account for what content is, or what kind of entities beliefs and other intentional states are. It does, though, pose an outer limit on what content can be: namely, that however content is going to be individuated it has still to be related to the explanation of human behaviour. That is no less than saying that content has to be able to support a rational account of human

[7] See Luntley, above n 5, 3–11.

[8] Cf *ibid* 1–11. For the foundational role of intentional states in any theory of content, see the claims of the 'face-value theory' in S Schiffer, *The Things We Mean* (Oxford, Clarendon Press, 2003) 11–48.

behaviour.[9] This constraint adds to the initial need to provide for an account of behaviour the further requirement of rationality: content is necessary not only in order to understand the way we experience the world, but also in order to account rationally for our behaviour (or intervention in the world); whereas 'experience of the world' might be taken to constitute something like the passive side, or the information-background of behaviour, the rationality requirement seems to flow directly from focussing upon behaviour as such. Thus, both claims incorporated into the doctrine of intentional realism are still within the triviality scope[10] of the initial transcendental argument (the fact of human behaviour).

As soon as one endorses the two minimal requirements of intentional realism, springing out from the fact of the existence of human behaviour and its impact upon the causal network of the world, one has a response to the so-called *constitutive task*, or the task of characterising the role of content in rationalising explanations of behaviour. Yet, what one still lacks is an answer to the way of individuating content. This seems to fall largely under the subject matter of the so-called *engineering task*,[11] or the task of connecting the material side of content, ie brain states, with the environment by using causal concepts. Strictly speaking, this second task is not on the same level of neutrality as the first, the constitutive task; in fact it presupposes that one has already opted to individuate content in a specific way, namely by holding that content is individuated by entities which are independent of the environment and which possess some (mysterious) representational abilities.

Be that as it may, I take the engineering task to express, in a more general way, the important task of the connection between thought and environment which is independent of the method of content individuation. Admittedly, if one treats this problem as an 'engineering task' that postulates the reconnection of intentional content with its environment through causal concepts, one is already 'biased' as to the method of individuation of content. Conversely, the 'engineering task' can take a completely different content if one individuates content in a *non-representationalist way*. In all, whichever way one chooses, the issue of the connection between thought and environment will be present; what is not obligatory, however, is that it will always take the form of a *physicalist programme*. In fact, I am going to argue that the more general issue that the 'engineering task' addresses can be better resolved if one avoids representationalism and the affiliated forms of physicalism. Since the problem of representationalism is going

[9] Luntley, above n 5, 4.

[10] It is widely accepted that the starting premiss of any transcendental argument should state a fairly uncontested, or trivially true, fact. See S L Paulson, 'On Transcendental Arguments, their Recasting in Terms of Belief, and the Ensuing Transformation of Kelsen's Pure Theory of Law' (2000) 75 *Notre Dame Law Review* 1775; also R Stern, *Transcendental Arguments and Scepticism* (Oxford, Clarendon Press, 2000) 3–13.

[11] See Luntley, above n 5, 7.

to reappear later,[12] I am going to offer a brief account of the way representationalism individuates content, with the aim of demonstrating some serious problems whose need for a solution will lead the discussion to a non-representationalist model of content individuation.

2.2.2 Representationalism[13]

For a long time, representationalism has been considered as the only option for intentional realism. Representationalism responds to the *constitutive task*, or the task concerning the intervention of intentional behaviour in the causal flow of the world, by assuming the existence of content-possessing entities of some kind that are independent from the environment.[14] Propositional attitudes like 'believing that', 'hoping that', 'wishing that', etc are attitudes towards such entities. This 'reification' of content is achieved through entities like, say, Platonic or Cartesian ideas. Clearly, the claim of the existence of independent entities is a powerful expression of the idea that content is self-standing and necessary in order to account for human behaviour: it rests upon the simple thought that something can be conceived as intervening in the flow of the world only if it is independent of it. The more independent this 'something' is, the better is the explanation it offers. And indeed one could hardly imagine anything more independent than entities that are revealed by a mysterious faculty (Platonic ideas), or by introspection (Cartesian ideas). Alas, the aftermath of those strong claims is the impossibility to establish any connection of those entities with the world, since in order for them to be representations of the world, they need somehow to be in some causal relation to it: hence, the 'engineering task' is doomed to fail from the beginning, as there is no way of offering any explanation that would connect these non-physical entities with the environment on an account that would be in accordance with the way the world works, that is, without assuming an obscure metaphysics. If, however, the engineering task fails, so does the constitutive task, for explanations of human behaviour can no longer be modelled in a satisfactory way.

Intentional realism, in the form of representationalism, has more chance to survive if one is able to provide an account that respects the engineering task by endorsing a physicalist ontology. This is the road that modern representationalist theories take. Here, thought is individuated by entities which are characterisable independently of the world, albeit, they can be connected to it causally. These entities are perceived as intentional states (beliefs, wishes, desires, etc) that intervene between the environment and our behaviour. These states feature in

[12] The problem of representationalism is going to reappear in connection with Lockean ideas and other mental intermediaries in the discussion of Wittgenstein's rule-following considerations; see Chapter 3.

[13] For the philosophical significance of representationalism for knowledge, see section 1.3.1.

[14] See Luntley, above n 5, 7–11.

causal explanations of behaviour while, on the other hand, they are themselves causally connected with what they stand for (bits of the world). In order to be able to engage into causal relations, intentional states must be shown to pick up the physical entities postulated by the engineering task, namely brain states. Thus, much of the success of the physicalist programme depends on the possibility of reducing belief or other intentional states to the level of physical brain states.

The programme of physicalism seems to undermine intentional realism by subordinating the constitutive to the engineering task. Even in their occult metaphysics, Platonic and Cartesian ideas capture the central claim of the constitutive task which is the 'reification' of thoughts as normative entities that can account rationally for behaviour. Conversely, physicalism, driven by the fear of succumbing to idealism, or to an obscure metaphysics, seems to arrive at the other extreme: by focusing upon the engineering programme it seems to bestow explanatory priority on the reducing brain states over the normative concepts (beliefs, etc): since it is more important to have entities that can feature in causal explanation, one should be able to disguise the normative states as physical states. After this move has been performed the constitutive and the engineering task can no longer be treated as being on a par. As a result, some amongst the physicalist philosophers choose to abandon the programme of preserving both tasks and, instead, embark on an eliminativist programme that gives up the constitutive level.[15] Yet any attempt to get rid of the latter is bound to bring about the cancellation of intentional realism.

But is the dilemma compulsory? Is it true, in other words, that one can either hold intentional realism to be true, or undertake the task of naturalising content, but not both at the same time? On the assumptions of representationalism, this seems to be inevitable. However, besides representationalism there seems to be one more way of individuating content which might be able to preserve both the intuition of intentional realism and the idea that thought has to fit in the physical universe (naturalisation of content).

2.2.3 The Priority of Thought

The main problem of physicalism becomes apparent with the reductionist move. This move, besides being powerless to establish the priority of brain states over normative states, demonstrates a further deficiency. In a counterintuitive way, it contravenes the rationale of its employment: reduction is allegedly employed in order to save the autonomy of thought by offering a workable, that is naturalised, explanation of human behaviour. Despite its noble intentions, it ends up declaring that intentional realism, or the normative autonomy of thought, is untenable.

[15] Amongst those philosophers count Paul and Patricia Churchland and Stephen Stich in his earlier work. See Luntley, above n 5, 8–9.

The roots of this failure lie deeper, though. They lie in the whole idea of representations as being independent of what they represent (the environment).[16] The reification of thought through entities that possess representational powers requires such strong assumptions that it ends up undermining the normativity of thought and the idea of intentional realism. The way representationalism is set up yields an understanding of the constitutive and the engineering task as being antithetical: either thought is independent and cannot be analysed (or reduced) to causal categories, or thought has no independence and is understood only through the categories of physics; in the first case there is no hope of ever establishing any connection between thought-as-blueprint and the environment whose blueprint it is. In the second, there is no way of adequately explaining human behaviour. In fact eliminativism, or the full reduction of the constitutive level, shows precisely the *aporia* connected to the dilemma. As soon as one realises that the categories of thought cannot be reduced to physics, one prefers to ignore them altogether, as being unreal or instrumental[17] and, instead, concentrate on what is palpable: the picture of the world through our best scientific theories.

These thoughts point in the direction of a viable alternative which could uphold the intuitions of both the constitutive and the engineering tasks. Such an account would have to rescue the normative level of thought while giving a description of how thought fits in the world without presupposing reduction. Clearly, against a representationalist background, it might seem extremely difficult to combine these requirements. Things seem totally different if one discards the notion of representation and alludes to the idea of a non-reductionist theory of naturalised content. Such a theory would rest on the assumption that the whereabouts of the normative entities of the constitutive level do not need to be remote from their worldly surroundings. Put in those terms, a theory of content will still be normative, while conceiving content as being shaped in the world. At the same time, it will hardly need to appeal to any kind of reduction of content-concepts, precisely because content will have already been conceived as being in touch with the environment. Obviously, reductionism seems to wither away, as soon as representations are disposed of.

A non-reductionist theory of content exploits the impossibility of analysing the normative concepts of the constitutive level in causal terms, by endorsing the thought that the constitutive and the engineering tasks stand side by side.[18] Such a theory contemplates the possibility of autonomous intentional content conceived in a way that is not cut off from its environment. In doing so it endeavours

[16] See also the discussion of the role of representations as *ultra-interpretations* in the context of Wittgenstein's criticism, Chapter 3.

[17] This is a more subtle version of eliminativism in which the constitutive level is not fully eliminated but treated instrumentally as a way of talking that one finds useful to employ, which, though, carries no real significance. See Luntley, above n 5, 8–9.

[18] Along these lines evolves the account of content offered by Luntley, above n 5, 11 *ff*.

to show that thoughts are not reducible to causal terms, ie they are autonomous, while, at the same time, they are not mysterious entities isolated from the world. Such a view establishes the autonomy of the normative constitutive level of thought through transcendental reasoning, while it proceeds to declare that the constitutive categories are characterisable only in an externalist way, that is, by showing that the environment is necessarily implicated in the constitutive account of content.[19] By performing this double move, the non-reductionist theory of content achieves threefold: it rescues intentional realism; it holds to the idea of a naturalised intentional content; it reconciles the constitutive with the engineering task by rejecting reductionism. In fact, the third achievement is made available because naturalised content is compatible with a causal account of the world. What it does not any more require is a reductive account of mental content in causal terms, since, from its constitution, it is involved in the world.

2.3 An Anti-representationalist Theory of Content

A non-reductive theory of content, like the one just sketched, can be taken to be of Fregean inspiration.[20] The most central claim of such a theory is that it identifies the structure of thought with the structure of language. This claim is not unqualified; it aims to capture the fact that the structure of thoughts can be, on the whole, individuated through linguistic structures.[21] As such it is narrower than the claim that the structure of language is constitutive of the structure of thought, or that language exhausts thought. The investigation into whether this stronger claim is true or not need not occupy us in the present context. Instead of offering a definitive answer as to which is prior, language or thought, one could characterise the connection between the two in a more neutral way, by alluding to something like *the semantics exhausts ontology thesis.*[22] This thesis contends that, to the extent that the building blocks of the environment (ontology) can be captured through the structure of thought, it can also be captured through the structure of language (semantics), avoiding thus a direct confrontation with the language/thought issue.

The semantics exhausts ontology thesis substantiates the idea that the study of the structure of thought precedes that of the structure of the world or, more cautiously put, that the 'burden of proof as to what kinds of entities there are' is inverted between semantics (thought) and ontology (the world); it says, more or

[19] See *ibid* 10, 11.

[20] The term is used by *ibid* 11 *ff*, in order to summarise externalist, non-reductive theories of content whose roots lie in the work of Gareth Evans and have been further developed by Lynne Rudder-Baker and A Clark. Similar ideas are to be found in the work of D Davidson, as well as in more contemporary philosophical work of Davidsonian aspiration such as that of S L Hurley; see the preface of her *Consciousness in Action* (Cambridge, Mass, Harvard University Press, 1998).

[21] See Luntley, above n 5, 11.

[22] *Ibid* 12.

less, that one could come to know ontological categories by attending to the structure of thought rather than by scrutinising the molecular structures of matter. To that extent, the Fregean strategy presents itself as an alternative to eliminativism and reductionism in general. Eliminativism, as discussed earlier, trusts physics and its picture of the world to such an extent as to postulate the harmonisation of the theory of content with an ontology deriving from physics; in doing so it fails to account in a satisfactory way for the rationality of human behaviour. Conversely, the Fregean strategy exploits the a priori necessity of thought for the justification of behaviour and goes on to proclaim that semantics, as a level of individuation of thought, comes in importance before ontology in the process of content formation. This comparison shows, in a rather instructive way, that if one wants to account rationally for behaviour, one has to admit the priority of thought and the concomitant priority of semantics.[23]

2.3.1 Normativity of Content

A Fregean theory of content takes intentional realism seriously and endorses the autonomy of thought. To that extent, it attempts to give a description of thought-content which is non-reductionist. But, in doing this, it does not presuppose that intentional content is independent of the mind and the environment. In fact, it purports to offer an account of content which will be compatible with our being physical creatures in a physical world; albeit, one that is not necessarily carved in a physicalist vocabulary. This account of content is also an account of the mind and the environment, precisely because mind, thought and environment are envisaged as interconnected, as opposed to independent as a reductionist account would have them.

In discarding the physicalist vocabulary, the non-reductionist account of content focuses mainly upon the normativity of content as it is revealed through the patterns that underlie our use of expressions. Meaning and understanding place obligations upon speakers to use the relevant expressions in a patterned way. Those patterns can be described independently of the physical mechanisms that underwrite our way of dealing with expressions (ie various brain states). Furthermore, they enjoy an a priori status since they constitute the necessary presuppositions of meaning and understanding and can be described in a non-empirical way.

[23] The question whether semantics in the present context is exhausted by formal semantics depends on the broader issue of the relation between thought and language. For present purposes suffice it to say that formal semantics (ie the structures of language) are indispensable for a mapping of thought which is normatively constrained. Later, in Chapter 3, it will be argued that formal semantics, lest it give rise to mind-world dualism, needs to be linked with the idea of practice. In that case formal semantic rules are supplemented with substantive norms which are constitutive for particular practices.

The elementary patterns within which meaning and understanding unfold are, for an account of Fregean aspiration, those of the assertive sentence (judgement). Words have meaning only in the context of sentences. This claim is conceptualised as the *context principle*.[24] The context principle narrows ontology down to the patterns expressions exhibit within the structure of sentences (as the elementary semantic structures). As a result objects are revealed through the patterns that certain words (names) exhibit within the context of sentences.[25] This is the case not only with names that denote concrete objects, but also with those that denote more abstract objects (like legal concepts (eg contracts), numbers, musical compositions, a game of chess, etc). Let us take the case of arithmetic which was also Frege's main concern.

Whether numbers are objects depends upon the claim that numerals are names.[26] To establish this claim it is not enough to look at whether numerals point towards objects. One reason for this is, of course, that numbers are abstract objects and hence not available to our senses. But to hold this as the decisive reason for our inability to establish the fact that numerals are names simply 'by looking around' is to miss the whole point. This is so because for something to be a name (ie name for an object) is not about its standing in a special relation to an object (as an ontological category). Rather, a sign is a name only to the extent that it demonstrates the appropriate pattern of use within the context of a sentence. Consequently the question whether numerals are names, and hence whether numbers are objects, turns upon the question whether they exhibit the appropriate pattern of use within the relevant sentences. Given that the rules which regulate patterns of use are those of grammar, the claim can be furnished as saying that numbers are objects if and only if numerals exhibit the grammar of names. In this way, in engaging in the a priori study of grammar, we unveil what kinds of objects there are. This study of grammar is a study of the patterns of thought and to the extent that thought is individuated through language, a study of language. The whole programme of studying semantics or the grammar of thought before or instead of ontology boils down to the claim that there is no non-conceptual or transparent experience of reality.

The fact that the sentence is the elementary unit of grammar should not remain unqualified. Sentences are never single-element units but composite ones, usually exhibiting a complex structure that contains several parts (names, predicates). Frege acknowledged this fact by endorsing the thesis that the meaning of a sentence (or thought) is a function of the meaning of its parts, or the *compositionality thesis*.[27] The compositionality thesis should not be taken to overrule the

[24] For a brief account of Frege's context principle and the primacy of the sentence/proposition see Luntley, above n 5, 16–18.

[25] The context principle can be combined with the following idea of Wittgensteinian origin: objects do not exist independently, but are integrated with other objects within certain arrangements of events (so-called *facts*). While sentences depict facts, names depict objects.

[26] See Luntley, above n 5, 17.

[27] *Ibid* 18.

context principle or the idea that the sentence is the context within which names acquire meaning. Were it the case, the result would be something like the claim that it is possible to offer an account of names independently of their grammar which is tantamount to saying that meaning presupposes a queer sort of connection between mind and object. Instead the compositionality thesis should be interpreted as giving expression to the idea that (assertoric) sentences express judgements which purport to depict structured bits of reality (facts). Being about facts, judgements are truth evaluable (ie they can be true or false), while isolated names cannot.

The antagonism between the context principle and the compositionality thesis will reappear in the discussion of mind-independence a few paragraphs from now. The issue of mind-independence arises with respect to the degree of objectivity attached to the existence of abstract objects. While the compositionality thesis corresponds to a strong notion of mind-independence, the context principle underpins a notion of mind-independence that is compatible with the condition of intelligibility postulated in Chapter 1. Accordingly, the latter will be deemed more suitable for the purposes of the project at hand. For now, let me turn to the Fregean argument for the existence of abstract objects.

2.3.2 The Fregean Argument for Abstract Objects

Frege employs the following argument in order to account for the existence of abstract objects. Although his argument relates specifically to numbers, it can be put to the service of the proof of the existence of other kinds of abstract objects, including legal 'objects' (norms, contracts and so on). Broader, the argument serves to illustrate how the ontological category 'object' is made intelligible in the first place: by demonstrating the appropriate role within the structure of judgment. Here are the premisses of the Fregean argument[28]:

(P) if a range of expressions function as singular terms[29] in true statements, then there are objects denoted by expressions belonging to that range[30]

(P') Numerals, and many other numerical expressions besides, do so function in many true statements

Therefore:

(C) There exist objects denoted by those expressions (ie there are abstract objects)

[28] See S Coyle, *On the Foundations of Legal Reasoning in International Law* (University of Glasgow, unpublished Doctoral Thesis, 1998) 89–90. See also B Hale, *Abstract Objects* (Oxford, Blackwell, 1987) 10.

[29] A singular term is any word in a sentence that has the function of referring or naming a particular object or thing. As such count usually: proper names (eg 'Aristotle', 'Altona'); singular definite descriptions (eg 'the man on the balcony'); and demonstratives (eg 'this cat', 'that boy').

[30] I use the argument as stated in Coyle, above n 28, 89, however without limiting the conclusion to numerical expressions.

The force of the argument lies in the semantic role singular terms assume within the environment of assertoric sentences.[31] This role consists in determining the truth-conditions of the sentence in the sense that its truth value can only be stated if the referential role of the relevant singular term is taken seriously (in Hale's words if 'the singular term discharges its referential function'[32]). Stated in this way, the semantic role of singular terms appears to have the ontological implication that there must exist objects to which the one or the other singular term refers.

There are two ways to understand the ontological charge of Frege's argument. One is to declare the priority of the referential function of the building blocks of the sentence. Here the truth of the judgment is derivative vis-à-vis the referential role of the names and predicates comprised by it. Conversely, one can take reference to substantiate within the environment of a true sentence. In the latter case truth will be prior to reference. Each of the two understandings yields an entirely different conception of objectivity. A robust explication of reference effects strong objectivity, one that is exposed to the mind-world gap intentional realism tried to bridge. On the other hand, the priority of judgement may evoke a suspicion of linguistic idealism or the view that content is a mind-made thing. Such idealism would again allude to dualism, albeit one deriving from the opposite end of the spectrum. Connectedly, it is of utmost importance for the nature and character of objectivity which of the two understandings of Frege's argument one chooses to follow; for, it seems, objectivity is a function of the relations between truth and reference; the judgement and its parts.

A succinct way to present the problem is in terms of mind-dependence/independence. The more robust mind-dependence/independence is set up the stronger becomes the amount of ensuing dualism and the higher the chances for a revival of scepticism. Instead, we must try to steer a middle way between extremes. This will be attempted via a discussion of two conceptions of mind-independence. Out of them one will be deemed compatible with the idea of grammar, while the other will not. The incompatible one corresponds to the intuitions of referential realism. Although referential realism is a possible interpretation of the Fregean project it is not a charitable one, for it is incompatible with Frege's primary interest in objectivity. In contrast, the second conception of mind-independence arises from a judgement-focussed explanation of the Fregean project, one that is neo-Kantian in flavour. The judgement-focussed explication reaffirms the centrality of grammar in an account of intentional content and paves the way for an understanding of objectivity which resists mind-world dualism and scepticism.

Perhaps the most successful attempt to do away with sceptical conclusions has been the effort to present grammar as a normative activity by conceiving of it as

[31] See Hale, above n 28, 12.

[32] *Ibid* 12.

a practice of rule-following. This view, which is to be discussed in the next chapter,[33] argues that, once linked to practice, rules of judging (grammar) stand in an internal relation to the criteria of content-individuation. In this case internality consists in that rules of judging constrain *directly* our interpretations or justifications about what can serve as content-giving. They do so, for they set the limits of intelligibility as to what may count as an interpretation and, otherwise, nothing that falls outside the practice can so count.

That objectivity and knowledge require the notion of practice can be illustrated as follows: what is central to the programme of intentional realism is the normativity of thought, which is capable of justifying action. For the idea of normativity to be established, two steps are called for: on the one hand, to refer to a medium that escapes the problems of traditional representations and, hence, guarantees intelligibility of content (it was attending to this task that led us to the notion of grammar); on the other, to ensure that the 'superior' medium avoids a slip-back into the mind-world dualism. The latter task requires, in turn, that two moves be performed.

First, to secure the primacy of grammar by reinstating the priority of judgement over its parts: considering that grammar states the structure of judgment, priority of the latter entails that grammar assumes primacy over all other determinants of content. Replace judgement with its parts and grammar becomes subservient to grammar-independent items (criteria and interpretations) which purport, with little success, to restore unity between the various parts of the judgement.[34] In this case, any effort to explain truth and reference as underpinning an intelligible notion of content fails and the outcome is scepticism.

The second move requires that we conceive of judging as a normative activity. This move purports to ensure that grammar does not deteriorate into any criteria. The idea of normativity is best redeemed through the idea of the rule, ie a normative entity which connects past and future instances of its application into a continuous series, in the light of the rationale it incorporates. The rule's rationale needs to be conceived of as determining content in the last instance. It is essential, as a result, that the rationale remain conceptually prior[35] to any criteria, be they of a mental or environmental nature. It is precisely this function that practice performs, for it is only in connection with it that the rule and its instances remain in contact. Consequently, in practice we encounter rules of

[33] See Chapter 3.

[34] For a very illuminating survey of the traditional problems of the unity of judgement (proposition), see Davidson, above n 4, part II.

[35] The relation of conceptual priority can be illustrated as follows: a concept X is prior to concept Y if Y is accounted for in terms of X, where X is not in turn accounted for in terms of Y; conceptual priority does not entail epistemic priority (it could be the case, in other words, that our knowledge of Y conditions our knowledge of X). For these matters, see S L Hurley, *Natural Reasons* (New York and Oxford, Oxford University Press, 1989) 10–11.

grammar at the bedrock of our fundamental capacity to form intentional content which can account for a link between thought and action in a principled way.[36]

While the second move will have to wait until Chapter 3, the remainder of this chapter will be devoted to developing the first move: beginning with a brief discussion of two alternative notions of mind-independence, I shall proceed to demonstrate the advantages of the notion favoured by the judgement-centred explication of truth and reference. This will lead, in turn, to an explanation of truth as emanating from inferential connections between assertive sentences; this will, in turn, give rise to a semantic conception of truth. The semantic conception of truth will, finally, determine the type of mind-independence which should be attached to existential claims of abstract objects and, as a result, the nature of objectivity which pertains to claims of knowledge: objectivity which is thought-dependent, as in being individuated within judgments and their mutual connections.

Before setting out to tackle the two different explications of mind-independence and objectivity, I shall briefly illustrate Frege's primary interest in the objectivity of thought-content. This discussion will set the context in which a judgement-related explication of truth and reference will emerge as the best explication of Frege's interest in the objectivity of thought.

2.3.3 Fregean Objectivity

Frege makes thoughts the centrepiece of his philosophical method. Although he is interested strictly in the objective logical structure of the sentences thoughts are embedded in, Frege's focus on thoughts may still create the impression of rebutting objectivity in exchange for some form of linguistic idealism.[37] This allegation is often linked to the traditional prejudice that any rejection of representationalism is tantamount to a refutation of objectivity. If content is a priori connected with our way of conceptualising the environment how can it be anything more than a subjective account? Moreover, the objection goes, if semantics exhausts ontology, how can any talk about the world amount to anything more than an account of signs and the way we use them?

Frege, in juxtaposing thoughts (the content of judgements) to ideas (the main unit of mental representations) never misses an opportunity to say that thoughts are objective entities whereas ideas are subjective. For Frege the subjectivity of ideas reflects the fact that we cannot communicate with them, since what we communicate with has to be shared by everyone. Conversely, thoughts are what we communicate with, hence they are shared by everyone. This is one reason that

[36] The danger this move purports to disable is illustrated in section 2.6.

[37] Or the idea that the environment is of a linguistic nature. Conversely, as mentioned earlier, the semantics exhausts ontology thesis is about the intelligibility of content rather than any claim in respect of the essence of the world, let alone the claim that everything there is to know is linguistic in essence.

supports the claim about the objectivity of thought. A second lies in the fact that thoughts and not ideas are the bearers of truth/falsity. And for Frege truth is always *objective.*[38]

Such remarks indicate the train of argument which can refute the accusation about a denial of objectivity: thought is truth evaluable, hence objective; it is not about something that is internal to the mind as opposed to, say, something external that lies out there (ie the environment). That is to say, grammar does not step into the place of ideas, while the world still occupies the other side of the dualist universe of the representationalist mind. Were it the case, the semantics exhausts ontology thesis would, of course, be neglecting the world-side in an unforgivable way. But this naïve picture makes sense only if one sees the claim for the priority of thought through the prism of representations and the concomitant mind-world dualism. The priority of thought thesis should not be understood just as an inversion of the dualistic picture that favours intentional activity (ie the formation of judgements) over perceptive activity (sense-data, the world). Such an inversion is, indeed, 'introvert' in the sense that it falls short of explaining the *aboutness* of thought by alluding to something like the priority of the Giving (intentional activity) over the Given (the objects of perceptual activity).

Instead, what the semantic exhausts ontology thesis should be taken to express is the idea that neither the Giving nor the Given enjoys ontological priority in accounting for content, which is another way of stating the rejection of mind-world dualism. Further, the rejection is not self-standing, an axiom that is endorsed without further evidence. It is, as suggested before, the only consistent conclusion of an account of content which purports to generate a justification of intentional behaviour.

The priority of the grammar of thought, as an integral part of the justification of behaviour, builds upon the idea that it is impossible to give an account of the reference of signs independently of their grammar. In pleading for this view it endorses the claim that grammar has an *explanatory priority* over reference and not that reference is non-existent. This claim lies at the heart of the anti-dualist argument as regards the relation of mind with the environment and does not purport to diminish the importance of reference. Instead, what the 'monistic' picture submits is that grammar and reference are inseparable and that the only asymmetry that occurs is the explanatory priority of grammar, generated by the need to justify intentional behaviour. Still, intentional activity (grammar), insofar as it reveals the ontological structure of the world, has to be supplemented by the inputs of perceptual activity. It is precisely at this point, the point of interface between mind, thought and the world, that the monistic picture needs a non-dualist vocabulary which avoids expressions that give rise to any impression of dichotomy. In a non-dualist account of content the environment is not really an input into something (the mind) which is later neatly organised into a pattern

[38] See for an accurate summary of these claims, Luntley, above n 5, 26–28.

(the grammar). This vocabulary is indeed misleading to the extent that it nurtures an introverted ontology. Here is a more appropriate way to put it: 'input' is already part of the a priori account of content; that is, content is (about) the world and grammar plays the role of the 'pilot' who navigates through the world and 'slices' it in accordance to the need to justify human behaviour.[39] When I point towards the Chrysler building saying: 'the roof demonstrates a fine example of art-deco architecture', grammar slices the environment to fit the judgement's content.[40] Here my judgement's content is not about something (eg an idea) which is different from the Chrysler building; nor does the Chrysler building have any relevance to my judgement's content other than the one dictated by grammar. Once dualism has been defeated there is no gap left between intentional activity and the world and, hence, no need to succumb to any kind of 'ranking' between them because both coincide in content formation the way grammar prescribes. That is to say, grammar or the structure of thought offers the transcendental justification for an equal participation of intentional activity (the Giving) and the world (the Given) in the process of content formation. Luntley makes this point with eloquence:

> Suppose that the metaphysical input to grammar is transcendentally justified; that is, it is not a gratuitous metaphysics plugged in just to get the right results, it is there in order that we cut content at just the points necessary to get that which rationally explains behaviour. That, then, is anti-representationalism, for it is the idea that the individuation of thought and its logical grammar is world-involving. The logical grammar of thought, the structure by which it is truth-evaluable, is not, then, a linguistic structure. It is a structure of how we are in the world. The possession of content is the possession of the world. Furthermore, if in our responsiveness to reasons, we take ourselves to be responsive to contents (beliefs, etc), this means that our responsiveness to reasons can be a direct responsiveness to the world. The world comes within the province of our thoughts, it falls within the space of reasons.[41]

The gist of those remarks is that content is world-involving and grammar is the structure of what exists, at least to the extent we are interested in, in accounting for human behaviour in a principled way. It is precisely this idea that the judgement-oriented explication of truth and reference will seek to corroborate.[42]

2.3.4 Anti-psychologism and Logic

The notion of objectivity in the context of a Fregean theory of content calls for further elucidation. Objectivity, here, refers to the logical form of thoughts and the patterns of (inferential) reasoning as opposed to the subjectivity of inner psychological states. Both the structure of thoughts and the patterns of reasoning

[39] Compare with Luntley, *ibid,* 26–30.
[40] The example derives from Hurley in *Consciousness in Action,* above n 20, 16.
[41] Luntley, above n 5, 27.
[42] See sections 2.4 and 2.5.

are the subject matter of logic. The juxtaposition between logic and psychology emerges, in Frege's own work, as a product of a rigorous effort to reject the view that logic is a psychological (hence empirical) category.[43] One of the main shortages of a psychologistic explication of logic is that the content of logic is empirically conditioned and therefore contingent: there could always exist some novel situation where new or different logical principles or laws might emerge, as it is always the case with different sorts of pain, pleasure, and so on. Frege opposed this picture by alluding to the fact that our judgements and the inferences upon which they rest do enjoy a degree of objectivity which makes it possible to ascertain whether they are correct or not, independently of inner psychological operations.[44] To that extent objectivity of logic springs out from the way things are: take for instance the principle of identity that says that every object is identical with itself ('t = t').[45] Independently of the psychologico-empirical mechanisms that underlie an identity judgement, there is a further necessity for the validity of that principle which has to do with the fact that every object is indeed identical with itself. This is a property of objects that is independent from the psychological groundwork of judgement-formation but nevertheless essential to the content of the judgement on self-identity. Put this way the issue of objectivity mainly expresses the idea that objectivity of judgement is linked with the manner the external world is, rather than with the inner mechanisms which support judgement formation. Frege says:

> Thus I can also acknowledge thoughts as independent of me; other men can grasp them just as much as I; I can acknowledge a science in which many can be engaged in research. We are not owners of thoughts as we are owners of our ideas.[46]

Now, given this notion of objectivity, there are two ways of interpreting it.[47] The first is the more crude way of Platonism. It rests on the somewhat naïve contrast:

[43] For a very clear exposition of the issue of objectivity in Frege's work, albeit in a clearly Kantian spirit, see T Ricketts, 'Objectivity and Objecthood: Frege's Metaphysics of Judgement' in L Haaparanta and J Hintikka (eds), *Frege Synthesized*, Synthese Library, vol 181 (Dordrecht, Reidel, 1986) 65–95. Conversely, Tyler Burge offers some exemplary analysis of Frege's quest of objectivity in a more realist spirit in his 'Frege on Sense and Linguistic Meaning', above n 3, 242–69.

[44] Think the objectivity of grammar as referring to the structure of a judgement minus what Russell called the propositional attitude or our disposition towards the judgement's content (the attitudes of assuming, wondering, asserting, etc). See also Coffa, above n 3, 67, where he mentions Bolzano's distinction between objective representations on the one hand and subjective representations and reality on the other. According to it objective representations consist neither in the object itself for 'the object is located in space and time', nor in any subjective representation, for those perish with the passing of time whereas the objective content of judgement persists. The analogy between objectivity of representations and objectivity of grammar is quite straightforward (although in the present context the talk of representations is not fully appropriate given the rejection of dualism).

[45] See Ricketts, above n 43.

[46] *Ibid* 72. The passage originally appears in G Frege, 'Thought' in M Beaney (ed), *The Frege Reader* (Oxford, Blackwell, 1997) 341. Note that Frege uses the word 'ideas' to refer to subjective psychological inner states.

[47] For a more or less similar distinction, see Ricketts, above n 43, esp 65–74.

external world (objective)—internal states (subjective). According to this unrefined classification if we want to find things that are objective we have to look into the realm of objects; hence if thoughts are to be objective they have to be themselves placed, as mind-independent abstract objects, next to the other concrete objects of the external world, according to the way Platonism prescribes.

An alternative way to interpret the notion of objectivity is to abide by Frege's interest to ground the objectivity of logic in an a priori way within the structure of judgements and the patterns of reasoning which aim to the formation of true judgements. Seen this way, objectivity refers to the a priority of the logical structure of judgments. This structure is a prerequisite in order to refer to objects (abstract or concrete) and therefore the notion of objecthood makes sense only against the background of judgements and the patterns of reasoning with them. To put it more vigorously, if thoughts need to be objective in the last instance, they have to claim an a priori objectivity which is prior to the notion of objecthood (reference). Rather it is the latter that rests on the former. On this account objectivity lies in the logical structure of judgements as they are employed within patterns of reasoning. In other words, *what is objective is something akin to the matrix of the thought* and retains some priority towards both our internal states and the way things might turn out to be (as depicted in true judgements). This structure reveals what kind of terms or building blocks can potentially form a judgement irrespective of the latter's truth or falsity. Admittedly, the grammar of thought is especially interested in the formation of true judgements and therefore not every combination of blocks will be satisfactory. This fact notwithstanding, truth and falsity depend upon the structure imposed by the grammar of judging.[48] That is to say, before anything can be judged as being the case or not, as existing or non-existing, it has to be incorporated or 'translated' into a judgement according to the way and under the constraints grammar imposes.

In order to deepen an understanding of the implications of each of the two options, I shall now turn to discuss two conceptions of mind-independence, the latter being traditionally identified as a condition for objectivity.[49]

2.4 Mind-independence and Realism

The Fregean argument for the existence of abstract objects depends, to a large degree, upon our ability to formulate true normative statements (premiss (p2) of

[48] This notion of objectivity shows a certain affinity to Andrei Marmor's conception of *logical objectivity*. This is the objectivity that applies to some type of discourse if it is possible to ascribe determinate truth values to the statements comprising the discourse (see A Marmor, 'An Essay on the Objectivity of Law' in B Bix (ed), *Analysing Law: New Essays in Legal Theory* (Oxford, Clarendon Press, 1998) 3–31 (at 6, 7)). One may say broadly that the objectivity of judgements lies in the fact that their semantic/logical structure makes them truth-evaluable.

[49] See Chapter 1.

the Fregean argument[50]). Clearly this ability relates to the question 'what makes legal/normative statements true?', or the question about the truth-makers of normative statements. We need, in other words, to account for the things (referents) via which normative terms 'discharge their referential function', as noted earlier. At this point emerges the issue of realism: if we want to argue for the existence of abstract normative objects, we need to be able to account for the referents of normative expressions as being mind-independent, or as being outside the mind, belonging to the environment and, thus, possessing a fact-of-the-matter nature. Conversely, if the things which normative statements target (ie their truth-makers), are of the mind's making, then there is nothing that could make normative statements in an objective way true. Put in this way, the issue of realism seems to be largely about mind-dependence/independence of the referents of legal statements. It seems, in other words, that some form of realism or Platonism is an inescapable condition for the success of the Fregean argument about the existence of abstract normative objects.

Be that as it may, a closer look at the mind-independence issue may reveal that the latter does not need to go hand in hand with realist ontology. This conclusion will be reached mainly through the remark that the semantics exhausts ontology thesis can guarantee a weak form of mind-independence, one that corresponds to claims of objectivity under conditions of intelligibility imposed by grammar. This weak notion of mind-independence may be substituted for mind-independence in the strong sense, namely one that presupposes realist ontology and a verification-independent notion of truth. Accordingly, I shall distinguish between two conceptions of mind-independence, out of which only the second will be inexorably connected with a realist ontology and therefore will be considered as incompatible with the semantic transformation of ontology:

(a) According to the first, the claim for mind-independence is the rejection of the idea that we have internally represented necessary and sufficient conditions that determine the extension of a term/concept. This tenet is compatible with, indeed necessitated by, the rejection of intentional items (formulas, representations, and so on) which may determine content conclusively. The most vigorous effort to reject ultra-determinants of the sort has been Wittgenstein's late philosophy. In rejecting those, Wittgenstein put forward the view that content is linked to a practice of rule-following. The dependence of content on practice makes it possible to distinguish between what we take to be the case and what actually is the case, for practices are external to minds and their constituents.[51] It follows that the first conception of

[50] See section 2.3.2.

[51] Many connect Kripke's and Putnam's externalist theories of meaning from the late 1970s with this tenet. This is not entirely accurate, for those theories rely heavily on the assumption that content determining practices are superior to inner representations just by virtue of the fact they are in closer proximity with the physical components of the environment. Clearly this view presupposes a strong version of mind-independence, for it assumes priority of the environment as regards matters of

mind-independence reconstructs objectivity against the background of the antithetical pair: intention-extension,[52] where both concepts are required to meet the standards of intelligibility imposed by grammar.

(b) The second notion of mind-independence is much more radical: here independence is conceived in relation to our way of gaining knowledge about the environment. On this stipulation, something is mind-independent if its being the case is independent (hence beyond) our ability to know it. Basically the issue here is that mind-independence means that truth is 'external to our judgements/language', whereas mind-dependence means the opposite. On this conception truth and reference are conceived against the background of an environment which in principle extends beyond our ability to know it, in the sense that our ability to know things is not a sufficient condition for the existence thereof. This conception of mind-independence reconstructs truth and objectivity as signifying verification transcendence.

On a first glance the two conceptions of mind-independence seem to entail each other: that is, only if we presuppose that the extension of terms (names, predicates) lie outside judgements it is possible to achieve truth and objectivity; and the other way round: sentences whose truth-conditions can be laid down in definitions, are products of our intentional apparatus and therefore not true as-a-matter-of-fact. But this coupling of the two senses of mind-independence, and derivatively of truth and objectivity, is by no means necessary. One reason for this is that the first meaning of mind-independence includes merely an epistemic claim as regards the possibility of making the distinction between analytic and synthetic truths. Conversely, the second notion of mind-independence entails a much stronger metaphysical claim, namely one about truth requiring the existence of an external (to our judgements) environment. In fact one can attain to the first conception of mind-independence without succumbing to the metaphysical aspect. For the next couple of sections I will try to show first that the metaphysical version is incompatible with the semantics exhausts ontology thesis

content individuation. This, however, is from a Wittgensteinian point of view just another case of ultra-representations or criteria that lead to radical indeterminacy. For a criticism of those views see the discussion in Chapter 3.

[52] Although the term *extension* belongs to the realist vocabulary its use should not be deemed inappropriate at present. It merely purports to capture the possibility that we may be wrong about the real content of a concept. For this to be possible one need allow that correctly formulated judgements, in whose environment extensions are settled, do not always depict facts. This requires in turn that it be possible to distinguish between true and false judgements. In this case truth need not be construed in a strong manner, namely as correspondence with the environment, but only as strong assertibility (or superassertibility). A sentence is superassertible 'if it is assertible in some state of information and then remains so no matter how that state of information is enlarged upon or improved'; for the notion of superassertibility see C Wright, *Truth and Objectivity* (Cambridge Mass, Harvard University Press, 1992) chs 1 and 2; also *idem*, *Saving the Differences* (Cambridge, Mass, Harvard University Press, 2003) ch 8.

and, secondly, that we still need to preserve the epistemic distinction between the extension and the intension of concepts.

The idea of an external world, whose existence lies beyond our ability to know it, relates to the desire to account for something that makes our statements true in an objective way. According to this longing, objectivity follows from the existence of objects that are located in an environment which is external to our minds and intentionality (referential realism). This somewhat naïve version of realism takes objectivity to supervene on objecthood with the result that truth relies on reference. Accordingly, the referential realist is someone driven by the commonsense intuition that our thoughts and linguistic structures can be objectively true only if there is a distance or 'slack' between those and the things that make them true. Justified as this idea may appear, it has an unexpected detrimental effect: it undermines objectivity by inducing a radical gap between mind and world. Notoriously, this gap, sooner or later, calls for some form of representationalism in order to be bridged. Either that or one will have to abandon any effort to account for the normativity of thought. In either case the price to be paid is high: it is the loss of any possibility for objectivity.

To this version of realism is usually juxtaposed some form of non-realism as being more successful in accounting for objectivity in the domain of truth and knowledge. The non-realist candidate which appears particularly promising in this respect is some variant of (Kantian) transcendental idealism.[53] According to it the intelligibility of the environment is subjected to a network of pre-given categories and schemata of experience, as well as the subsequent incorporation into the form of *Urteile* (judgements). The categories and further the *Urteile* (judgements) constitute the conditions for the existence of the physical world (*Gegenstände* or objects) which cannot exist independently of them; up to this point transcendental idealism implicates an ontological relativism. However, relativism at the ontological level does not amount to relativism at the level of truth and objectivity: the relativisation process that experience undergoes through the implementation of the categories or the *Urteile* seems to amount to a non-sceptical conception of truth and objectivity, for—according to what may be assumed to be the implied premiss—transcendental conditions of experience are taken to constitute a common denominator, or something like objective constraints of truth and knowledge. According to this Kantian, or rather neo-Kantian, view it is absolutely consistent to accept both the thesis that objects cannot exist independently of their incorporation into the form of valid *Urteile* and the thesis that truth is not relative.[54] Truth in this case will be constructed

[53] Transcendental Idealism is commendable for one more reason: it is part of the same rationalist tradition to which Frege also belongs. For a historical reconstruction that brings out the continuity of the rationalist tradition see Coffa, above n 3. For a critical presentation of (neo-) Kantian transcendental idealism, see C Heidemann, *Die Norm als Tatsache* (Baden-Baden, Nomos, 1997) 266–72.

[54] See *ibid* 271.

along the lines of the Tarskian convention T.[55] This verificationist version of non-realism need not be very strong[56]; the non-realist could accept the possibility of true sentences that are not (yet) known. What the non-realist would object to, however, is the existence of true sentences that are, in principle, unknowable (the latter is what the realist would accept). According to this explication transcendental idealism presents itself, as regards the issue of knowledge, as a case of empirical realism. From a neo-Kantian point of view this version of non-realism is advanced as an attractive alternative to referential realism, which holds that conditions of experience exist as such, a claim which further gives rise to the belief that objects exist independently of perceivers' experience (the Kantian '*Ding an sich*').[57] The challenge which the realist must meet is to find a way to bridge the gap between his private world of sensations and some mind-independent reality constituted by the co-ordinates of experience. The strong notion of reality, in other words, which referential realism nurtures increases by far the possibility that private sensations fail to grasp external reality. As a result referential realism amounts to scepticism about the external world.

Referential realism in this naïve version seems to completely succumb to the Myth of the Given,[58] namely the idea that the external world can guarantee the justification of our judgements on objective grounds and that, as a result, our judgements do not fail to make contact with the environment. Linked with these claims is a strong taste of scepticism and the resulting failure to connect thoughts with the states of affairs they purport to depict. But if the threat appears clearer in the case of naïve realism, not every form of non-realism remains intact either.

In particular, non-realist tenets with a strong verificationist component are vulnerable to similar objections, for they distort the priority of semantics over ontology.[59] In order to ensure that judgements make contact with the world, non-realism is required to generate justifications which are capable of incorporating environmental impacts into the 'space of reasons', ie the conceptual space

[55] For a detailed discussion of the Tarkian formula see section 2.5.2.2.

[56] Verificationism in this context means simply that understanding a sentence consists in grasping the sort of information states that would verify it. As such this version of verificationism is weaker that the one tendered by Logical Positivism; the latter contains the claim that a sentence is true only if there is actually evidence that warrant its assertion. See the discussion in section 2.6.

[57] It is worth noting that Kant's talk of the *Ding an sich* is a very ambiguous part of his philosophy and indeed provides the ground on which Kant could be judged as being a realist. The sort of realism that can be ascribed to Kant is that of referential realism, for he denies the possibility of ever gaining epistemic access to the *Ding an sich*. On the other hand it is questionable whether even this sort of realism could be associated with Kant. Conversely, it seems that the interpretation of the *Ding an sich* which best coheres with the rest of Kant's work is one that takes it to express an *abstract schema*: the object that is abstracted from all its features and properties, about which the only thing that can be said is that it is the object. For a detailed discussion of these issues see Heidemann, above n 53, 261–66. For a realist interpretation of Kantian philosophy, see R Langton, *Kantian Humility: Our Ignorance of Things in Themselves* (Oxford, Clarendon Press, 1998).

[58] See J McDowell, *Mind and World* (Cambridge Mass, Harvard University Press, 1994) 4 *ff.*

[59] A more detailed discussion of verificationism, with a view to illustrating its shortcomings, will be tendered in section 2.6.

circumscribed by well-formed judgements. At this point lurks the danger of a revival of the Myth of the Given in the guise of strong verificationism. Strong verificationism makes an appeal to external constraints which is not very different from the, perhaps more direct and primitive, appeal of naïve realism. Both appeals are joined in their failure to generate the required justifications. John McDowell identifies this point very elegantly when he says that what appeal to the Given amounts to is a brute impact of the exterior, one we cannot be held responsible for:

> But it is one thing to be exempt from blame, on the ground that the position we find ourselves in can be traced ultimately to brute force; it is quite another thing to have a justification. In effect, the idea of the Given offers exculpations where we want justifications.[60]

According to this critique, all strong verificationism can offer are exculpations instead of justifications. To that extent, non-realism does not seem to constitute a better alternative to naïve realism. Both positions seem to be trapped in a fruitless dualism which needs to be compensated by an appeal to the Myth of the Given.

In contrast to both naïve realism and some strong verificationist version of non-realism, a transformation of ontology performed along the semantic exhausts ontology thesis is in a position to uphold objectivity and truth without retreating to radical mind-world dualism and the sceptical *impasse* attendant to it. This transformation of ontology through the semantics exhausts ontology thesis relocates criteria of objecthood within the objective structure of inferential reasoning. This is so, not because we cannot have anything better than a judgement-related objectivity, on the supposition, say, that we can never make contact with the environment. Rather this is the case because, on a non-dualist understanding, the environment is necessarily implicated in the constitutive account of content which judgement-formation generates. That is, the content of our intentional states is already shaped in step with how things are. To use a somewhat daring expression, standards of truth and correctness are at the same time external while *already in-the-judgements.* Now, the difference is that externality has to do with what is objective (as opposed to subjective) in a logical sense, as Frege tried to imply. Understood thus, grammar, or the structure of thought, is no more than the structure of the world which impinges upon us 'from outside' as opposed to mental pictures and representations. It is this structure we are required to master if we want to engage in judging and reasoning.

In this context, in order to establish what a name stands for (its reference) it is necessary to attach that name to a true judgement which depicts a fact. The semantic priority of the judgement over its parts is, in a sense, justified by the composite structure of the environment which the judgement reflects: yet, in a trivial way, the formation of judgements, as of every 'whole', presupposes the

60 See McDowell, above n 58, 8.

understanding of its parts. Be that as it may, understanding those parts need not be independent of their being embedded in judgements: using predicates and names in judgements requires that we understand the way they function within multiple judgements: saying that an a (table) is F (red) implies that we already understand both how the name a functions in judgements of the form Ga, La, etc ('the table is blue', '. . .is yellow', etc) and how the predicate F functions in judgements of the form Fb, Fc, etc ('the chair is red', 'the door is red', etc). In other words, names, predicates and other terms can only be grasped within judgements, yet, once understood, they result in knowledge which is about those names and the objects they denote and not just about the judgements that include them or the facts they denote.[61]

A further important aspect of the priority of truth over reference is the fact that in uttering a judgement one places oneself under the normative requirement of the binary distinction true-false. If the judgement is false one should be ready to withdraw it. Conversely something that looks like a judgement but is not uttered under the obligation of withdrawal is not really a judgement. Thus the caveat of withdrawal captures the very essence of the normativity grammar imposes on content. It is the normativity of the logical structure of judgements which makes them truth-evaluable. This structure has to be thought of as logical as opposed to linguistic, for the grammatical structures of ordinary languages cannot account, in a necessary way, for the way sentences are truth-evaluable. Luntley puts it in an acute way:

> The study of grammar involved is . . . seen to be the study of that structure of our thought and language that makes it truth-evaluable. That is to say, the priority of semantics over metaphysics amounts to the claim that it is by studying the structure of our thought necessary for it to be aimed at truth that we uncover the structure of the world. Semantics provides an account of the structure of thought. It provides an account of the structure of language that makes it suitable for thinking and saying things that can be true or false. In so far we restrict metaphysics to what can be thought about or talked about, then a study of thought and talk will, ipso facto, be a study of the general structure of what is. On such a view, semantics gives us the outline structure of

[61] See Luntley, above n 5, 22. Also Coffa, above n 3, chs 4 and 5. On the formation of judgements and the connections between linguistic patterns of use and ontology see the classic and exemplary treatise of Quine, 'Speaking of Objects' in his *Ontological Relativity and Other Essays* (New York, Columbia University Press, 1977) 1–27 (at 1–16). Quine shows, in the best way, how the structures of language manage to 'reveal' objects around us by demonstrating that, the more complex are the judgements one is able to form, the more refined is one's ontology. Of course, Quine's purpose is to undermine the objectivity of conceptual schemes by showing how tightly they are connected to various linguistic structures. His demonstration has, nevertheless, been exploited in the opposite direction, the one I am also using; for such an account see the bulk of Donald Davidson's work and for a quick summary his recent 'Seeing through Language' in J Preston, *Thought and Language* (Cambridge, Cambridge University Press, 1998) 17–27.

what is thinkable. The only metaphysical issues left untouched by such a study will be the issues concerned with the unthinkable. It is not clear that that amounts to anything at all.[62]

2.4.1 Which Mind-independence?

The move towards grounding reference on logic renders the second of the two senses of mind-independence obsolete or even mistaken. Be that as it may, the semantic explication of reference is still perfectly compatible with the first notion of mind-independence, the one based on our ability to distinguish between something's being of the mind's making or not. To be more precise, the talk is of the ability to distinguish between terms whose content is fixed by their intension and those whose content is fixed by their extension. Accordingly, 'bachelor' is a term, whose meaning can be given through an analytic, intentional definition ('unmarried man'), whereas 'moon' is a term whose meaning is fixed by its extension, ie the actual body in space which revolves around the Earth. This distinction is perfectly intelligible and necessary within the framework of a semantic transformation of ontology. It is intelligible because a judgement-based explication of reference still makes the distinction between judgements that are about things that are mental constructions or mind-dependent and those that are parts of the environment or mind-independent. An ontology which is exhausted by semantics still can tell apart the mind and its artifacts from the environment and, for this reason, can make the distinction between the extension and the intention of a term. Cyclops are certainly creatures that do not exist as part of the environment, and for that reason the content of 'Cyclops' will be given by an (intensional) definition. On the other hand, the meaning of the concept 'horse' will depend on the way horses are. 'The way horses are' will be laid down in a number of judgements which succeed in articulating perceptual data about horses into coherent knowledge and cohere with one another. It is not false to depict the whole process by saying that a true judgement about elements of the environment is no more than the way of uttering perceptual data according to the structure of the thought and without contradicting previous judgements.[63]

The foremost intention of non-representationalist theories of intentional content is to account for the *direct impact* of the environment upon the formation of our intentional states and not to ostracise it from this formation-process. The emphasis such theories put on the a priori elements of intentional activity is not motivated by an interest to 'purge' a priori elements of intentionality from the 'imperfections' of the environment; rather it rests on the belief that the a priori maps 'what is the case'. To that extent these theories endorse the view

[62] Luntley, above n 5, 23.

[63] That said, a judgement about the environment involves always experiential input, while judgements concerning , say, Cyclops do not (unless one considers the information derived from mythology books to be of that kind). It is, more or less, this difference that makes the first notion of mind-independence also necessary, apart from intelligible.

that truth and reference are environment-involving. What they reject is the possibility that content be conceived of outside the context of well-formed judgements. That said, we still need a notion of mind-independence which, despite not amounting to knowledge-independence, can still demonstrate that meanings are not mental constructs, are 'not in heads', but, instead, are linked with the way things actually are.

2.4.2 Objectivity and Norms

The preceding discussion has illustrated a possible way to refer to normative (legal, moral and so on) entities in an objective manner, by taking them to be more than mere mental constructs. This possibility must be fleshed out by remarking that the issue of mental intermediaries (or representations[64]) cuts across that of mind-(in)dependence. For as long as mental intermediaries form the groundwork of a theory of content, all content remains mind-dependent *in a strong sense*. In this case there is no content whatever which is not of the mind's making. Accordingly, concepts depicting intellectual constructs (eg concepts of arithmetic: 'two', 'addition') remain mind-dependent as much as do those purporting to depict the environment ('tree' or 'table'). As soon as we reject mental representations, however, content becomes mind-independent with respect to every domain: empirical as well as abstract concepts acquire a certain distance from minds by ceasing to be mental constructs. Undeniably, even then, concepts depicting intellectual or abstract entities will bear a grater affinity to minds, in virtue of their being rational constructions (mind-dependence *in the weak sense*). Yet, even such concepts, continue to enjoy a relative independence from minds to the extent they derive their contents from networks of judgements inferentially related to one another. In this case, both the rule-governed structure of inferential reasoning as well as the dependence of rules of inference on the practice of their application, ensures that conceptual content escapes the radically subjective surroundings of minds.

On the face of it, even if normative concepts are called into existence by rational means (eg definitions) their content need not be exhausted by those means or, which is the same, be stipulative (analytic). The content of such concepts will still depend on the latter's ability to pick out properties in virtue of a network of judgements that stand in inferential relations to one another. To that extent the content of such concepts will be amenable to 'new' discoveries. Judgements of the sort are not analytic definitions or, in any other sense,

[64] For a discussion of representations see section 2.2.2 and Chapter 3.

statements about things in minds.[65] Treating them as such is a major misunderstanding that owes its origins to the mind-world dualism and the concomitant need for intermediaries which purport, in vain, to generate some kind of contact between the two.

Conversely if one does away with the dualist picture, judgements are conceived of as being about the environment. And in this case it is, of course, possible to distinguish between a definition that captures some functional or other internal features of a concept and a judgement that refers to extensional properties picked out by the same concept. The criterion here is that a judgement of the second kind will always provide us with additional or genuine knowledge concerning the content of the same concept. This can be demonstrated by using an example from the area of *colour.* Colour concepts are often compared with normative concepts to the extent that colour properties constitute secondary qualities of objects, or properties that do not exist independently of perceivers' powers but are conceptually linked to experience.[66] Imagine someone, say John, who spent all his life in a black and white room studying all aspects of colour in great detail to the effect that he came to know all definitions and descriptions of how and in what way different surfaces reflect light in order to produce the different colours and their variations.[67] One day John exits his room and the first thing he comes across is a patch of green grass. And he exclaims 'Ah! This is 'green''. Such a judgement which involves the environment is adding a new portion of knowledge in John's colour expertise, regardless of the fact that he already knew all definitions concerning 'green'. This case can easily be transferred to the field of normative knowledge. Regardless of whether one has the most perfect definition of a legal concept, say, 'contract' or 'beneficiary', there will always be room to infer from the network of existing judgements a new judgement which increases one's amount of normative knowledge. Insofar as this is the case, normative judgements are not about things in the head.

[65] Definitions can be taken to perform a semantic reduction of normative concepts akin to the one performed by other non-normative psychological concepts (as in the cases of emotivism and projectivism). All these reductionist moves rest normally on some form of eliminativism which holds that there are no genuine properties in the target domain of normative concepts. In most cases such forms of eliminativism amount to the complete elimination of normative concepts and their replacement through concepts which are considered to be able to pick out genuine properties (in this case properties of mental or psychological states). For a discussion of eliminativist views in moral and legal philosophy, see G Pavlakos, 'Normative Knowledge and the Nature of Law' in S Coyle and G Pavlakos (eds), *Jurisprudence or Legal Science?* (Oxford and Portland Oregon, Hart Publishing, 2005) 89–125.

[66] For a detailed discussion of the relation between secondary qualities and normative properties in the context of legal theory, see *ibid* 112 *ff.*

[67] The example paraphrases a similar example from F Jackson, 'Epiphenomenal Qualia' in *idem, Mind, Method and Conditionals,* International Library of Philosophy (London, Routledge, 1998) 57–69 (first published in (1982) 32 *Philosophical Quarterly* 127); see also in the same volume his 'What Mary Didn't Know', 70–75 (first published in (1986) 83 *Journal of Philosophy* 291) and the anti-reductionist argument based on the same example in M Tye, *Consciousness, Colour, and Content* (Cambridge Mass, MIT Press, 2000) 4–5.

With the issue of mind-independence, temporarily at least, out of the way, I shall turn to discuss standards of correctness for judgements. Given that the referential function of names and predicates has been explained away in the context of judgement, it is important to illustrate in more detail judgements' ability to track truth. The explanation should focus on what is it about true judgements which manages to discharge the referential role of their parts. What must be avoided, on pain of circularity, is any recurrence to the referential function of the parts of the judgement. Instead, the explanation that is advanced draws on the way judgements interlock when we reason.

2.5 Inferentialism and Truth

In the judgement-focused account of ontology pursued here, when we talk about the objective grammar of thought we refer to those patterns which govern the formation of judgements and the inference of valid (true) judgements from other valid (true) judgements (this is the process of reasoning). These patterns or laws are, trivially, identified as belonging to the realm of logic, ie as being laws of logic. Laws of logic are general norms which apply universally to processes of reasoning that enable us to connect thoughts with truth-values (by forming valid judgements). In embodying such standards, laws of logic form the basis of communication which, otherwise, cannot be achieved through subjective inner psychological states. As a result, the objectivity of grammar consists in the general and universal laws of logic. Those laws have as their subject matter the formation of correct judgements. To that extent they constitute the standards for the formation of correct judgements. Depicting this connection between logic and truth Frege says:

> Just as 'beautiful' points the way for aesthetics and 'good' for ethics, so do words like 'true' for logic. All sciences have truth as their goal; but logic is also concerned with it in a quite different way: logic has much the same relation to truth as physics has to weight or heat. To discover truths is the task of all sciences; it falls to logic to discern the laws of truth.[68]

At this point, the most crucial question for the issue of ontological commitment is where one is going to locate the standards of truth, which is to say, correct reasoning. As illustrated before, a Platonist explication which reifies standards of

[68] See G Frege, 'Thought' in M Beaney (ed), *The Frege Reader* (Oxford, Blackwell, 1997) 325–45 (at 325).

correctness as objects that can be associated to thoughts according to a name-bearer relation, would undermine the central importance of judgement. Conversely, the judgement-focused[69] explication of Frege's programme resists the idea that logic, as consisting of the standards of judging, is about judging itself in a pure form. It is not the case, in other words, that the laws of logic generalise over the forms of statements as regards their truth, thus amounting to the use of schematic letters and a truth predicate.[70] Within the Fregean project logic seems to realise a more substantive role. The basic laws of logic generalise over everything and every property. They do not mention the one or the other specific thing nor do they generalise over things in relation to the one or the other property. The point is namely that in Frege, laws of logic, or standards of reasoning, do not substantiate externally to concrete judgements in a manner that would require a meta-language to describe the way those standards apply to the judgements for the latter to be true (correct). Instead, the more substantive conception of logic which resides in the Fregean programme aims to reveal the standards of reasoning within the context of the judgement.

2.5.1 The Predicate 'True': an Example

A very good way to elucidate this point is by taking the predicate 'true'. For Frege the attachment of this predicate to our statements is not required because truth is not an (external) property that we need to attach to our thoughts through judgements. Any definition, in a meta-language, of the concept of truth taking it to be a property of thoughts, say in the way that the correspondence theory of truth takes it to be, would imply that we need a judgement in order to connect thoughts with the property of truth in the same way that we need some other recognitional capacity in order to connect a chair with the property of being red. But the capacity to recognise anything as having some property is not more than making a judgement. If this is the case then it seems that judgements are of two kinds: those that assign properties to things (as the property of being 'red') and those that assign the specific property of being true specifically to thoughts. Such a conclusion is absurd. Its absurdity derives from overlooking that any judgement of the form 'the chair in front of me is red' does not assign any property to the corresponding thought but merely fulfils the requirements for a true thought by associating it with a whole network of inferential reasoning.[71]

[69] For a very interesting exposition in this spirit, see Ricketts, above n 43, as well as his 'Logic and Truth in Frege' (1996) LXX *Aristotelian Society, Supplementary Volume* 121. Instead of judgement-focussed one could say Kantian. I think, though, that using the former leaves less room for misconceptions.

[70] As Ricketts remarks this is a more contemporary idea of logic, see above n 43, 76.

[71] Truth is in a way connected with the process of judging through reasoning. If thoughts can be viewed as isolated propositions 'corresponding' to some 'frozen' bits of reality, judgements are incorporated in chains of reasoning and are connected with other judgements in a way that makes them permissible (true) or false (impermissible).

In a way, truth is not a property to be assigned to something (a thought) but relates to the method that properties are assigned to things through judgements. If the judgement assigns the property in a successful way then the corresponding sentence is true. And the success of such an assignment is constituted through the valid inference of the judgement from other judgements and not on the basis of an extra judgement that aims to connect the original judgement/thought with the property of truth (the way truth is specified by a meta-language). On the contrary, supposing the latter would lead to an infinite regress: every time we would form a judgement in order to connect a thought with the property of 'being true' according to the conditions set in some definition of truth, say 'correspondence with reality', we would need a further judgement in order to connect the thought that the first thought is connected with the property of truth ('corresponds with reality') anew with the property of truth (as a 'correspondence with reality'), and so on.[72]

The important lesson to be drawn from the discussion so far is that truth and the other standards of correctness of judgements cannot be given on a meta-level, externally to judgements. Of course, this is not to say that there are no standards or that they are in some way ineffable. Frege takes those standards to be of the maximal generality and not to be inferred on the basis of the laws of any other domain of knowledge (or discipline).[73] Amongst the standards for the correctness of judgements count the laws of logic and the principles of inference (like, for instance, the *modus ponens* argument) which Frege takes to be distinct from the former. Be that as it may, in the Fregean system, the standards of correctness are not provided by statements *about* the judgements of a domain of knowledge, but are demonstrated *through* the judgements within the domain of knowledge.[74] Meeting or failing those standards is not a property that is ascribed to our thoughts through judgements; it is the appreciation within our reasoning of the constraints standards set to our reasoning:

> The recognition of a thought to be contradictory is not a judgement to the effect that a thought has some property. It is rather an apprehension manifested by the refusal to affirm the thought while affirming the opposite. Similarly to recognise that one thought implies another is to be prepared to accept the second on the basis of the first.[75]

[72] See Ricketts, above n 43, 77–79; and for a more detailed account of the infinite regress, his 'Logic and Truth in Frege', above n 69, part II. Having said that, a judgement-immanent account of truth would not be impossible. In section 2.5.2.2 I shall attempt to mould such an account under the rubric 'semantic theory of truth'. A semantic theory of truth will provide for a definition of truth, albeit in such a way that the definition will remain within the requirements of the present reading of Frege's conception of truth.

[73] See Ricketts, above n 43, part II.

[74] This conception of correctness dovetails with the idea that following grammatical rules, ie rules that guarantee the meaningfulness of our sentences, does not consist in any act of matching language with the world but, instead, depends on the practice of their application. Later Chapter 4 will make use of such practice-immanent conceptions of correctness with an eye to illustrating the activity of judging as a reflexive practice that is underpinned by reasons. See Chapter 4.

[75] See Ricketts, above n 43, 84.

This conception of truth and the other standards of correctness as being made explicit within judgements yields a picture of the grammar of thought according to which the latter is realised within the process of our inferential reasoning. To locate the grammar of thought, as containing standards of judging, within the process of reasoning has the seminal effect of locating objectivity within language. This is one of the most important transformations that the so-called *linguistic turn* achieved during the transition from the nineteenth to the twentieth century. After taking this step the environment is no longer conceivable in terms other than those of language. If what is true or false, consistent or inconsistent, depends on criteria which are made explicit within our reasoning, then truth and falsity are not a matter of correspondence to, or description of, something external that lies 'out there' but, instead, a matter of reasoning. Moreover not only truth, but, as we will see in a moment, also existence, becomes a matter of reasoning. Patterns of inference set the framework within which the ontological segmentation of entities into objects (as names) and properties (as predicates) takes place or, to say with Quine, 'to be is to be the bound of a variable'. This paradigm-transformation of philosophy, as already stressed in many previous occasions, is precisely the opposite of the subjectivism and the scepticism fostered by the idea of a radical mind-world dualism. It rests on the conviction that judgements are not combinations of (subjective) ideas in our heads whereas the criteria of truth lie 'out there'; that our judgements are subjective until they come to match (how then?) the world. Rather, the underlying assumption of the linguistic transformation is that we escape our subjectivity at the moment we succeed in forming valid judgements and in reasoning successfully. At that point we start *participating* in the world.

Truth and correctness are, thus, interwoven with the way the grammar of the thought unfolds as we go along making valid inferences and, more broadly, reasoning successfully. Two further aspects of the way grammar is enmeshed with the process of judgement-formation will be illustrated next.

On the one hand, one aspect concerns the fact that grammar enables us to distinguish between grasping a thought and its being true or false. It is often the case that despite not being in a position to ascertain a judgement's truth or falsity, we still can understand it. Here grammar provides the *intelligibility conditions* of content. On the other hand, the second aspect refers to the fact that our judgements, when taken together as a whole, generate a handful of constraints in respect of the truth or falsity of any new judgement. In this second function grammar generates *criteria for coherence.* In this context the truth of a judgement will always depend upon the inferences that previous valid or true judgements generate. Both in its intelligibility and coherence aspects grammar constrains in an a priori way the truth-conditions of judgements. Take for instance the following two judgements:

J1: all Mediterranean countries are warm

and

J2: as a Mediterranean country, Greece is extremely cold.

As they stand those two judgements are logically (that is a priori) incompatible. Even if we do not have any other information regarding their truth-values, their combination forces us to say that one of the two is false. This conclusion can be based merely on the structural features of the two judgements: on a first level we are able to grasp the two corresponding thoughts without having any information about their being true or false. This ability derives merely from the fact that both J1 and J2 are 'codified' in the same way, ie as grammar prescribes. This codification is the inescapable condition for their intelligibility. Notice now how the code (the logical structure) generates substantive conclusions: since both judgements are captured in the same structure a kind of unity appears between them. It is no longer enough that J1 and J2 are individually intelligible, but need to exhibit a joint intelligibility or *coherence*.[76] Now coherence, postulated by the a priori character of grammar, is in a position to allow or disallow, in an a priori way, potential inferences concerning the truth of the two judgements.[77] Assume for a moment that J1 is a true judgement and that we inquire on the cognitive content of J2. The intelligibility and coherence conditions would a priori render invalid an inference of the form J1 $\rightarrow$ J2, without requiring any further information about J2.[78] In a way, namely, the structure of grammar transfers knowledge about the content of J1 to the content of J2 through (inferential) reasoning. Understood in this way logical patterns impose standards according to which we are able to determine the truth or falsity of our judgements on the basis of inferential reasoning. They enable us to appreciate inconsistencies, agreements or analogies between the premisses of our reasoning without resorting to the notion of reference. Inasmuch as reasoning is more of a form of reason-giving rather

[76] In the context of practical reasoning the requirement of coherence cannot be satisfied by mere inferential or deductive reasoning as further evaluations are needed. In legal reasoning it is the case that coherence requirements are met by a two level reasoning. There the first-order or internal justification concerns the syntactical intelligibility and the inferential coherence of legal propositions, whereas the second-order or external justification is more about their practical appropriateness (see N D MacCormick, *Legal Reasoning and Legal Theory* (Oxford, Clarendon Press, 1978) chs 2, 5, 7 and R Alexy, *Theorie der juristischen Argumentation. Die Theorie des ratinalen Diskurses als Theorie der juristischen Begründung*, 2nd edn (Frankfurt am Main, Suhrkamp, 1986) 273–347. For a very comprehensive review of coherence theories in philosophy and law, as well as for an original statement, see Susanne Bracker, *Kohärenz und juristische Interpretation* (Baden-Baden, Nomos, 2000). For an excellent critical analysis of arguments from coherence in law see S Bertea, 'The Arguments from Coherence: Analysis and Evaluation' (2005) 25 *Oxford Journal of Legal Studies* 369.

[77] One should be careful to avoid any misunderstanding: what is a priori here is the structure of thought and the postulated coherence and not truth itself. Were the latter the case there would be no further need to reason! The claim is rather that the a priori structure of grammar recasts the problem of truth as a matter of inferential reasoning in a manner which avoids the representationalist vocabulary of reference. That said, it is still the case that empirical judgements are synthetic: in other words, there is room for an infinite number of novel judgements as regards what is the case. It is just the truth of those judgements that is going to be decided on the basis of our hitherto valid judgements (this should make perfect sense in the light of the non-dualist assumption that the building blocks of the environment are reflected in grammar and vice versa. On this assumption anything that does not exist or is not the case can only amount to a false judgement.)

[78] The underlying symmetry between thought and environment emerges here quite graphically: true facts block inferences that lead to false conclusions.

than of comparing signs (or groups of signs) with correlating objects, truth and falsity become the subject matter of justification. Truth is no longer a question of deciding in a crude/direct way if something of the mind's making refers (corresponds) to something that exists out there in the world. Once truth has been substituted, under the aegis of the 'semantic exhausts ontology' thesis, for reference, it is not possible to explain truth by evoking anew reference. Grammar provides a different means of deciding matters of truth (and, no doubt, reference): this is justification through valid inferential reasoning. Thus, the talk about truth and falsity can be already restated as talk about justified or not justified (inferential) reasoning. Hence, what is not justified will also be not the case (will be false) and vice versa.[79]

Attendance to the forms of inferential reasoning is in the position to reveal the structure of the environment which dovetails with the structure of thought and is a priori. The existence of a common underlying structure implies that it is also public in the sense that it is intelligible in an objective way, independently of inner mental processes. It is this assumption that led Frege to distinguish between the process of causal explanation of a person's beliefs (psychology) and the justification of those beliefs (logic).[80] It is the latter, justification through inference, and its underlying structures that are objective and with which Frege's interest exclusively lies. Construed this way judgement formation is based on our ability to appreciate logical patterns, inconsistencies and implications within a process of reasoning. Making or using judgements amounts to no less than mastering the ability to agree and disagree, to reason with others and, to put it in a nutshell, to communicate.

2.5.2 Conceptions of Truth

Attendance to inferential connections between judgments buttresses the judgment-centred explication of grammar which, in turn, underpins an intelligible notion of objectivity. It is time to investigate now which conception of truth corresponds to the inferential explication of grammar. In what follows I shall discuss two different accounts of truth. Whereas the first, the *correspondence theory of truth*, encourages a retreat to the priority of the referential role of names and predicates (ie the building blocks of judgement), the second, the *semantic*

[79] Clearly this point requires a more in depth analysis in order to be established, one that escapes the scope of the book. Perhaps a pertinent line of argument would be to assume that some notion of justification, which comprises possible alongside actual judgements, succeeds to ground the point tendered. For a detailed treatment of inferentialism see the seminal work of R Brandom, *Making it Explicit* (Cambridge Mass, Harvard University Press, 1994); *idem*, *Articulating Reasons* (Cambridge Mass, Harvard University Press, 2000); for recent efforts to connect the work of Brandom with legal theory, see M Klatt, *Theorie der Wortlautgrenze* (Baden Baden, Nomos, 2004); G Bongiovanni, A Rotolo and C Roversi, 'The Claim to Correctness' in G Pavlakos (ed), *Law, Rights and Discourse* (Oxford and Portland, Oregon, Hart Publishing, 2007).

[80] See Ricketts, above n 43, 74–75.

theory of truth, dovetails with an account of reference within the environment of judgement. Although none of the answers tendered in what follows should be taken to provide final answers to what is an extremely complicated topic, it will be possible to reach a temporary 'ceasefire' for the purposes of this book.

2.5.2.1 Truth and Correspondence

The *correspondence theory of truth*[81] takes sentences to be true in virtue of their correspondence to facts, where facts are considered to be parts of the environment that are characterisable independently of language and grammar. To that degree correspondence theories of truth are usually employed in the context of representationalist theories of thought and content. Hence, the main problem that any correspondence theory faces is to explain why the world is made out of facts, while maintaining that those facts are characterisable in a non-semantic way. The problem emerges because *facts* are not natural entities but 'entities' that are suited to be related to true judgements. Therefore *facts* presuppose that we have categorised the world in a way appropriate for making true judgements; but if the world has been 'cut' into facts then it has been already subjected to the same categorisation as that of judgement, namely the categorisation of grammar. As a result the correspondence theory, in its representationalist version at least, will already rest on language, despite a claim to the contrary.

Contrary to what the correspondence theory assumes, a semantic explication of truth need not make any concession towards idealism if thought-content is conceived as being world-involving, according to the idea of anti-representationalism. Anti-representationalism assumes that thought-content cannot be characterised independently of what it is about, ie the environment or the world. At the same time thought-content is structured according to the logical patterns of grammar. Hence it is possible to account for content (the world) through grammar. But in doing so one already accounts for what is the case. To that extent grammar aims to truth. Truth is the justificatory reason for the concept of logical grammar. Judgements are truth-evaluable in virtue of their embeddedness in patterns of inference which reveal the judgements' segmentation into distinct logical parts. As a result, the concept of truth can be analysed through the logical structure of grammar, as a semantic concept. In fact truth can be taken as constituting the basic semantic concept which mediates between logical grammar and the environment, to the effect that *ontology may be understood as supervening on grammar.*

2.5.2.2 The Semantic Conception of Truth

The basic idea of a semantic theory of truth is that the truth of judgements can be systematically computed from an account of their semantic structure. The

[81] For a brief account see Luntley, above n 5, 60–63. And for a more detailed account, K Taylor, *Truth and Meaning* (Oxford, Blackwell, 1998) ch III.

semantic theory aims to show that the combinatorial structure of judgements, as revealed through the inferential patterns in which they are embedded, determines their truth-conditions. Hence the definition of truth which the semantic theory arrives at is a recursive definition of truth.[82]

The semantic theory aims to demonstrate how the truth-conditions of any judgement expressible within first order predicate calculus can be derived from an account of the structure of the judgement in conjunction with an assignment of semantic values to the judgement's components. Any judgement in natural language which is expressible in first order predicate calculus will be amenable to a transparent display of the judgement's logical grammar. To that extent the semantic theory draws upon the *syntax of a language*, or the logical rules according to which something is a well-formed sentence in that language.

For any sentence S of a language L the semantic theory will provide a systematic account of what it is to say of S that it is true in L. This account will be recursive in the sense that it will give the truth-conditions of the sentence by ascribing semantic values to the atomic components of the language. A further condition is that the account of what it is for S to be true in L will be given on the meta-level of a meta-language ML. That is, the sentences within which the truth-conditions of S will be specified will be sentences not of L but of ML. Thus for any S in L the conditions of its being true will be given in the ML according to the clause:

(1) 'S' is true if and only if p,

where p are the conditions specified in ML. Here both the name 'S' as well as the predicate 'is true' do not belong to L but to ML. Further the condition given in p will be a way of expressing in ML what is for any sentence of L to be true. This would roughly amount to a translation of each of the sentences of L into the ML. In that way clause (1) will provide an explication of the predicate 'being true in L' for any sentence of L by drawing upon the recursive definition of the syntactic structures of L-sentences.

Let us take L to be a fragment of, say, German whose atoms are whole sentences and ML to be English. Then the specification of the truth-conditions of the L-sentence 'der Tisch ist schwarz' will be given by:

(1)' 'der Tisch ist schwarz' is true if and only if the table is black.

Along these lines, clause (1) provides the basic assignment of the conditions under which the atoms of a language possess a semantic value. When those atoms are taken to be whole sentences (as here 'der Tisch etc'), then the assignment of the conditions under which they possess a semantic value is already an account of truth-conditions, since in that case atoms are sentences and the semantic value of

[82] A semantic theory of truth will typically be modelled against the background of Tarski's theory of truth. For an account of the latter see A Tarski, 'The Semantic Conception of Truth and the Foundations of Semantics' reprinted in S Blackburn and K Simmons (eds), *Truth* (Oxford, Oxford University Press, 1999) 115–43; for further analysis see S Soames, *Understanding Truth* (New York and Oxford, Oxford University Press, 1999) chs 3 and 4; also Luntley, above n 5, 60–88.

sentences is truth (or falsity). But the point of the semantic theory of truth need not be as trivial as that. A semantic theory can gain the truth-conditions of any sentence *recursively*, by deriving them from the *semantic conditions* of sub-sentential units, that is without presupposing the concept of truth.[83] As a result, the truth-conditions of any sentence will be derived from the semantic conditions for singular terms and predicates. The semantic conditions for a singular term will be the conditions under which the term has a semantic value, namely the conditions under which it stands for an object (or, the conditions under which it refers). Similarly the semantic conditions for a predicate will be those under which it has a non-empty extension. Those conditions normally will have to be assigned on the base level of the theory in an extensional way, namely by establishing a certain relation between the atomic units of L and the world. According to a standard characterisation, the assignment of semantic conditions will be given through the concept of *satisfaction*.[84] Along these lines, the concept of truth will be defined via the semantic conditions of sub-sentential units which, in their turn, will be satisfied in an extensional way on the base level of the theory.

The 'extensional' satisfaction of the semantic conditions of sub-sentential units need not be radically different from the 'satisfaction' of the truth-conditions of any sentence according to clause (1). Take for instance an atomic, sub-sentential unit: the name 'Tisch'. On the base level of our semantic theory, the name 'Tisch' will acquire a semantic value along the lines of the clause:

(2)' 'Tisch' refers to table,

or, in the general form:

(2) 'F' refers to F

By ascribing a semantic value, clause (2)' discharges the referential function of the name 'Tisch' in a way that can make true the statement 'der Tisch ist schwarz'; namely by presupposing the existence of the object table. In this sense it can be said that the formal condition for any expression F to refer, or for clause (2) to be true, is the possibility of formulating an existential sentence of the form $(\exists x)(Fx)$ [or in our example: 'there is something that is a table'].[85] Hence the formal condition of the possibility to refer to an object can be stated as:

(3) 'F' refers to F $\Leftrightarrow (\exists x)(Fx)$.

Whenever it is possible to write an existential sentence of the above form there is an object denoted by the expression F. Further, it is the case that any assertive sentence which contains expression F can be taken as having a referential relation towards the object denoted by expression F, in virtue of which the sentence is made true. Therefore one could skip, as it were, clause (2)' and simply say that an assertion 'refers' to an object to the point that it is possible to restate the assertion as an existential sentence.

[83] See *ibid* 64 *ff.*

[84] *Ibid* 69–70.

[85] See the detailed analysis in Heidemann, above n 53, 309–17.

As a result, a semantic account of truth which is recursive will contain an account of reference for the sub-sentential units which amounts in turn to an account of the existence of the objects referred to. According to this account, any expression F (eg table) is thematised as an object through the use of its name 'F' (eg 'Tisch') within an assertive sentence (like in 'der Tisch ist schwarz'). If, further, the sentence is true then there exists an object that is denoted by the expression. The formal conditions for that are exhausted in the possibility to rewrite the assertive sentence as an existential sentence within which the expression F functions as a predicate (in our example: 'there is something that is a table'). Put in more general terms: the existence of an object will be established through the employment of an assertive sentence which implies an *affirmative existential sentence.*

This method for accounting for the existence of an object can be regarded as complementary to the Fregean strategy that was illustrated earlier.[86] There, the existence of an object was granted when an expression exhibited the appropriate role (that of a singular term) within the context of a true sentence. Under the light of the present account one can add: *an expression exhibits the appropriate role when it is possible to restate the original (assertive) sentence as an affirmative existential sentence in which the expression under consideration functions as a predicate.* This extension is perfectly consistent with the listed criteria for singular termhood since the latter imply the possibility of forming affirmative existential sentences in which the candidate-terms for singular termhood function as predicates. What is more, it decides an ambiguity as regards the priority of judgement over its parts, which is in-built in the Fregean argument for abstract objects.

Regarding the 'extensional' definition of reference in clause (2) there are two further points worth commenting on: the first concerns the assumed fundamental character of a definition of reference within a semantic theory of truth; why, in other words, should clause (2) be more 'basic' than truth-clause (1) in establishing some sort of link between language and reality? Prima facie there doesn't seem to be any reason for such a differentiation. But if this is the case then a new worry arises: do, perhaps, both (1) and (2) fall short of linking language with the world? The answer one is going to tender to those two questions depends largely upon the stance one chooses to adopt towards representationalism. If we accept representationalism, then we assume that it is possible to characterise the language and the world independently of each other. If we do so, then it does not really matter at which level of the theory we undertake the task of re-establishing a link between the two (when defining truth and reference). Any level would be as futile as any other. Conversely, if we reject representationalism then, again, it does not really matter at which level we undertake to define truth and reference; this time, though, the reason is that the link between language and

[86] *Cf* section 2.3.2.

world is already there! It is the idea of anti-representationalism: that there is no thing such as environment which is not mediated by thought (language) and its categories. When we look through the spectacles of anti-representationalism two things strike us as natural.

First, that any account of reference or truth cannot but be semantic, for the only way to 'slice reality' is through grammar. Accordingly, it does not really matter which of the two, reference or truth, we are going to make the basic level of an account of how language and the world make contact; for, in anti-representationalism, the issue of contact has been settled at an earlier point, through the concept of grammar. Of course, as argued earlier, it is probably more suitable to set truth at the basic level since the structures of grammar unfold predominantly on the level of sentences. Besides, the Fregean strategy demonstrated that a range of expressions denotes objects to the extent they function as singular terms in true assertive sentences; this was further supplemented with the remark that the existence of an object rests on the availability of restating assertions as existential sentences in which singular terms function as predicates.

Secondly, not everything that is formulated in linguistic structures is a linguistic entity. In clause (1), the right-hand side is the fact of the *table's being black*, rather than some linguistic item which needs to be connected to something extra-linguistic. The fact that the table is black is what makes the sentence 'der Tisch ist schwarz' true. With respect to it, a semantic account of truth does, after all, deliver a kind of correspondence theory, in a very different sense, however, than the usual understanding of the term assumes. What is depicted by the right-hand side of base-clauses are *facts*; not in any metaphysical or representationalist sense, ie as independent from grammar, but facts as a category that makes sense only in the context of grammar: 'the facts appealed to are the facts as categorised by human thought and language, but so what? There is no other kind'.[87] Further, it is possible to recast those facts as higher-order (or abstract) objects through nominalisations of the sentences that depict them. Along these lines, chapter VII will argue that legal norms can be explained as higher-order normative facts.[88]

To summarise: a semantic theory of truth accounts for truth and reference on the basis of the semantic features of judgments and the (inferential) relations that obtain between them. To that extent, truth and reference are subjected to *constraints from grammar*. Constraints from grammar are consistent with the idea of 'anti-representationalism' which chooses to individuate content through the structure of thought.

[87] Luntley, above n 5, 71.
[88] See section 7.5.2.

2.6 Grammar, Criteria and the Need for Practice

The last section of the chapter purports to deal with a danger arising from a potential interpretation of grammar which will be labelled *criterial.* Criterial interpretation interrupts the normative potential of grammar by rendering grammar a static structure which, in order to generate content, needs to be fed with content-giving data. Those data are, then, grouped together into definitions which, due to the a priori nature of grammar, assume the status of ultra-determinants which account exhaustively for content.

Staticity of criteria is juxtaposed to the normative programme of intentional realism. The latter purports to work out a theory of content-individuation which is capable of justifying intentional action. To this end it is required that a normative link be put in place between content and behaviour. Grammar can play the role of such a constraint only if its rules are explicated as bearing an internal relation to interpretations—be they of events, intentions or actions—which function as criteria that shape the contents of our thoughts. Conversely, any prioritisation of such interpretations over rules of grammar reopens the mind-world gap, for any item which purports to be final arbiter of content is prone to lead to a hopeless regress of interpretations and the sceptical impasse that attaches to them.[89]

The most striking case of reduction of grammar to criteria has been that of Logical Positivism (henceforth, LoP). In the first half of the twentieth century, LoP undertook the effort to account for ontological categories by adducing a grammar which comprised rules of syntax for logically reconstructed natural languages. Soon, however, in an effort to reconcile rationalism with empiricism, LoP ended up postulating empiricist criteria which determined the application of grammar. These criteria were grouped together into forming analytic definitions that would account exhaustively for thought-content. With this move LoP reinstates mind-world dualism, for the stipulated criteria remain hopelessly in need of a further criterion to connect them with grammar.

2.6.1 Logical Positivism and the Construction of the Environment

Painting with a broad brush, LoP combines two philosophical intuitions, one of a rationalist or idealist character and another of an empiricist or phenomenalist spirit. The former comprises the view that objective criteria for knowledge are to be found in the structure of thought which is a priori and can be revealed through a logical analysis of language (grammar). Moreover, by attaining this structure, one may reconstruct the structure of the world. On the other hand, phenomenalism—the empiricist component—postulates that all knowledge be reduced to elementary sensations (sense-data). It was the latter idea that

[89] See section 3.2.1.1.

prompted LoP to propose a reduction of all meaningful sentences to elementary Ur-sentences about objects of our immediate acquaintance (the notorious *Protokollsätze*[90]). Connectedly, any domain of discourse that did not correspond to sense-data of some sort was deemed meaningless for there was nothing there to *verify* the relevant sentences.

Surprising as it may sound, both components of LoP—the rationalist and the empiricist—can be traced back to the reductionist metaphysics of logicism of Frege and Russell.[91] These philosophers had attempted to reduce arithmetic to logic with a view to laying down a foundation for the complex concepts of arithmetic. Such reduction was meant to do away with obscure metaphysical questions regarding the ontological status of mathematical entities ('what are numbers?') and, instead, substitute in their place the far more transparent language of logic. In this way mathematicians would stop raising 'subversive' questions and instead continue to make use of the otherwise highly successful conceptual tools of arithmetic.[92] This programme was subsequently transferred by Russell into the domain of epistemology in an attempt to account for the existence of the external world[93]; albeit with one important difference: this time the fundamentals of the reduction were located in the data we are acquainted with through our senses (sense-data). On this strong empiricist supposition everything else we know and understand has to be reducible to sense-data. Connectedly, the grasp of a concept or proposition does not derive from any logical or semantic structure, as it did in the case of the reduction of arithmetic to logic, but originates directly from objects of our acquaintance. Conversely, any understanding of the meaning of words or sentences presupposes our grasp of concepts and propositions, for the latter, owing to their proximity to sense-data, are more 'basic' or fundamental in the chain of reduction. Russell's strategy of working his way up to meanings from elementary foundations of experience gives away a certain amount of confusion between semantic and ontological issues, one that Wittgenstein would revisit more and more in years to come.[94]

[90] See R von Mies, *Positivism* (Cambridge Mass, Harvard University Press, 1951) ch 8; also O Neurath, 'Protocol Sentences' in A J Ayer (ed), *Logical Positivism* (New York, Free Press, 1959) 199–208.

[91] There are a lot of good works on the movement of logicism. For a historically minded one see Coffa, above n 3, chs 11, 12, 14.

[92] It could be said that the reductionist programme of logicism corresponds to two different kinds of reduction in the case of mathematics and in that of epistemology. In the former reduction serves the purpose of replacing systems of expressions, whose usefulness is granted but no proof of their validity is available, with other systems that are less problematic. Conversely, in the case of epistemology the main aim is to substitute in the place of ontologically demanding categories a method construction from elementary sense-data. For a discussion of reductionism and its different variants in the historical context of logicism, see Coffa, above n 3, 214–18.

[93] B Russell, *Our Knowledge of the External World*, (London, Allen & Unwin, 1972); in this book Russell proclaims; 'the study of logic becomes the central study in philosophy: it gives the method of research in philosophy' (*ibid* 243, as quoted by Coffa, above n 3, 208).

[94] Wittgenstein, despite blending elements of Russell's phenomenalism in his own early work, would complain early on about the reduction of the meaning of signs to sense-data. One of the

Until the latter's criticisms would become louder and clearer, however, the logicist programme and the unexpected twist it took in the field of epistemology would be the two main sources of inspiration for Rudolph Carnap and the Vienna Circle.[95]

In *der Logische Aufbau der Welt*, the *opus magnum* of LoP, Carnap takes up the motivation and the conceptual tools of logicism, albeit giving a different turn to the logicist project, at least in the form Russell had applied it to the philosophy of knowledge.[96] Although Carnap's programme incorporates a fair amount of empiricist elements, not least amongst them a verificationist theory of meaning,[97] his implementation of the constructivist enterprise is much more faithful to the rationalist inspiration of logicism than Russell's own epistemology. One reason may lie in the fact that Carnap was very keen on demarcating his philosophy from the 'substantive' metaphysical doctrines of empiricism, idealism and realism.[98] Another possible explanation is that Carnap was embedded in the Kantian tradition[99] of German-speaking philosophy, a tradition that was far more amenable to the formal aspirations of logicism than those of the other substantive metaphysics.

The difference between empiricist and rationalist versions of constructivism may be depicted as follows: empiricist programmes place their faith in elementary sensations which they take to enjoy the highest degree of objectivity and certainty. As a result, in them, principles of construction are designed in order to 'transfer' the apodictic power of elementary sensations to the higher levels of the construction. On the contrary, rationalist constructivism is highly suspicious vis-à-vis any kind of sense-data acquired through the sensory apparatus of individuals which is deemed messy and unreliable. Connectedly, in this case, the

earliest complaints can be found in the much-quoted passage from the *Tractatus*: 'Die Logik muß für sich selber sorgen' in L Wittgenstein, *Tractatus Logico-philosophicus* (Frankfurt, Suhrkamp, 2003) and in English translation by D F Pears and B F McGuinness (London, Routledge and Kegan Paul, 1961) para 5.473. For a very illuminating discussion of this passage, see P Hanna and B Harrison, *Word and World: Practice and the Foundations of Language* (Cambridge, Cambridge University Press, 2004) 77–94.

95 I shall confine the discussion to Carnap. I would hope that this choice is justified by Carnap's central role in the promotion and development of LoP. For a reliable sample of the views of the main exponents of the Vienna School, see Ayer, above n 90.

96 R Carnap, *Der Logische Aufbau der Welt* (Hamburg, Meiner, 1961).

97 Although verificationism is not explicitly part of the *Aufbau*, it is safe to assume that its emergence was enabled by the ideas of that book.

98 *Cf* Carnap, above n 96, 5–6.

99 As far as the idealist strand of the *Aufbau* goes, Carnap's constructivist programme greatly resembles the Kantian tradition, and in particular the neo-Kantian intuitions shared in the German-speaking world by many contemporaries of Carnap. That said, Carnap's programme was in many respects superior to other contemporary neo-Kantian philosophies, despite sharing with them a similar interest. The reason lies in the fact that Carnap was using a far more developed conception of semantics incorporating logical tools which allowed a more 'neutral' metaphysical standpoint than neo-Kantianism.

point of construction is to embed lower-level evidence, contaminated by too high an amount of subjectivity, into the objective, or intersubjective structure of the construction.

Empiricism entails the metaphysical thesis that the world is exhausted by states of affairs which are immediately encounterable in experience. This thesis amounts to a prioritisation of empiricism over rationalism which not only undermines claims of objectivity in many areas of non-empirical discourse but, what is worse, weakens the claims of LoP in the domain of scientific knowledge, contrary to all intentions of LoP. This results from undermining LoP's most original intuition about logic and language being antecedent to truth and knowledge; in other words, the intuition that in order to know a proposition (ie to establish its truth) we must first know which proposition we are talking about. The latter knowledge, however, requires that propositions be individuated by the appreciation of the logical structures of our sentences, rather than some 'magical' or 'immediate' grasp of items that are individuated by sense-data (as in phenomenalism) or the environment (as in realism). Consequently it is semantics that determines content and not anything external to it.

Indeed one of Carnap's main concerns in the *Aufbau* was to refute the view that content-individuating entities are antecedent to logic and language. The latter view is linked with the possibility of asking the questions that traditionally form the subject matter of (referential) realism: 'are there really xs?', 'is there really an external world?'. To this Carnap objected that it is not even possible to coherently raise those questions, for their formulation already presupposes the semantics of a language. Consequently, the meaninglessness of such—and other similar metaphysical—questions derives from the fact that they fall outside the constructivist framework, rather than the impossibility to verify them by way of reference to any scientific data (in other words, meaninglessness is not matter of verification). On the face of it, there is a strong argument for the priority of rationalism over empiricism in LoP, despite the emphasis placed on the language of phenomenalism.[100]

[100] For a convincing explication of the *Aufbau* along these lines, see M Friedman, *Reconsidering Logical Positivism* (Cambridge, Cambridge University Press, 1999) 90–91 and especially 108–13. Also S Paulson, 'Zwei Wiener Welten und ein Anknknüpfugspunkt' in C Jabloner and F Stadler (eds), *Logischer Empirismus und Reine Rechtslehre* (Wien and New York, Springer, 2001) 137–90. Paulson bases his argument for Carnap's rationalism on Carnap's statement that phenomenalism is only one of the possible starting points as regards construction in the *Aufbau* (others being physicalism etc). Others disagree: see H Putnam, *Words and Life* (Cambridge Mass, Harvard University Press, 1995), where he argues that Carnap's phenomenalism (which he calls solipsism) is conceptually connected with LoP: phenomenalist sense-data will always be defining for LoP insofar as the final criterion for knowledge remains focussed on the individual's sensations.

2.6.2 Verificationism

Be that as it may, Carnap ended up embracing phenomenalism's damaging effects by subscribing to the dogma of verificationism. Although a few years would pass before the dogma found its precise formulation, its beginnings can be identified in Carnap's *Aufbau*. Using a rather broad brush[101] we may identify two variants of verificationism. The former, with respect to meaning, entails that that we can 'think of' possible states of affairs which would verify our propositions, those that have been already individuated by the semantic structures of language. This instance of verification is of low intensity for it does not require that the stipulated states of affairs be also available (or that we have access to them), hence it is compatible with the priority of semantics over ontology. Verification becomes more demanding—and loses in convincingness—in its second variation, when it is postulated with respect to truth. Then it says that a proposition is true (hence knowable) if and only if it can be actually verified (or has been already verified). This postulate was destined to found its sharpest formulation in the so-called verificationist conception of meaning and truth which was advanced in the 1930s by a number of thinkers (logical positivists in Continental Europe and A J Ayer in England). On the assumption that the possibility of knowledge depends on our ability to verify propositions, those philosophers required that one evoke facts which are either elementary sensory inputs, statable in basic, observational, proto-sentences of science (the notorious *Protokollsätze*); or, alternatively, reducible to such facts (and the relevant *Protokollsätze*). This conception of truth as verifiability can become very restrictive—almost suffocating—for content and meaning, for according to it meaningful are only the sentences for which it is possible to identify true propositions (or existing states of affairs). Notably, its results were particularly damaging with respect to normative discourse: if one postulates that criteria for the use of normative terms and, further, conditions of normative knowledge be fully located in sensory input of some kind, it is most likely that none of the things we refer to as normative, nor the language we use in so referring, would satisfy the specified condition, for normative entities do not 'emit' anything which can be recorded by our senses or regulate our use of normative terms. Departing from such positions the movement of LoP ended up repudiating whole areas of discourse (most of traditional metaphysics, morality, ethics) as meaningless because they lacked support by any piece of scientific knowledge.

However the connection between the two kinds of verification, the one with respect to meaning and the other with respect to truth, is not a necessary one. In

[101] For an informative summary of the main ideas of verificationism, see J Skorupski, 'Meaning, Use, Verification' in B Hale and C Wright (eds), *A Companion to the Philosophy of Language* (Oxford, Blackwell, 1999) 29–60.

order to relate them to one another one must be labouring under two suppositions, both of which are reminiscent of the (rather bold) metaphysics of Wittgenstein's *Tractatus*: that, on the one hand, a sentence has meaning only if it is possible to picture some state of affairs; on the other, to conceive of reality as the totality of items (states of affairs) which are encounterable immediately in experience. As indicated earlier, Carnap makes an unwarranted move to that picture of the world. In order to follow the details of it we need now to turn to Carnap's ontology (although he would be very unhappy with the term).

2.6.3 The Metaphysics of the Aufbau

In the *Aufbau*, Carnap undertakes the task to reconstruct ontological categories on the basis of a system of logico-syntactical rules which he borrows from the 'new logic' elaborated by Whitehead and Russell in the *Principia Mathematica*.[102] Despite falling squarely into the philosophical tradition of replacing ontology through semantics, the constructive strategy of Carnap (his *Konstitutionssystem*) fails at the end of the day to offer an individuation of ontological categories in purely formal terms for it subjects their validity to the experiential data available to the observer.[103] Let us see why: the construction technique in Carnap generates ontological categories through the interaction of higher-order objects (concepts) with elementary sensations which form the basic level of the construction. Connectedly objects are constructed in the light of higher-order objects (Carnap calls them quasi-objects) when they 'interact' with sense-data. Quasi-objects (or concepts) have the form of unsaturated functions F(x); hence anything that can occupy the place of the variable is rendered an object at the lower level and so on until one reaches the elementary sense-data. Thus in order to construct a red object, say a ripe apple, one would have to saturate the function that stands for the class of red things with some sense-data originating in the observer. Once an object has been constituted one may follow the reverse procedure and break it down into its elementary constituents which, as one would expect, consist in sense-data. As a result any construction is valid only to the extent that it contains, in latent form, the possibility of reduction.

A similar procedure applies *mutatis mutandis* at the basic level of the construction, the one with respect to the elementary sense-data which form the starting point for all construction. Given that those cannot be broken down into simpler counterparts, they are 'analysed' by being subjected to a covert process of synthesis (Carnap calls it *quasi-analysis*). Quasi-analysis is the process whereby

[102] This is basically the theory of types that Russell and Whitehead developed in their *Principia Mathematica* in order to deal with a number of paradoxes in set theory (most typical amongst them the so-called liar's paradox). See Carnap, 'The Old and the New Logic' in Ayer, above n 90, 133–46, [139–40].

[103] For the constructive strategy in the *Aufbau* see Friedman, above n 100, Coffa, above n 3, 214; and Paulson, above n 100.

the constituents of elementary sensations are individuated by subsuming them under the unsaturated component of quasi-objects (concepts). In this case quasi-objects represent, roughly, certain resemblances between clusters of sense-data (hue, saturation and so on).[104]

There is a certain amount of flexibility in this constructive structure, for what is a concept on one level of the construction may assume the role of a quasi- or higher-order object on a different level. This flexibility encourages Carnap to say that there is no conclusive reason for taking any of the levels of the constructions to be basic; thus it is possible to insert at the lower level physical objects or indeed the sensations of every observer as opposed to those of one observer only. What matters for the construction, so Carnap tells us, is the structure of the construction itself. Owing to its formal character it fosters an ontological pluralism while it presents itself as metaphysically neutral. Metaphysical neutrality is what makes the constitution system so basic that any metaphysical claim or question which attempts to transcend it becomes meaningless.

Truth be told, Carnap's system, in its formal-semantic aspect, suggests a kind of ontological liberalism, for anything that is admissible from the point of view of the semantic structure (or the constitutional scheme) is a candidate for existence (ie can be an object). From the point of view of legal theory, this is a most convenient idea which could be put into the service of an account of normative entities. Such an account would have been capable of demonstrating that propositions of law are individuated by semantic structures and, as a result, of reaffirming the priority of language over ontology, a priority that is essential for the possibility of objectivity in law. Unfortunately Carnap's thesis for metaphysical neutrality collapses because of his insistence on the reduction to sense-data as a condition for constitution. This condition goes much deeper than a first look may suggest: far from confining itself to actual objects, phenomenalist reduction goes into the heart of ontology: not just actual objects but also ontological categories must succumb to it. To put it differently, reduction, ie the possibility to carry out the construction in reverse order, must hold not only for 'saturated functions' but, what is worse, unsaturated functions as well.[105] This is precisely the point of committing the unwarranted move to the metaphysical picture that assumes the world is exhausted by states of affairs immediately encounterable in experience (the verification theory of truth). No sooner is this picture in place,

[104] Some commentators (Paulson, above n 100) identify in this a strong proof of idealism, for it appears that sense-data come never in a raw, unconstructed form. Be that as it may, one should not forget that the relation of resemblance between sensations—which underpins the notion of quasi-analysis—is a problematic concept not least because of its solipsist nature. As a result the construction of sense-data becomes circular for it derives its force not from any rational structure but, instead, from the category of resemblance between sensations.

[105] Putnam thinks along the same lines when he remarks that the solipsism of Carnap's phenomenalism will always reappear no matter which interpretation of the raw data of the construction is taken. Unsurprisingly, in addressing this point, Putnam intends to show that, to the extent phenomenalism is solipsistic, it fails to make any contact with the environment (this handicap he labels *Brentano's problem*). See his *Words and Life*, above n 100, ch 4.

however, than anything which cannot be subsumed under the reduction formula is rendered meaningless. Accordingly, content ceases to be a matter of semantic structure—as the rationalist intuition of LoP would want it—and becomes an issue of sense-data. Such data are considered as forming criteria and definitions which are defining for the content/meaning of concepts and propositions. This move is especially damaging for law: unless one is prepared to reduce all law to sense-data, one would have to reject the possibility of meaning and knowledge regarding the legal domain.

To sum up: Carnap misses the opportunity to fully cash in the pluralist benefits of the semantics exhausts ontology thesis, for his constitution system rests on the supposition that every 'construction' has to be reducible to sense-data. His insertion of sense-data into the construction formula causes the cancellation of the most beneficial component of the semantic exhausts ontology thesis: ie the priority of semantics as regards content and knowledge. In order to avoid this conclusion one would need to couple the priority of semantics over ontology, the rationalist element of LoP, with a different conception of the semantic structure; this would require that one abandon the idea of phenomenalist reduction as a necessary component of the construction strategy and replace it with an intersubjective structure capable of generating content. Logical positivists never managed to deliver along those lines, for they were too concerned to avoid building a philosophical edifice that bears no relation with the environment.[106] It would take a few more years and some intense philosophical thinking before Wittgenstein would come up with a radical conceptualisation of grammar as a practice of rule-following, moving away once and for all from phenomenalism and the world-view it presupposed.

[106] See von Mies, above n 90; and Neurath, above n 90.

3

Grammar and Rule-following

3.1 Introduction

Grammar was introduced in order to guarantee a notion of intelligible content, one that would guard knowledge from scepticism. We saw that the most important source of such scepticism is the mind-world dualism which pertains in equal portions to realism and some mentalist understanding of intentional content. Conversely, the idea of grammar is apt to close the gap by introducing the view that the environment does not exist independently from our ability to use propositional language as a condition of regarding something as an object (or else our ability to judge).[1] Thus what makes our thoughts true and leads to knowledge is subject to constraints from grammar, specified as the set of norms which govern the form and inferential relations between judgements. Along these lines, judging is the condition for articulating what is the case in a manner that is *fundamental*. Consequently, nothing outside grammar may assume priority in determining content. The opposite would cause grammar to deteriorate into criteria, as the case of Logical Positivism has illustrated graphically.[2] Criteria are beset by the exact same problems as mental intermediaries, for they allow a gap between mind and world to open, one that is beset by the familiar devastating consequences. How, then, to illustrate the fundamental character of judging without evoking another type of intermediary?[3]

In embarking on this enterprise, I shall turn to the late work of Wittgenstein[4] which contains a painstaking effort to disclose the foundation of intentionality (the ability to form contentful thoughts). What is interesting about this work for present purposes is the thoroughness with which Wittgenstein scrutinises (and

[1] I owe this formulation to Carsten Heidemann.

[2] See section 2.6.

[3] It should be remarked in passing that this requirement cannot be met simply by postulating anti-representationalism. For grammar to develop its anti-representationalist powers, a separate demonstration of its fundamental character is called for, one that excludes all other determinants of content.

[4] The most representative work of this period is, of course, L Wittgenstein, *Philosophical Investigations*, translated by E Anscombe, 3rd rev edn (Oxford, Blackwell, 2001).

eventually rejects) a plethora of possible determinants of intentional content.[5] Endorsing Wittgenstein's conclusion, I proceed to identify the *capacity to follow a rule, as the capacity to engage in normative activity,* as the foundation of all content. Rule-following constitutes a practice which constrains the ascription of content to mental states, linguistic signs and tokens of behaviour. Practices are sufficient for dismantling sceptical arguments, because they open up anew the possibility to refer to standards/criteria as objective constraints of content: while outside practice any criterion can be equated to its sceptical counterpart, under the cupola of practice criteria can be employed coherently in order to justify judgement and behaviour. What criteria cannot do inside practice is to fully determine content; to carry, as it were, the full burden of content formation. But this they cannot do anyway, for as soon as they are stripped of the protection of practice they collapse into their sceptical counterparts and from there to unintelligibility. Thus, in the end, criteria are rendered effective only to the extent they derive their capacity for determinate content from a more fundamental level of rule-following.[6] This, then, will be the structure of the chapter:

The opening section is about rejecting gap-openers in the form of anything that purports to function as a final arbiter of content (ultra-interpretations[7]). Ultra-interpretations are marked by the claim that they possess properties which are intrinsically content-determining. The discussion is introduced with a dilemma: either all standards of content lead to scepticism or there are some privileged standards which escape this fate. Both horns of the dilemma fail to produce content. In illustrating the reasons for the failure I take the opportunity to illustrate the shortcomings of some typical examples of ultra-interpretations (mental intermediaries and Platonic entities).[8]

Wittgenstein's solution of practice is presented in sections 3.3 and 3.4. Absent a more detailed positive account of practice (Wittgenstein, in fact, spends the larger part of the *Philosophical Investigations* in giving a negative account of practice!) the exact content of practice has been the object of much controversy. I begin by examining and rejecting two prominent interpretations of practice which fail to go beyond dualism: the communal interpretations of Saul Kripke and Crispin Wright. The former is rejected on the grounds of its scepticism, while the latter on those of its behaviourism and the loss of normativity it effects. The behaviourist view is given special attention, for it will re-emerge in Chapter 5 in an effort to refute a particular reconstruction of legal practice. Following this, a more successful interpretation is presented. According to it rules bear an internal

[5] Intentional content is used throughout as synonymous with meaning.

[6] Along the same lines see S L Hurley, *Natural Reasons: Personality and Polity* (New York and Oxford, Oxford University Press, 1989) chs 2, 3 and 5; also N Stavropoulos, *Objectivity in Law* (Oxford, Clarendon Press, 1996) 147–59.

[7] The term derives from Hurley, above n 6, 35.

[8] For a detailed account of intermediaries, see S Kripke, *Wittgenstein on Rules and Private Language* (Oxford, Blackwell, 1984) 7–54, where he offers an exemplary reconstruction of Wittgenstein's arguments in *Philosophical Investigations*, above n 4, paras 134–242.

relation to their applications. Internality in this context guarantees that rule-following constitutes the most fundamental level as regards intentionality. All other criteria or grounds spring out from rule-following and become intelligible only against the background of the latter.

Section 3.5 turns to update the discussion on truth, tendered in chapter II, in the light of the remarks on rule-following and practice. In Chapter 2 I argued that the priority of judgement necessitates the priority of truth over reference, which, in syntactic terms, corresponds to the priority of sentence over its parts (names and predicates). This priority was secured against the background of a semantic conception of truth. In this chapter I turn to further elaborate on that conception by supplementing it through a use theory of content: the pragmatic account that emerged from the preceding sections of this chapter is now put into the service of linking truth to the conditions for asserting sentences. This gives rise to a pragmatic conception of truth, one that necessitates an understanding of truth conditions as assertion conditions. On this conception truth becomes compatible with the role of grammar as the most fundamental instance of rule-following.

The chapter concludes with some clarifications on the relations between rule-following (practice) and grammar. Although Wittgenstein does not specify the type of rule his rule-following considerations apply to, it is rules of grammar I have most in mind in the present context. For it is those rules which, in the most abstract sense, point the way for intentionality (just as beauty does for aesthetics and goodness for ethics, to paraphrase Frege[9]). Of course Wittgenstein does not purport to bestow only rules of grammar with content-giving abilities; for him any practice (and the rules that lie at its 'bedrock') is content-giving. However, in contrast to other, less fundamental practices, grammar conditions the possibility of judging as such; hence, it forms the condition for the possibility of every other practice. The claim about the fundamental character of the practice of grammar is illustrated through the following line of reasoning: (p1): rule-following must guarantee normativity of content; (p2): normativity requires ability to refer to reasons; (c): rule-following must enable reference to reasons. Reference to reasons is only possible if we can conceive of them as subjects of predicative sentences. For that, however, one needs the referential structure of grammar. It follows that grammar is the most fundamental practice. With respect to this conclusion two further points are touched upon: first, the reflexive character of rule-following; secondly the worry—of a realist origin—that, unless the fundamentality of practice is explained in terms of a close link with the environment, practice might turn into another intermediary.

[9] See G Frege, 'Der Gedanke. Eine Logische Untersuchung' in *idem*, *Logische Untersuchungen*, 4th edn, G Patzig (ed) (Göttingen, Vandenhoeck & Ruprecht, 1993) 30–53.

3.2 Rule-following and Content

Recent exegesis[10] has treated Wittgenstein's rule-following considerations and the related private language argument as being about the content of intentional states, thus inscribing it into the discussions concerning relations between mind and world within contemporary philosophy of mind and epistemology. Understood this way, the argument is an attempt to clarify the reason why concepts we employ end up signifying things (objects, states of affairs, value-properties, etc) in a way that is objective to anyone using them. Thus, the first step is to address the problem of the content of those mental states that constitute the outcome of our perception or the ground upon which our intentional action rests: why is it the case that these states (beliefs, desires, and so on) have one content rather than another, thus being able to tell us something determinate about the world, irrespective of the fact of their being true or false, and therefore to cause our intending to do something, irrespective of the fact whether we succeed or fail at doing it? Understanding why content is determinate or certain sheds further light on our understanding of how there can be a distinction between being correct (level of perception) or successful (level of intentional action) in one context and mistaken in another. In this respect the problem of content or the *problem of aboutness* refers both to the level of experience or perception as well as to that of intentional action.[11]

The problem of content or *aboutness* is certainly a variation of the question about the relation between mind and world. This is the reason why the way one is going to account for the determinate character of concepts' content is very much dependent upon one's understanding of the mind-world relation. Thus a Platonic philosopher would respond to the riddle of content by invoking a mysterious power of entities as such which have the ability to impinge upon minds. For the Platonic philosopher:

> If the question arises of whether someone meant *add two* rather than *quad two*, and so of whether he is wrong about addition or right about quaddition, it is in some way answered by the superior status of addition in this respect.[12]

On the other hand a Cartesian or *lato sensu* mentalist philosopher would try to solve the problem of content by appealing to some intrinsic qualities of objects stemming from the opposite direction, ie that of the mind. In this case they are

[10] See in particular G P Baker and P M S Hacker, *Wittgenstein: Rules, Grammar and Necessity*, vol. 2 of an *Analytical Commentary on the Philosophical Interpretations* (Oxford, Blackwell, 1988); S L Hurley, *Consciousness in Action* (Cambridge Mass, Harvard University Press, 1998); J McDowell, 'Wittgenstein on Following a Rule' reprinted in A Miller and C Wright (eds), *Rule-Following and Meaning* (Chesham, Acumen, 2002) 45–80.

[11] Hurley, above n 10, 221 *ff.*

[12] *Ibid* 223.

images, formulations of rules, experiences or feelings that possess the mysterious power to draw the world towards the mind and in this way to bridge the mind-world gap.

The relations between mind and world are a central part of Ludwig Wittgenstein's later philosophy, notably his considerations on rule-following and the private language argument. With them Wittgenstein purports to refute both Platonic and mentalist explanations of content as futile and unsatisfactory. For him Platonic constructions of the world's intrinsic mind-drawing powers are inasmuch idle as are their correlative mentalist constructions of those world-indicating powers that are intrinsic to minds.[13] There is, however, enough evidence to suppose that this rejection seems only to be symptomatic of a more general and all-encompassing rejection. Platonism and mentalism are, according to this assumption, rejected only as the most extreme and therefore naïve versions of a deeper problem: deep-rooted mind-world dualism. As long as this gap is maintained not only absurd Platonic or mentalist intrinsic qualities of items (worldly and mental respectively) fall short of bridging it, but so does any other kind of entity, be it Platonic, mentalist or other, which purports to be intrinsically content-determining (ultra-interpretation[14]). To that extent Wittgenstein's account might well be taken to emerge on the level of the theory of meaning but cannot be convincingly restricted there, thus excluding any considerations in the realm of epistemology or the account of how we acquire knowledge of the world.[15]

In an influential essay[16] from the 1980s, John McDowell has suggested that Wittgenstein, in putting forward his rule-following considerations, attempted a fresh look at what constitutes a standard or a pattern of content. On this reading Wittgenstein does not want to reject all patterns but merely to dispel certain misconceptions we connect with the natural thought that it should be possible to know which applications of our expressions are correct and which wrong. In searching for an adequate conception of standards we are asked, like Theseus and his Argonauts, to steer between the two mythical monsters, Scylla and Charybdis. Scylla embodies the loss of *objectivity* that arises from a conception of content that takes it to be an instance of interpretation. Charybdis on the other hand embodies the loss of *normativity*. Here, what has to be avoided is an explication of content along lines which reduce it to non-normative facts that fail, at the end of the day, to relate to it (normativity in this sense is meaning-relatedness).

[13] *Ibid* 223.

[14] For the term see above n 7.

[15] For a brief overview of the epistemological relevance of a 'private language', see B Wilson, *Wittgenstein's 'Philosophical Investigations'* (Edinburgh, Edinburgh University Press, 1998) 7–16.

[16] McDowell, above n 10.

3.2.1 A Dilemma and the Loss of Objectivity

Let us have a look at the (notably very ugly) face of Scylla: this reflects basically the idea that all standards of meaning are rendered inert because they stand in need of interpretation: that, in other words, anything which may determine content will fall prey to a regress of interpretative moves which fails to generate a distinction between correct and wrong applications of a sign. To that extent, Scylla is about the loss of objectivity. Mc Dowell links the loss with a dilemma that arises from para 201 of the *Philosophical Investigations* (PI):

> This was our paradox: no course of action could be determined by a rule, because every course of action can be made out to accord with the rule. The answer was: if everything can be made out to accord with the rule, then it can also be made out to conflict with it. And so there would be neither accord nor conflict here. (PI, para 201)

The first horn of the dilemma is para 201 itself. It says that any fact or other sign we look for in order to back our use of an expression will turn out to be in need of further interpretation itself and so on until we end up losing sight of the distinction between following a standard and thinking we follow it. The second horn is the intuitive idea that there might be some interpretation that is not itself in need of interpretation, something like a super-interpretation. Such an interpretation would be capable of bridging the gap between the instruction or the rule, one received in learning an expression and the use one is going to make of it. Interpretations of this kind are likened to a super-rigid machine or to rails that extent into the future. But this view is unattainable too, because it leads anew to the need for more interpretations.

To the two horns of the dilemma correspond the two philosophical traditions of Cartesianism (or mentalism) and Platonism. In their attempt to account for content both rely on entities which purport to mediate between minds and the world in a determinate manner (ie *intermediaries*). Such intermediaries are alleged to escape a regress of interpretations, for they are equipped with intrinsic content-fixing powers. In the *Philosophical Investigations* Wittgenstein discusses (and eventually rejects) a plethora of intermediaries.[17] For present purposes I will confine the discussion to the most characteristic cases; that said, the arguments

[17] Wittgenstein, above n 4, paras 134–242.

put forward below can be generalised to apply to all intermediaries.[18] Intermediaries probably are the most characteristic cases of ultra-interpretations, or entities which claim to be intrinsically content-determining.

3.2.1.1 Intermediaries

Since the Myth of the Given[19] cannot be sustained in its full range one has to introduce intermediaries which undertake the task of bridging the mind-world gap. The relation between intermediaries and dualism is circular: insofar as intermediaries are introduced to generate content, they perpetuate a state of dualism. And vice versa, dualism feeds the need for entities which are capable of bridging the mind-world gap.

Concepts (or their meanings) are embedded in symbols and words within languages. We use words in order to describe worldly things (material and non-material), to express thoughts, judgements, desires and hopes. For some reason we take our words to mean or signify the same thing each time we use them. Surprisingly enough we even take words from different languages to signify the same thing each time we use them. But our words (or language) do not have any kind of natural connection with the world (at least under the dualistic conception). The fact that we nevertheless keep on using words and understanding them does not account for the kind or the nature of the determinacy of meanings or the concepts' contents. What is it that connects language with the world in such an unambiguous way that we keep on understanding meanings in one way and not another? If a dualist wants to account for this connection he needs to introduce a *tertium*; an intermediary between mind and world, which has to be of a double quality: on the one hand to be of the same substance as linguistic units are—i.e. mental—and on the other hand to stand in a privileged relation or, rather, connection with the external world. According to this idea words need to be reinterpreted into an intermediary that has its own 'lines of projection into the world'[20] or, in other words, its own powers to represent the world. This double hypothesis constitutes what has been called a *dog-legged*[21] theory and can readily be shown to suffer from a double deficiency: first, the reinterpretation of our words and symbols into another medium might not be as unproblematic as these theories take it to be. Secondly, the representational powers of the intermediary might themselves be in need of interpretation in a

[18] For a detailed discussion of intermediaries see the classic work of Kripke, above n 8, 7–54.

[19] This is the idea that our judgements never fail to say something about the world, owing to the latter's (somehow magical) ability to guarantee an objective justification of our judgements. The term was first introduced by Wilfrid Sellars, *Empiricism and the Philosophy of Mind* (Cambridge, Mass, Harvard University Press, 1997) and has since been employed regularly in discussions concerning the mind-world problem; see amongst others J McDowell, *Mind and World* (Cambridge Mass, Harvard University Press, 1994); Hurley, above n 10.

[20] See S Blackburn, *Spreading the World* (Oxford, Clarendon Press, 1984) 43.

[21] *Ibid* 42.

way that would cancel the unambiguous character of the representation. Representation would be in this case substituted by a chain of interpretations or the need for a new intermediary that would be able to provide determinate outcomes, hence a *regressus ad infnitum* would arise. The gravity of these deficiencies depends, of course, upon the nature of the intermediary employed. If the representative medium is grounded on the side of the mind (like say the Lockean *ideas*), then it is much more likely that the regress will emerge at the level of representing the world, since the mentalistic character of the intermediary will make it fairly easy to connect it to things like words and concepts. And vice versa: if the intermediary employed counts as a distillation of the world (akin to, say, Patonic forms) then it is much more likely that the regress lurks on the level of the connection of the medium to linguistic entities.

3.2.1.2 Ideas

Locke uses the concept of *ideas* in his theory of understanding in order to account for the way we connect determinate meanings to our words. In doing this he places himself in the philosophical tradition of Aristotle and Hobbes in which Ideas are the mental likenesses which men form, whenever their minds are confronted by things which belong to the external world.[22] Locke believes that our ideas as mental representations of the world are hidden somewhere in 'our Breast'.[23] We on the other hand come to make use of our words as the signs of our ideas in order to record our thoughts in our memory or to expose them in front of others. This connection is no natural connection between particular sounds and certain ideas, but a voluntary one. This is so because for Locke: 'words in their primary or immediate Signification stand for nothing, but the Ideas in the Mind of him that uses them'.[24] This passage reveals a lot about the place of ideas in Locke's theory of understanding. Since words are voluntary they cannot signify anything with a natural or inevitable necessity. *Ergo*, according to Locke, they can only be used by men to signify things they know. So far so good, as long as the implied premiss is that we cannot make signs signify something, unless we have to a certain extent some knowledge of that thing.[25] But Locke's argument suppresses another premiss, namely the premiss that our words can only be used to signify ideas, because ideas are all we (can possibly) know. In the Lockean universe everything we know about external, worldly objects, other people and abstract entities, we know only derivatively through the immediate knowledge of our ideas. Hence, our knowledge of things like chairs, clouds, the sun, numbers or other people is not immediate but just a reflection of our genuine knowledge of the respective (or corresponding) ideas that hide in our breast. Which fact, of

[22] For a brief account see Blackburn, above n 20, 41–42.

[23] As cited in *ibid* 41.

[24] This is the expression Locke uses at the beginning of ch 2 of book 3 of his *Essay Concerning Human Understanding*; *cf* Blackburn, above n 20, 41.

[25] Blackburn, above n 20, 41.

course, makes it very difficult to have any reason to suppose that we know anything about the world, and that there is something more in the world apart from our ideas or, to put it differently, that we are not just brains in a vat connected to a powerful evil computer which supplies us with stimuli.

The inability of the theory of ideas to account for our knowledge about the world appears to be connected with a serious problem on the level of content. How is it possible to relate our words or concepts to the external world through the medium of ideas? The whole point behind the theory of ideas was to provide for a reliable medium that would be related to the mental fabric of our words and concepts, but which, simultaneously, would be able to establish connections with the world in a more determinate way than our linguistic symbols do. Ideas can certainly meet the first demand since they are as much mental as linguistic symbols are, but fall short of succeeding in their second task; namely the task to provide for a determinate connection to the external world. They seem to be as inappropriate for this task as words are. The assumption then that words point out through such things as ideas to a different class of things which are part of the external world, would seem somewhat improbable. It would be rather the case that we would need a new medium in order to get ideas out of 'our breast' and connect them to the external world. But if we are in need of something like new ideas in order to reinterpret our ideas a dangerous regress would be *ante portas*! It would be pretty much like trying to get someone to understand that a painting might represent a landscape by showing him more and more paintings.[26]

It seems that the theory of ideas, at the end of the day, is doomed to fail in accounting for the meaning or the content of concepts and, broader, intentional states. But this is the case for any other theory which introduces intermediaries as private reproductions of reality (what Blackburn calls dog-legged theories).[27] Reproductions of this sort are supposed to explain how words can be understood to refer to an environment that they themselves reproduce. These reproductions must themselves be taken as representative of the external world, and in this respect we do not have any satisfactory explanation of what it is to so take them.[28] If we need to introduce another medium in order to illuminate the powers of the first reproduction, we face the danger of sliding into a regress like the Atlas problem[29]: the regress, namely, which occurs when providing an explanation of why the world stands in its place by saying that it is carried on the shoulders of Atlas and when we are asked who carries Atlas, then change the subject. This danger will always lurk as long as we do not explain the representative powers of the original medium and instead introduce a new medium that seems to require the same kind of explanation as the original. Furthermore this danger will be

[26] *Cf ibid* 42.
[27] *Ibid* 40.
[28] *Ibid* 43.
[29] This is a paraphrase of Blackburn's term 'elephant problem'. *Cf* Blackburn, *ibid*, 43–44.

present as long as the indeterminacy of words and concepts is relocated in explanatory indermediaries and then anew in the intermediaries' interpretative methods (or media).

The lack of any direct, intrinsic connection of words with the things they signify has, in the first place, generated the need for an explanation of the fact that we understand them in one way and not another. The answer was that if we are to understand them in a determinate way, then we need to know what they signify. In order to know what they signify, the argument goes, we must have a way of representing to ourselves what they signify in a more reliable way. This is the moment where ideas are employed. But this is also the moment where the indeterminacy of words is transferred to the explanatory indermediary (ie to ideas): if ideas are just a way of representing things to ourselves then they do not seem to be less voluntary than words when applied. In this case we are once more in need of a new medium (something like second-order ideas) in order to know what our original ideas represented. This absurd regress would only be interrupted if it would be possible to introduce an intermediary which is essentially representative, ie its existence within our minds would guarantee that we know in a determinate way which part of the external world is represented.[30] Such an intermediary should not just be a way of representing things to ourselves, but the way of representing things *erga omnes*:

> A medium whose mere presence ensures that it also represents the right thing . . . a medium which carries its own interpretation with it, so there is no possibility of misunderstanding what is thought of, once it is present.[31]

In contrast to ideas, whose private character renders them insufficient in accounting for the explanation of meaning and content, the new medium's explanatory power has to rely on its direct representative character irrespective of the fact of being located in minds.

3.2.1.3 Images

Images seem prima facie to be a strong candidate as a solution to the problem of the perfect representational intermediary. First, they possess a sort of self-evident ability to intrinsically represent particular objects or aspects of the world by their mere presence, in the way a photograph 'copies' those bits of the world which the camera points at. Secondly, the forming of images seems to be a rather uncomplicated and non-mysterious ability of our minds. Images were the main ingredient of the so-called picture theory of meaning which Wittgenstein endorsed in his early work and later renounced. However, a closer look on images reveals a series of problems that prevent them from being able to account for meaning and understanding.

30 *Cf ibid* 44.
31 *Cf ibid* 44.

Blackburn demonstrates this inadequacy against a simple thought experiment.[32] He imagines a landscape which contains unthinking objects and a number of mirrors or pictures which respectively reflect or picture those objects. Then he goes on to remark that the mirrors, in whatever angle they are located, do not add any more significance to the landscape, as the one that was already there before any mirrors or pictures:

> The landscape and its pictures may reflect each other perfectly well, but this in itself gives us no ground for saying that the pictures . . . are thinking of features of the landscape, any more than that the features of the landscape signify the features of the picture.[33]

The point, in other words, is that the employment of images in order to explain meaning and understanding could amount to a circular argument. The way we take an image to represent one or another feature of the environment depends rather upon our method of projection of the picture on the world and not upon an intrinsic feature of the picture itself. Wittgenstein tries to point to this with a simple example.[34] He imagines an old man climbing up a hill; then he concentrates upon his image carefully. Could it not be, he asks, with a high probability, that the old man is rather sliding backwards down the hill? What decides which is really the case is not a quality intrinsic to the image but the interpretation one imposes on it. On the other hand, if one tries to justify the interpretation by saying that the image has to be taken in this way 'because the man is climbing up the hill', then one starts going in circles and misses the whole point; namely, that images were introduced as the very intermediary to explain how we understand these words in the first place. Thus, the conclusion is that the image of the man cannot account for the meaning of the expression 'a man is climbing the hill'.

Images thus fail to account for understanding despite the fact that they were put forward as the ideal representational medium, owing to their intrinsic ability to literally represent things, but because a picture is susceptible to interpretations and also because a picture's mere presence is not by itself sufficient to guarantee any particular way of taking it. Thus images are proven to be incapable of putting an end to the regress of interpretations. And if images cannot halt the regress of representations then nothing can. This failure might give rise to the suspicion that the problem does not lie with images or representational media in general but with the original reasoning that generated the need for representation; namely, the argument that the need to take words in a determinate way has to amount to the need to find a way to (objectively) represent to ourselves what it is that they stand for. It might be, on the contrary, that representational media and images in particular are not indispensable for the content of our thoughts in the first place let alone for understanding.

[32] See *ibid* 45.
[33] *Ibid* 45.
[34] As mentioned in *ibid* 46–47.

Wittgenstein tries to make a case against representational media in a theory of content by considering what happens when we ask somebody to 'fetch a flower from the meadow'. According to an image-based theory of understanding this person would have to determine a mental picture of, say, a red flower, or a red patch, which he holds until he finds a real flower that corresponds to it. But Wittgenstein goes on to object to this picture:

> this is not the only way of searching and it isn't the usual way. We go, look about us, walk up to a flower and pick it, without comparing it to anything. To see that the process of obeying the order can be of this kind, consider the order 'imagine a red patch'. You are not tempted in this case to think that before obeying you must have imagined a red patch to serve you as a pattern for the red patch which you were ordered to imagine.[35]

By highlighting the regress Wittgenstein wants to show that the image of the flower cannot explain the understanding of the imperative 'fetch a flower' because it itself presupposes the understanding of that imperative:

> [The image] can only figure in an explanation if we understand that *it is the right image* . . . knowing which is the right kind of flower is not explained by knowing that the flower matches some given pattern, unless we also know that it is the right kind of pattern. But recognising patterns to be the right ones is no easier than, or different from, recognising flowers.[36]

The need to represent to ourselves objects or aspects of the world seems rather to complicate things than to contribute to a solution of the problem of content and meaning. Representations just re-present the world and along with it they re-produce the problem of meaning. In fact they duplicate the problem of meaning: apart from the initial need to connect the world to our language, an additional need emerges: to connect language with our images which are supposed to account for the language-world relation![37]

3.2.1.4 Platonic Entities

Platonic standards can be treated in a similar manner, for whatever they turn out to be, metaphysically speaking, their success will at the end of the day depend on their ability to make contact with minds. In other words, the difficulty arising with respect to Platonism is that of picking, in each case, the right Platonic entity. Usually the latter task will involve anew some mental image which will raise the sceptical regress of interpretations.[38] To that extent Platonism turns out to be a truncated case of intermediaries.

[35] L Wittgenstein, *The Blue and Brown Books* (Oxford, Blackwell, 1974) 3.
[36] Blackburn, above n 20, 49.
[37] Similarly *ibid* 50.
[38] *Cf* Kripke, above n 8, 53–54.

3.3 Conceptions of Practice

Given the mind-world gap no conceivable intermediary is in the position to efficiently bridge it. Such intermediaries as ideas, images or Platonic rails at the end of the day merely raise a regress of interpretations and, hence, fail to promote the idea of meaning and understanding. However, aside from the unanimity that prevails in respect to the negative conditions of meaning, there seems to be little agreement about what positively makes content possible. Wittgenstein's well-known appeal to practices as the vehicle of meaning and understanding has not been interpreted or understood in a uniform way.

Wittgenstein's appeal to practice is a composite argument that mainly combines two individual arguments: the so-called *practice* and *use arguments*.[39] The use argument departs from the insight that all questions about meaning can be rephrased as questions about use. According to Wittgenstein: 'for a large class of cases—though not for all—in which we employ the word 'meaning' it can be defined thus: the meaning of a word is its use in the language' (*Philosophical Investigations*, para 43).[40] This definition is usually taken to support an argument for the impossibility of a private language. One should be careful at this point: private languages or, in other words, uses of concepts or private ascription of contents to concepts are according to the use argument not meaningless *lato sensu*, ie unintelligible in terms of syntax and grammar, but meaningless *stricto sensu*, ie deprived of any practical consequences, useless.[41] It is this lack of an ordinary or reputable use that deprives any private language from real meaning. Employing private definitions, to use a favourite analogy from the *Philosophical Investigations* (henceforth PI), is tantamount to my right hand offering money as a gift to my left hand. Wittgenstein comments on this exchange that it is futile because 'the further practical consequences would not be those of a gift'.[42] Analogously, in the case of the private definition, the practical consequences would not be those of ascribing meaning to our expressions: if one says 'I have something' referring to a private object in one's mind, this expression would pass the normal grammatical and logical tests for meaningfulness, but not the test of use. 'I have something' is, in this case, practically meaningless since we have no idea what a more detailed description of a private object would be.[43]

The use argument is further supplemented by the so-called practice argument. Within the practice argument the use-criterion of meaning is taken to denote use as part of a concrete practice. Wittgenstein stresses the point that the "appropriate 'mental accompaniments' plus the appropriate behaviour, do not constitute

[39] See Wilson, above n 15, 17–24 and 45–56.

[40] *Ibid* 45.

[41] See *ibid* 45–56, who even distinguishes an autonomous 'consequences argument' within the PI, *ibid* 14–16.

[42] Wittgenstein, above n 4, para 268.

[43] This is more or less a summary of the presentation in Wilson, above n 15, 52–53.

following a rule, making a chess move, being guided by a signpost. There must also be a practice in each case, to which the behaviour in question conforms or belongs".[44] At this point it should be said that Wittgenstein's appeal to practices is strongly founded on the insight that content is normative. It is this conception of content as rule-following that leads Wittgenstein to appeal to practices, since rule-following before anything else, or aside from everything else, is practice or performance.[45]

At the same time there is a big controversy among commentators which type of practice Wittgenstein deems capable of achieving the amount of normativity content requires.[46] Does the practice of a single individual suffice, or must one recur to more public forms of practice? Wittgenstein does not seem particularly concerned to clarify which kind of practice he is postulating (public or private). His concern within the practice argument is rather to connect content with use and practice. After having shown, in numerous passages of the PI, that all intermediaries between a rule and its application cannot guarantee the determinacy of content, he points to practices as the solution to the regress resulting from interpretations and other intermediaries. If it is for meaning to be construed as a normative notion then there must be something which renders rule-following more fundamental than any other interpretation. Conversely if rule-following is reduced to any other criterion, then it succumbs to a battery of sceptical argument, as Wittgenstein argues in para 201 of PI.[47]

As a result Wittgenstein's remedy, ie practice, is therefore presented not merely as a supplement or an alternative to the discredited intermediaries but as something radically different from them. Following a rule, producing meanings, is according to this insight not an interpretation:

> It can be seen that there is a misunderstanding here from the mere fact that in the course of our argument we give one interpretation after another; as if each one contented us at least for a moment, until we thought of yet another standing behind it. What this shows is that there is a way of grasping a rule which is not an interpretation, but which is exhibited in what we call "obeying the rule" and "going against it" in actual cases. (PI, para 201)

What is then the advantage of practices over interpretations and other intermediaries? Does it, furthermore, make a difference if one talks about public practices instead of private ones? In what follows I am going to discuss a number of conceptions of practice which fail to ground the foundational character of rule-following with respect to content. Broadly speaking, those strategies fail on either of two grounds: either because they conceive of practices as themselves being in need of further interpretation; or because they reduce practices to

[44] *Cf ibid* 18.

[45] See McDowell, above n 10; and Hurley, above n 10, 225 *ff*. Against this idea is Wilson, above n 15, Appendix, 134–45.

[46] See instead of others Hurley, above n 10, 225 n.

[47] See section 3.2.1.

entities and/or events which are normatively inert. Having rejected those deficient conceptions of practice I turn to discuss an alternative conception of practice which manages to capture the foundational character of rule-following with respect to content. It is this conception of rule-following grammar needs to be linked with. Grammar as practice can, then, surmount mind-world dualism and amount to knowledge.

3.3.1 Private Practice

There are a number of commentators who believe that the practice of an individual is enough in order to escape the regress of interpretations. Blackburn takes the example of the born Robinson Crusoe who develops a technique for solving a Rubik's cube washed onto his island, in order to show that a solitary individual could develop a practice or technique and could abide by rules. This thought, however, appears to be in conflict with a number of remarks in the PI which, prima facie, deny the possibility of private practices. Thus Wittgenstein says in para 199:

> It is not possible that there should have been only one occasion on which someone obeyed a rule. It is not possible that there should have been only one occasion on which a report was made, an order given or understood; and so on. To obey a rule, to make a report, to give an order, to play a game of chess, are customs (uses, institutions).

Or in the more famous para 202:

> And hence also 'obeying a rule' is a practice. And to think one is obeying a rule is not to obey a rule. Hence it is not possible to obey a rule 'privately': otherwise thinking one was obeying a rule would be the same thing as obeying it.

These remarks have led many commentators to object that practice, at least in the way Wittgenstein employs the term, means communal or public practice. Under this scheme we can indeed regard a born Crusoe as having his own 'private', as it were, practice, but we can only do so by projecting upon him the point of view of our own community. Blackburn comments on this objection that:

> it is not clear what this means, nor whether it gives the community any particular prominence in the creation of meaning . . . The problem that Crusoe poses is that he does have a practice (follows a rule) regardless of how we or anybody else think of him. Of course . . . it is our judgement that he is following a rule. But this does not bring our community or any community far enough into the picture. It would be our judgement that an island has a tree on it. But whether an island has a tree on it is quite independent of how we or any community describe it, or even of whether any community exists to describe it.[48]

[48] See Blackburn, above n 20, 84–85

And then he goes on to observe that one must not fall into the trap of automatically equating practice with public practice, since this equation requires an independent argument showing that the practice of isolated individuals cannot count.

But even if individual practice can indeed be considered as a valid candidate in accounting for meaning and understanding does it do the job any better than the discredited interpretations? Let us consider the famous example of the student who applies the rule 'add two'.[49] Our student having counted by twos all the way up to 1,000, he then goes on: '1,004, 1,008 . . .' and so on. Upon our challenge he responds that he is not making a mistake, that this is what he was doing all along and that this agrees with his prior uses of the rule 'add two'. And indeed why are we entitled to think that he is wrong in applying the rule of addition rather than being right in applying another rule, say that of 'quaddition' (which is his own private use of the rule 'add two')? Appeal to his prior uses of the rule does not help more in order to give a determinate answer as to which is the actual meaning of the rule in question. Every party could 'read' in the student's prior uses one's own interpretation precisely because uses and practices do not interpret themselves anymore than anything else (images, ideas, etc) do. The student's own appeal to the agreement of his present application to his prior uses of the rule cannot stop us from imposing on him our own interpretations:

> It doesn't help . . . to appeal to the agreement of the application in question with his other applications up to now, because what's at issue just is what determines whether those previous applications agree with this way of going on or that one; they don't interpret themselves.[50]

Clearly (private) practices do not prevent the regress from arising, because they are themselves open to multiple interpretations. They more or less behave like private sensations, images and ideas. Hence any practice can be made out to accord with the rule, or to conflict with it (PI, para 201). Private practice or the practice of an individual does not seem, therefore, to be a reputable candidate in resolving the regress which threatens meaning. Private practices are proved to be trapped in the mind-world dualism in the same way that images or ideas are and therefore they end up merely being one amongst many other intermediaries. But intermediaries are inescapably subjected to multiple interpretations and are, for this reason, incapable of guaranteeing meaning and understanding. These remarks lead to the conclusion that private practice can be fruitful only if it is conceived in a distinctively different way from mental entities like images, ideas and other relevant intermediaries. In other words if it is for private practices to have any worth in the account of meaning and content, one has to seriously address the problem of mind-world dualism. As long as one accounts for

[49] See the discussion in Hurley, above n 10, 225–29.
[50] *Ibid* 227.

(private) practices within the realm of dualism one is going to face the same problems that emerge from the employment of mental intermediaries.

3.3.2 Communal Practice

Inserting an interpretation between a representation and what is represented does not explain the connection between them. The reason is simply that interpretations are themselves open to new interpretations and so on. The regress amounts to a total inability to explain meaning and understanding with the notorious effect that no course of action can be determined by a rule, because every course of action can be made out to accord with the rule. Private practice does not seem to be able to offer a solution out of the regress. Be that as it may, Wittgenstein refers to practice in his effort to offer a solution to the problem. What is more, he links practice to a collective perspective while contrasting public practice with private practice (as in the famous para 202 of the PI, cited earlier).

With respect to communal variants of practice I shall discuss two views: the sceptical solution and the behaviourist view. The sceptical solution[51] arises from the belief of some commentators that the regress cannot be entirely avoided, hence that one has to learn to live with it. As a result the sceptical solution does not aim to dispense with the regress but only to limit its devastating conclusions.[52] The sceptical solution fails, however, because it conceives of rule-following as ex post acceptance, one which stands in need of further interpretation in order to be linked to any rule. Things are not different with respect to the behaviourist solution. This view attempts to rescue objectivity of content by relating rule-following to the external behaviour of community members. The reduction, however, effects a loss of objectivity, for facts of

[51] 'A 'sceptical solution' to a sceptical problem is one that begins . . . by conceding that the sceptic's negative assertions are unanswerable'; see McDowell, above n 10.

[52] For a recent revival of the discussion between those who endorse the sceptical solution and those who reject it, see George Wilson, 'Semantic Realism and Kripke's Wittgenstein' (1998) 83 *Philosophy and Phenomenological Research* 99 (who defends Kripke's interpretation); and M Kremer, 'Wilson on Kripke's Wittgenstein' (2000) 85 *Philosophy and Phenomenological Research* 571 (who criticises Kripke's views).

behaviour are no more self-explanatory than intermediaries of sorts. The discussion concludes that none of the reviewed communal views manages to establish practice as a foundation for content, the result being that the gap between mind and world survives.[53]

3.3.2.1 Sceptical Solution

Saul Kripke thinks that the dilemma of para 201 is inescapable and needs to be embraced.[54] His conclusion is that there is nothing which can be kept immune from the regress of interpretations; therefore one should merely attempt to offer something like a sceptical solution. His sceptical solution effectively accepts the first horn of the dilemma and introduces the idea of community as a means for toning down its devastating conclusion. (The gist of Kripke's position is that all, not just idiolectic or private, content is an illusion.) Kripke's sceptical solution urges us to give up a truth-conditional conception of meaning in favour of justification conditions. The idea is that justification conditions, instead of relying on an ultimate interpretation (say, the rigidity of the external world) in the manner of the truth-conditional conception, consist in standards that are internal to the practice of a linguistic community. In this train of thought, what counts as a successful application of an expression is one that secures the *acceptance* of the individuals in the linguistic community. On the face of it, conditions of justification function as justifications that are less damaging because they hold sway over the entire linguistic community.[55]

This view strives to play down the regress by substituting communal practice in the place of interpretations and other intermediaries. Communal practice, on this account, is something not entirely different from interpretations. It is rather something like a safer criterion for arriving at more determinate interpretations, owing to its being grounded in the way the majority of the members of a community happens to apply meanings. However, acceptance on behalf of the community carries too thin a credential for grounding determinacy of content. Acceptance fails to render practice foundational because, unless it is buttressed through reference to acceptance- or ratification-independent[56] standards, it leads to circularity: any token of acceptance will be susceptible to multiple interpretations for there is nothing outside acceptance itself to determine its content. One way to sidestep this problem is to modify the sceptical solution by pointing to constraints which block the regress of interpretations. This is what the behaviourist solution purports to do.

[53] The criticism of those views follows McDowell, above n 10.

[54] See Kripke, above n 8.

[55] A note of caution: not any community-based understanding should serve the same aim—once the framework of the dilemma is discarded communal practice acquires a very different meaning. This is the 'correct' interpretation of Wittgenstein's rule-following considerations defended in section 3.4.

[56] The term comes from McDowell, above n 10.

3.3.2.2 Behaviourist Solution

Crispin Wright[57] approaches the dilemma of para 201 from a different perspective: Wright thinks that Wittgenstein's point was to save objectivity by purging its constituents from the misconceptions stated in the dilemma. On his view Wittgenstein is trying to debunk the insufficiencies that lurk inside what we usually take to constitute a pattern or standard of meaning. However, purging patterns form their shortcoming allows us to retain the idea of the pattern. Wright identifies as the main shortcoming of patterns which fall within the ambit of the two horns of the dilemma the fact that they are idiolectic. The signs or standards that Wittgenstein rejects after due consideration, on the supposition that they themselves stand in need of justification, are on Wright's view unsuitable to function as standards for content, because they rest on a leap of faith, or an inspired guess on behalf of the rule-follower. The rule-follower assumes that he has a privileged way of accessing those standards and then just hopes that everybody else does in the same manner. This is probably easier to bring out in the case of Platonic standards, yet Wright seems to think that the problem is the same as regards also every type of interpretation (which is the first horn of the dilemma). How then to retain objectivity? Wright tells us that there is scope for some amount of objectivity within the practice of a community. Communal practice in this case seems to impose a pattern of correctness for the individual. However, this pattern hangs in the air for it itself is unfounded. The reason is that there is no standard as far as communal applications go. These *may* not be deemed right or wrong, for any standard of application could anew be argued to belong to an idiolect, albeit one pertaining to the community as a whole. As a result the community is not right or wrong, but 'it just goes'.[58]

Conceived in this way, communal practice is constructed in pure behavioural terms. Its content consists in pointing out just how one has learned—through communal practice—to react to specific situations.[59] Although this view manages to sidestep the problem of intermediaries it is questionable whether it manages to preserve the idea that the relation between a rule and a course of action is more than a relation between brute movement and its casual explanation. On the face of it, the main problem of the behaviourist solution is that it fails to provide for an '*innerness*' or *certainty* of content. Moreover, when compared to the discredited intermediaries it does not seem to demonstrate any serious advantage. It is true that inner entities (like images or ideas) were private to such a high degree that, at the end of the day, they were incapable of generating objectivity. But, at least, they were fulfilling the purpose of their employment, namely to relate

[57] See C Wright, *Wittgenstein on the Foundations of Mathematics* (London, Duckworth, 1980) as quoted by McDowell, above n 10.

[58] *Ibid.* 5.

[59] *Ibid.* 55 *ff.*

meaning to something indisputable.[60] If the problem there was that mental entities were placed in the heads, hence too remote from each other for meaning to be possible, in the behaviourist account the problem is even more acute: public or community practice is taken to be totally independent of any stable pattern, hence to be totally random or contingent. The account of meaning and understanding from the sceptical solution's point of view more or less amounts to the following picture: at the basic level of any language-game, there are no normative elements (rules) to be found. We merely have brute facts (movements, sounds, etc), which need to be interpreted in order to obtain meaning. This interpretation cannot be idiolectic but has to be performed on a communal basis in order to guarantee objectivity. The criterion of objectivity is in this case the fact that the community, or the larger part of the community happens to agree in doing this rather than something else (which, on another interpretation, could also be shown to fall under the same course of action).

3.3.2.3 Charybdis and the Loss of Normativity

The idea of a forsaken, empty of normativity, bedrock is precisely what McDowell tries to capture with the image of Charybdis.[61] McDowell explores this problem by scrutinising further Wright's conception of objectivity and showing that it actually fails to relate to the issue of content, in the sense of guiding (normatively) our applications of linguistic expressions. The problem with Wright's conception of purged standards, the conception of 'it just goes', is that it replaces a normative notion of meaning with a descriptive one. There is nothing in the facts that constitute the practice of a community at the level of 'it just goes' that could serve as guideline for meaning. But how does Wright reach his conception of objectivity anyway? And what are the details thereof that render it descriptive? Let us have a closer look at his arguments.

In establishing the futility of the kind of pattern Wittgenstein allegedly rejects Wright employs the following *modus tollens*:

P1: if possession of a concept were conceived as grasp of a ratification-independent pattern -> idiolectic understanding of the expression

P2: the idea of idiolectic knowledge is an illusion

C: no ratification-independent patterns

First the justification of P2: the picture of idiolectic meaning leads to the consequence described in the first horn of the dilemma of para 201: conflation between following a rule and thinking that one follows it. P1, on the other hand,

[60] McDowell seems also to acknowledge this point when he writes: 'The idea of interpretation seemed hopeful because it promised to enable us to attribute, to items [he refers here to ideas, images, etc] that are in themselves normatively inert, a derivative power to impose a normative classification on items in the world outside the mind'; see J McDowell, 'Meaning and Intentionality in Wittgenstein's Later Philosophy' in *idem*, *Mind, Value and Reality* (Cambridge Mass, Harvard University Press, 1998) 263–78 (at 265).

[61] *Cf* above n 10.

stands for the view of what it is to manifest understanding to others. Instead of postulating ratification-independent standards Wright's view turns to instances of behaviour which count as manifesting understanding to others; one that is characterisable without command of the language in question (that is, not in terms of the contents of their thoughts). Otherwise one could say that 'such and such' is the case. The latter would imply importing into the picture some truth-conditional, hence ratification-independent, understanding of patterns and then go back to the first horn of the dilemma of para 201.

It seems that Wright is moved by a noble motive: to reject the idea that assigning a meaning is forming a hypothesis about something concealed behind the surface of one's linguistic behaviour. However, there is more than one way to cash in this idea:

(a) to remain at the surface of behavioural facts about the use of expressions (as shallow as the 'signs' castigated by the dilemma of para 201). In this case the linguistic practice of a community is put together by brute facts and some feelings of commitment ('basic level');
(b) or to say that the outward linguistic behaviour should be characterised in terms of the contents of the thoughts expressed in utterances.

This is, then, the face of Charybdis: the devastating effect of the *basic level* which causes all meaning to dissolve in behavioural regularity and random brute facts that cannot bridge the gap between the rule and its application. In this universe, initiation into a common language consists in acquisition of linguistic propensities describable without the notion of meaning (conflation of bedrock and sub-bedrock).

To follow a rule is equated here to an ex post ratification according to the reactions of the community. This behaviourist account falls short of being able to generate a persuasive account of why meaning and understanding are possible, let alone of persuading us that it is Wittgenstein's intended solution in relation to the problem of the indeterminacy of content. The main reason is that such an account of the community's practice is circular and derives its normativity from its normality/regularity (in the sense of habitual repeating). Therefore, it fails to generate a satisfactory concept of content (or any concept of content at all).[62] This failure becomes apparent whenever a dispute arises among the members of a community about the true meaning of a previously established (and now challenged) communal practice. Then easy cases are transformed to hard cases,

[62] McCulloch demonstrates accurately the inconclusiveness of the *sceptical conclusion*: 'If Wittgenstein really has demonstrated that understanding cannot be explained in terms of inner processes, the contemplation of ideas, the grasping of senses and so on, then all we are left with are dispositions to use words. So if they cannot deliver an account of meaning and understanding, *there are simply no such things* ... But the outcome here is spectacular: there is no such thing as meaning, and there is no such thing as correct understanding of language' in G McCulloch, *The Mind and its World* (London, Routledge, 1995) 104.

which cannot be answered through a 'shared' background, for the 'divided', or better, disputing community can no longer generate safe criteria of meaning orientation.

3.3.3 Summary

All in all, the discussion points to the same direction: irrespective of which type of practice (private or communal) one chooses to insert at the bottom of one's account of meaning, one needs to deal with the same problem: practices do not interpret themselves more than does any of the other 'discredited' mental intermediaries.[63] This amounts to the fact that every practice is open to multiple interpretations with the effect that any practice can be brought into accord with a rule or into conflict with it. The question which practice agrees with a rule or with a prior practice cannot be answered by pointing to the fact of the agreement. Agreement is what we are trying to establish. It would be a useless *petitio* to use it for justifying it anew. Wittgenstein's words illustrate vividly this point:

> One does not learn to follow a rule by first learning the use of the word 'agreement'. Rather, one learns the meaning of 'agreement' by learning to follow a rule.[64]

And in another passage:

> It is no use, for example, to go back to the concept of agreement, because it is no more certain that one action is in agreement with another, than that it has happened in accordance with a rule.[65]

If practices are conceived as another intermediary they do not seem to escape the regress which renders mental intermediaries useless in accounting for content. If no sign or image as such can generate its own interpretation, neither can any practice (or agreement in practice). This amounts to the conclusion that agreement in content does not follow automatically from agreement in practice.[66] But the communal solution (in both its sceptical and behaviourist variations) is grounded on exactly the opposite conclusion. It starts by recognising the inability of private sensations, images and even private practice to account for determinate contents and meanings, only to go on, later, to say that community agreement in practice can establish determinate meanings. In other words it starts by stating that nothing stable underwrites content and then goes on to make a strong case that content is guaranteed by the contingent fact that we happen to agree in doing this rather than that. This is like first saying that meaning, on the account of private entities, is impossible because of the contingent or indeterminate

[63] See the discussion of Hurley, above n 10, 229–33.

[64] See L. Wittgenstein, *Remarks on the Foundations of Mathematics*, 3rd edn, G H von Wright, R Rhees and G E M Anscombe (ed) (Oxford, Blackwell, 1978) 405; quoted in Hurley, above n 10, 233.

[65] Wittgenstein, above n 64, 405; quoted in Hurley, above n 10, 233.

[66] This seems to be also the point of McCulloch, above n 62, 82.

character of these mental entities, while on the other hand trying to ground meaning on another contingent factor, namely the fact that we happen to agree in doing this rather than that. But if nothing underwrites meaning (because everything that could be taken to underwrite it is contingent—this seems to be the implicit premiss of the sceptical solution), then it is inconsistent for the sceptic to help himself to something he has already denied (meaning based on contingent practices). Susan Hurley writes:

> it is not an adequate answer to say that the solution that practices provide is a sceptical one, that nothing underwrites content, and that we just, contingently, happen to agree in doing this rather than that. This answer simply fails to take the point: the problem, if there is one at all, runs as much to action ... as to sensation or anything else. Unless it's defused, it deprives us even of arbitrary, groundless decisions ... If the absurd conclusion is in force, we're not entitled to talk about what we just do, whether contingently or not, about our practices or decisions or choices or anything intentional in the way needed, because they are content-presupposing; this would be a case of the sceptic helping himself to resources his own argument denies him.[67]

Disclosing an inconsistency within the sceptical line of argument will not do any good to the effort to rescue content. On the contrary: it might be the case that the consistent sceptic conclusion is that one should discard meaning *tout court*. This is probably the most likely conclusion to draw anyway after having diagnosed the radical indeterminacy of both mental intermediaries and practices (be they private or communal).

This rather pessimistic conclusion need not follow, however. On a general level it can be refused on the grounds of a transcendental argument.[68] The first premiss of the argument states something which, according to our trivial experience, is the case: 'meaning and content seem to be possible since we communicate'. The second premiss focusses on the conditions for the possibility of such meaning and content: 'meaning is possible upon the condition that there is something underlying it which is not contingent'; or in its negative form: 'if it is for meaning to be possible it should not be dependent upon mental intermediaries or any other contingent items (practices included)'. Then the conclusion more or less amounts to something like: 'there is something underlying meaning which is not contingent or indeterminate in the way mental intermediaries are'. This conclusion is far from clear about what this thing might be in positive terms. But if we take the powerful intuition of the transcendental argument combined with Wittgenstein's insistence on practices, we might be able to have a fresh go at practices and try to find a way not to treat them as contingent.

Thus, an important requirement for a fruitful exploitation of practices is to conceive them in a way that is consistent with Wittgenstein's prescription that there is a way of grasping a rule which is not an interpretation. Practices must be

[67] *Cf.* Hurley, above n 10, 233–34.
[68] For a similar strategy *cf* McDowell, above n 10, 66–69.

reconstructed as being interpretation-free (or *ratification-independent*) items or patterns, which lay at the level of the 'bedrock' or, in other words, at the bottom of any language, where justification reaches an end.[69]

3.4 Beyond Mind-World Dualism

A number of commentators,[70] who by and large share the concerns of the previous analysis, attempt to steer between the Scylla of mentalism and the Charybdis of scepticism by suggesting a different reading of Wittgenstein's discussion of practices and agreement. According to this view, practices are to be understood as something totally distinct from intermediaries. Wittgenstein's appeal to practices does not aim to compare them with all previous discredited intermediaries in order to make a case for their superiority. What Wittgenstein actually does, the argument goes, is to claim that a practice is not a third thing standing between a rule and its applications, hence that it is not a medium like the rest. This reading rests predominantly on para 201 of *Philosophical Investigations* where Wittgenstein stresses the point that 'there is a way of grasping a rule which is not an interpretation'.

On this 'alternative' reading the relation between the rule and acts of its application is, rather, internal. Rule and acts of following make contact at the level of language[71] preventing therefore any gap to arise and any intermediary to be essential for bridging the gap. It is this internal relation or, in other words, 'what we call 'obeying the rule' and 'going against it' in actual cases' (PI, spara 201) that provides for a way of grasping the rule which is not an interpretation. This emphasis on the interdependence between rules and acts of abiding by the rules offers a solution out of the infinite regress which usually undermines the employment of any intermediate entities. Baker and Hacker write:

> The apparent logical gulf between a rule and its 'extension' arises from the mistaken assumption that understanding a rule is at least partly independent of how it is projected on to actions. But however it is formulated or explained, a rule is understood only if it is correctly projected. To be ignorant or mistaken about what acts are in accord with it is to be ignorant or mistaken about what the rule is.[72]

But if the understanding of a rule is not at all independent of how it is projected on to actions, this means that the mind-world dualism can no longer be sustained. Meaning and content, once alleged to inhabit the mind, are now placed within the broader contexts of human action. It is the context of action or, in other words, practices, which generate intentional content and guarantee the

[69] *Cf* McDowell, *ibid*, 274.
[70] For a comprehensive account see Hurley, above n 10, 235 n; also McDowell, above n 10, *passim*.
[71] *Cf* Hurley, above n 10, 235.
[72] Baker and Hacker, above n 10, 97.

possibility of meaning and understanding. Practices constitute the bedrock 'where our spades are turned' (PI, para 217) and where every interpretation or 'justification' reaches an end:

> Giving grounds, however, justifying the evidence, comes to an end; but the end is not certain propositions striking us immediately as true, ie it is not a kind of seeing on our part; it is our acting, which lies at the bottom of the language game.[73]

On this pragmatic reading of Wittgenstein, meaning and understanding have to be placed within this 'acting' if they are to be something more than a blind reaction to a situation, or to be an attempt to act on an interpretation and still be a case of going by a rule. The pragmatic account takes practices and rules to constitute a normative groundwork which is neither contingent upon, nor susceptible to, interpretations. In this way the pragmatic account escapes the sceptical impasse and generates objectivity and knowledge.

3.4.1 Pragmatism and Objectivity

The pragmatic account does not allow the mind-world gap to open in the first place. Practices are here constructed as parts of the environment that can account for mental content and meaning. This account does away with dualism in a simple and straightforward way and spares one from the need to seek entities which, in order to be able to bridge the mind-world gap, need to possess self-interpreting properties (like images or ideas). Therefore practices do not need to be thought of as self-interpreting entities or, on Hurley's successful expression, *ultra-interpretations.*[74]

Ultra-interpretations are in a very strong way connected to dualism: if the mind is radically separated from the world then the need arises for entities within the mind which possess the property to create (powerful and self-evident) connections to the world. This is the test that all ultra-interpretations fail: there is no such thing as one that can provide for its own interpretation in an unambiguous and indisputable way; hence, all ultra-interpretations end up being extended into an endless series of interpretations which prevents them from fulfilling their task as self-standing, ultimate points of reference or ratification-independent patterns. The ultra-claim to provide definitive interpretations, which is encapsulated in ultra-interpretations, is, through their failure to do so, transformed into an unfulfilled ultra-burden that exposes their total dependence on a radically sceptical *regressus ad infinitum.* Ultra-interpretations are rendered radically sceptical not on the ground of their initial claim (this is perfectly anti-sceptical), but

[73] *Cf* Wittgenstein, *On Certainty*, G E M Anscombe, G H V Wright and P Denis (eds) (Oxford, Blackwell, 1975) para 204.

[74] *Cf* Hurley, above n 6, 35.

because their inability to live up to the claim deprives them of any possibility to stand as ratification- or verification-independent patterns which alone would provide for objectivity.

On the other hand, practices, on the pragmatic account, can be considered as *ratification-independent patterns* which enjoy objectivity; or, to use a somehow informal expression, practices are, in a way, able to provide for their own interpretation, only this is possible because it is happening without the dualist part, ie not within a special realm which is independent of the environment. To say this might sound somewhat inconsistent with the previous remark that there is nothing which could provide for its own interpretation. Nevertheless, the ability of self-interpretation seems in a way to be implicit in the assumption that practices in the pragmatic account enjoy the status of ratification-independent patterns: because how else, if not through its ability to be self-interpreting, can a pattern be ratification-independent? To that extent, in order to regard practices as foundational for content we must regard them as self-interpreting.

The alleged inconsistency is untangled by the fact that practices, as accounted for in a pragmatic theory, do not actually pose the claim of being self-interpreting entities or ultra-interpretations because they do not need such a strong claim: unlike images, ideas and Platonic entities, they are not hidden in isolated vats (minds) and therefore their objectivity is the result of their public character and not of their capacity for a second-order re-production or picturing of the reality. Whereas ultra-interpretations need to be reinterpreted and brought into accord with each other, practices lie on the same level as either minds and world and, therefore, are common to all minds. Conceived of this way practices do not need a second- (or third-, fourth- . . . or νn-) order interpretation (or any interpretation at all, which is the same as saying that they come already interpreted) in order to constitute a common ground for all minds. It follows that practices do not succumb to an infinite regress but are ratification-independent, ie objective. Minds acquire their common ground as they partake of practices and not because they possess entities which re-present the world. In this way the pragmatic account of practice establishes a normative link between mind and world by beginning at a mind-independent point (practice) rather than something that exists in one's mind. In the spirit of this pragmatic or contextualist reading of Wittgenstein's account of practices, Hurley writes:

> [Wittgenstein's] point is . . . that it is a mistake to conceive of the relation between the mind and the world in such a way that the need to postulate intrinsically self-interpreting entities of any kind arises . . . He appeals to practices . . . not as [such entities], but because he conceives them as identified in relation to and constitutively engaged with the world. His appeal to them is in effect a repudiation of the conception of the mind as independent of the world that gives rise to the problem which makes [self-interpreting entities] seem necessary.[75]

[75] *Ibid* 35–36.

On the face of it, one may say that pragmatism and mentalism raise an equally strong claim to objectivity and knowledge. Owing to their different relation to dualism, however, each of those claims leads to completely different results.

Mentalism holds to something like *objectivity in the mind* by postulating the existence of entities within the mind (images, ideas and other ultra-interpretations). Ultra-interpretations, or representations in the mind, are conceived of in such a way that they cannot be linked to the world unless the proper interpretation is employed. They just stand there in the mind as normatively inert entities, or 'mental' signposts which, in themselves, do not signify anything before they are interpreted. What we need in order to establish a normative connection to the world 'is not that item, whatever it was, considered in itself, but that item under the right interpretation'.[76] But then the question 'which is the right interpretation' cannot be answered by the fact of the mental signpost's standing there, with the result that any interpretation could be made to be the right one. And if one tries to block this indeterminacy by further employing another item from 'the restricted inventory' of mental items one can appeal to, the story repeats itself:

> It does not matter what item, from the restricted inventory, we pick on as a plausible candidate to be what someone's putting the right interpretation on, say, the heard instruction "Add 2" (or anything else) might consist in. Whatever it is, it cannot be what we hoped it would be, since considered in itself it in turn just "stands there like a sign-post". We might be tempted to require putting the right interpretation on the item that was supposed to be an interpretation, but that is clearly to embark on a regress, which looks as if it must be hopeless. The item that is supposed to be the right interpretation of the first putative interpretation will shrink in its turn, under the requirement of fitting into the restricted inventory of available items, into something that "just stands there". So the very idea of a person's understanding, as something that determines a distinction between behaviour that is in accord with the understanding and behaviour that is not, comes under threat.[77]

Content as being in accord with or as abiding by a rule, as a normative enterprise in other words, seems to come under threat in the mentalist account. If mental items and processes in general are like signposts with versatile use, then accord to a rule, or a thought, or an intention is akin to accord with a contingent interpretation; which is to say accord to nothing or accord to anything. Thus, instead of taking states of affairs in the world to correspond to forms of mental content in a determinate way, dualism forces one to relate mental content to contingent interpretations. Along these lines, if one has a thought about, say, today's rainy weather in Hamburg, what is decisive for the content of one's thought is not 'that today rains in Hamburg' but an interpretation which, if one is lucky, might establish the link between the weather in Hamburg and one's

[76] See McDowell, above n 60, 265.
[77] *Ibid* 266.

thought.[78] Without that amount of luck, however, any weather in Hamburg can be taken to constitute the content of the thought. Along these lines, interpretations amount inevitably to an infinite regress which undermines the possibility of establishing any connection to the environment, the further result being that a general or global scepticism arises. Content and understanding go astray along with the possibility to connect to the environment. They fall pray to the dualistic trap by becoming dependent upon a contingent chain of interpretations which nurtures radical scepticism about meaning, content and the environment.

Pragmatism, on the other hand, argues for *objectivity in content and meaning* by establishing a normative link between mind and world (through practice). Dualism collapses and ultra-interpretations are rendered unnecessary. Practices stand on their own as objective, ratification-independent patterns which provide all minds with common contents. Objectivity in content and meaning, on this account, amounts to determinacy of content and can account for knowledge. Pragmatism must be carefully distinguished from crude Platonism: Platonism allows the mind-world gap to open and then tries to bridge it, thus succumbing to the futile logic of intermediaries. On the contrary pragmatism's main contribution is that it prevents in the first place the gap from opening. For this reason pragmatism can be regarded as modest objectivism. Interpretations are incapable of establishing the normative link between worldly states of affairs and mental contents. It is rather language-games, practices and forms of life that are able to conceive content as a normative concept by generating the normative link between mind and world. Accordingly, the pragmatic account discards the idea of interpretation as the last instance of grounding content and meaning and focusses upon language-games, practices and forms of life as the successful candidates for a normative explication of content and meaning.

The paradox—on the level of the theory of meaning—which emerges from the fact that ultra-interpretations behave as ratification-dependent (non-objective), albeit self-interpreting, entities while practices as ratification-independent (objective), albeit non-self-interpreting patterns, can only be untangled if—on the level of the theory of knowledge—the issue of dualism is properly addressed: one is then able to understand that objectivity in the mind (ultra-interpretations and other items) becomes modesty on the level of meaning, content and the world, whereas objectivity about meaning, content and the world rejects the existence of all intermediaries.

3.5 Meaning, Use and Truth

In line with his remarks on rule-following and practice Wittgenstein advanced an explanation of the meaning of linguistic expressions which relates meaning to the

[78] This is a modified version of an example offered by McDowell, *ibid*, 270–71.

way language is used in communication. The 'use theory of meaning', as it came to be known, has had a strong impact on the philosophy of language in the second half of the twentieth century.[79] Disregarding differences in detail and elaboration between the different variations of the theory, there is a shared core consisting of the thesis that use exhausts meaning. The gist of the thesis is that, in accounting for the meaning of words and sentences, one has to attend to the ways those are actually employed by the speakers of a language. In doing so one comes to grasp the rules that govern use and, hence, meaning. The result can be generalised to intentional content, granted the equation between thought and language which was defended earlier.[80]

The *use theory of content* can be combined with the semantic conception of truth in order to show that the truth-conditions of a sentence are identical with the reasons we have for asserting the sentence within the language-game (or practice) of grammar. As Chapter 2 demonstrated, what individuates truth-conditions on the semantic conception of truth is the grammatical structure of the assertive sentence. However, what we have discovered in this chapter is that grammar, far from coming in a static form, waiting to be supplemented by phenomenalist sense-data,[81] is practice. Analogously, truth-conditions cease to depend on anything other than the use speakers subject sentences to, when they engage in the practice of grammar. The use of sentences within the practice of grammar is marked by the elementary activity of using an assertive sentence (making an assertion). Making an assertion, to that extent, is the most fundamental activity in the pragmatic transformation of grammar and must be given priority over all other activities.[82] When specified in the context of making an assertion the truth-conditions of a sentence amount to no more than assertion conditions.

[79] For a succinct albeit comprehensive exposition, see J Skorupski, 'Meaning, Use, Verification' in B Hale and C Wright (eds), *A Companion to the Philosophy of Language* (Oxford, Blackwell, 1999) 29–59. For a contemporary version of a use theory of meaning see P Horwich, *Meaning* (Oxford, Clarendon Press, 1998) ch 3.

[80] See section 2.3.

[81] As the logical positivists and the epistemology of Russell's and Whitehead's *Principia Mathematica* would have it. See section 2.6.

[82] Later, in Chapter 7, I will discuss a number of other rules that are linked to the pragmatic dimension of grammar, rules which express a number of claims on behalf of those who engage in the practice of grammar. Such pragmatic rules broaden the normative inventory of grammar by making explicit the communicative dimension of language. Seminal in disclosing this dimension has been the work of Karl-Otto Apel, Jürgen Habermas and Robert Alexy. For the relevant literature see section 7.5.1.

3.5.1 Asserting a Sentence

The starting point is the assertion of a sentence.[83] The rule which specifies the conditions for correctly asserting a sentence S in language L takes the form[84]:

(rule of assertion): S is correctly used in order to make an assertion in L if and only if one is justified in believing, of the proposition that is expressed by the use of S, that it is true.

Thus to correctly assert a sentence means that one is justified in believing that the sentence is true, in the broadest sense of the word 'true'. Accordingly, assertion and truth are connected within a rule that specifies the conditions for the correct use of affirmative sentences. As a result the rule of assertion provides for a notion of correctness that relies on some form of epistemic justification[85]: one undertakes a correct use of a sentence as long as one is justified in believing that the corresponding proposition is true. Put in this way, however, the notion of correctness (and the relevant rule of assertion) appears to refer to propositions as some entities of some extra-linguistic nature, different from that of sentences. On a first look this creates a difficulty, for taken conjointly, the premisses 'the meaning of a sentence is exhausted by its correct use (or the rule that governs that use)' and 'the correct use of a sentence relates to the truth of the corresponding proposition', yield the conclusion that the meaning of a sentence turns on the truth of a proposition. Were one to conceive propositions as being extra-linguistic entities, the project of explaining meaning and content in a language-immanent way would collapse.

In order to avoid this conclusion, the use theory of meaning proceeds to explicate the notion of the proposition in a language immanent way. In other words, propositions as corresponding to sentences (and concepts as corresponding to concept-words), must in turn be associated with the way we use language. This, however, is far from unusual or contradictory. In fact the whole programme of explaining meaning via use rests on the assumption that there are no entities external to language that are self-interpreting, so as to be able to account for the meaning of linguistic signs.[86] The only 'source' of meaning is the use of a sentence according to some normative standards. Understood that way, to talk of concepts and propositions is simply to talk indirectly of the use of expressions and sentences within particular languages. To grasp a proposition or a concept is to normatively respond to a rule according to which some sentence or expression is employed in a language. Along these lines, talking about propositions and concepts is nothing more than talking about language-understanding in an

[83] The discussion will stay on the level of sentences since the rules that govern the use of words are determined in connection with the way a word contributes to the assertion conditions of a sentence; see also Skorupski, above n 79, 32.

[84] In the formulations of the rules for assertion I follow roughly Skorupski, *ibid*, 32–40.

[85] *Ibid* 32–33.

[86] This is a characteristically Wittgensteinian idea and is discussed in detail in Chapter 4.

abstract way, ie without specifying the particular language. This is to say, concepts and propositions have no explanatory role in an account of meaning as use.

Specified thus, the use-theory of meaning is, to talk with Michael Dummett,[87] a full-blooded theory of meaning which does not rely on extra-linguistic concepts or propositions in order to account for meaning, but proceeds to explain what it is to possess a concept or grasp a proposition as part of the account of meaning. It is for that reason that the use theory incorporates an epistemic claim: the priority of language in the explanation of meaning yields an account of what it is to be justified in believing that a sentence/proposition is true. This account is epistemic in that it contains an analysis of what it is to know that a sentence/proposition is true: in the full-blooded theory of meaning-as-use, this consists in the 'practical ability to tell when it is right to utter [a sentence] assertorically: to recognise information states as warranting or not warranting that kind of utterance of the sentence'.[88]

3.5.2 Assertion and Truth

The satisfaction of the epistemic claim of the use theory of meaning requires some account of the truth conditions of a sentence-as-proposition. Such an account can be given by a semantic theory of truth as the one discussed in the first part of this chapter. According to a semantic theory of truth, the truth conditions of a sentence will be given by the conditional[89]:

(truth-conditional formula): Sentence S is true in language L if and only if it is the case that proposition P.

This formula discharges the epistemic claim raised by the rule of assertion: S is correctly used to make an assertion if and only if one is justified in believing that the sentence is true; and the truth-conditional formula provides the truth-conditions for S in L. Stated in those terms the truth-conditional explication of meaning need not be incompatible with a language-immanent explication of propositions and concepts. However, the claim raised by a 'full-blooded' semantic theory poses some further constraints upon the truth-conditional explication of meaning. Those constraints refer, as mentioned before, to the way one is allowed to understand the relation between propositions and sentences. In particular, the concern arises in connection with the way one is going to demarcate the epistemic issue of 'grasping a proposition' or 'possessing a concept'. There are at least two ways to conduct such an enterprise.

The first way is to explicate the epistemic issue as exceeding the boundaries of a theory of meaning. To abide by that option entails that one distinguishes, more or less, between two phases in one's account of the meaning of a sentence S.

[87] See M Dummett, *The Seas of Language*, softback edn (Oxford, Clarendon Press, 1996) i–xvii; and the discussion in Skorupski, above n 79, 38 *ff.*

[88] Skorupski, *ibid*, 39.

[89] See section 2.5.

Accordingly, to know the assertion of S in L is, first, to know its truth-condition and, secondly, to know the epistemology which links with that truth-condition.[90] While the first issue belongs to the subject matter of a theory of meaning, the latter does not. On this understanding what the theory of meaning, and its truth-conditional part, account for is merely the 'things' of which linguistic expressions are true (namely the propositions of which sentences are true). However, the theory of meaning seems to remain silent in respect to the epistemic question 'how does one come to know the truth-conditions of a proposition'. This question has to be answered via an epistemological account which transcends the boundaries of any theory of meaning and content and accounts for extra- or pre-linguistic entities or connections.[91]

I take it to be pretty obvious that such a solution is not what a full-blooded use theory of meaning aims for. Therefore I will consider the second route for tackling the epistemic issue of 'grasping a proposition' to offer a more satisfactory solution. This holds, roughly, that the theory of meaning has to go beyond a truth-conditional part that merely 'stat[es] what expressions of the language are true of and deriving from that truth-conditions for sentences of the language'.[92] In fact it has to explain what it is to know the truth-conditions of a sentence. But in doing so it merely evokes the assertion conditions of a sentence. This is perfectly consistent with the point of a full-blooded theory of meaning; namely, that grasping truth-conditions is never over and above mastering assertion conditions.[93]

Arguably, this furnishing of truth-conditions suggests a verificationist understanding of the assertion conditions and, derivatively, of the concept of meaning.[94] Having said that, verificationism in respect to meaning is to be distinguished from verificationism in respect to truth. The first version says that understanding a sentence consists in grasping what information states would verify it irrespective of those states' actual existence or availability. (Put in slightly different terms, it is the idea that a sentence is meaningful if and only if one is able to conceive or 'simulate' what sort of evidence would be adequate for asserting a sentence.) In contrast, verificationism in relation to truth holds that truth is verifiability. A sentence is true if and only if there actually is evidence warranting its assertion. Leaving the second conception aside, some version of verificationism about meaning could be made compatible with a flexible pragmatic account of meaning as use. For that to work one needs to evoke a looser version of verificationism about meaning which, roughly, holds that a sentence is

[90] Skorupski, above n 79, 37.
[91] This is, roughly, the solution that Skorupski suggests, *ibid* 48–54.
[92] *Ibid* 38.
[93] See above n 87.
[94] For a detailed discussion of the topics in this and the next paragraph, see Skorupski, above n 79, 40–45.

verifiable if one can describe, at least in principle, what it would be like to encounter in experience the state of affairs which makes a sentence true.

This version of verificationism escapes the narrow or *stricto sensu* verificationism about truth that was endemic in the thought of the Vienna Circle and the work of the early Wittgenstein.[95] Verificationism *stricto sensu* holds that the meaning of a sentence is determined by the actual availability of a state of affairs for which the sentence functions as a picture or mirror. For this to hold, an ontology is presupposed which postulates reality as consisting of a totality of states of affairs.[96] In this context understanding a sentence implies that one is able to experience in a direct way whether the relevant state of affairs obtains. In contrast to this idea a more flexible version of verificationism about meaning can be taken to share insights with the later work of Wittgenstein. On this approach the meaning of a sentence is related to the methods of verification rather than some picturable state of affairs which would verify it. Linking the concept of meaning to the method of verification bestows meaning with a significant amount of flexibility: meaning is made dependent upon the method of verification; further, since there are many different methods to verify a sentence, meaning becomes perspectival or context-related. This yields a pluralistic understanding of the assertion-conditions of a sentence which eventually leads to a rather *liberalised* conception of meaning and content.[97] Assertion conditions as consisting in the method of verification eventually are taken to incorporate the consequences of an assertion for rule-following as well as the operations which license it. This broadening of the concept of meaning towards incorporating practical consequences is particularly acute in the late work of Wittgenstein. There, understanding an assertion is more than to be told when one is licensed to make that assertion; one needs to know what consequences flow from that assertion for action.

On this liberalised understanding, practice becomes constitutive for the determination of meaning. Understanding a word or a sentence is to know what can be done with it in practice. Connectedly the liberalised conception of meaning transcends verificationism (as a method for establishing assertion conditions) and is recast as a practical concept (as emanating from the *consequences* that the use of words and sentences entail in our everyday practices of communication). *Meaning (and, further, content) as practical concept* dovetails with a picture of intentionality which extends beyond mind-world dualism. In it, the mind is directed at the environment not via self-interpreting entities but via the normative constraints action imposes on thought and vice versa: one is only entitled to those assertions which do not conflict with the content of one's true thoughts (eg

[95] See section 2.6.

[96] For the affinity with the ontology of Wittgenstein's *Tractatus Logico-Philosophicus*, see Skorupski, above n 79, 40–45.

[97] *Cf* M Luntley, *Contemporary Philosophy of Thought and Language* (Oxford, Blackwell, 1998) ch 12.

my thought that the book is on the table before me, commits me to holding true claims about how my movement will be impeded by that particular book, or how the movement of other objects will be impeded or enabled by it). On this approach intentional content is generated according to patterns of practice. To put it differently, normativity of content does not flow from the environment as such, as there is hardly anything out there that possesses intrinsic normative properties. In contrast, normativity comes from the direction of practice: content is generated along the lines of how thought engages with the network of our practices.

The dimension of the (inter)action of agents with the environment invests meaning with an evaluative aspect: as meaning is generated along the way action 'meets' the environment, the various instances of this 'meeting' are interpreted in the light of the evaluations that underlie action. In this sense it is action that provides for the evaluative character of meaning considering that the environment, as such, is valueless. In the light of the values that underlie action the *consequences* of understanding a sentence in one rather than another way become significant for the determination of meaning. To that extent, meaning becomes dependent upon the consequences that understanding, in the light of action, entails. For instance the consequences that the act of asserting entails for action points to the rule that one should be truthful when asserting something (imagine asserting untruthfully to a blind person that the staircase he is about to descend has 10 instead of 12 stairs—just to use an example where the consequences for action are fairly clear!). Hence consequences for action point to the normative constraints of meaning and demarcate meaning as a normative concept throughout.

3.6 Practice, Realism and Reasons

In the last section of the chapter I shall guard against a misconception or even fallacy committed by a number of prominent contemporary defenders of the pragmatic approach who work within analytic philosophy.[98] The misconception is that, lest idealism arise, a constitutive link must be presupposed between environment and practice. In fact, I will argue, unless this is taken just to express a caution against mentalism, it would lead to a new dualism and its devastating conclusions. Conversely, I shall argue that for meaning to remain normative something like priority of practice must be defended. Practice forms the locus within which mind and environment make contact, and this locus has to be conceived of as lying at the bedrock of any effort to explain content. Postponing a detailed discussion until Chapter 4, I will just outline the conditions for priority. The latter will point to two seminal elements of the pragmatic account, which are

[98] Donald Davidson, John McDowell and Susan Hurley, just to mention the most familiar names from the discussion so far.

interdependent: first, the existence of a fundamental practice (or language-game) which involves the rules of grammar and forms the background of any other intentional activity (or practice); notably, this language-game conditions our ability to form intentional content by depicting facts in our judgements; secondly, the reflexive character of rule-following. Unless practices were understood as normative they would dissolve into brute facts of behaviour. For that to be avoided, judging must be conceived of as a principled or reflexive activity which is subject to constraints or reasons which are adduced for distinguishing false from right ascriptions of content. This reflexive dimension, or dimension of depth, requires that it be possible to refer in a justificatory manner to the rules of any practice. Again, here, this is rendered possible on the basis of the fundamental language-game of grammar, which allows us to 'objectify' rules and reasons with a view to justifying any practice.[99]

3.6.1 The Realism Fallacy

There is a fear amongst contemporary defenders of the pragmatic or contextualist approach working in the analytical tradition: the fear that any prioritisation of practice will lead to idealism and from there back to dualism. Because of this fear, such philosophers resort to a kind of moderate realism. With a view to dispelling this fear I shall focus on the work of S Hurley, assuming that her views are in broad agreement with a number of other prominent philosophers who work in the area.[100]

Hurley conceives of the contextualist account as standing within a philosophical tradition which, beginning with Kant, attempts to undermine the naïve idea about the unquestionable character of perceptual experience. Philosophers belonging to this tradition argue that neither is there a pre-given unity of things nor can our experience of them be taken for granted. Hence, perceptual experience is not something given which imposes itself upon the mind. According to a characteristic Kantian expression, 'Combination does not lie in the objects'.[101] It has rather to be reconstructed through the spontaneous activity of synthesis (Kant), which is predominantly an activity- or agency-involving procedure. However, Hurley goes on to argue, agency or intentional action cannot be, in

[99] Conceived of this way, practices have depth. Depth allows for disagreement, error and correction. Conversely the communal model of practice seems to take practice to be exhausted by its behavioural surface or the mere fact of agreement between its participants. The main disadvantage of such flat understandings of practice is their inability to account for determinate content, for they must succumb to an infinite regress of interpretations. For the notion of depth see the extensive discussion in Chapters 4 and 6.

[100] I allude to such names as John McDowell, Donald Davidson, Tyler Burge and, amongst those working in legal theory, Nicos Stavropoulos.

[101] *Cf* Hurley, above n 10, 240. See also Hurley, above n 6, chs 2, 3 and 5.

turn, taken to enjoy any primitive or inherent ability to generate content, since that would require an answer to the problem of how intentional content is possible in the first place:

> How can the activity of synthesis have the transcendental role of making content possible, when any role it plays will presuppose that intentions with content are possible? The view that unity depends on the transcendental role of the activity of synthesis leaves unexplained the source of the unity presupposed by conceiving of synthesis as an activity to begin with, as an expression of agency as opposed to merely a series of natural events.[102]

The problem of content is therefore as much a problem for action as it is for experience. By shifting from the unquestionable character of experience to some kind of intentional action which enjoys a strange charisma of pre-given content, one is just postponing the settlement of the problem of content and meaning, thus asymmetrically favouring the Myth of the Giving over the Myth of the Given. Both myths are equally misleading since no act (like no experience) can provide for its own content (or interpretation) and therefore one has no good reason for favouring one over the other.

Hurley notes that holding to the Myth of the Giving while rejecting the Myth of the Given leads in many ways away from realism, into various forms of idealism. But to rescue some form of realism, one need not return to an insensitive form of the given. It is much more fruitful to elaborate a balanced account (an instance of which she takes the contextualist account to be) which would unify action and experience in a way that would demonstrate that only perceivers are agents and vice versa.[103] Such an account would reject both myths and still be able to subscribe to realism. In this light Hurley suggests that Wittgenstein's appeal to practices (ie forms of life) should be read not as a practice-oriented asymmetry but as a way of avoiding both myths by recognising the interdependence of experience and practice within forms of life:

> We can correct the traditional philosophical subordination of agent to subject without going to the opposite extreme. We can adopt a sophisticated, activity-laden view of

[102] *Cf* Hurley, above n 10, 241.

[103] This seems to be also the pivotal insight of Karl-Otto Apel, which underlies his programme of the transformation of the Kantian Critique of Pure Reason into a 'Critique of Language'. Apel locates the commencement of this enterprise in the *Tractatus* where Wittgenstein is taken to argue that language is not merely the (transcendental) condition of the possibility of describing facts but at the same time the condition of the possibility of the facts themselves as existing states of affairs. Language is in this way taken to be inescapably interwoven with experience. What Wittgenstein does not yet see in the *Tractatus* is that language, apart from its semantics and syntax, has also a third pragmatic level. This last level concerns agency among speakers and can be shown to transform language and communication into an agency-related activity. This pragmatic level, Apel holds, constitutes, together with the other two levels of language, a transcendental condition of experience (as the existence of facts as states of affairs) and therefore can be assumed to indicate that the role of the perceiver and the agent cannot be disconnected convincingly. For a brief, albeit reliable, account of the evolution of Apel's argument, see K-O Apel, *From a Transcendental-Semiotic Point of View*, M Papastephanou (ed) (Manchester, Manchester University Press, 1998) 9–42.

> experiential content, without taking intentional content as primitive in the ways associated with the Myth of the Giving. What is needed, rather, is to understand why it is no accident that only perceivers are agents, as well as why it is no accident that only agents are perceivers: to understand the interdependence of perception and action. There is no apparent reason this cannot be done compatibly with realism.[104]

In a similar vain Donald Davidson proclaims:

> In giving up the dualism of scheme and world, we do not give up the world, but re-establish unmediated touch with the familiar objects whose antics make our sentences and opinions true or false.[105]

Such worries are either overstated or misconceived. They are overstated if they purport to emphasise the mind-independent character of practice. Obviously, if practice is to ground objectivity of content, it must be strictly separated from mental representations.[106] To that extent it is important that all paths to individualist or mentalist interpretations of practice be blocked. However, in so doing, one need not postulate any priority and/or independence of the environment over practice. Conversely, it suffices to conceive of practice as the locus of individuation for both mind and world by postulating its conceptual priority over either of those. Conceived of in such terms, conceptual priority ensures that mind and environment are *equiprimordial* in a manner which precludes the mind-world gap from arising.[107]

On the other hand, those worries are wrongheaded if they are taken to require that practices be individuated by some unadulterated conception of the environment, one that is unmediated by practice. Any attempt to individuate practice in this manner will amount to reinstating environment as a criterion of content which is more fundamental than practice. From what we know so far, anything that is more fundamental than rule-following constitutes an ultra-interpretation and is bound to lead to indeterminacy and loss of content. Given the lengthy demonstration the latter point has been subjected to so far, I shall turn directly to discuss how individuation along the specified lines may lead to the priority of environment.

Such priority may be construed as conceptual priority and independence: the environment (E) is conceptually prior and independent with respect to practice (P), if P is accounted for in terms of E, where E is not in turn accounted for in terms of P.[108] Conceptual priority and independence need not entail epistemic priority. In other words, the conceptual priority relation allows for the dependent term, in our case P, to be epistemically prior. This does not contravene Hurley's

[104] *Cf* Hurley, above n 10, 242.

[105] See D Davidson, 'On the Very Idea of a Conceptual Scheme' in his *Inquiries into Truth and Interpretation* (Oxford, Clarendon Press, 1984) 198.

[106] Such is the mind-independence that was deemed compatible with the idea of grammar; see section 2.4.

[107] See section 3.6.2.

[108] For the relation of conceptual priority and independence see Hurley, above n 6, 10–11.

argument: practice, although enjoying epistemic priority over the environment, is still conceptually dependent on it. The next step is to establish a link between environment and content. Conceptual priority is transitive: if X is prior and determines Y, and Y determines Z, then X also determines Z. Translated into the present context, this relation entails that if the environment is constitutive (as in, prior and independent) of practice then it becomes the foundation of content. But conceiving of the environment as the foundation of content reopens the problem of ultra-interpretations with the all too familiar devastating consequences.

3.6.2 The Priority of Grammar

Conversely practice must be conceived of as being prior and independent from both mind and world. It is only then that dualism is avoided. Although a full elaboration of this point has to be postponed for some other occasion,[109] I would like to briefly mention a key requirement for the conceptual priority and independence of practice. This is the requirement that practice provides for the normativity of content. Practice was introduced as a means for avoiding the mind-world dualism that springs out from entities which purport to determine content conclusively (ultra-interpretations). Such entities cannot be placed at the bottom of an account of intentionality, for they fall pray to a regress of interpretations which gives rise to so radical an indeterminacy as to render intentional thought and action unintelligible. But in replacing ultra-interpretations, and the strong sense of objectivity those represent, practice runs the danger of losing hold of the determinacy of content.

This danger was very clearly demonstrated in the efforts of Kripke and Wright to offer a communal solution to the problem of rule-following.[110] We saw there that, in attempting to steer away from the Scylla of mentalism, communal interpretations of practice move straight into the camp of indeterminacy (Charybdis). The only remedy out of the impasse is to conceive of practice as a normative activity that lies at the bottom of intentionality. Having distanced ourselves from a strong, albeit devastating, notion of objectivity, the one that pertains to ultra-interpretations, it is essential to preserve the modest objectivity that is linked to the idea of normativity. To that extent, an explication of practice as the foundation of intentionality is inexorably connected with the requirement that practice be a source of normativity. Intentionality, on this conception, presupposes the existence of a foundation which is normatively efficacious. 'No foundation without normativity' sounds the slogan of intentionality, hence, if practice is to form this foundation it should be conceived of as a normative activity.

[109] Some insights in this direction are to be found in Chapter 4.
[110] See section 3.3.2.

Normativity requires that 'moves' within practice be not contingent but, conversely, capable of justification with reference to normative standards of sorts (reasons). It follows that, insofar as practice purports to be the foundation of intentionality, it must be in a position to account for a justified ascription of meaning to tokens of movement/speech within practice. Justifications and other principled ascriptions of meaning should not deteriorate into a regress of interpretations but remain dependent on the activity of rule-following. So conceived, justifications are essential for content, precisely because they do not purport to exhaustively determine content (were they to do so, in the familiar fashion of ultra-interpretations, they would be claiming to be more fundamental than practice), but merely to indicate our ability to adopt a reflexive attitude when we engage in rule-following. In other words, as far as the pragmatic conception of practice goes, justifications, interpretations and criteria make sense only to the extent they demonstrate the normative character of practice and remain tied down to the authority of a rule that extends well beyond (and behind) them.

A tentative response to the requirement of normativity as reflexivity is to structure practice in such terms as to guarantee the ability to *refer* to reasons which do not open the regress of interpretations. As was argued earlier, this ability is made available by the rules which govern the structure of judgements and the inferential relations obtaining between them (rules of grammar). It is within the practice of grammar that intentional activity can be thematised, in the sense that reasons for action and content can be itemised, referred to and adduced for supporting or discrediting the various moves within practice. As a result, it is essential that a basic or foundational practice (or language-game) be presupposed, one that constitutes the bedrock of all intentional activity: the practice of grammar[111] (or of *judging simpliciter*, as I shall call it in Chapter 4). This foundational language-game underlies all other cognitive practices because it allows us to realise the condition of normativity/reflexivity which is required for practice to function as foundation of content. What is more, placing grammar at the bottom of intentional activity shifts the boundaries of scepticism to the extent of dismantling it: while the mind-world dualism nurtures scepticism by attaching content to a plurality of conceptual schemes, the positioning of grammar at the bedrock of intentionality establishes a unique benchmark. To put it in the words of a classic passage from Donald Davidson[112]:

[111] For the role of a foundational language-game in an account of meaning and knowledge, see K-O Apel, *Transformation der Philosophie*, vol 2, *Das Apriori der Kommunikationsgemeinschaft* (Frankfurt am Main, Suhrkamp, 1973) and in English translation by G Adey and D Frisby as *Towards a Transformation of Philosophy* (London, Routledge and Kegan Paul, 1980) 165. Along similar lines see Philip Pettit's distinction between basic and non-basic rules of intentionality, in *idem*, *The Common Mind*, 2nd edn (New York and Oxford, Oxford University Press, 1996) 79–81.

[112] See Davidson, above n 105, 198.

> Without the dogma [of dualism] … relativity goes by the board. Of course truth of sentences remains relative to language, but that is as objective as can be.

It is the reflexive dimension of rule-following I turn to next, with an eye to demonstrating the relations that pertain between a fundamental and other kinds of practice. This will allow me to set up the parameters for the detailed discussion of objectivity and knowledge with respect to law undertaken in the second part of the book.

4

Practice, Normativity and Reasons

4.1 Introduction

The discussion so far has pointed to two requirements for practice as a source of determinate intentional content. On the one hand, avoidance of the dualism of mind and world requires that practice be specified as the foundation of intentional content in thought and action. On the other hand, practice needs to be furnished with a normative component with an eye to resisting the scepticism or relativism associated with a regress of interpretations. In this chapter I argue that both requirements point to an account of content I shall call *pragmatic rationalism*. This combines the pragmatic conception of practice discussed in the last chapter, with a rationalist understanding of normativity.

The pragmatic conception takes all judging to depend on a practice which escapes mind-world dualism by arguing that environment and thought are equiprimordial, for they arise simultaneously within practice.[1] However the pragmatic understanding lacks, on its own, the resources for guaranteeing normativity and determinacy of content. Broadly speaking the challenge pragmatism faces in this respect is to steer clear from understandings of practice which either lead to a regress of interpretations or otherwise evoke the bad effects of mind-word dualism.[2] This is where the rationalist component comes in; *rationalism* proposes that normativity be understood as resting on constraints of content which are internal to practice, albeit capable of normativity. Such constraints create a *space* between membership or participation in the practice and exhaustive appreciation of its contents. Thus, it is possible that, notwithstanding one's competent use of a concept in everyday communication, one may

[1] To be more precise, this is true if 'environment' is taken to signify a reality that is ontologically structured in facts, objects and properties. Intriguing as it may be, the possibility of an unstructured or unadulterated reality falls outside the scope of this book, for the reasons explained in Chapter 1.

[2] Two such failed attempts were discussed in the last chapter: on the one hand, the interpretations of practice by S Kripke and C Wright in section 3.3.2. On the other, a strong realist explication which takes practice to be answerable to an unadulterated or pure reality (section 3.6.1).

still fail to have full knowledge of the concept's content.[3] In this manner the rationalist idea allows for error, correction and discovery while respecting the fundamentality of practice.

As a result, it becomes a central task of the view proposed here to specify the structure and nature of rationalist constraints. In this context three central tasks are to be undertaken. First of all, rationalist constraints will be specified as reasons that guide judging as a form of activity. Secondly, it will be shown that the idea of rationalist constraints requires that grammar be conceived of as the most fundamental content-giving practice. Finally, it will be suggested that a grammatical structure, in whose light content formation emerges as a normative activity, renders all agents who partake of it autonomous. Autonomous agents may be, further, conceived as persons who raise certain claims to objectivity and correctness, to the effect that not any reason proposed in a particular domain of judging may be deemed valid. With the concept of personhood in place, pragmatic rationalism arrives at a robust explication of the depth of practice, such as can underpin claims of knowledge in contexts as contested as law, morality and ethics. What is more, it may do so without being compelled to step out of the realm of judging (practice), in some desperate search for superlative grounds of knowledge, a search that is likely to lead to scepticism and its discontents.

The chapter opens with a discussion of the normativity of rule-following (section 4.2). The nature of constraints as reasons is considered: How are reasons to be understood? What are they metaphysically speaking? When do they stay within grammar and when do they constitute ultra-interpretations? What conditions must they fulfil? Section 4.3 deals with some objections to the reflexive character of practice. Section 4.4 is about the requirement of distinguishing between two levels of practice, as a condition of referring to reasons. Relations between the different levels of practice and some implications for the status of judging agents as persons are proposed. Finally, section 4.5 anticipates a possible objection and attempts to connect the first with the second part of the book.

4.2 Reasons and the Reflexive Character of Practice

It was argued earlier that it is a distinctive mark of the pragmatic explication of intentionality that it substitutes normativity for a strong objectivity. Normativity requires that practice pose constraints to thought and action (for, as was argued earlier, in the pragmatic account thinking is an activity). This necessity of constraints for normativity is linked to the need for determinacy: unless we presuppose that there are constraints for content which cannot be put in

[3] See T Burge, 'Frege on Sense and Linguistic Meaning' in *idem, Truth, Thought, Reason: Essays on Frege* (Oxford, Clarendon Press, 2005) 242–69; and the discussion in sections 6.2 and 6.3.

question (call these ratification-independent), content becomes impossible.[4] Ratification-independence is not unlimited, however: it is sustained by and within the boundaries of practice. In other words, insofar as the fundamentality of practice is accepted, constraints must be in principle accessible from within the practice for every participant. Far from guaranteeing that constraints are automatically known by the participants of practice, this caveat simply ensures that there be nothing, capable of constraining practice, which is unfathomable from the point of view of the participants of the practice, even if it will take a lot of hard thinking and many failed attempts (over a very long time) before they 'discover' it.

There is, of course, the possibility to question constraints in a more radical manner, namely by attacking practice itself as a reliable guide to truth and knowledge (for all we know, after all, there is nothing guaranteeing that practices do not practice collective illusion!). There is much less in this worry than meets the eye, for it is considerably more difficult to challenge practice *tout court* than isolated criteria. Practice (or at least a certain level of it[5]) refers to such general or thin presuppositions for articulating content that, indeed, even an attempt to challenge it would have to presuppose it. To the extent this is true, we should not worry if content remains relative to practice, for practice is as objective as can be (paraphrasing slightly Davidson when talking about language).[6] Consequently, it may be said that practices rely on a more fundamental agreement, one that cannot be undermined without losing the concept of content (and action) *tout court*: this agreement is an agreement in form of life. That said, a question still stands: how to conceive of constraints more precisely?

[4] See J McDowell's 'transcendental' argument in *idem*, 'Wittgenstein on Following a Rule' reprinted in A Miller and C Wright (eds), *Rule-Following and Meaning* (Chesham, Acumen, 2002) 45–80; also the discussion in section 3.3.3 and 3.4.

[5] This is the practice arising from the rules of grammar as the most fundamental form of practice. *Cf* section 4.4. Also see P Pettit, *The Common Mind: An Essay in Psychology, Society and Politics* (Oxford, Oxford University Press, 1993) 76–81, who distinguishes between a basic and a non-basic level of rule-following (practice); K-O Apel adopts a similar distinction when he pronounces: "one language game at least is excluded [ie form scepticism] and presupposed as a transcendental language-game"; see *idem*, *Transformation der Philosophie*, vol 2, *Das Apriori der Kommunikationsgemeinschaft* (Frankfurt am Main, Suhrkamp, 1973) and in English translation by G Adey and D Frisby as *Towards a Transformation of Philosophy* (London, Routledge and Kegan Paul, 1980) 165. For a thorough and exemplary discussion of Apel's views compare with C Roversi, 'Constitutionalism and Transcendental Arguments' (2008) 59 *Northern Ireland Legal Quarterly* (forthcoming). Another philosopher who takes the view that thought has a reflexive structure (albeit, confining his claim to philosophical thinking) is E Tugendhat, 'Überlegungen zur Methode der Philosophie aus analytischer Sicht' in A Honneth *et al* (eds), *Zwischenbetrachtungen im Prozeß der Aufklärung* (Frankfurt am Main, Suhrkamp, 1989) 305–17.

[6] D Davidson, 'On the Very Idea of a Conceptual Scheme' in *idem*, *Inquiries into Truth and Interpretation* (Oxford, Clarendon Press, 1984) 183–98 (at 198).

4.2.1 Constraints as Reasons

Constraints can be represented as *reasons* for abiding by rules of practice. Speaking broadly, the idea of reasons reflects better the fact that the ascription of content to thoughts is the result of an activity, for activity is constrained by reasons rather than causes. It could be objected that some constraints—in particular those connected with naturalistic aspects of the environment—perform a more basic function of individuation in virtue of a direct connection they have with naturalistic aspects of the environment.[7] On the face of it, such constraints cannot be understood as reasons but need to be specified along the lines of their basic content-individuating ability, which is of a causal nature. This view evokes anew the suspicion of dualism and should be rejected as inconsistent with the pragmatic explication of practice which takes practice to be fundamental for content. Consequently, there is no reason for bestowing constraints of any particular domain with a privileged role by taking the domain to which they belong to comprise special content-giving powers which are exempted from practice. Constraints are intelligible as such only within practice—and to the extent they do so they constitute reasons for acting and judging within the practice.

4.2.1.1 Reasons as Facts

Reasons as constraints of rule-following can be various things. In the light of our representation of content through linguistic structures (sentences) we may say that the things which can constrain our judgment and action are the parts of the environment which are depicted by our sentences.[8] To cut a long story short, possible candidates for reasons are objects, properties and facts. Two remarks are owed here: first, to say that objects, properties and facts are reasons or constraints is not paradoxical; it does not purport to resuscitate an essentialism of sorts; nor should it be taken as evoking a 'direct' relation between practice and environment. As explained earlier, the referential function of language, and in particular the environment of the sentence, accounts for an exhaustive depiction of ontological categories.[9] Translated into the conceptual scheme of language, objects, properties and facts make sense as objective constraints for judging, conceived of as a rule-governed activity. Secondly, facts are more fundamental than objects and properties, due to the priority of referential function which was ascribed to sentences: within the judgement-oriented explication of grammar, it is the

[7] This objection derives form realist theories, see S L Hurley, *Natural Reasons: Personality and Polity* (Oxford and New York, Oxford University Press, 1989) chs 5 and 6.

[8] Along the same lines, see Pettit, above n 5.

[9] This has been the rationale throughout Chapter 2.

environment of the assertive sentence within which all other ontological categories are disclosed. As a result, the most basic constraints (reasons) of rule-following are facts.

One should guard against thinking that such facts refer only to naturalistic aspects of the environment. Instead facts should be conceived more liberally, as comprising not only natural but also legal, moral or other social facts. Such facts, for instance, can be normative in that they are about rules and principles.[10] The necessity of importing a liberalised conception of facts is demonstrated by the need for differentiated explanations which arises in different contexts. Not any kind of intentional content yields a scientific explanation of the type naturalistic facts generate, despite the widespread belief that any proper explanation has to be of the causal type.

4.2.1.2 Reasons and Rational Explanation

Consequently it would be unwise to restrict our inventory of reasons for content by arguing that *only* facts which can generate causal explanations (eg naturalistic facts) are productive of content. This view has been encouraged by the habit of many philosophers to refer to causal explanations when discussing constraints of content.[11] However, such a view is extremely restrictive. A fact-as-reason can stand in a causal relation to a token of thought or action without amounting to a full causal explanation. What is more, naturalistic explanations are not always illuminating in non-scientific contexts: the point is that, although in most cases it is possible to redescribe any given fact in naturalistic terms, the resulting explanation may fail to explain the thought or action targeted by it. The case of colour is a good example: suppose that my belief about the pen being red is caused by the fact that the pen lying on the table is red. Suppose further that I am not satisfied with this explanation but want a full scientific explanation. With a view to obtaining it, I replace 'red' with such concepts that refer to the properties physics tells me are responsible for producing the effect of redness on the retina of my eye. The amounting explanation, although exemplary in causal terms, is far from successful in explaining what caused my *belief* regarding the colour of the said pen. The same conclusion should be, *mutatis mutandis*, extended to explanations relating to social contexts: my belief that if I park in front of the delivery entrance of Karstadt I am bound to be fined, is caused by the (normative fact) that 'parking before … is forbidden'.

In those and other similar cases what is in issue is a rational explanation.[12] Rational explanation is juxtaposed to causal explanation in the following sense: causal explanation purports to illustrate a strict causal connection between

[10] See above the referential function of grammar (Chapter 2) and the detailed discussion on how to depict (legal) normative facts in section 7.5.2.

[11] This is the case with Donald Davidson and Tyler Burge as Hurley remarks, see *Natural Reasons*, above n 7, 95.

[12] Hurley, above n 7, 96–98.

constraints, which are conceived of naturalistically, and tokens of thought or action. The causal connection is here of the type that pertains to scientific explanation. Conversely, rationalistic explanations purport to explain content by linking thought and action with non-naturalistic reasons. Although it is still possible to speak of a causal link in this context, any talk of cause will involve a much looser understanding of the term. To accommodate this possibility, some philosophers have proposed the term *causal relation* to cover cases of loose causality involved in rational explanations.[13]

The need for retaining a loose notion of causality can be justified in a further manner: non-naturalistic reasons can, in most cases, be redescribed as naturalistic facts, giving rise, in effect, to causal explanations. Although such explanations may be illuminating to a certain extent, they usually fail to offer a full explanation as the cases of colour and social norms have illustrated. Thus non-naturalistic reasons possess an autonomous explanatory force (rational explanatory force) which drops out when they are redescribed in naturalistic terms. At the same time rational explanations constitute themselves a form of description, for they themselves rest on facts (albeit non-naturalistic). Although non-naturalistic facts are not capable of causing anything in a scientific sense they are still about entities whose occurrence is necessary for the existence of a token of thought or action. Besides, non-naturalistic facts can, on many occasions, be underpinned by naturalistic facts or events which constitute a scientific explanation at a different level of description. This is usually what relations of supervenience purport to achieve by linking higher-order non-naturalistic facts with lower-order facts describable by the vocabulary of science.[14]

Insofar as reasons which can generate explanations are much wider than the class of naturalistic reasons, it is appropriate that rational explanation be given lexical priority over causal explanation. This priority is justified in light of the central role action plays for thinking and the notion of constraints as reasons it generates (within the context of a pragmatic understanding of practice). Thus it would not be inappropriate to talk of rational explanation as an overarching conception of explanation with causal explanation only to take over when explanation targets naturalistic content.

4.2.2 Conditions for Reasons

I turn now to discussing a number of additional requirements for reasons that are relevant in the present context. Reasons must simultaneously be motivationally

[13] Such philosophers include Davidson and Burge. See Hurley, above n 7, 97.

[14] For reasons to be taken up in Chapter 6, supervenience will be deemed of low importance for legal and more general, normative contexts. See also G Pavlakos, 'Two Conceptions of Universalisation' in Z Bankowski and J MacLean (eds), *The Universal and the Particular in Legal Reasoning* (Aldershot, Ashgate, 2006).

efficacious and objective.[15] The capacity to motivate lies, as it were, in reasons' universality: reasons need to be universal in the sense that they ought to be abided by in an indefinite number of situations, whenever a judging-subject attempts to form a true judgement about any state of affairs involving the same reason.[16] Thus the motivational dimension can be represented by the obligation to judge something as being X (rather than Y) in light of reason R. On the other hand, reasons need to meet a requirement of objectivity: that they be in an appropriate manner accessible to judging subjects. Philip Pettit[17] breaks down this condition into three distinct qualities: reasons must be independently identifiable; directly identifiable and finally they should be fallible.

4.2.2.1 Independent Identifiability

Independent identifiability expresses the idea that any reason must be identifiable or determinable by a finite subject independently of any particular instance of application. Thus judging-subjects should be capable of generalising a reason to future cases, although their being finite would not allow them to have knowledge of the infinite number of instances the reason applies. On Pettit's proposal, this is possible by taking any finite set of applications relating to a reason to instantiate a relationship of exemplification: this is a three-place relationship between a set of applications (or examples), the relevant reason and the subject for which the said examples stand. The three-place constellation allows for a finite set of examples to exemplify just one reason for a particular judging subject, contrary to the fact that no finite set of examples can instantiate a determinate reason (as Wittgenstein went in great length to argue in his *Philosophical Investigations*).[18]

4.2.2.2 Direct Readability

The condition that reasons be directly readable, means that finite thinkers must be able to read straight off what they require. Direct readability is a different way to say that the rule and the reasons that guide its application stand in an internal relation to one another. It follows that direct readability does not imply that rule-following must be groundless or unreasoned but only that it is fundamental

[15] Those follow from the more general requirement that the rule and its interpretations (criteria of application) stand in an internal relation. See Chapter 3. Pettit, above n 5, 82–83, introduces a similar set of distinctions between what he calls objective and subjective conditions. In his distinction, objectivity refers to the motivational capacity of reasons, while subjectivity captures their capacity to be accessible from the point of view of judging subjects. A change of terminology was deemed necessary in order to avoid a possible clash with the terms used in the discussion of the normativity of legal reasons, in section 7.4.

[16] A more detailed discussion of the motivational relevance of reasons is offered in the context of legal reasons, see section 7.4.2.

[17] Pettit, above n 5, 82 *ff.*

[18] For more details on the potential of the exemplification condition see Pettit, above n 5, 86–88. For a powerful, reconstruction of Wittgenstein's arguments, see S Kripke, *Wittgenstein on Rules and Private Language: An Elementary Exposition* (Oxford, Blackwell, 1984).

with respect to intentional content and action. To that extent it should be possible to identify reasons which, by constraining the application of rules, block an infinite regress of interpretations. Notably direct readability can be explained as a disposition or inclination arising from the exemplification of a rule by the thinking subject. One note of caution should be added here: the disposition postulated here is not like any other disposition which is bound to fall prey to a regress of interpretations.[19] In contrast to regress-invoking dispositions, the kind proposed in this context derives its authority from the reasons it refers to and not vice versa: it is not the disposition, in other words, that is presupposed (as, say, some magical quality of thinkers) in order to group together various instances of application into forming the appropriate constraint or reasons. But instead the disposition arises when the rule/reasons are understood as a result of the exemplification that takes place between the thinking-subjects and a set of examples or instances of application.

4.2.2.3 Fallibility of Reasons

Finally, the condition of fallibility submits that reasons for rule-following may be fallible. This is the important idea that our judgements are not true by stipulation: it is often the case that the reasons we relied on in forming a judgement turn out, on further inquiry, not to have been the right ones. Fallibility is, to that extent, an important condition for objectivity, for it guarantees that there is still room for discovery and correction as regards our judgements. Insofar as this holds true, fallibility becomes a key condition for the insight that content is not mind-dependent throughout but, instead, that it is possible to distinguish between right and wrong judgements.[20]

At the same time, the type of objectivity that goes along with fallibility respects the foundational character of rule-following. This point can be illustrated as the possibility to retain meaningful disagreement. Disagreement remains meaningful when it displays itself as a case of different beliefs against a background of same content (same content-different belief cases). Same content requires that the practice of judging function as a deep level of conceptual agreement ('form of life') against whose background content and communication are secured. In the light of a form of life, divergent beliefs constitute intelligible instances of disagreement about reasons rather than effecting a breakdown of content and communication. On the contrary, were every divergence in belief to constitute a difference in 'form of life', the possibility of communication would be disabled and all content would be lost. As a result, the type of objectivity enjoined by fallibility does not rest on a radical mind-independence of content, one that is exempted from a most basic conceptual scheme ('form of life') that guarantees

[19] For a critique of dispositions as another intermediary, see Kripke, above n 18, 24; also see the discussion in section 3.2.

[20] See the remarks on two kinds of mind-dependence in section 2.4.

communication. Notwithstanding the existence of such a conceptual scheme, there is a lot of room for error and correction with respect to reasons for judging. Hence, objectivity manifests itself as the space for disagreement between meaningful judgements, the latter constituting partial disclosures springing out from a common background.

4.2.2.4 Reflexive Rule-following

The possibility of identifying reasons which satisfy all the above conditions warrants the conclusion that rule-following has a reflexive dimension. A reflexive dimension entails that practice is not a mechanical exercise which unfolds independently of those who judge, say by aligning the content of thoughts to items which pre-exist the capacity of thinkers to judge. The reflexive dimension implies that thinkers have the ability to critically assess the various instances of applications of rules. What is more, the reflexive dimension of rule-following can be used in underpinning an understanding of agents who are capable of rule-following as persons. The claim in this respect would roughly be that anyone who may engage in reflexive (as opposed to mechanical) rule-following is autonomous. The proposed concept of the person is of particular interest in the context of philosophical programmes which aim to connect intentionality with a substantive idea of communication (eg discourse theory).[21] Such theories are usually beset by a difficulty to explain the substantive content of communicative practices in the light of their reluctance to import a metaphysically loaded conception of the person. Conversely, in the context of the conception advanced at present, personhood remains substantive without exceeding the boundaries of the communicative practice. This is made possible by a more substantive notion of rule-following which points at the necessity of reasons—then reasons are taken to constitute the constraints of what is possible or permissible vis-à-vis rule-followers as persons.[22]

4.2.3 An Objection to the Reflexivity of Practice

An objection attempting to question the reflexivity of grammar argues that any reference to constraints or reasons would anew lead to a regress of interpretation, for reasons constitute nothing more than a fresh kind of self-interpreting entities (ultra-interpretations)[23]; however, the objection continues, anything that purports to be an ultra-interpretation has to succumb to the same objections

[21] For the centrality of the concept of the person in discourse theory, see R Alexy, 'Diskurstheorie und Menschenrechte' in *idem*, *Recht, Vernunft, Diskurs* (Frankfurt Main, Suhrkamp, 1995) 127–74.
[22] See also the discussion in section 4.4.
[23] For the meaning of ultra-interpretations, see section 3.2.

Wittgenstein raised against entities which purport to be intrinsically content-determining.[24] Conversely, the objection submits, rule-following must be deemed reflexive in a *minimal* sense: by allowing that it be possible for thinking subjects to *name* the rule they are following and to be given the option to act against it. Those two conditions should exhaust the matter of reflexivity.

The minimalist conception of reflexivity (one that impugns reasons as normatively inert) draws heavily on the particular requirement that rule-following remain automatic or direct. In other words that an intentional thinker should be in a position to 'directly' read-off the meaning of a rule without further reflection. For, otherwise, the regress of interpretations would arise.[25] Two defences can be advanced against this argument: first of all, the whole idea of directness (if Chapter 2 was right) is about not placing anything other than rules at the bottom of intentionality, and not about claiming that content, thought and action are groundless. Yet, this is exactly what the minimalist view ends up with, if we take practice to consist of habitual moving or of a basic (ie groundless) disposition to act in a certain way.[26] This problem takes a bolder form in the case of a behavioural reading of rule-following, akin to the one proposed by C Wright and discussed in the last chapter: the behaviourist position attempts to reduce rule-following to the contingent fact of convergence between the behaviour of those who partake of the practice.

A second reason for disallowing the minimalist view is the need to account for objectivity of content through fallibility (and, hence, objectivity). Fallibility is a key consequence of the rejection of mind-world dualism and the idea of ultra-determinants: under dualism, any course of action (any judgement) could be made to accord with a rule, which is to say, no one could ever go wrong as long as following a rule remains about conforming externally (groundless) with a pattern of behaviour. Conversely, fallibility requires that, in principle, we be in a position to know when we are right and when wrong, as a result of which it becomes possible to correct our views. What is more implicit in fallibility, or enabled by it, is disagreement. Disagreement remains an option only if it is possible to have different beliefs about the content of a rule, albeit without losing sight of the meaning of the rule.[27]

4.3 Grammar as the Fundamental Practice

Perhaps the most important requirement for the reflexive character of judging is that it be responsive to reasons. Reference to reasons renders the referential

[24] For articulating this objection, I owe many thanks to Carsten Heidemann and Stefano Bertea; for the shortcomings of self-interpreting entities, or ultra-interpretations, see in detail section 3.2.

[25] For the condition of directness, see Pettit, above n 5, 82 and 88–90.

[26] See for the difference between following and simply conforming to a rule, Pettit, above n 5, 76–77.

[27] On this point see the discussion in Hurley, above n 7.

apparatus of grammar central to the present project and calls for a distinction between two levels of judging: a fundamental one which relates to grammar and another one that relates to all other practices of judging: let me refer to those as *judging simpliciter* (JS) and *judging in a domain* (JD) respectively.[28] While JS grounds the ability to refer to reasons as one that is pivotal for conceiving of ratification-independent constraints of practice, JD remains domain specific in the sense that it purports to articulate the reasons that constrain the judgements of a particular cognitive practice.

4.3.1 Judging Simpliciter

JS is the thinnest or most general way of conceiving of the practice of judging as reflexive. It refers broadly to the ability to supply reasons which constrain ascription of content. To that extent, JS does two things: first, it lays down the rules which delineate the semantic structure of judgments as well as the inferential relations that hold between them (rules of grammar)[29]; secondly, grammar points out the need for depicting reasons when judging.[30] Although the practice of JS cannot determine any substantive features of reasons as regards particular contexts of judging, it can still, on the basis of the above two features, impose limitations on the structure and ontology (or metaphysical make-up) of reasons: thus, to the extent that judging is confined by grammar, it would be contradictory to allow as reasons items which are pre- or non-propositional or linguistic.[31] Finally, the rules of JS can be revealed through transcendental reasoning, as a result of which they enjoy a priori status.[32]

4.3.2 Judging in a Domain

JD relates to the various practices of judging within particular (or concrete) cognitive contexts (eg law, morality, physics etc). In effect, JD refers to rules that

[28] For a distinction between two levels of rule-following, of which one is more basic than the other, see Pettit, above n 5, 76–81. His distinction, even though cast in different vocabulary, reflects a very similar rationale to the one followed here.

[29] See above section 2.5. Chapter 7 will add a corpus of pragmatic rules to the existing semantic rules of grammar, as a result of the pragmatic recasting of the latter as practice, see section 7.6. For the content of those pragmatic claims, also *cf* section 4.4.

[30] It should be borne in mind that, owing to the centrality of the sentence for judging, reasons are, basically, facts. This stands in line with the judgement-oriented explication of grammar, which was put forward in section 2.5. For the priority of facts also *cf* section 4.1. As regards JS itself, its role is not to generate reasons but, instead, to set up the possibility of referring to reasons, those that spring out from the various domains of judging.

[31] The equation between propositional and linguistic holds only on the assumption that propositions are individuated semantically, along the lines of the semantics exhausts ontology thesis, defended in Chapter 2.

[32] For the transcendental reasoning adduced by discourse theory with an eye to grounding fundamental rules of judging, see Chapter 7.

pertain to the domain (call them substantive rules). Substantive rules constitute a more specialised level of normativity which regulates adequately the practice of judgement formation with respect to a cognitive domain. As opposed to rules of JS, the rules of JD are directly connected with the reasons that constrain their application. This should not come as a surprise: rules of JS, at least prima facie, point at structural features of judging amongst which counts the need to refer to reasons. The formal connection between rules of JS and reasons within a domain makes it the case that rules of JS demarcate a level of normativity which, although constrained by the general need to refer to reasons, is not constrained by any reasons in particular. Conversely rules of JD are directly responsible to the reasons of the domain. To that extent, it is possible with regard to JD to speak of reasons and rules interchangeably.[33]

It is important to notice here that with respect to any cognitive domain the practice of judging and the practice of acting within the domain form a *continuum*: in other words it is not possible (nor desirable) to draw limits between, on the one hand, engaging in an activity and, on the other, forming conceptual content with respect to the domain this activity demarcates (for instance, it is futile to say that the level of judging about a correct move in chess is different from the level of playing chess—doing so would reopen the gap between rules of grammar and criteria which Wittgenstein vehemently strove to bridge). Instead it should be admitted that all substantive practices possess a cognitive dimension and, vice versa, that all cognitive moves are embedded in a substantive practice. Hence the reasons for acting and the reasons for knowing within a domain are not disconnected.[34] To that extent I shall refer to 'the grammar of a domain' as the set of rules and reasons (general conceptual or formal and domain-specific or substantive) which regulate domain-specific judgments. Notably, I will use this concept when I turn to examine Hart's efforts to account for the grammar of law: Hart's primary and secondary rules will be taken to constitute the rules of legal grammar, rules which prescribe the formation of judgements within the legal domain.[35] Inquiry into these matters, notwithstanding its high degree of abstraction, is far from idle as regards the practice of law. Linked to issues of judgement formation are a number of important questions which have dominated the debates in legal philosophy since the early days of this discipline: questions about the truth-values of legal propositions; the existence of norms; the meaning of legal language; and the possibility of right answers in adjudication.

[33] There is still a reason for distinguishing between rules and reasons in a domain: this relates to the difference in degree of fallibility reasons and rules admit of. While reasons are fallible throughout, rules can be conceived of as embodying a more ideal dimension, one that is put together by those reasons which have survived critical inquiry.

[34] This shows that the distinction between JS and JD is possible (and desirable) only for analytical purposes.

[35] *Cf* Chapter 5.

The two most important consequences linked to the possibility of distinguishing between two levels of judging are the fact that practices have depth; and the fact that the two levels of judging stand in a hierarchical relation to one another.

4.3.3 Depth of Practice

First a few words on the fact that practices have depth: the dimension of depth is precisely what normativity of rule-following requires and, conversely, what any shallow conception of rule-following akin to the behaviourist reading[36] eschews. The dimension of depth shows that partaking of a practice cannot simply consist of performing a series of movements. Instead any movements—including cognitive movements which allow for the inference of conceptual content—must be underpinned by reasons if they are to form instances of following some rule within the practice. To that extent reasons allow for the possibility to dig below the (behavioural) surface of the practice and discover the grounds upon which the participants act. Depth can be represented as our ability to depict reasons that underlie the surface of the practice. This ability to depict (internally to a practice) substantive reasons which demarcate the cognitive domain in question is enabled by the (structural-formal) rules of grammar which, at the same time, delineate the ontological limits of what we can know. The practice of grammar, apart from pointing to the necessity of rule-following as a reflexive activity,[37] first and foremost, allows us to 'objectify' the reasons that form the grounds of our justifications (those that are required by judging qua reflexive activity). By objectifying the reasons which underpin a practice we make it possible to refer to them in order to justify our judgements within the practice—it is this possibility that upgrades judging to reflexive rule-following.[38]

Truth be told, any talk of objectification within a practice-oriented explication of knowledge has an amount of precariousness about it. Notably, any attempt to refer or single out any items as forming the grounds of reflexive rule-following harbours the danger of opening up a gap between rules and criteria of application, a gap that is catastrophic, along the lines sketched earlier. Be that as it may, it should be possible to avoid the gap (or to defuse its catastrophic effect) at the level of the objectification JS makes possible, for the following reasons: first, objectification becomes possible *within* the cognitive practice and not outside it; this ensures that objectified reasons will not turn into practice- or rule-independent criteria which purport to determine content, with all the devastating

[36] See section 3.3.2.2.

[37] This function will be explained further in the last chapter; there I will supplement the semantic-syntactical rules of Chapter 2 with so-called pragmatic rules by using some of the arguments of discourse theory; these rules are deemed necessary for understanding JS as a practice rather than a static structure, one that would reproduce the pitfalls of the grammar of logical positivism, see section 2.6.

[38] The idea of depth will be employed in the second half of the book (Chapters 5 to 7) with an eye to exploring the nature of substantive reasons for judging in the legal domain.

consequences that are familiar to us by now.[39] What is more, such reasons can only make sense as reasons or grounds in the light of their being embedded in a practice, for otherwise they would be marking an instance of uncertainty with respect to which practice one is engaged in signifying, as a result, an unintelligible instance of conceptual disagreement.[40] The internality of the objectification is available to us because of the interconnection between JS and JD, or the fact that every substantive practice is at the same time a cognitive activity (ie that cognition is an instance of action). A second reason relates to the fact that, unless we make room for referring to reasons for judging/acting, it is impossible to grasp the reflexive element of rule-following. Thus, conceiving of rule-following as reflexive requires that we allow for a momentary opening of what, owing to its internality to practice, is a harmless gap. Again this is possible because of the general structure of JS which is embedded in the grammar of particular domains. The ability to refer to reasons in this manner is essential for conceiving of rule-following as being constrained, for otherwise the whole idea of practice deteriorates to non-normative constructs. A final reason for the harmlessness of objectification is the nature of JS itself as a practice: JS is the one practice which points to the fact that all other substantive practices are reflexive; hence it must make room for the structural capacity to represent reflexivity by accommodating the possibility to refer to reasons.

4.3.4 Priority of Grammar

The second remark concerns the very important issue of the relations that obtain between the two levels of judging (JS and JD). We saw that JS or the practice of grammar is the practice that makes it possible to refer at all to reasons. In light of the fact that normativity within a domain depends on the ability to refer to reasons, it seems to follow that the practice of grammar (or JS) is more fundamental than the practice of JD. What does this fundamentality mean in practical terms?

By enabling reference to substantive reasons within a specific domain, rules of grammar render judging a reflexive activity which comprises two levels of normativity: on the one hand, rules that enable (moreover, require) reference to reasons at the most general level of judging simpliciter; on the other, rules which are attached to particular cognitive contexts and track domain-specific substantive reasons. Interactions between the two levels of normativity are too complex to be dealt with in the present context. With a detailed account waiting for some other occasion, it is pertinent to offer some remarks on one aspect of the interaction which is of particular importance in the context of this book. This is the issue of hierarchy or priority between the two levels of grammar: do rules of

[39] See the discussion throughout Chapter 3.

[40] See above section 4.2.2.3 on the fallibility of reasons.

grammar at the most general level of judging constrain the content or the form of the substantive reasons to be found in the various domains?

To answer this question one needs to recall the double function of the rules of grammar as conditions of judging simpliciter. These rules do, roughly, two things: first, they lay down the structure of judgement. This structure delineates the ontological limits of what we can know, and, consequently, creates the conditions for linking the content of our thoughts to the world (environment). On this function, rules of grammar impose limits to what can constitute a substantive reason in a particular domain. Broadly speaking, those limits are specified by the semantic structure of grammar and rule out any putative reason that relies on non-propositional or non-conceptual items, namely items that purport to exist beyond the boundaries of any semantically structured conceptual scheme.[41] On top of it, rules of grammar acquire a second function, one of far greater importance in the context of legal content. This consists in their ability to demarcate the space of reasons as a space of autonomy for those who partake of any activity of judging. Within the space of autonomy judging subjects acquire the status of persons. With respect to the latter, the second feature of the rules of grammar marks a substantive constraint with regard to what may constitute a valid reason for judging. The next section tracks in more detail the connections between grammar and personhood.

4.4 Grammar, Persons and Autonomy

Rules of grammar allow conceiving of practices as being constrained by reasons. In prescribing that judging in any domain be responsive to reasons, grammar furnishes practices with a 'deep' structure that can ground claims of objective knowledge, albeit without giving up the primacy of the practice, a move that could invite sceptical objections of the type discussed earlier.[42] No sooner are rule-following and practice furnished with a reflexive element than the status of the agents, who partake of them, undergoes an important change. Agents who engage in reflexive rule-following, I shall argue, become autonomous in a minimalist sense, one that is linked with the very nature of rule-following. What is more, by expanding on this minimalist idea of autonomy, one can argue that the idea of rule-following effects a fully-fledged notion of autonomy, which is capable of underpinning a more robust conception of the person. Notably, the latter possibility becomes available only with respect to evaluative or prescriptive discourses, where the activity of rule-following points at a principle of universalisation as a requirement of normative validity. This qualification aside, with the introduction of the concept of the person, pragmatic rationalism arrives at an

[41] *Cf* the semantics exhausts ontology thesis in Chapter 2.

[42] See Chapters 1 and 2.

evaluative-substantive conception of practice. In this respect pragmatic rationalism can underpin claims of knowledge in domains such as law, morality and ethics, by invoking the concept of the person and excluding reasons that would speak against the autonomy of persons *qua* rule-followers.

The argument will be constructed in three steps. First, it will be shown that rules of grammar constitute a source of autonomy in a minimal sense. This will be demonstrated against a link between the concept of the rule and such concepts as freedom and responsibility. The second step purports to connect the idea of reflexive rule-following, as being enabled by the rules of grammar, with what Kant takes to be the supreme principle of morality. This move sets the background for linking the normativity of grammar with a substantive notion of autonomy. The connection is demonstrated against the idea of universalisation. Although the latter is adduced by Kant to demonstrate validity-conditions for moral rules, universalisation seems to perform a more fundamental function, one consisting in its ability to capture what is specifically normative about reasons in general. Drawing on a recent demonstration of the ability of universalisation to ground the obligating force of moral reasons, I argue that universalisation pertains to reasons in general as much as it does to moral ones. Consequently, insofar as we wish to capture practices as instances of reflexive activity—and we saw that the philosophical account of content and knowledge has given us many a good reason for so wishing—it is necessary that we conceive judging as involving universalisation.

It is only through the third step of the argument that one arrives at a more substantive notion of autonomy and personhood. This step is the least satisfactory of the three, although it relies on an idea that seems to be well-established in contemporary Kantian scholarship: this is the idea that agents capable of universalising reasons are to be valued intrinsically. Kant argued for this idea by suggesting that the supreme formula of morality (the rule of universalisation) admits of an alternative, albeit synonymous, formulation, which it has become common to refer to as the formula of humanity as end-in-itself.[43] Although the logical steps that lead to the alternative formulation wait yet for a full demonstration, I adduce a popular argument attributed to Christine Korsgaard which roughly does the job. What is far more important in this context is the existence of a widespread consensus amongst scholars that the capacity of universalising judgements bestows on those who can exercise it moral value. Let this be considered to suffice for present purposes. If this is accepted, then the reflexive version of rule-following grammar supports leads to a conception of agents capable of rule-following as persons. Although personhood develops its full potential with respect to practical reasons only, its roots lie already in the notion

[43] See for instance A W Wood, 'The Supreme Principle of Morality' in P Guyer, *The Cambridge Companion to Kant and Modern Philosophy* (Cambridge, Cambridge University Press, 2006) 342–80.

of rule-following as an activity constrained by reasons, for only the latter can support the idea of a morality that is responsive to reasons, along the lines Kant has argued.

4.4.1 Rule-following and Autonomy

In what ways does agents' capacity to handle reasons affect their status? In previous pages the sceptical and behaviourist explications of practice were rendered incapable of capturing the idea of a normativity that is bound by reasons.[44] In rejecting such interpretations, of key importance has been the understanding that those conceptions, by eschewing a normative explication of reasons, run the danger of falling below the threshold of a normative explication of practice. By contrast, the pragmatic reading that was advanced in their place made prominent the role of practice as activity that is constrained by (a) reason(s).[45] Of key importance to the ability to refer to reasons was deemed to be the idea of grammar—that most fundamental of all practices—on whose background it is possible to refer to reasons when we judge in any specific domain, by ascribing properties to objects or depicting facts in the environment. In virtue of undertaking this task, rules of grammar come to stand for the most basic level of (reflexive) normativity. This level is not available to any animal being, but only to those who are capable of making sense of it as an instance of reflexive activity. In appreciating the reflexive character of those rules such beings become autonomous, where autonomy amounts to something like the freedom to willingly abide by a normative standard.

The connection between rules of grammar and autonomy may be best demonstrated through the kinship rules bear to freedom and responsibility. Succinctly put, rules imply that agents are left with a range of choices as regards their application. Choice entails freedom to the extent that agents can exercise their discretion with regard to the various possible applications of the rule. Theirs, however, is a bounded freedom, for agents, in exercising their discretion, remain answerable vis-à-vis the rule. In other words agents assume responsibility for their choice and, to that extent, are prepared to accept criticism or, at least, they think it appropriate that they be under an obligation to offer reasons for their choice. It is in this special interplay of freedom and responsibility that autonomy substantiates. Notably this minimal notion of autonomy, or something close to it, is highlighted by Kant in his *Groundwork for the Metaphysics of Morals* when he discusses thinkers' capacity to judge.[46] There are various passages in this work where Kant is suggesting a link between the capacity to judge and

[44] See section 3.3.2.

[45] It is precisely because agents are involved in this activity that they end up partaking of reasons.

[46] See I Kant, *Groundwork for the Metaphysics of Morals*, T E Hill Jr and A Zweig (ed) (Oxford, Oxford University Press, 2002); all quotations derive from this translation. Pagination refers to the *Akademie Ausgabe* of Kant's works.

autonomy. Thus in section one of chapter 3, entitled 'Freedom must be Presupposed as a Property of the Will of all Rational Beings' (4:447) he argues:

> But it is impossible to conceive of a power of reason that consciously regards its own judgements as directed from outside; for in that case the subject would attribute the determination of his power of judgement to some impulse, not to his reason. Reason must regard itself as the author of its own principles independently of alien influences. It follows that reason, as practical reason, or as the will of a rational being, must regard itself as free (4:447).

Later on he says:

> We see now that when we think of ourselves as free, we transfer ourselves into the world of the understanding as members and we recognise the autonomy of the will together with its consequence, morality; whereas when we think of ourselves as under obligation, we view ourselves as belonging to the world of sense and yet simultaneously to the world of understanding (4:453).

And in a further, longer, passage:

> But since *the world of understanding contains the ground of the world of sense and therefore also of its laws*, it thus gives laws directly to my will (which belongs entirely to the world of understanding) and must be conceived as thus lawgiving. Therefore, although I regard myself from one point of view as a being that belongs to the world of sense, I shall have to recognise that, as an intelligence, I am subject to the law of the world of understanding—that is, of reason, which contains this law in the Idea of freedom, and thus in the autonomy of the will. I must therefore regard the laws of the world of the understanding as imperatives for me and see the actions that conform to this principle as duties (4:453–4:454, underlined in the original).

Its thin status notwithstanding, the wider implications of a minimal notion of autonomy should not be underestimated: it may show that there is a minimum capacity of agents which, even if it falls short of making them fully autonomous, is nevertheless able to impose certain constraints on what can constitute a normative constraint within any practice. The constraints imposed on reasons by this minimal idea of autonomy may be explained in terms of a quality or property of *reasonableness* agents acquire through the capacity to judge. An argument, demonstrating this thesis may take the following form:

(P 1) To the extent that judging is a reflexive activity, it is about adducing reasons

(P 2) It follows that those who engage in judgment confer meaning to portions of the environment (for, to speak with Wittgenstein, nothing in the world carries a label with its name on it).

(P 3) To that extent, anyone who engages in judging, ie who can handle rules of grammar, has the capacity to confer meaning upon the environment—call this the *property of reasonableness.*

(P 4) It follows that anyone who engages in judging is a bearer of reasonableness.

(P 5) This implies that anything which purports to be a substantive reason in the context of a concrete cognitive practice must preserve the reasonableness of judging subjects.

Conversely, a putative substantive reason which would lead to violations of rationality would infringe on reasonableness and, therefore, would need to be disqualified from counting as one. Such violations usually occur as instances of syntactic, semantic or pragmatic errors and can be illustrated through the form of an *argumentum ad absurdum* which spots an inconsistency (or contradiction) in the use of language (be it at the level of syntax, semantics or pragmatics). One particular instance of this kind of argument is especially well suited in disclosing the rules of grammar as the necessary conditions of a well-formed judgement. This is the so-called transcendental argument which aims at revealing the necessary conditions for statements that describe true states of affairs (a true state of affairs in this context would be the fact 'that we all engage in judgments').[47] A special form of transcendental argument (so-called *transcendental-pragmatic*) will be deployed in the last chapter with an eye to formulating those amongst the rules of grammar which establish the activity of judging as necessarily involving reason-giving.[48]

4.4.2 Grammar and Universalisation

Is it possible to press the meaning of autonomy further at home? This possibility becomes available no sooner than it becomes clear that the features associated with the thin notion of autonomy (ie choice, freedom, responsibility) are merely partial expressions of a more central phenomenon, namely the reflexive character of rule-following, which, in turn, stands for no other thing than the normativity of practice—the same normativity that was deemed a prerequisite for an account of content, which steers clear from scepticism and relativism.[49] So if one wished to specify further the notion of autonomy, a good move would be to focus closer on normativity. Is there any way of explicating normativity in such a manner as to draw further insights with respect to the autonomy of rule-followers? A most apposite idea for capturing the meaning of normativity, indeed one that has a well-established meaning in the philosophical debate, is that of universalisation. Although Kant originally employed universalisation in the context of ethics and

[47] *Cf* Chapter 7; for transcendental arguments in the context of legal theory, see S Paulson, 'On Transcendental Arguments, their Recasting in Terms of Belief, and the Ensuing Transformation of Kelsen's Pure Theory of Law' (2000) 75 *Notre Dame Law Review* 1775 ; C Heidemann, 'Hans Kelsen and the Transcendental Method' (2004) 55 *Northern Ireland Legal Quarterly* 358; C Roversi, above n 5; for transcendental arguments in general see the classic texts by P F Strawson, *Individuals: an Essay in Descriptive Metaphysics* (London, Methuen, 1959); *idem*, *The Bounds of Sense: an Essay on Kant's Critique of Pure Reason* (London, Methuen, 1966); and B Stroud, 'Transcendental Arguments' (1968) 65 *Journal of Philosophy* 241.

[48] See Chapter 7.

[49] See Chapters 1 to 3.

morality with an eye to stating an intrinsic characteristic of moral judgements, it is possible to work our way towards a thinner conception thereof, one that captures what is specifically normative about rules in general.

Such a thin notion of universalisation pertains to a recent proposal in Kantian scholarship which uses the idea of universalisation in order to capture the absolute normative character of practical reasons. On this view,[50] Kant chooses the principle of universalisation as the supreme principle of morality because it is particularly apt in accounting for the absolute normative character of practical reason. This is the requirement that an act be correct only if it be backed by reasons such that are inherently normative, ie they are not reducible to any other non-normative criteria.[51] Most notably, Kant attempts to capture normativity through the idea of duty. Along these lines he argues that, unless our acts are performed out of duty, they cannot be bestowed with moral worth (ie they are not correct). The idea of duty is further explicated through the law-like structure of principles. It is the law-like form that may give rise to duties, for it is it that captures the essence of normativity. Thus acting from duty means acting from a law-like principle because that principle so commands. A further consequence of this requirement is that what gives an act its value are not its consequences but the motive enshrined in the principle. Conversely, if the value of an act depended on its effects then the act would not conform to the principle but to whatever random outcomes follow from it. But then, it would fail to have been performed out of duty. The gist of this argument is that in order to understand agency in normative terms we need to relate its motives to a principle that is intrinsically normative. Famously Kant goes to great lengths to demonstrate that there exists only one principle which can live up to the requirements of normativity. In his *Groundwork of the Metaphysics of Morals* he formulates this principle as a formal rule of universalisation[52]:

> Act only in accordance with that maxim through which you at the same time can will that it become a universal law.

Leaving aside the specific reference to practical reasons, this way of explicating universalisation with respect to practical reasons may turn useful in demonstrating in the most radical sense the reflexive (or normative) character of the rules of grammar. This demonstration will be crucial in attaching to grammar a fully-fledged notion of autonomy, one that bestows inherent values on all agents capable of reflexive rule-following.

[50] See S J Kerstein, *Kant's Search for the Supreme Principle of Morality* (Cambridge, Cambridge University Press, 2002) ch 4.

[51] Failure to specify non-reducible normative reasons would lead to something like G E Moore's open-question argument which threatens normative standards with indeterminacy, see his *Principia Ethica,* revised edn (Cambridge, Cambridge University Press, 1993). Either that, or we would need to refer to a further reason or meta-reason in whose light those reasons would regain normative significance.

[52] Kant, above n 46, 4:421.

In postulating that only maxims that can become universal laws may underpin action, universalisation expresses in the most succinct way an intuition that has been of great importance for the contextualist account of content in Chapter 3[53]: that, namely, no reasons or criteria should guide conceptual activity (judging), other than those that may be shared within the space of a public practice. This idea led us to reject private constructs, Platonic forms and conventionalist descriptions as falling below the threshold of what it takes for anything to be a reason for judging. Understood as a rejection of dualism and an invitation to spell out the irreducible normativity of the practice of judging, universalisation turns out to dovetail with the task performed by the rules of grammar.[54] Thus it is possible to transcribe Kant's moral principle in a manner that is in line with the intuition about the normativity of intentional content:

> Judge only in accordance with reasons that at the same time you can will that they be depicted as objective grounds for your judgement.

Superficial objections aside, this reformulation of universalisation may be utilised in order to pinpoint what is most fundamental about normativity, namely the reflexive capacity to consider reasons for following (or abstaining from) a rule. This capacity is so central to rule-governed activity that permeates standards of any level or kind, be they rules of judging or rules that lay down duties and obligations. At the same time, reflexivity is introduced at the most basic level through the rules of grammar, and it is there that the idea of universalisation comes first into existence, even though in a very minimalist manner.

4.4.3 The Formula of Humanity as End-in-Itself

Universalisation shows that the reasons which constrain our judgements must live up to a certain standard: they cannot be conceived of as private standards or criteria, but instead as criteria that can be shared by every participant in a practice. Now this type of constrained normative activity is bound to generate special standards with respect to normative questions. When I ask 'what ought I to do?' my answer, in order to be in line with a normative activity, must denounce 'private maxims' and abide by a public rule. Along these lines, this first meaning of universalisation, the one pertaining to normativity in the most general sense,

[53] Cf Chapter 3.

[54] A connection in this context is argued despite the fact that Kant is talking about external action (captured by morality, law, etc), while judging involves merely conceptual activity. Two reasons may be adduced in support of the argued connection: as it has consistently been argued thus far, all levels of action are conceptually mediated to the extent that there is no level of action that could be conceived of independently of the judgements that generate those concepts on whose basis the action is performed. On the other hand, it has been the centrepiece of an argument against dualism, and the scepticism adjacent to it, that judging is not an internal, purely mental activity but, instead, one that substantiates within a public practice of rule-following. Insofar as this holds, acting and judging may be represented as the two sides of the same coin. Compare also with the discussion in section 7.3, where an argument for the unity of the normativity of action and judging is tendered.

entails a second, more substantive, meaning of universalisation, one that pertains especially to judgements answering the question 'what ought I to do?'. In this latter context normativity generates duty/obligation by sanctioning only those moral rules that every agent could will that they become universal laws. This aspect of universalisation, Kant tells us, is capable of generating a more robust notion of personhood in that it bestows inherent value on agents capable of answering the practical question.

To illustrate the inherent value of persons we need to relate the idea of universalisation as normativity with that of universalisation as a validity condition for practical reasons.[55] As we know from Kant, agents capable of universalisation in the second sense possess value in virtue of that capacity. Roughly speaking, Kant takes the principle of universalisation to demonstrate the rational character of practical reason, from which follows that anyone capable of rational thinking is also capable of practical reasoning. In virtue of this capacity it is suggested that rational thinkers are valuable-in-themselves. Kant himself does not offer a more detailed argument for that conclusion. Instead what we find is the bold claim that the universal moral law, which stands for the idea that morality is rational, implies the proposition that agents posses inherent value to the extent that they should not be utilised as means to the pursuance of ends that have been specified in their absence[56]:

> So act that you use humanity, as much in your own person as in the person of every other, always at the same time as end and never merely as a means.

The missing link from Kant's argument can be reconstructed if we take on board the thought that, in order to attach values to states of affairs, we must engage in acts of evaluation, or value-judgements. The latter are no less than instances of practical reasoning. It follows that, given that practical reasoning is the means for predicating value of states of affairs, there is no other source of value external to rational thinkers. Hence, in virtue of their being the only and last instance of practical reasoning, rational deliberators are rendered the source of all value, which is to say, they are absolutely valuable.[57] Adopting the argument to the vocabulary of the present discussion, we may give it the following form[58]:

(P 1') To the extent that judging is a reflexive activity, it is about adducing reasons.

[55] Thus, the argument as regards the absolute value of persons is confined to practical reasons. It may be possible, nevertheless, to argue that all types of reasons are practical in virtue of their link with public practices. Even though such an argument might be possible it will not be followed up in the present context.

[56] Kant, above n 46, 4:429.

[57] This is, in compressed form, the argument adduced by Christine Korsgaard on a number of occasions: see her *The Sources of Normativity* (Cambridge, Cambridge University Press, 1996) chs 3 and 4.

[58] In developing the following argument I relied on a reconstruction of Korsgaard's reasoning offered by W J FitzPatrick, 'The Practical Turn in Ethical Theory: Koorsgaard's Constructivism, Realism and the Nature of Normativity' (2005) 115 *Ethics* 651 (at 662–63).

(P 2') In practical contexts such reasons are moral reasons.

(P 3') Moral reasons are instances of evaluation with respect to certain aspects of an otherwise value-free environment.

(P 4') Therefore, anyone who engages in moral judgement is capable of conferring value upon certain aspects of the environment.

(P 5') But if judging subjects can confer evaluative meaning upon objects or facts of their choice, then they must regard themselves (and others who partake of the same activity) as autonomous (which is to say as bearers of value).

(P 6') To that extent, anyone who engages reflexively in practical reasoning is a bearer of moral value *qua* reason-giver.

Having established the most substantive of the elements of pragmatic rationalism, the concept of the person, I turn now to discuss some amongst its most important consequences.

4.4.4 Constraints from Persons

The substantive dimension of pragmatic rationalism, which corresponds to the concept of the person, is relevant primarily in practical/evaluative domains of judging (eg law, morality, ethics). That said it may underpin a unifying account of those domains, in illustrating the impossibility of drawing strict lines between the reasons of different domains. In this latter function the concept of the person guarantees something like the unity of practical reason and will be taken up in the last chapter with an eye to offering an argument for the unity between law and the other domains of practical reason.[59] In what follows, I turn to discuss the two aspects of the substantive dimension of pragmatic rationalism in order.

4.4.4.1 Scope of the Constraints

First, a few thoughts on the question of the scope of substantive constraints grammar imposes on domain-specific reasons. Those are of a varying degree and intensity: in value-free domains such constraints aim at preserving the reasonableness of judging subjects by avoiding logical or other contradictions. Conversely, in practical/ evaluative contexts constraints from grammar aim at safeguarding the inherent value of reason-givers as fully-fledged autonomous agents (persons). Whereas in the former case constraints from grammar circumscribe a thin conception of autonomy, one comprising merely a general ability to handle reasons, the latter case designates a more substantive notion of autonomy, one that is linked to the inherent value of reason-givers. In this context a further argument for the unification of the two conceptions of autonomy would need to demonstrate the possibility of communication between the various domains of judging. The possibility of such communication may be brought home along the

[59] See Chapter 7.

lines of the concept of universalisation. Universalisation illustrates how, in placing grammar at the bedrock of all judging, we may conceive of conceptual content across domains as irreducibly normative. Owing to this function grammar becomes the common denominator of all forms of judging. No sooner has it been rendered the common denominator of judging, than a link between all domains of judging is established. There are two possible ways to make sense of this link.

On the one hand, it could be considered as a weak link; one merely suggesting that the various domains of judging stand next to each other, with none amongst them claiming priority over the rest. In this context, the fully-fledged meaning of autonomy (persons as ends-in-themselves) is inescapable only in the sense that sooner or later every judging subject is bound to engage in moral argument, as it is rather hard to imagine a conceptual argument to the effect that someone can consistently avoid judging in the moral-evaluative domain.[60] That said, the weak link can happily accommodate the idea that persons need not be at all times autonomous in a strong (moral) sense; the moral 'picture' of agents may remain latent in the background of the different domains of judging.

On the other hand, it is possible to evoke a strong link between domains of judging. In this case, the substantive notion of autonomy, the one arising within the domain of moral reasoning, is rendered dominant, in the sense that agents preserve their moral status as persons across the various domains of judging. An adequate illustration of this point requires the demonstration of the priority of the moral domain, as the one that gives rise to the strongest possible meaning of autonomy. The priority of the moral domain is effected by something like the *self-referentiality* of judging in the moral domain. Self-referentiality, far from constituting some kind of logical circularity, simply is a succinct way of saying that the meaning of a moral judgement must not contradict the autonomy involved in the capacity to judge. The point can be made in more detail as follows: judging in the moral domain does not merely aim at determining the status of agents in this domain alone but, what is more, the status of anyone who partakes of judging *in abstracto*, for, somehow, when we judge in the moral out of all other domains we judge about the conditions of judging. This should not come as a surprise, considering that morality purports to fully determine the status of persons, while personhood is intertwined with the capacity to judge. Hence any insight in the status of persons deriving from the moral domain may claim authority over any other domain of judging. Clearly, then, the issue of the extent of import of an evaluative conception of judging into non-evaluative domains, as well as the level of JS, touches upon the core of intentional thinking,

[60] For the inevitability of making practical judgements, see the transcendental reasoning employed in section 7.5.

our capacity for knowledge, as well as issues of understanding and communication. That said, it cannot be further explored within the limits of this book, save for some occasional remarks in the final chapter.

4.4.4.2 Unity of Practical Reason

The second issue that needs to be addressed with respect to constraints imposed by grammar is the issue of the unity of practical reasons. The explication of normative reasons, as resting on public practices of universalisation, guarantees the continuity of practical reason. Although practical reasons are generated in different contexts by distinct practices (law, morality, ethics, etc) the idea of universalisation helps to bring out the rationale which is common to all of them. Thus, despite differences between various types of practical reasons (be they legal, moral or otherwise practical) it is possible to relate them to one another as a result of their being instances or outcomes of a practice of universalisation.[61] In substantive terms this comes down to a claim that all such reasons must respect the idea of personhood which attaches to any practice of universalisation. To that extent, the idea that agents who partake of a public practice of universalisation are absolutely valuable constitutes a material constraint vis-à-vis the content of practical reasons: no reason may be permitted that infringes upon the absolute value of persons. Such infringement would be assumed any time persons were prevented from partaking of the practice of universalisation or, even, when reasons for action would consistently fail to satisfy a public test of universalisation. In that respect the concept of personhood, as one that is intertwined with the idea of universalisation, cements the unity of practical reason, by grouping together the various forms of practical reasons. Notably, such unity is perfectly compatible with a weak link between the various domains of judging, as explained in the previous section.

4.5 Pragmatic Rationalism

It is time to illustrate how the remarks submitted so far can bear on the idea of pragmatic rationalism. This offers me the opportunity to restate the main ideas of the first half of the book in a succinct way.

Wittgenstein's slogan 'logic must take care of itself' pointed the way to grammar as the most suitable means for dealing with the dualism of thought and content. Following this, the idea of grammar was refined with a view to

[61] This seems to be in tune with the idea that law is a special case of practical reasoning, which is increasingly becoming a common thesis amongst non-positivist legal theorists. Instead of others, see R Alexy, *The Argument from Injustice* (Oxford, Clarendon Press, 2002); R Dworkin, 'Introduction' in *idem, Justice in Robes* (Cambridge Mass, Harvard University Press, 2006); N Stavropoulos, *Objectivity in Law* (Oxford, Clarendon Press, 1996).

underpinning an anti-representationalist theory of intentional content. Anti-representationalism in the contemporary philosophy of mind marks the most coherent effort to defeat mind-world dualism and the concomitant scepticism, by demonstrating a constitutive link between mind and environment. Along these lines it was argued that grammar serves the purposes of anti-representationalism in the best way, for it constitutes a common ground for conceiving of both mind and world, disallowing as a result the mind-world gap. Then a problem was identified with respect to the various possible interpretations of judging, not all of which can safeguard the anti-dualist intuition of grammar. Two such interpretations were discussed and juxtaposed: criteria as ultra-interpretations and rule-following. While the former was deemed to be unsuitable for overcoming the problem of dualism, one particular version of rule-following was illustrated to be successful in bridging the gap between mind and environment: the pragmatic conception of practice.

In contrast to other conceptions of rule-following, the pragmatic view steers away from a relapse into dualism by enjoining the fundamental character of practice with respect to thought and action. In placing rule-following at the bedrock of intentionality the pragmatic conception demonstrates successfully how reference and truth are connected with our practices of judging in a constitutive way. Here, neither the environment nor the mind can claim priority, for both arc articulated against the background of practice. On the other hand, far from being a self-validating process, practice supplies the resources for accounting for error, correction and improvement. Being the vehicle for both the mind and the environment, practice may still underpin a corrective activity by pointing at facts which play the role of environment-dependent constraints for the ascription of content. Such facts can be conceived of as reasons which determine rule-following as the most fundamental intentional activity. Consequently, the pragmatic conception safeguards the normativity of intentional content by linking rule-following to reasons.

An issue arises with respect to the nature of normative reasons: how to conceive of them if not by linking them to the more robust understandings of objectivity that pertain to realist criteria of truth and reference? In contrast to the latter, normative reasons need to remain internal to practice. Notwithstanding internality, reasons can still uphold the distinction between correct and incorrect judgements, for, despite arising within the practice, they are not readily knowable to judging subjects. The idea of a foundation which can work as a standard for our thoughts, albeit without transcending our cognitive powers, is characteristic of the rationalist tradition in philosophy. In order to make it work in the context of a pragmatic conception of practice we need to make out a level of practice as more fundamental than all other levels, in that it makes it possible to refer to reasons as constraints of rule-following. This would, then, guarantee the normativity or determinacy of reasons without resorting to any external to practice criteria which may give rise to indeterminacy. This is the function grammar fulfils: through its rules it is possible to depict reasons for judging without stepping out of the practice of judging altogether. Instated as the foundation of practice, grammar can redeem the rationalist intuition that it is possible to think wrong thoughts, simply because we can never have full knowledge of all aspects of our conceptual scheme.[62]

The two parameters of rule-following, its pragmatic element of practice and its rationalist explication of normativity, enjoin an understanding of intentional content which can be labelled *pragmatic rationalism*: this is the idea that there are deep standards (reasons) of cognition and action which, however, are embedded within our practices of judging. Those standards allow for a distinction between right and wrong judgements in virtue of the deep dimension of the practice of judging. The latter is effected by the multiple layers of reasons which can potentially be depicted within the two levels of practice (dimension of depth). Owing to its deep structure, judging-as-practice is autonomised from particular instances of its application; from particular users (even if those are whole communities); and from reductive explanations (as in behaviourism). Thus practice becomes a relatively autonomous level of normativity which secures objectivity and knowledge. In this environment, deep reasons might occasionally elude rule-followers even though they should be in principle always discoverable through a deepening of the inquiry (otherwise dualism would arise).

4.5.1 A Priori and a Posteriori Elements of Practice

This distinctly rationalist idea of a deep, albeit practice-dependent, foundation of content is usually enabled on the supposition that there exist a priori reasons which assist us to access the deep structure of content formation. In being a priori such reasons remain objective enough to deliver the amount of determinacy which a normative conception of content requires. At the same time, those a priori reasons form themselves part of the same structure of content formation which they supply with normative criteria. Given that pragmatic rationalism adduces the foundational level of judging, ie grammar, with an eye to explaining the deep structure of content, it follows that the property of being a priori must be ascribed to the rules of grammar.

Rules of grammar are a priori. To begin with, they are rules of logic (syntax and semantics) which demarcate the space of reasons for judging by: (1) allowing reference to facts; (2) relating judgements inferentially to one another (relations of coherence, consistency, etc). Finally, they are rules that (3) set up pragmatic conditions for the use of sentences. The latter category of rules extends beyond the domain of logic in incorporating rules that demarcate pragmatic operations undertaken by judgements. Such rules comprise claims which aim to secure interpersonal conditions for the happy employment of a plethora of pragmatic operations which are carried out through a purpose-oriented use of symbols,

[62] As such aspects count the various reasons which constrain content-ascription.

better known as speech-acts (claiming, commanding, asserting and so on). The most important function of those claims is the introduction of interpersonal obligations between speakers, such that bestow an evaluative meaning on communication and understanding. This meaning supplements the dimension of autonomy that is involved in the activity of judging: in revealing the justificatory contexts between agents, such pragmatic claims illustrate how judging is reason-giving or reflexive in such a deep sense that it bestows on agents inherent value, along the lines the Kantian formula of humanity as end-in-itself has suggested. Lest confusion arise, pragmatic rules of grammar are likely to underpin a fully-fledged notion of autonomy (and personhood) only in connection with practical or obligation-imposing contexts.[63] In such contexts, as opposed to theoretical ones, the happy employment of judgements requires that judging subjects stand with each other in a pragmatic relation of mutual recognition as autonomous persons.[64] Such pragmatic relations are the corollary of the substantive meaning of the autonomy which pertains to anyone who can universalise practical reasons. The a priori character of the rules of logic and the pragmatic claims for interpersonal communication will be demonstrated in Chapter 7 through the employment of a transcendental argument.[65]

In contrast to rules of grammar, the reasons for judging in a domain are mostly a posteriori: such reasons relate to the concrete facts that are depicted by judgements within specific contexts of action and cognition. Thus moves of chess, rules for performing a contract or guidelines for queuing are all contingent on the specific context in which they arise. In this case the domain of judging (or language-game, to borrow a more familiar term) is not fundamental; hence, we may conceive of alternative configurations of the domain in question (ie a different way of playing chess or fulfilling contracts and so on), without implicating ourselves in a contradiction. That said, it is still possible to allow for degrees of necessity with respect to particular domains of judging. On a common definition of necessity, necessary is a proposition p if and only if p is true in all possible worlds. This formulation may, for present purposes, be transcribed as requiring that there be reasons such that they are true irrespective of the particular configuration a language-game has come to assume. A common way for revealing such enduring reasons is conceptual analysis. This form of analysis

[63] See above section 4.4.3; and the discussion in section 7.6.3.

[64] This relation is depicted, for instance, in the so-called *discourse rules* which are developed within the discourse theory. See R Alexy, *Theorie der juristischen Argumentation* (Frankfurt, Suhrkamp, 1978) and in English translation *A Theory of Legal Argumentation: The Theory of Rational Discourse as Theory of Legal Argumentation*, R Adler and N MacCormick (trans) (Oxford, Clarendon Press, 1989); and J Habermas, 'Diskursethik – Notizen zu einem Begründungsprogramm' in *idem, Moralbewußtsein und kommukatives Handeln* (Frankfurt am Main, Suhrkamp, 1983) 53–125; and in English translation 'Discourse Ethics: Notes on a Program of Philosophical Justification' in *idem, Moral Consciousness and Communicative Action*, C Lenhardt and S Weber Nicholsen (trans) (Cambridge Mass, MIT Press, 1992) 79 n.

[65] See sections 7.5 and 7.6.

focuses on the way a concept is employed within larger units of speech (sentences) with a view to stating necessary conditions for the happy employment of that concept.[66] Such conditions can be restated as reasons that constrain our (practice of) judging with respect to the domain demarcated by the respective concept. Necessity, however, need not be a priori.[67] In other words, it may be the case that we discover that, say, the concept 'queuing' presupposes a certain bundle of conditions and that anything that does not meet the stipulated conditions is not an instance of queuing. This discovery, far from arising on the basis of pure speculation, springs out from our engagement with the concrete practice of queuing. In being founded on experience (a posteriori) such conditions cannot claim absolute validity, for they remain responsive to the fallibility that is latent in future new configurations of the practice. Here, necessary conditions resemble, to use a familiar metaphor from Wittgenstein, the bank of a river where water flows.[68] While the flowing water stands for the numerous possible configurations a particular practice (eg queuing) may assume in the actual world, the bank symbolises something like the *point* of queuing; this point would involve some set up that ensures that people are served on a first come/first served basis. Although this rationale is not impervious to change (imagine rules of queuing for disabled or aged people—there, the first come/first served rationale might be overridden by other considerations: for instance, severity of disability and so on), it may still constitute something like the horizon of our understanding of the practice of queuing. All in all, necessity in this context stands for something like a relative a priori.

But there is a stronger sense in which we may conceive necessity; namely as signifying an absolute or genuine a priori. This is the case when certain reasons in a particular domain reflect fundamental limitations of judging simpliciter (JS). Painting with a broad brush indeed, we may distinguish between two different categories of a priori reasons. The first would include value-neutral reasons, which arise from the overall architecture of pragmatic rationalism. A clear instance of such a reason is the postulate that all domain-specific reasons in a domain must be accessible from within the domain. Thus, it cannot be the case that reasons constraining the practice of chess are unfathomable or are to be found outside the activity of playing chess. The second category is value-laden and includes such reasons as demonstrating the substantive meaning of autonomy enshrined in the activity of judging (as explained earlier[69]).

This category of reasons is mostly confined to practical domains—law being one of them. In Chapter 5 it will be demonstrated that the conceptual analysis H

[66] For a detailed analysis of conceptual analysis see section 5.2.

[67] This is one of the major contributions of Saul Kripke to modern modal philosophy in *Naming and Necessity* (Oxford, Blackwell, 1980); see discussion in Chapters 1 and 6.

[68] See L Wittgenstein, *On Certainty*, G E M Anscombe, G H V Wright and P Denis (ed) (Oxford, Blackwell, 1975) paras 96–99; and for discussion see P F Strawson, *Scepticism and Naturalism* (London, Routledge, 1985) 14–21.

[69] See section 4.4.

L A Hart engages in amounts to reasons that argue for a necessary connection between law and obligation. This necessity is not granted by presupposing that 'law' is a rigid designator,[70] referring to something akin to a practice-independent substance or essence (this would be more the view of interpretivism[71]), but instead by arguing that, within the constraints of a practice of judging, it is impossible to conceive law in non-normative terms or, what amounts to the same claim, that necessarily law is obligation-imposing. Of course what remains open in Hart's analysis, as will be argued in Chapter 5, is how much legal obligation really comprises. Although for Hart legal obligation can be analysed in conventionalist terms, the Practice Theory of Law—which is put forward in Chapter 7—argues that the necessity of the fact that law is obligating must be brought into line with the substantive meaning of autonomy enshrined in the activity of judging: here what matters is not merely the universalisation of reasons, in the sense that no reason can be inert of normativity, but, what is more, universalisation as the activity that bestows on persons inherent value. In light of this premise the content of legal obligation needs to be conceived of in accordance with all other obligating reasons, which compete for the definition of the content of autonomy (and personhood).[72]

4.6 Where does Law Fit in All This?

The second part of the book attempts to offer a more detailed discussion of legal practice with an eye to underpinning a conception thereof that lives up to the conditions of pragmatic rationalism, as stated in this chapter. The main requirement for legal practice to underpin claims of objectivity and knowledge is that it possess depth. The dimension of depth signifies the reflexive element of practice, which equips participants with the ability to adduce grounds for the truth of the propositions they employ. After discussing two seminal efforts to explicate practice in Chapters 5 and 6, those of conventionalism (Hart) and interpretivism (Dworkin), Chapter 7 will undertake an attempt to reconstruct depth along the lines of pragmatic rationalism. While the two former accounts are accused of reinstating ultra-interpretations and other sceptical facts, which fall prey to indeterminacy, the Practice Theory of Law (PTL, for short) succeeds in redeeming legal practice as an instance of reflexive rule-following by exploiting the

[70] As rigid designator is described any expression that has the same referent across possible worlds. The intuitive idea behind rigidity is that the actual referent of an expression (if any) projects onto all possibilities. Typical examples here are proper names (eg 'Aristotle') and natural kind terms (eg 'water'). See S Kripke, *Name and Necessity* (Oxford, Blackwell, 1980) 77–78; for a succinct discussion of rigidity, see R M Sainsbury, 'The Essence of Reference' in E Lepore and B Smith (eds), *The Oxford Handbook of Philosophy of Language* (Oxford, Clarendon Press, 2006) 393–421 (at 416–519).

[71] See Chapter 6.

[72] See the discussion in section 7.6.

lessons gained from pragmatic rationalism. In the light of PTL, law is explicated as a constraint-generating concept, one that can satisfy claims of knowledge by individuating reasons non-sceptically in the context of a reflexive practice of judging and acting.

Before concluding the chapter and, with it, the first part of the book, I feel that I need to deal with a common criticism frequently adduced against the type of analysis that has been undertaken thus far: this is the objection that the philosophical analysis of intentional content is irrelevant or, even, futile with respect to law.[73] This objection seems to have taken shape as a reaction to recent positivist strategies that argue for an understanding of legal practice as an instance of automatic or non-reflexive rule-following.[74] This strategy purports to block reflexivity in understanding and applying the law, with an eye to disrupting the chain of justification which would make inevitable an extension of legal reasons into the domain of general practical reason (including morality). It seems to me that both the positivist thesis and the anti-positivist objection are wrong-headed. In particular the anti-positivist objection would be much better off if it appropriated the philosophical critique of bad or sceptical versions of determinants of content and instead elaborated an account along the lines of pragmatic rationalism.[75]

In any case, the objection of irrelevance should be rejected for one more—in fact, far graver—reason: that, namely, it is absurd to treat legal content separately from any other type of content and therefore to subject it to a different analysis of conditions of objectivity and knowledge. The contrary would suggest the suspect view that non-legal content has it easier than legal content; that, namely, the former can get away with indeterminacy and scepticism free of any duty to justify knowledge while the latter cannot.[76] Notwithstanding the higher complexity of the legal realm, once practice has been placed in the centre of all intentional activity, the account of intentional content must remain uniform for all cognitive domains. Such an account needs to show that practice is in the position to disarm bad sceptical scenaria by replacing sceptical criteria and attendant dualism with a

[73] See along these lines S Hershovitz, 'Wittgenstein on Rules: the Phantom Menace' (2002) 22 *Oxford Journal of Legal Studies* 619.

[74] For the positivist line of arguing, see in particular A Marmor, *Interpretation and Legal Theory*, revised 2nd edn (Oxford and Portland, Hart Publishing, 2005); the anti-positivst argument that buys into the premisses of the positivist account of rule-following is to be found in Hershovitz, above n 73. In contrast Stefano Bertea in a recent paper attacks head on the very premiss that rule-following can be automatic or unconscious. See *idem*, 'Remarks on a Legal Positivist Misuse of Wittgenstein's Later Philosophy' (2003) 22 *Law and Philosophy* 513, where he also offers an exemplary reconstruction of the positivist reasoning. The reflexive character of rule-following is also explicitly endorsed by N MacCormick, *Institutions of Law* (Oxford, Oxford University Press, 2007) ch 16.

[75] For a similar strategy see S Bertea, above n 74. See also N MacCormick, above n 74.

[76] It is characteristic that the view that indeterminacy infects all types of meaning in the same manner is shared by acute philosophers in both the positivist and the non-positivist camp. See for instance Herbert Hart's views on the indeterminacy of general meaning in *The Concept of Law*, 2nd edn (Oxford, Clarendon Press, 1994) 124 *ff*; and Nicos Stavropoulos' views on semantic content in his *Objectivity in Law* (Oxford, Clarendon Press, 1996) chs 2 and 3.

'healthy' account of criteria, along the lines demonstrated earlier. This leads to the view that practice either is suitable for underpinning all types of content or it is not. But if we answer in the affirmative, then it must follow that the reason practice succeeds remains stable across the board, irrespective of cognitive domain. And, if this reason turns out to be the capacity of practice to be reflexive or responsive to reasons, then it is this capacity that underpins truth and reference in any of law, science, maths, biology, sociology or physics. Of course, in each of the above, the entities depicted or referred to by our propositions will differ metaphysically speaking (in being either empirical or practical or abstract). However, logically speaking, that is, from the point of view of grammar, they will all share the same property: that of a good reason within a rule-governed practice.

Part Two

Knowledge and Legal Theory

5

Conventionalism and the Grammar of Law

5.1 Introduction

Hart's method can be conceived of as one of two principal efforts in contemporary legal philosophy to account for legal knowledge through the means of a structure of judging (grammar).[1] In his *opus magnum*, *The Concept of Law* and a number of spin-off works, Hart elaborated an account of legal phenomena by drawing on the conditions under which the participants in a legal system make statements about the law. Despite his sustained efforts to furnish his task with an adequate philosophical account, Hart fails to represent the practice of law as a normative activity, along the lines pragmatic rationalism suggested in Chapter 4.[2] As a result, his account falls short of generating legal knowledge.

First, I discuss Hart's method of conceptual analysis for arriving at rules of grammar that open up the possibility of intelligible legal knowledge (section 5.2). Against this background, legal practice is reconstructed as one that gives rise to (legal) obligations. The latter are embedded in norms (legal rules) that constitute distinct objects of (legal) cognition. Then the discussion moves on to Hart's distinction between an external and an internal explication of obligation. In sustaining this distinction, Hart attempted to present legal obligation as a hybrid concept that collects in it empirical as well as normative elements. In presenting these two aspects as equivalent Hart hoped to have replaced an account of law delivered in obscure moral terms with one that firmly relied on the conventional characteristics of legal practice, albeit without eschewing the normative character of legal practice. This move left Hart with an inconsistency regarding his account of legal obligation, or so I argue (section 5.3). In particular, the inconsistency

[1] The other is that of Hans Kelsen's; see S Paulson, 'Zwei Wiener Welten und ein Anknknüpfugspunkt' in C Jabloner and F Stadler (eds), *Logischer Empirismus und Reine Rechtslehre* (Wien and New York, Springer, 2001) 137–90.

[2] See Chapter 4.

manifests itself as a failure to account for the fact that legal agents, in justifying their actions, appeal to normative reasons rather than any conventional facts providing for their own interpretation.

More importantly, however, Hart's failure to explain legal obligation springs from a deeper failure to employ coherently the results of his conceptual analysis in order to arrive at a normative conception of grammar: contrary to his discovery that law is principally a practice of obligation, Hart concluded that law rests on a series of behavioural facts which determine the content of its elements (rules). In the fashion of earlier positivist philosophies which failed to generate a pragmatic understanding of grammar[3] this conclusion disengages criteria of objectivity from the normative background of a practice so that the operation of understanding and applying legal concepts ceases to be an instance of reflexive rule-following and becomes a hopeless effort to hold together a set of disconnected items that bear a random relation to the practice of law. However, what the idea of grammar, as a set of rules, requires for taking shape is the dimension of normativity, a dimension that can be guaranteed only as long as one remains inside a practice. Absent this normativity, which is what stepping out of practice entails, grammar dissolves into items that are normatively inert. It is precisely this loss of normativity which appeals to convention or agreement are needed to compensate for, albeit with poor results, as the case of Hart's positivism illustrates.

The deficiency of this account is demonstrated by two important criticisms of Hart's account (section 5.4). First, the *incompleteness thesis*: this corresponds roughly to Ronald Dworkin's claim that Hart's analysis identifies too little as law, and his subsequent attack against the philosophical method of conceptual or semantic analysis. In pointing out the impoverished character of Hart's concept of law, Dworkin suggested that what actually shapes the content of legal obligations is a much richer network of normative reasons (principles, policies, etc) which can only be brought into light if one identified legal practice as extending in much greater depth below the surface Hart had based his external conception of obligation on. The second criticism comprises the *connection thesis.* This argues that legal obligation is connected to moral obligation as a matter of conceptual necessity. This thesis will be discussed in more detail in the final chapter by drawing upon recent work by Robert Alexy.[4] There, it will be argued that conceptual or semantic analysis may be developed to indicate a grammar of obligation which reveals the depth of legal practice by disclosing the continuity between legal and moral reasons. It is with respect to this type of grammar that the normativity essential to intelligible knowledge may be redeemed as regards the realm of law.

[3] For a pragmatic account of grammar, one that connects it with the activity or practice of judging, see section 4.3.

[4] See section 7.6.

5.2 Conceptual Analysis and the Grammar of Law

In the opening pages of his most celebrated work, *The Concept of Law*, H L A Hart declares his dissatisfaction with most of the earlier attempts to answer the question "what is law", for they had merely amounted to *partial* revelations of the truth about law's nature.[5] Instead, he suggests that a fresh start be made in order to reveal the *whole truth* of the matter. What this fresh start consists in is easy to tell from the opening three chapters of the *Concept of Law*. Hart, in applying the lessons of his contemporary analytical philosophy,[6] attempts to answer the question about the nature of law through an analysis of the meaning of legal expressions, as it manifests itself in the day-to-day use of legal language by a legal community (conceptual analysis).[7]

The attribute 'analytical' applies to philosophical theories that approach philosophical questions through an *analysis* of linguistic meaning.[8] Roughly speaking, two key ideas run through the many variants of analytical philosophy. The first is that an analysis of meaning can reveal the nature of the object of the philosophical enquiry. This idea is coupled with the assumption that language is some kind of interface between minds and the environment (the world), hence, by mastering linguistic meaning one can make contact with the world. The second idea is that the analysis of meaning has to attend to the ways language is actually used by competent speakers. This second thesis is especially associated with a particular stream of analytical philosophy, the so-called ordinary language philosophy. Although ordinary language philosophy is not synonymous with analytical philosophy, for the purposes of the present discussion I will assume so. Two reasons may be given for this simplification: first, ordinary language philosophy is the most influential school within the movement of analytical philosophy; and secondly, ordinary language philosophy is perhaps the one part of analytical philosophy that had an impact on legal theory throughout the twentieth century.

The focus on usage was a key point of the late philosophy of Ludwig Wittgenstein.[9] Through it he attempted to replace those theories that tried to

[5] There is an interesting parallel running between Hart and Frege as regards their intention to 'clarify' or 'replace' earlier muddled philosophical efforts. See H L A Hart, *The Concept of Law* 2nd edn with a postscript edited by P A Bulloch and J Raz (Oxford, Clarendon Press, 1994) ch 1; and G Frege, 'Logik in der Mathematik' in *idem*, *Schriften zur Logik und Sprachphilosophie. Aus dem Nachlaß*, G Gabriel (ed) (Hamburg, Felix Meiner, 2001) 92–165.

[6] See H L A Hart, 'Jhering's Heaven of Concepts and Modern Analytical Jurisprudence' in *idem*, *Essays in Jurisprudence and Philosophy* (Oxford, Clarendon Press, 1983) 274–77.

[7] For a clear exposition of conceptual analysis in law see N Stavropoulos, 'Hart's Semantics' in J Coleman (ed), *Hart's Postscript: Essays on the Postscript to the 'Concept of Law'* (Oxford, Oxford University Press, 2001) 58–98. For the role of conceptual analysis in philosophy, see F Jackson, *From Metaphysics to Ethics* (Oxford, Clarendon Press, 1998) ch 2.

[8] For a thorough discussion of the method of analysis in philosophy and its impact on legal theory, see J Stelmach and B Brożek, *Methods of Legal Reasoning* (Berlin and New York, Springer, 2006).

[9] See section 3.5.

explain meaning independently of language, by alleging a one-to-one correspondence between words and objects. The problem with that explanation of meaning was that it implicitly relied on a prior understanding of the expression in question. Take for instance the word "car". In explaining to someone the meaning of "car" as "the word car designates the object *car*", one is relying on the fact that she or he already understands "car". Instead, a non-circular explanation requires attending to the different ways speakers use the expression in question and to the implicit rules that guide the various instances of its use.[10] Mastering those rules equals grasping the meaning of the relevant expression. What is more, knowledge of the conditions and/or criteria for the use of an expression conveys knowledge about the nature of the objects to which the expression applies. For instance, to know the rules for the correct use of "car", ie to know when it is appropriate to use "car", amounts to knowing the essential properties of cars, ie what kind of things cars are.

Applied in the domain of law the idea of analysis comprises the study of legal concepts in general and the concept 'law' in particular.[11] As already noted, this study is not just a semantic study directed at an illustration of the meaning of 'law' but aims deeper. It aims at shedding light on the nature of law by conveying knowledge with respect to the essential properties of the entities 'law' applies to. Two different versions of analysis can be distinguished in this context, the first—conceptual analysis—being a clear instance of meaning analysis, while the second—transcendental reasoning—is a less obvious one.

Conceptual analysis in the field of legal philosophy requires that the legal philosopher study the various instances of the application of 'law'[12] and make explicit the rules that guide speakers in using it. To that extent, it is assumed that the essential features of law can be revealed through the (semantic) rules that guide the use of legal concepts. In particular, conceptual analysis comprises two levels: the first is a priori, for it purports to state rules for the use of legal expressions that reveal a priori features of law.[13] *In concreto*, these rules have the form of *analytic* sentences, namely sentences that we are justified in holding true just by grasping their meaning (eg the sentence: "legal rules give rise to obligations").[14] The second instance of analytical jurisprudence consists in stating rules

[10] The latter, according to Wittgenstein, cannot be taught but are a matter of 'natural uptake', one that substantiates through one's participation in a linguistic community. For a brief, albeit accurate review of the ideas connected to the use theory of meaning, see J Skorupski, 'Meaning, Use, Verification' in B Hale and C Wright (eds), *A Companion to the Philosophy of Language* (Oxford, Blackwell, 1997) 29–59.

[11] For the historical background of analytical jurisprudence, see Hart's lucid exposition in 'Jhering', above n 6, 271–77.

[12] Inverted commas are used throughout the chapter in order to refer to the concept *law*.

[13] A priori true are those sentences whose truth can be established independently of any empirical proof.

[14] See Hart's discussion on the relation between legal rules and obligation in *The Concept of Law*, above n 5, 79–91.

for the use of legal expressions that are a posteriori true.[15] These rules have the form of sentences that are *synthetic*, namely true in virtue of our empirical evidence with respect to the use of legal language. In stating these, the legal philosopher has to look into the actual instances of the application of legal expressions by the legal community. Thus, if lawyers use "manslaughter" whenever someone kills intentionally upon having been provoked, then semantic rule SR applies: "'manslaughter' applies to any instance of intentional killing following provocation". What is more, given that any semantic rule reveals something about the nature of law, one is justified in holding true that provocation is an essential property of manslaughter.

Before turning to see how these general thoughts apply to Hart's own method, one last word on the difference between semantic rules that are analytic (a priori true) and those that are synthetic (a posteriori true): all rules the legal philosopher arrives at through conceptual analysis are supposed to be revealing necessary or essential features of law. Be that as it may, analytic rules indicate features of law that somehow are more fundamental than those revealed by rules that are merely synthetic. The reason is that the former do not depend on experience and, to that extent, are non-revisable. That law is the source of obligations, for instance, is a necessary feature that is part of the conditions of applying 'law' (i.e. of its meaning), irrespective of experience. Being what they are, analytic rules guide the practice of a legal community but, at the same time, transcend its boundaries and constitute objective, practice-independent criteria against whose background it is possible to judge the correctness of the practice of any community. In contrast, synthetic semantic rules, like the one quoted earlier for manslaughter (SR), allow for revision in the light of new empirical evidence: if the perpetrator was indeed provoked, yet the killing took place 48 hours after the act of provocation, the condition of provocation may be rendered a necessary albeit not sufficient condition for applying "manslaughter" to the facts of the case. Such rules are interlaced with the actual empirical conditions for applying legal terms and depend heavily on both the natural environment and the actual practice of the legal community. (Thus, *different* legal communities apply "manslaughter" in different ways, although *all* legal communities make this pattern of behaviour punishable.)

Conceptual analysis leads Hart to the general conclusion that it is impossible to capture law's nature through definitions that fix necessary and sufficient conditions for 'law' because such definitions tend to misrepresent as essential certain features of law that are only contingent. Instead, Hart takes conceptual analysis to point at a new type of criteria that guide users in their applications of legal expressions. Contrary to necessary and sufficient conditions, criteria of the new

[15] A posteriori true are those sentences whose truth can be established only by reference to empirical proof.

type cannot generate 'final', rigid definitions of legal concepts but are revisable or, in Hart's words, *defeasible* in the light of new circumstances the community runs into.[16]

Hart famously attributes the open-textured character of all (and not just legal) meaning to the ignorance of fact and the indeterminacy of aim:[17] it is impossible for legislators to anticipate in the wording of a statute the complexity of the environment and the concomitant impact it has on agents' aims. Think of the rule 'no vehicles are allowed in the park'. Suppose that it was enacted in the late nineteenth century with a view to controlling the increasing amount of 'urban noise' that came as a result of the rapid industrial development of those days. Now imagine that more than a century later an accident occurs in the same park when a remote-control toy car causes injury to an old lady who is taking her afternoon walk. When the case is brought before the court a determination of the legality of the conduct that caused the injury is required. For that the judge will have to answer the preliminary question whether the toy car falls within the meaning of the concept 'vehicle' of the statute. For certain, any definition of 'vehicle' which is fixed by facts or aims pertinent to the context of the original legislation would fail, for the simple reason that no Victorian legislator could ever foresee the hundreds of types of vehicles that would have appeared a century or so later, nor the diversity of aim that agents (including legal officials) would connect to them. Instead, the present day judge must arrive at a definition of 'vehicle' that reflects the facts and the aims of the case at hand. This will most likely bring about a revision of the criteria for 'vehicle' pertinent to earlier definitions, and will amount to a fresh, more precise understanding of its meaning. (Thus, for instance, the existence of self-propelled artifacts that serve play might be deemed irrelevant to the meaning of 'vehicle' in a statute regarding parks.)

Hart tells us that the concept 'law' behaves in a way not dissimilar to 'vehicle'. It is not possible to provide for an exhaustive definition of 'law' that would account for all legal systems at all times. Instead the criteria such a definition comprises are revisable in the light of new circumstances, the idiosyncrasies of different contexts (societal formations) and the various aims that agents associate with them. The effort to uncover those various aspects sheds light upon the nature of law and its relation with other forms of normativity (morality, ethics, courtesy and custom, only to mention the most important of them). This endeavour unfolds through the method of conceptual analysis, or the systematic exposition of the (semantic) rules that guide the use of legal expressions.

[16] These ideas are expressed in H L A Hart, 'Jhering' and 'Positivism and the Separation of Law and Morals' in *Essays in Jurisprudence and Philosophy*, above n 6. Strictly speaking, revisability should be distinguished from defeasibility, for the two concepts describe phenomena with different logical structures. See the highly insightful discussion in B Brożek, *Defeasibility of Legal Reasoning* (Zakamyce, Kantor, 2004); also J Hage, *Studies in Legal Logic* (Dordrecht, Springer, 2005) ch 1.

[17] *The Concept of Law*, above n 5, 128.

Semantic rules reach beyond the level of meaning and language in that they make explicit criteria for correct applications of legal expressions ('is X a legal rule?', 'is Y a contract?', and so on). In being about correct applications of legal expressions, these criteria relate to both the level of *how we talk about law* and the level of *how law actually is (law's reality)*. Given certain constraints with respect to our ability to grasp anything independently of thought and language there might not be a way to plainly state where the boundaries of the two levels lie. It is important, however, not to obscure either level, but instead to be aware of their synchronic impact upon any theoretical inquiry into law's nature. Awareness with respect to both levels is perhaps the best way for guaranteeing theoretical open-mindedness in our quest for a correct understanding of the nature of law. On the face of it, correctness does not consist in a final, absolute grasp of 'the truth' about law (be it in the form of a theory or a definition) but in an ongoing effort to bring the two levels of language and reality into accordance. In practice, such an effort implies that the theorist remains conscious, at all times, of the fact that the whole truth cannot be inferred only from the way we employ legal language or only from a direct, unmediated grasp of law's reality. Instead, the theorist is asked to realise that proximity to truth requires constant awareness of the fact that thought and language are responsible to reality while, at the same time, any grasp of reality is responsible to, or has to fit with, the way we articulate thoughts in language.

Explicated as above, the valuable exercise of conceptual analysis invites the legal theorist to engage in an ongoing process of refining definitions of legal concepts with a view to achieving a more accurate understanding of the nature of law. Refinement is possible by revising existing criteria or introducing new criteria in the light of new considerations. Although the process of revising old and introducing new criteria is far from being linear, it is appropriate to say that it contributes to an overall increase in *legal knowledge*, or knowledge with respect to law's nature. A pertinent question arising in this context is one about the exact relation between the increase in legal knowledge and the various kinds of considerations the theorist takes into account in bringing about the increase. In other words: in what proportions do considerations about the use of legal language (call them *semantic considerations*) combine with considerations about the reality of law (call them *empirical considerations*) in order to generate legal knowledge? Although Hart advances conceptual analysis as a dynamic theoretical exercise for arriving at case-sensitive definitions of 'law', he never specifies in detail which part thereof draws upon semantic and which upon empirical considerations.[18]

[18] To get a sense of the intense contemporary debate on the nature of conceptual analysis in law, see Stavropoulos, above n 7; also V Rodriguez-Blanco, 'A Defence of Hart's Semantics as Nonambitious Conceptual Analysis' (2003) 9 *Legal Theory* 99. For a recent defence of the role of definitions in law, see N MacCormick, *Institutions of Law* (Oxford, Oxford University Press, 2007) ch 16.

In the light of our earlier distinction between an a priori and an a posteriori part of conceptual analysis, it is not difficult to illustrate Hart's expositions as accommodating both levels of inquiry. Semantic considerations are gained through the a priori part of conceptual analysis: here the theorist locates semantic rules at a high level of abstraction which guide speakers' understanding of 'law' irrespective of particular circumstances (ie concrete legal systems). The criteria for a definition of 'law' introduced by such rules are fixed by reference to characteristics of law that transcend specific contexts: characteristics whose rejection would lead to a loss of the meaning of 'law'. At this level, law is shown to share essential features with other forms of normativity like morality, custom and etiquette, while all of them are sharply contrasted to non-normative regularities of behaviour (habits). On the other hand, empirical considerations pertain to a posteriori conceptual analysis: here the theorist aims to state rules for using legal language in a manner that successfully depicts the empirical features of concrete contexts (for instance, those of a particular legal system or type of legal systems). The level of abstraction for these rules is low and they amount to criteria for 'law' that are immediately responsible to (and revisable on the grounds of) empirical features of the context under consideration. In a moment we will see that, in Hart's theory, such criteria play the role of differentiating 'law' from other types of normativity (morality, ethics, custom and etiquette) for they refer to features of 'law' that were developed through the specific functions that legal institutions came to perform within particular societal formations (German, English, US and so on) or types thereof (depending on the criterion of classification: Western, Muslim, Capitalist or Traditional).

For the following two sections I shall be reviewing Hart's conclusions regarding law's nature that derive from the two levels of conceptual analysis he employs.[19] Employment of a priori conceptual analysis and the involvement of semantic considerations will be related to his explanation of the normative character of law as a necessary relation between 'law' and 'obligation'. On the other hand, reliance on empirical considerations by way of a posteriori analysis will be shown to underpin Hart's explication of law as the outcome of a social convention.[20] Along these lines, the two levels of conceptual analysis effect a

[19] Lest any misunderstanding occur, it should be made clear that Hart never referred explicitly to the method of conceptual analysis let alone drew any distinction between an a priori and an a posteriori part thereof. To that extent, the exposition at hand is a reconstruction of Hart's thought in the light of the remarks made earlier in this chapter. Be that as it may, it is a reconstruction that purports to take seriously what in Hart's work is, philosophically speaking, the most valuable and innovative part, namely his attempt to apply the theoretical tools of his contemporary analytical philosophy to the analysis of law. This endeavour is what invests Hart's work with an unprecedented depth for Anglo-Saxon legal theory and manifests its intellectual superiority vis-à-vis his predecessors. As a result, any serious attempt to evaluate Hart's substantive conclusions about the nature of law ought to make explicit the methodological assumptions of his theory.

[20] A possible objection to this classification is that the conventional character of law can be considered a priori, thus reserving the characterisation of the a posteriori only for the legal conventions of particular legal systems. This objection rests on the misunderstanding that any

system of norms which constrain the use of legal expressions and, if grouped together, may serve as a grammar for generating legal knowledge. Despite its potential, however, Hart's grammar fails, at the end of the day, to live up to the demands of legal knowledge. The failure will be shown to stem from the explanation of legal obligation Hart puts forward, one that effects an impoverishment of the grammar of law by rendering its rules responsible to criteria which are external to the practice of a legal community, instead of the other way round.

5.2.1 The Normative Character of Law: Law and Obligation

Early in the *Concept of Law* Hart arrives at the conclusion that legal rules are a species of social rules on a par with rules of morality, ethics, custom, etiquette and so on. This conclusion rests on a general analysis of normative speech, one that makes explicit the fundamental semantic rules that guide the use of regulative expressions and sentences amongst speakers of a language. Insofar as semantic rules refer to actual properties, it is possible for Hart to argue that the various forms of legal, moral, ethical and other rules share a number of core characteristics and, hence, may be grouped together under the genus 'social rules'. To that extent, the a priori part of Hart's conceptual analysis undertakes the task to illustrate the essential characteristics of normativity generally speaking.

Hart argues that in using social rules, speakers treat them as shared standards of behaviour, standards that can be employed in order to justify or criticise one's own or others' conduct. To that extent, the language of rules presupposes or is necessarily accompanied by the *critical reflection* that some regular pattern of behaviour is a correct standard of conduct: Hart labels this kind of reflection 'the critical reflective attitude'.[21] The critical reflective attitude comprises two aspects: one subjective, consisting in the reasons speakers have for treating some pattern of behaviour as a binding standard; and one objective, consisting in speakers' demonstration of doing so (a demonstration that usually consists in the actual ways speakers employ normative language in order to criticise, praise or advise others). The latter aspect constitutes, more or less, an empirical fact that can be located in the environment. It should be pointed out that what is crucial for the existence of any rule are not the *actual* reasons speakers have for treating a

necessary proposition is also a priori. This equation is mistaken. As we know since Saul Kripke's *Name and Necessity* (Oxford, Blackwell, 1982), a proposition can be necessary while being a posteriori. The basic difference between a priori and a posteriori necessity may be represented as follows: a priori necessary is a proposition that is true irrespective of how the actual world is like. Conversely, a posteriori necessary is a proposition, if it is true with respect to how the actual world is like. An example of the former is the proposition 'water is the transparent stuff that we drink'; while of the latter: 'the stuff water consists of is H_2O'. It follows that the proposition about the conventional character of law must be deemed a posteriori, for it derives from how things actually are (it derives from our actual experience of legal systems). For these distinctions in detail and with examples, see Jackson, above n 7, 46–55. I am indebted to Dimitrios Kyritsis and Bartosz Brożek for drawing my attention to the above objection.

[21] See Hart, *The Concept of Law*, above n 5, 55–61.

pattern of behaviour as a correct standard (subjective aspect) but merely the fact that they do so (the objective aspect). To that extent, the upgrading of a pattern of behaviour to a rule acquires an objective standing and becomes empirically transparent to the theorist. This should not come as a surprise: Hart's preoccupation with a neutral, value-free description of law led him to overemphasise the importance of the objective aspect and even substitute it in the place of the subjective one.[22] This gave rise to a number of important problems with respect to his account of normativity because the objective, factual aspect of the critical reflective attitude cannot by itself sustain the required connection between the existence of a normative standard on the one hand and the reasons agents have for acting, on the other. This point will be taken up in more detail shortly.

In an attempt to flesh out the critical reflective attitude, Hart takes it to indicate the presence of an *obligation*. On the grounds of the concept of obligation Hart distinguishes social rules from two other related phenomena, habits and acts of brute force.[23] Habits are, as it were, incomplete rules; they comprise a regular pattern of behaviour but there is no element of critical reflection that this pattern is a valuable standard of conduct. On the other hand, acts of brute force may indeed entail a certain amount of regulatory power, even though they fall short of generating obligation. What they generate, instead, is the feeling that one is obliged to act in a certain way. To demonstrate this he uses the gunman example:[24] when held up at gunpoint and asked to hand over their money, any reasonable person would be expected to comply with the order. However, in doing so he or she would not be treating the gunman's order as giving rise to an *obligation* but would rather experience feelings of *being obliged*.[25]

To sum up: Hart's analysis of the use of legal language leads him to the conclusion that for something to be a legal rule it is necessary that the members of a legal community hold the belief that it is a valuable standard of behaviour. It is only under this condition that a rule can be seen as giving rise to an obligation rather than amounting to an instance of brute force (being obliged). The

[22] Hart was a relativist with respect to morality. As a result he thought of agents' reasons for treating something as a standard of behaviour as being utterly subjective and incapable of supporting objective scientific judgements about the existence or non-existence of rules. In contrast, agents' behaviour was a much more reliable medium for underpinning such judgements. For Hart's relativism in conjunction with his positivism, see his five theses on positivism in 'Positivism and the Separation of Law and Morals', above n 16, 57.

[23] Hart reserves the term obligation for moral and legal rules only, for he understands obligation as resulting from the threat of serious social pressure; see *The Concept of Law*, above n 5, 85–87. This is not a very clear distinction given that other kinds of social rules (etiquette or courtesy) may also be accompanied by the threat of social pressure that can be serious enough. Social pressure might have an impact on the intensity of the perceived obligation but not on its existence. The latter rather depends on whether some practice is treated as a standard of behaviour, which is to say as a rule.

[24] Hart, *The Concept of Law*, above n 5, 82.

[25] *Ibid.* Hart uses the case of the gunman with an eye to rejecting John Austin's definition of law as a set of commands backed by threat. Such a definition, Hart submits, is incapable of distinguishing between a legal rule and the command of a gunman, precisely because it fails to apprehend the element of obligation that is in-built in law.

necessary link between rule and obligation, however, is not peculiarly confined to law but encapsulates an essential feature of normativity in general. To that extent, Hart concedes that law is a species of normativity and legal rules a species of social rules.

5.2.2 Law in its Own Right: Convention and Authority

Despite appearances it would be wrong to assume that Hart confuses legal rules with other kinds of social rules. On the contrary, he is very keen on distinguishing the domain of law from other areas of social normativity and in particular morality. The part of his theory that undertakes this task focusses on the empirical differences between practices of law on the one hand and practices of morality on the other. In a more philosophical vocabulary, this part of the Hartian analysis intends to establish sufficient features for the existence of legal rules as opposed to necessary ones, a task that was undertaken by the general part of his theory.

Hart compares practices that give rise to legal rules and those that give rise to moral rules with an eye to illustrating that the former are different in content or rationale from the latter, irrespective of their both sharing the property of being normative (ie of being considered as valuable standards of conduct that give rise to obligations). Moral rules surface as the result of long-standing practices when at a particular point in time the participants of the practice form the belief that some regular pattern of behaviour is a valuable standard of conduct. Owing to the length of the whole process, there is an assumption that the relevant beliefs give rise to obligations that are firmly grounded on a lengthy process of deliberation. In taking their time, so to speak, the participants have had the opportunity to contemplate the various aspects of the practice, to soberly evaluate its effects and even to review and improve some of its components. As a result, the practice raises a strong claim to correctness with respect to the rules it generates. In short, moral practices are about establishing rules of conduct that lay down obligations that reflect the fundamental evaluations of a community about what is right and wrong. These rules emerge from a lengthy process of deliberation, testing and revision that invests them with an increased amount of practical authority.[26]

Hart points out that such rules of morality would have formed the core of traditional legal systems within small-sized communities. In such groups of limited membership all law was required to do was to offer a rough indication of what kind of conduct is permitted or forbidden with a view to guaranteeing the preservation of the community. In this respect, law is indistinguishable from

[26] For such a reading of Hart's theory, see J Waldron, *The Dignity of Legislation* (Cambridge, Cambridge University Press, 1999) ch 1. Waldron's reading seems to be apposite for capturing legal positivism's concern for moral neutrality.

morality, both systems consisting of basic rules of obligation that evolve through a long process of deliberation. Hart calls these rules *primary rules*.[27] But contemporary legal systems seem to be the result of an entirely different process, embodying a rationale that is radically different from the one underlying primary rules. Apparently, at some point in their history, owing mainly to a considerable increase of their membership, most societies developed patterns for modifying or replacing their primary rules in a *deliberate* way without 'taking their time' and without being interested, or at least principally interested, in the correctness of the amounting rules. Those patterns had a number of other characteristics, most important amongst them being the fact that change or modification of primary rules was entrusted to specific people or bodies of people (judges, state officials, legislative bodies). Those patterns soon rose to the status of standards of conduct vis-à-vis those who administered the corpus of primary rules and gave rise to a new type of rule, what Hart calls *secondary rules*.[28]

On the face of it, secondary rules are the expression of a rationale that is radically different from the one underlying primary rules: their purpose is not to create obligations that are valid unconditionally, in virtue of their being the considered outcomes of a long-standing deliberation, but instead to effectively administer the system of primary rules (to that extent *secondary rules are rules about primary rules*). This feature makes secondary rules indifferent vis-à-vis the content of the obligations that primary rules incorporate. Instead, secondary rules focus on whether primary rules are being created or modified according to the set of conditions specified by them. What is more, Hart maintains that the rationale of secondary rules is much more than a local phenomenon within modern legal systems: in fact, the whole idea of law as we know it today is permeated by the idea of secondary rules, for every developed legal system is founded upon a special secondary rule, one that is the most general secondary rule of the whole system, the so-called *rule of recognition*.[29]

The rule of recognition contains the criteria of legality (or *validity*), which is to say the criteria for distinguishing between those rules of obligation that are part of the legal system and those that are not (but, instead, form part of morality, custom, ethics, courtesy and so on).[30] Criteria of validity acquire the status of conditions that are necessary and sufficient for something to be a legal rule. Thus they replace the lengthy process by which non-legal social rules are being

[27] As primary, Hart characterises those rules that give rise to rights and duties, the most common example being the rules of criminal law. For a detailed discussion see Hart, *The Concept of Law*, above n 5, ch V *passim*.

[28] Secondary rules are rules that authorise legal subjects to create, modify or otherwise alter primary rules; see *ibid*.

[29] *Ibid* 94–117.

[30] For Hart this is the actual criterion for distinguishing between law and morality. Often he refers to some other differences between legal and moral rules such as the feeling of shame pertaining only to the latter and the generalised social pressure pertaining exclusively to the former. These, however, fall short of doing the analytical job of distinguishing between law and morality, as Hart himself seems to believe when talking about primitive legal systems.

established. Criteria of validity are content-independent and focus merely on the formal-factual conditions that must obtain for the valid creation or modification of the rules of the system. To that extent, criteria of legality or validity are necessary not because they can be known independently of experience (a priori) but because they can be known only with respect to the actual features of each and every particular legal system (a posteriori). This fact implies that there is no unique rule of recognition but a plethora thereof; in fact there are around as many rules of recognition as there are legal systems. Furthermore, it is important to point out that each and every rule of recognition plays the role of a *constitutive convention* with respect to some legal system: it is a *convention* because it owes its existence to the contingent fact of a decision or agreement, on behalf of a community, to treat some set of conditions as constituting criteria of validity for its legal system. It is constitutive because the legal system a rule of recognition corresponds to cannot exist outside it. Consequently, rules of recognition carry a striking resemblance to rules of games, for they too are the product of choice and are also essential for the existence of the relevant game (eg chess is what it is because of its rules and otherwise it does not exist independently of them).

5.3 The External and the Internal Aspect of Rules: Legal Theory's Split Personality

It was suggested earlier that Hart's conceptual analysis of legal language comprises two parts. One part is interested in the most abstract conditions for a meaningful use of 'law' (what was labelled *semantic considerations*) and therefore is not conditioned upon the empirical features of any concrete legal system (ie it is a priori); and another part is interested in concrete conditions for the use of 'law' (what was labelled *empirical considerations*) and therefore focusses on the empirical features of particular legal systems (a posteriori).

We saw that the former type of conceptual analysis led Hart to the conclusion that law gives rise to obligations (in other words, it is normative), while the latter to the conclusion that law is conventional. Together the two modes of analysis—each on a different level of abstraction—tell us what is necessary to know in order to arrive at a full understanding of the nature of law. Along these lines, if one wanted to refer to legal concepts or use legal language meaningfully, one would have to know at least that law is about obligation.[31] If, however, one wanted to refer meaningfully to a particular legal system, say the English or the German, one would have needed more information: one would have needed to know the constitutive convention of that system (its rule of recognition) and the criteria of validity specified by it. The former type of knowledge is a priori,

[31] To the extent that conceptual analysis is interested in stating semantic rules for the use of concepts the same point can be made by saying that in order to use properly 'law' one needs to know the semantic rule (SR): 'legal rules give rise to obligations'.

having to do with the way we understand 'law' in its most general form, while the latter is a posteriori, arising from the empirical study of the facts and events that comprise the constitutive convention of the system under consideration.

At this point it is justified to ask: in our understanding of legal phenomena, which of the two carries more weight for the fullest possible understanding of legal phenomena: empirical considerations or the conceptual connection between law and obligation? Admittedly, empirical considerations can be deemed weightier in a trivial sense: given that there is no such thing as ideal law, existing over and above all actual legal systems, it follows that all theoretical enquiry takes place with reference to one or more concrete legal systems and, hence, relies on empirical observations about the facts that put together the constitutive convention (or the rule of recognition) of each one of them. To that extent, our knowledge of the phenomenon law is inescapably interwoven with our knowledge of particular legal system(s). Be that as it may, our question purports to address a less trivial point: in determining the nature of law, even in relation to concrete legal systems, a *conceptual issue* arises which might not be possible to settle through reference to empirical considerations regarding a constitutive legal convention. This aspect stems from law's conceptual relation to obligation. This relation implies that it is not possible to determine the content of 'law' independently of the content of 'obligation'. However, the latter cannot be determined on the basis of a legal constitutive convention because it comprises a large amount of non-legal components: in assessing the existence of an obligation one often has to consider, apart from legal reasons, reasons of a moral or ethical nature.[32] Think for instance of *civil disobedience*: in assessing their legal obligations 'legal dissidents' often refer to reasons that exceed by far the 'space' of legal validity demarcated by the relevant rule of recognition. As a result, the content of 'law' can only be partly determined on the basis of a legal convention, for the latter fails to deliver a full account of obligating reasons. Recast in those terms, the question about the priority of the empirical or the conceptual becomes a question about the relation between law and the other realms of normativity.

Hart decides, somehow surprisingly considering his conceptual analysis of 'law', on an analysis of 'obligation' in empirical or value-free terms. When in Hart's theoretical system someone asks—what does it mean to know that 'law' is intertwined with 'obligation'? —Hart seems to want to avoid an answer that would involve the fullest possible set of reasons giving rise to obligations (obligating reasons), for such an answer would have to include all relevant moral or ethical obligating reasons. Such a consideration of the complete set of reasons,

[32] This is the case irrespective of the way we understand morality: if morality is understood as comprising a system of rules that are universally valid, then obviously these rules escape the validity criteria of a legal rule of recognition. On the other hand, even if morality is understood as conventional, then again the rules it comprises cannot be accounted for through a legal convention but, instead, one would need to locate the appropriate moral convention that specifies criteria of moral validity.

Hart points out, is beset by a number of disadvantages.[33] First, in the light of a vast plethora of value-systems, many of which are mutually incompatible, there is no determinate or objective way to arrive at uniform answers with respect to what gives rise to an obligation in a particular case. Secondly, in postulating completeness of the relevant obligating reasons, such an account becomes extremely time-consuming and extremely difficult, if not impossible, ever to achieve. Finally, and perhaps more importantly, an analysis of legal obligation premised on the fullest possible account of obligating reasons would eschew what for Hart is the most central feature of modern legal systems, namely the existence of a practice giving rise to a secondary rule of recognition. In omitting this important aspect, any analysis of law would be mistaking all legal rules for primary rules, a fact true of traditional legal systems—whenever law and morality were not clearly demarcated—but definitely not true of the highly complex modern legal orders.

For all these reasons Hart opts for an explication of legal obligation that actually does away with obligating reasons. Hart suggests that a legal obligation obtains if and only if the conditions of legal validity are in place. More importantly, these conditions do not comprise obligating reasons (be they moral, ethical or other) but consist of external facts that can be observed and recorded in an objective way (enactment in Parliament, issuance by the appropriate official and so on) and are recorded by the system's rule of recognition. By way of introducing the concept of legal validity, Hart breaks the continuity between legal and other kinds of obligation. Legal obligation becomes an empirical concept that may be asserted on the basis of a series of descriptive facts, whereas for asserting moral obligation some reference to actual obligating reasons is required.[34] Thus, the *reduction of legal obligation to legal validity* signifies a tactical trade-off between the alleged *shortcomings* of a 'deep' analysis of obligating reasons and the *objectivity* that pertains to the empirical facts to be found on the 'surface' of the behaviour of those who comply with legal rules.

Hart's reduction is available on one important condition: unless his theory were to count as an incomplete report of legal phenomena, it should still be possible to deem accounts of rules in terms of validity conditions *equivalent* to accounts of rules in terms of obligating reasons (call this the *equivalence condition*). In other words, the description of the facts that lie on the *surface* of the behaviour of those who comply with some legal obligation should carry the same informational value with a *deep* account of the reasons that give rise to the obligation in question. This requires that the legal theorist be able to switch between the two accounts without failing to depict the correct nature of legal

[33] See Hart, 'Positivism and the Separation of Law and Morals', above n 16, 82–87.

[34] We said earlier that it is possible to capture even moral obligation as referring to external features of speakers' behaviour. Such an analysis, however, would be even less convincing than in the case of law for it is impossible to identify a unique set of facts (ie a constitutive convention) that is responsible for generating moral rules.

phenomena. Hart attempts to meet the equivalence condition by alluding to the existence of two aspects of rules or two standpoints for understanding legal phenomena. The first, the so-called *internal aspect* or point of view, pertains to anyone who has developed vis-à-vis a legal system what was earlier referred to as the critical reflective attitude; in other words anyone who treats the rules of the system as valuable standards of behaviour. Hart reserves this role for the participants of a legal system. The second, the so-called *external aspect* or point of view, pertains to someone who is 'observing' the members of a legal community from some distance, that is, without necessarily sharing the belief that the rules shared by the members of the community are valuable standards of behaviour. The ability to switch between the two points of view is crucial for Hart's reductionist account of legal obligation.

On any superficial understanding of 'obligation' it is reasonable to expect that, insofar as someone believes that some rule is a valuable standard of behaviour, he or she should be in a position to offer reasons for corroborating that belief. As argued earlier, however, Hart considers any attempt to refer to the deep structure of obligation to be wrongheaded. Instead, on the validity-based account he puts forward, one should be able to justify one's belief by saying something like 'this is a valuable standard of behaviour because it has been validated according to the conditions set in the rule of recognition'. For the latter to count as a faithful depiction of legal obligation two conditions must be in place. The first condition is that it is possible to replace the notion of obligation with some other notion that is indifferent vis-à-vis obligating reasons. This task was carried out by Hart's analysis of the conventional character of law as a practice that gives rise to secondary rules, an analysis that, as indicated above, purported to demarcate law from morality, while substituting obligating reasons with the content-indifferent and formalistic notion of legal validity. The second condition requires that there be an external, empirical aspect to each and every legal obligation which corresponds to the facts of legal validity set down in a constitutive legal convention (rule of recognition). For this Hart turns to the *behaviour* of those who are acting under a legal obligation, ie those who occupy the internal point of view with respect to a legal rule. Uncontrovertibly, such behaviour can be described in value-free terms, without making reference to obligating reasons of any kind but merely by referring to the external, empirical components thereof. In particular, when the behaviour under consideration is the behaviour of those who regard the practice that gives rise to secondary rules as obligatory,[35] then its external components coincide with the criteria of validity spelled out in a rule of recognition.

It is at this instant that the external point of view assumes supremacy in Hart's system: once divested of any reference to substantive (moral, ethical) obligating

[35] Hart believes that in order to locate the rule of recognition of any legal system the theorist must focus on the practice of the legal community; see the discussion in *The Concept of Law*, above n 5, 79–91.

reasons, legal obligation can be easily asserted from the point of view of someone who does not associate obligating reasons with legal standards, someone whose viewpoint is external to the legal practice of the community under consideration (someone who occupies Hart's external point of view). To that extent, the internal point of view and the existence of legal obligations is conditioned upon the possibility of a description of facts from the external point of view.[36] Critics of Hart have pointed out that such a possibility is to be rejected. It is not just that any description from the external point of view fails to depict (the content of) legal obligations, but also that Hart's notion of legal validity runs out of resources when it is asked to explain the validity of the rule of recognition.[37]

The exchange of the internal for the external point of view signals the departure from a grammar that may ground a viable notion of objectivity, hence legal knowledge. In substituting isolated criteria for deeper normative reasons, Hart loses sight of the rationale in whose light law can be reconstructed as a meaningful practice, as opposed to a collection of contingent occurrences. As a result, the order between rules of grammar and semantic criteria is inversed: rules of grammar cease to be embedded in a practice of rule-following which, in virtue of possessing normative impetus, may impose an order upon criteria and, instead, are subjected to the authority of contingent events. To that extent Hart's account is not too dissimilar to the sceptical and behaviourist explications of practice that were discussed in Chapter 3.[38] In both cases, communal practice dissolves in a series of criteria which purport to function as final arbiters of normativity, over and above practice itself. No sooner criteria assume priority over rules, however, than the grammar of law becomes devoid of the dynamic structure which is required for legal knowledge and becomes static in the fashion of the grammar developed by the philosophy of logical positivism.[39] Static grammar falls short of grounding objectivity, for it conceives of criteria as ultra-determinants which can never coherently account for the space between wrong applications of grammar and those correct ones that constitute knowledge. I shall next turn to two important criticisms of Hart with an eye to demonstrating in more detail the failure of Hart's conceptual analysis to amount to a grammar appropriate for knowledge.

[36] This is despite Hart's insistence that the external point of view is parasitical on the internal point of view. The latter would instead require that the notion of legal validity be dependent on substantive obligating reasons, a thesis that traditionally has been associated with theories of natural law.

[37] See section 5.4.

[38] See section 3.3.2.

[39] See section 2.6. The predicament of a static grammar is connected with a conventionalist account of practice (which was discussed in section 3.3.2). For both strategies, take certain empirical entities (sense-data in the former case; behavioural data in the latter) to constitute the final arbiters of intentional content. In either case the normativity of content, as springing from a practice that is responsive to reasons, drops out.

5.4 Two Criticisms

Hart's positivist and value-free account of law stands and falls with the possibility to switch between the external and the internal point of view, in other words, to capture legal obligations in purely descriptive terms, through the notion of legal validity, without referring to the deep structure of obligating reasons. Given the centrality of the notion of validity to such an account it is not surprising that Hart's idea of a rule of recognition has been the focus of much critical discussion since the appearance of *The Concept of Law.* Roughly speaking, there are two lines of criticism that can be distinguished for present purposes. First, it has been argued that the notion of legal validity actually fails to account for the totality of types of legal obligation arising within a legal system (call this the *incompleteness thesis*). The second argument gives rise to a deeper objection: that it is insufficient to understand the practice of law as resting upon a secondary rule of recognition that generates criteria of validity because a full understanding of legal obligation requires association with other types of obligation (call this the *connection thesis*). Taken conjointly, the two criticisms demonstrate the inability of Hart's grammar to ground legal knowledge.

5.4.1 The Incompleteness Thesis

The incompleteness thesis says that no rule of recognition can offer a complete account of legal obligation for any legal system X. The *locus classicus* of this argument is Ronald Dworkin's *Taking Rights Seriously.* In it Dworkin argues that Hart's notion of legal validity falls short from giving a complete account of legal obligation.[40] Focussing on the judicial practice of modern legal systems Dworkin points out that judges, more often than not, consider as authoritative for their cases standards that have not yet passed the test of any rule of recognition. These standards, which Dworkin labels *principles* and *policies,* give rise to legal obligations not in virtue of some test of validity, but because they are justified on moral or ethical grounds. The fact that such standards actually figure in legal justifications shows that, after all, Hart's account of legal phenomena was not that accurate. But accuracy is only a minor concern in this case; the realisation that (some) legal obligations may exist independently of a rule of recognition puts Hart's conception of legal validity into serious doubt and generates the need for a new understanding of legal obligation, one that is capable of accounting for obligations of the principle or policy type. Dworkin, in later works, deepens his critique with his argument from the *semantic sting.* This locates the reason for incompleteness in the conception of legal meaning based on semantic criteria

[40] R Dworkin, *Taking Rights Seriously* (London, Duckworth, 1977) chs 2 and 3. A somewhat different argument that arrives at similar conclusions can be found in R Alexy, *The Argument from Injustice: A Reply to Legal Positivism,* S L Paulson and B Litschewski Paulson (trans) (Oxford, Clarendon Press, 2002) 71–74.

specified by a rule of recognition. The gist of his criticism is that if one assumes a semantic theory of legal meaning then any form of disagreement surrounding legal meaning must be deemed meaningless. This, however, would fly in the face of the actual fact of disagreement between lawyers. Dworkin convincingly shows that very often legal discourse consists of instances of passionate disagreement about the real nature of law or the true meaning of a legal precept, disagreement that arises with respect to concrete cases and becomes pervasive of most instances of adjudication. Accordingly, disagreement should be shown to be more meaningful than a sheer logomachy over semantic criteria and definitions. This could only happen if we assumed an object of disagreement which extends beyond the practice of disagreement itself (which is linguistically confined). Along these lines, Dworkin postulates the possibility of a strong notion of objectivity with respect to legal claims, one requiring that the essence or nature of law lie outside language, which might or might not succeed in capturing it.

The significance of these ideas can be illustrated by utilising the vocabulary of propositions: on Dworkin's conception, propositions of law are individuated with respect to the real substance of legal entities; that is, antecedently to the way we use language within the boundaries of a practice. The full-blown version of this idea can be found in Dworkin's notorious claim that it is possible for a community to go wrong with respect to the true meaning of legal sentences. Why is it so? Because, for Dworkin, it is always possible to have a proposition individuated by the essential properties of a case, which, as a result, escapes the semantic rules of the community: thus, there may be a true legal proposition (lp) despite the fact that the community has no place for it in its conceptual (or semantic) scheme. Meaning does not depend on what semantic rules tell us but on how things really are, legally speaking. Thus proposition p may be a proposition of law irrespective, or even *in spite* of, the criteria specified in a Hartian rule of recognition.[41]

Dworkin's line of argument puts the finger on a key deficiency of Hart's grammar: it is a grammar that lacks the resources for distinguishing between right and wrong applications of its own rules. This ability can be illustrated through the dimension of depth. A deep grammar is one that is not exhausted by the surface behaviour of those who engage in a practice of rule-following regarding its rules but, instead, possesses a deeper layer of normativity which can serve as a measure of correctness for the various instances of rule-following. The dimension of depth is what bestows grammar with normativity, for it allows

[41] This seems to me to be a distortion of the semantic view, for semantic explications of propositions need not exhaust truth and falsity: they merely sketch the possible ontological combinations of the building blocks of the world. A semantic explication of ontology does not say when a proposition is true or false; it merely says which propositions are candidates of truth and falsity. Thus, even on a semantic explication, we can have a validly formulated sentence that still fails to correspond to anything in the world (say a sentence about Unicorns). *Cf* my discussion of Hart's semantic analysis 'Law as Recognition: H L A Hart and Analytical Positivism' in T Murphy (ed), *Western Jurisprudence* (Dublin, Round Hall, 2004).

objective judgements about isolated applications of its rules to be performed from within a practice; judgements that otherwise would have been impossible, had the practice been exhausted by the shallow items identified by Hart's external point of view.

Be that as it may, Dworkin's eagerness to highlight the possibility of right answers with respect to legal questions caused him to overemphasise the importance of the distance between, on the one hand, behaviour lying at the surface of a practice and, on the other, deep reasons that are responsible for the normative force of the practice. His insistence on this point, which has been taken up and expanded by his proponents, threatens with another complication as I shall suggest in the next chapter: that of conceiving normative reasons (principles and policies) as something that exist independently of the practice of a legal community. This assumption is corroborated by Dworkin's frequent rejection of any explication of legal practice through the means of semantic analysis. Considering the central role language (semantic considerations) play in the constitution of any social or other practice, it is almost unavoidable to conclude that Dworkin, in rejecting semantic analysis *tout court*, is almost claiming that practices themselves are insufficient or inadequate for appreciating the normative reasons that guide participants in their behaviour.

5.4.2 The Connection Thesis

If the incompleteness thesis was about the lack of depth of Hartian grammar, the connection thesis purports to provide a positive account of deep normative reasons with respect to legal practice. In doing so it advances an attack on Hart's understanding of the very rationale of legal practice which purports to keep law distinct from morality. In a nutshell, the connection thesis says that legal obligations stand in the same line with moral obligations and, hence, that a full understanding of legal practices requires that certain moral and ethical reasons be drawn into the picture.[42] The reason given is that the practice of law should not be understood as *principally* being about the existence of a secondary obligation of recognition, one about recognising criteria of validity, managing legal material and allowing for deliberate changes of the rules of the system. Instead, the connection thesis argues, legal practice needs to be understood as

[42] There is a plethora of authors that can be interpreted as arguing for the connection thesis. For present purposes suffice to include in them R Dworkin, *Taking Rights Seriously*, above n 40; *idem*, *Law's Empire* (London, Fontana, 1986) and R Alexy, *The Argument from Injustice*, above n 40. In addition, most natural law theorists could be interpreted as endorsing some version of the connection thesis; see, especially, J M Finnis, *Natural Law and Natural Rights* (Oxford, Clarendon Press, 1980). Hart himself speaks of a minimum content of natural law that necessarily pertains to every legal system. Far from making any reference to substantive moral reasons, the latter constitutes more of a prudential safeguard against forms of government that would lead to the disintegration of social life altogether. Such forms of government, Hart says, should not qualify as legal systems; see Hart, above n 5, 193–200.

being directly answerable to primary obligations that exist independently or, perhaps, alongside the secondary obligation of recognition. On this understanding, the obligation of recognition is rendered secondary, albeit in the sense that it is amenable to a number of primary obligations that precede the process of recognition.

The connection thesis can be stated as the upshot of a critical enquiry into the foundation (or the validity) of the rule of recognition. A generic version of this argument might run along the following lines: Hart informs us that the rule of recognition is not valid as a legal rule (ie the notion of legal validity does not apply to it) but, instead, its existence must be explained in a different way to that of legal rules. However that may be, the rule of recognition is still the source of an obligation, albeit one of the secondary kind: the obligation vis-à-vis officials to recognise as legal only those norms that pass the validity test. What are, then, the grounds of this obligation? In the case of legal obligations the answer to this question has been rather unproblematic, for, in their case, validity exhausts obligation and no association to the content of other obligations is prima facie necessary. With respect to these, one could simply refer to the facts of validity in order to point out the existence of the relevant legal obligation. This option is not available as regards the existence of the rule of recognition, given that conditions of validity cannot be conceived of independently of the rule of recognition (in fact, they presuppose it). It follows that one has to look elsewhere for a source of validity. Hart attempts to locate a source of validity by conceiving of rules of recognition as species of social rules and then subjecting them to his account of the genesis of social rules. The problem with this explanation is that it cannot sufficiently distinguish secondary from primary obligations. Hart touches upon this problem when he discusses the difficulty in drawing distinctions between different types of primary obligation (especially legal and moral) in early communities. What we find, instead, in those societal formations are just primary obligations that result from the same process of creation: a complex process of 'maturation' where social practices evolve in the light of pre-existing primary obligations that determine the evolution of new rules and the content of the obligations they contain. To that extent, social rules that impose obligations are of a uniform type and form a coherent normative web that grows slowly with time.

But the said inability to distinguish *between different types of primary obligation* might also extend to our inability to *distinguish between primary and secondary obligations in the first place.* More specifically, it might be hard to demarcate the obligation embedded in a rule of recognition from all other (primary) obligations that arise from the social practices of a particular community. Given Hart's model of genesis of social obligations it would be hard to justify a separate, *sui generis* kind of obligation that could come into existence independently of all other (pre-existing) social obligations. For, even if it has been possible to detach *legal validity* from an obligation for justification, Hart would still admit that *social validity* is inherently answerable to reasons that are embedded in primary rules. To claim otherwise would amount to treating rules of recognition as legal, something that certainly flies in the face of his explication of rules of recognition as social. In the light of these remarks, every rule of recognition needs to observe the same reasons that primary rules do, and it can only be exempted from those if there is a good justification, namely one that in turn rests on an obligation-imposing primary rule (at least for as long as one remains within Hart's model of social normativity). To that extent, any rule of recognition is a covert primary rule.

The revolutionary conclusion of the connection thesis is that no single set of criteria of validity can be final but, instead, that criteria are revisable in the light of obligating reasons that are embedded in primary rules.[43] On the face of it, even Hart's own contention that the whole enterprise of law is essentially about validity is a *substantive thesis* that derives from obligating reasons rather than a 'cool', value-free description of the facts of a distinct social practice (law). Once, however, it has been exposed as a substantive thesis, Hart's analysis might look far less convincing as an understanding of legal phenomena considering that it has to compete with a plethora of other substantive theses that openly accept the relevance of moral obligations in determining legal validity. This conclusion suggests the contribution of the connection thesis to the project of a grammar for law. It would supplement the incompleteness thesis by indicating the lines a reconstruction of the deep normativity of legal practice should run along: legal reasons would need to be conceived of as standing in a continuum with moral reasons, for any attempt to construct an insular, value-free notion of legal obligation, as Hart would have it, is bound to collapse.

5.5 Conclusion

Hart's philosophical account falls short of the demands of legal knowledge. The reason for this has little to do with the fact that it is a semantic theory or that it relies on the method of conceptual analysis. It has more to do with the fact that, in developing a grammar for law, he prioritises criteria of application over rules of grammar. This he does by focussing on the surface of the practice of a legal community while missing out on the obligating reasons that confer a deep normative structure upon the practice. Yet, it is solely by taking into account the dimension of depth that one can make room for error and correction regarding beliefs about the law, both operations being crucial for an account of legal knowledge.[44]

There is a plethora of theories which share the kernel of the incompleteness and connection theses and claim to have worked out answers to the problems

[43] This is the upshot of the criticism of N Stavropoulos, *Objectivity in Law* (Oxford, Clarendon Press, 1996) ch 3.

[44] See section 1.2.

faced by Hart. Yet not any such theory should be given equal weight with respect to an account of the normative depth of legal practice. The reason is that not any theory, which superficially identifies the shortcomings of Hart's analysis, can compete with the most valuable of his achievements, namely the reconstruction of legal phenomena on the basis of a grammar. This achievement constitutes such an important contribution to legal philosophy that it renders it a very subtle issue to judge whether a philosophical account of law really is an advancement vis-à-vis Hart's own theory. It follows that for an account of law's normativity to succeed, it would have to build on Hart's account, not fall behind it by giving up his valuable idea of a grammar of law. Accordingly, some theories, as in the case of most variants of natural law, will have to be rejected outright, for, by postulating a strong realism regarding normative properties, they violate the condition of intelligibility which was outlined in the opening chapters of this work. Such theories will not occupy us further in this work.

More interesting is the case of Ronald Dworkin's interpretive theory of law or *interpretivism*, as it has come to be known in recent years. In putting forward interpretivism, Dworkin has claimed to be steering a middle way between natural law theories with a strong realist outlook and semantic theories like Hart's. Ambitious as Dworkin's course may be, it cannot succeed. The main reason is that interpretivism fails to occupy the middle space Dworkin would have it doing. In its early steps, interpretivism remains too close to Hart's semantic project and, to that extent, falls prey to the exact same objections this chapter raised. In later work Dworkin moves on to reject all kinds of semantic theory. There, his hostility to any notion of semantic analysis coupled with a strong rhetoric of objectivity almost forces upon the reader the conclusion that Dworkin's theory is incompatible with the idea of a grammar and intelligible objectivity in a manner almost as strong as that of the realist theories of natural law. Stavropoulos' more level-headed effort to cash in Dworkin's stake and rescue interpretivism by appealing to a different semantic analysis is probably the most interesting effort up till now to replace the thin philosophical underpinning of interpretivism offered by Dworkin. Despite its philosophical subtlety and degree of sophistication, even Stavropoulos' semantic rehabilitation of interpretivism has to fail as the next chapter will illustrate.

Having rejected interpretivism's attempt to retrieve the dimension of normative depth, which is missing from Hart's philosophy, I shall, in the last chapter, put forward what I think is a more appropriate account, by making combined use of the ideas of pragmatic rationalism, which were advanced in Chapter 4, and the main theses of the discourse theory of law.

6

Interpretivism and the Menace of Essentialism

6.1 Introduction

Conceptions of knowledge which rely on the one or other idea of grammar purport to safeguard intelligibility. Intelligibility guards against radical scepticism, by preventing a gap from opening between, on the one hand, what may constitute an object of knowledge and, on the other, subjects of knowledge. By postulating a grammatical structure which underwrites our thoughts and at the same time arranges the world in intelligible segments, such philosophies guarantee that the world is accessible to our minds, hence that our efforts to reach it are not as hopeless as sceptics would have it. In disarming sceptical moves, however, it would appear that grammar-based theories give up also a fair amount of objectivity or certainty, for what grounds knowledge, ie grammar, is no longer something external to minds—hence it is very easy to lose hold of any standard for judging whether our beliefs add up to knowledge or constitute merely subjective ideas. But if this were the case, would it mean that intelligibility can only be won at the price of a new scepticism (generated by what was earlier labelled 'the prison-house of language')?[1]

Chapter 3 addressed this concern with respect to Hart's attempt to ground a grammar of law. It was argued there, that Hart's analysis of the concept of law took a wrong turn when it replaced normative (or obligating) reasons with conventional criteria. Such conventional criteria fail to compensate for the loss of objectivity that derives from the rejection of the idea of an external, mind-independent environment which (causally?) determines the contents of our thoughts.[2] Hart arrived at his impoverished notion of grammar by representing legal practice as a flat enterprise which is exhausted by facts of behaviour identified through a secondary rule of recognition. In explicating legal practice in

[1] See section 1.3.1.

[2] One may even conceive of conventional criteria as being on a par with the idea of an external world as regards the hostility to grammar. In both cases what is being prioritised are determinants of content (ultra-interpretations) which do away with the priority of grammar as a determinant of conceptual content. Ultra-interpretations are discussed in section 3.2.

this manner, Hart deprived its participants of the possibility to make room for error or to engage in corrective intervention as regards particular moves within the practice. Conversely, the opposite would require one to make reference to a set of standards which constitute something like a deep rationale of the practice,[3] standards to which the participants may refer in order to pass judgements of correctness with respect to events which otherwise satisfy the list of criteria incorporated by the relevant rule of recognition. Reference to the normative depth those standards demarcate opens up the ability to distinguish between right and wrong applications of legal expressions and, thus, restores the objectivity that is necessary to knowledge, albeit without retreating behind the threshold of intelligibility grammar generates. As such these standards would correspond to the two conditions pragmatic rationalism has set for an explication of practice as reflexive activity: ratification-independence, ie the ability of standards to extend beyond the mere acceptance arising out of a convention; and secondly, practice-immanence, in the sense that standards remain in principle accessible from within practice.[4]

In this chapter I shall begin to look into conditions of depth as a requirement of a normative conception of legal practice which avoids slipping into the shortcomings of Hart's analysis. The first station in this journey is to refer to the theory that, more than any other in the field of jurisprudence, has emphasised the importance of the dimension of depth for the understanding of (legal) practice: Ronald Dworkin's interpretive theory of law (or interpretivism, as it has come to be known in recent years). If Dworkin's analysis were to succeed, it could be employed for fleshing out legal practice, with an eye to grounding intelligible legal knowledge. Despite accounting for the depth of legal practice Dworkin's theory will, in the end, be rejected as a viable conception of legal knowledge for, at least in its prevalent version, it enshrines a notion of objectivity which is incompatible with the condition of practice-immanence postulated by pragmatic rationalism. To that extent, it retreats behind the threshold of intelligibility as a prerequisite of knowledge.[5]

In section 6.2 Dworkin's conception of interpretivism is explained. The key concept for capturing the condition of depth is the *interpretive nature* of law. This matches the complex nature of legal phenomena, a complexity that requires the processing of a multiplicity of data, by the means of a theory (interpretive theory). The theoretical propositions involved in the required synthesis raise claims of objectivity which need to be settled by interpretivism. The issue of

[3] These standards would mainly comprise all those norms that correspond to Hart's idea that law is a primary practice of obligation, which is the main conclusion of his conceptual analysis of legal practice. See section 5.2.

[4] See section 6.5.

[5] See section 1.4.

objectivity is a key point as regards the metaphysical commitments of interpretivism, hence its compatibility with the condition of practice-immanence, propounded by pragmatic rationalism. On the face of it, interpretivism seems to allow for two different conceptions of objectivity. While the first is still compatible with the idea of a ratification-independent grounds, which underlie legal practice, the other identifies depth as a strong foundation which can only be found outside legal practice. The latter presents itself as incompatible with the idea of grammar, as the deep structure of a cognitive practice (or a practice of judging).

Section 6.3 attempts to explore the possibility of ascribing to interpretivism a modest notion of objectivity with a view to giving it a rationalist twist. On the rationalist conception,[6] what generates objectivity as regards cognitive moves or claims within a practice is a deep level of normativity, a deep rationale, which is not readily accessible to the participants of the practice, although it can be revealed on more careful reflection about the conditions of the practice (to that extent, it does not transcend the boundaries of the practice). This rationale comprises the norms for putting forward cognitive claims within a practice (judgements). The priority of judgement over non-conceptual or non-propositional content is a concept crucial to the rationalist project, as argued elsewhere.[7] An immediate consequence of this priority is the commitment of rationalism to a semantic or grammar-related understanding of content, for judgements cannot be conceived independently of a semantic structure. Thus, no theory that prioritises judgement, ie is rationalist, can afford to reject the semantic structure of cognitive content. Its semantic flavour notwithstanding, the rationalist project is different from Hart's philosophy in a key respect. Although both are semantically oriented, the rationalist programme redeems the lost objectivity of conventional facts by explicating rules of grammar as forming the normative bedrock of a practice of judgment formation. On the other hand, not all of Hart's philosophy should be rejected out of hand as non- or anti-rationalist: in particular, the part of Hart's conceptual analysis we labelled a priori retains a high relevance to the disclosure of the deep structure of judging, for it respects the order between judgement and non-propositional/conceptual content that is essential to rationalism. What reverses this order, and, as a result, fails to live up to the rationalist project, is, instead, Hart's prioritisation of the empirical data his a posteriori conceptual analysis generates. It being the case that the latter do not abide by any deep rationale, it is only the power of an arbitrary convention that can explain their binding status. This move, however, only creates the appearance of normativity, for conventional facts constitute unconnected criteria that fail in their task to found knowledge.

[6] *Cf* section 4.5.

[7] *Ibid.*

Section 6.4 is devoted to the demonstration of interpetivism's anti-rationalist metaphysics. Although Dworkin's early work seems to leave room for reading the interpretivist programme in the light of the rationalist agenda, in more recent work the same author lapses towards a more robust notion of objectivity which blocks the rationalist reading. Likewise, a recent move by Nicos Stavropoulos to underpin interpretivism by an alternative semantic framework has to fail.[8] The reason is that, in rejecting Hart's conventionalism, those moves are mistaking every rationalist project as conventionalist. However, in stepping out of the practice, as an antidote to conventionalism, these moves disturb anew the order between judgement and non-conceptual or non-propositional content: the correctness of judging no longer derives from *practising a set of norms*, but stands in a (causal) relation of acquaintance with practice-independent essences.[9] No sooner is this move accomplished, however, than the idea of practice is replaced by the debilitating idea of practice-independent criteria.

Finally, the discussion offers the opportunity to address the more salient issue of the relation between, on the one hand, the normativity of content formation and, on the other, the normativity of action, one that will be exploited in the last chapter of the book. In the light of the criticism of interpretivism, it is disclosed how positivism's failure is deeper than mere failure to refer to the proper conditions/grounds of existence for legal rules (namely, to pick substantive reasons for action, as opposed to conventional criteria). Had it been only of the latter kind then a supplementation of positivism with the dimension of depth interpretivism proposes, would have sufficed for redeeming the lost normativity of law. But it does not; it does not because what is more crucial is to understand legal practice as a cognitive activity that *is capable* of delivering knowledge of the kinds of reasons law is really about. In that latter respect, positivism and interpretivism are companions in failure. This is a failure to live up to the demands of legal practice as a successful cognitive activity. It is precisely this aspect of legal practice that the last chapter will attempt to redeem, by outlining the main tenets of a fresh account of legal phenomena, which borrows the philosophical intuitions of pragmatic rationalism (Chapter 4).

6.2 Interpretivism and the Depth of Practice

The dimension of depth with respect to a cognitive practice roughly indicates the possibility of establishing a critical distance between what the participants of a

[8] I am referring to N Stavropoulos, *Objectivity in Law* (Oxford, Clarendon Press, 1996).

[9] In particular, it seems that interpretivists are trying to steer a middle way between rationalism and realism, one that is doomed to lead to inconsistency. See section 6.4.2.

practice happen to do and what the practice actually requires.[10] This distance opens the possibility of making objective judgements about what is right and wrong as a matter of the practice in question, by allowing participants to dive below the surface of the practice and discover salient standards with respect to what the practice commands. That said, the mere fact of depth does not yet settle the nature of those standards or the type of objectivity they profess. Whether, at the end of the day, objectivity fails or succeeds will depend on what kinds of things one considers to be the components of the normative bedrock of the practice. Consequently, for the idea of objectivity to be viable, depth should not violate the conditions of modest objectivity that were laid down in the opening chapters of the book. It is against those conditions that Dworkin's conception of depth needs to be measured.

In Dworkin's work depth and the related issue of objectivity are closely intertwined with what he takes to be law's interpretive nature. To put it in a nutshell, this interpretive nature is marked by two elements. The first is the existence of a distinct category of facts which have a *sui generis* ontological status in virtue of their complexity (interpretive facts).[11] Complexity, in this context, is the result of a combination of the factual aspects of some social practice (say, the practice of courtesy) and the values pertaining to that practice, those values that constitute something like the *point* of the practice, to borrow a familiar Dworkinian term.[12] Consequently, an interpretive fact (say, about the obligation of courtesy to concede one's seat to elderly people) cannot be fully located in, or analysed into, either only descriptive or only evaluative components.[13] Even though some of the facts of the practice, as well as of the values that inform it, bear on the existence of the relevant interpretive fact (obligation of courtesy) neither of them is in a position fully to determine its existence. To put it in the

[10] The availability of such distance underpins the main difference between random convergence of behaviour and meaningful practice. See J McDowell, 'Wittgenstein on Following a Rule' reprinted in A Miller and C Wright (eds), *Rule-Following and Meaning* (Chesham, Acumen, 2002) 45–80; see also the discussion in section 3.2.

[11] See R Dworkin, *Law's Empire* (London, Fontana Press, 1986) ch II; see also N Stavropoulos, 'Interpretivist Theories of Law' in *Stanford Encyclopaedia of Philosophy* (Winter October 2003 edn), available at htpp://plato.stanford.edu/archives/win2003/entries/law-interpretivist/, section 1. For complexity in the context of an interpretive account of ethics, see G Sreenivasan, 'Interpretation and Reason' (1998) 27 *Philosophy and Public Affairs* 142 (at 144).

[12] One assumption that remains undiscussed by Dworkin is that the point of a practice can be characterised independently of the facts that constitute it. This assumption is not as self-evident as Dworkin might assume, for moral theories with a more naturalistic outlook might want to argue for the possibility of reducing points (or values) to facts. What raises further concern in this context is that Dworkin has in the past evoked supervenience in order to illustrate the relation between the point of a practice and the facts that constitute it; see his 'On Gaps in the Law' in P Amselek and N MacCormick (eds), *Controversies about Law's Ontology* (Edinburgh, Edinburgh University Press, 1991) 84 *ff*. Far from failing to corroborate the degree of independence between fact and value, which Dworkin's idea of interpretive facts would require, supervenience rather represents amongst contemporary philosophers a more elegant way of expressing the reduction of values to facts.

[13] Another problem concerns values: Are they also interpretive facts? Or does Dworkin assume a naturalistic explication of value?

language of propositions: the truth of an interpretive proposition[14] is not fully determinable by either descriptive or evaluative propositions, although it may supervene[15] on both. The reason for this is that there is no mechanical formula for relating descriptive propositions to evaluative ones in a way that could establish a one-to-one correspondence between the members of the two sets of fact and value. Another way to put it is to say that descriptive and evaluative facts are *asymmetric*,[16] for it is possible that the facts of a practice support a greater number of values than those the point of the practice actually comprises, and vice versa: that the evaluative point of the practice excludes some of the latter's factual constituents.[17]

Complexity gives rise to the second element of interpretive nature, that of interpretation. Given that interpretive facts are neither readily available in the environment, nor fully determined by either the descriptive or the evaluative facts of a practice, an account of their origin is called for. Interpretivism pictures the origination of interpretive facts as an instance of construction which materialises within interpretive judgements. Judgements of this kind generate interpretive facts by undertaking a 'creative' projection of the evaluative point of the relevant practice onto its factual constituents. Along these lines, an interpretive judgement which states what the law requires in a particular case undertakes an interpretation of the institutional facts of the relevant practice (be they political, legislative or adjudicative) in the light of the evaluative point of the practice. In addition, interpretations must satisfy the two criteria of fit and justification.[18] Fit

[14] 'Any proposition would count as interpretive that states principles which are not part of formally instituted legal norms; for instance, the proposition 'no one should profit form one's own wrong' in *Riggs v Palmer*, see R Dworkin, *Taking Rights Seriously* (London, Duckwoth, 1977) ch 2 (at 23).

[15] For the notion of supervenience see F Jackson, *From Metaphysics to Ethics* (Oxford, Clarendon Press, 1998); J Kim, *Supervenience and Mind: Selected Philosophical Essays* (Cambridge, Cambridge University Press, 1993); E E Savellos and Ü D Yalçin (eds), *Supervenience: New Essays* (Cambridge, Cambridge University Press, 1995); in moral philosophy see R M Hare, *The Language of Morals* (Oxford, Clarendon Press, 1952) 80 *ff* and 153 *ff*; *idem*, *Freedom and Reason* (Oxford, Clarendon Press, 1962) 19 *ff*;. Dworkin uses the concept of supervenience in his paper 'On Gaps in the Law', above n 12.

[16] In the context of the contemporary debate on moral particularism, asymmetry is often captured through the phenomenon of *supersession*: any norm that is stated in general language is superseded by an infinite number of new circumstances that escape the normative field of the norm. For a succinct discussion see G Pavlakos, 'Two Conceptions of Universalisation' in Z Bankowski and J MacLean (eds), *The Universal and the Particular in Legal Reasoning* (Aldershot, Ashgate, 2006).

[17] It is important to notice that Dworkin's theory attempts to rule out an explication of interpretative facts as sums of pre-existing parts. On such a reading an interpretive fact rests on a more basic layer of descriptive facts about a legal community which needs to be purged from all irrelevant facts through interpretation. For Dworkin the existence of an interpretive fact is not gradual: it does not exist before its construction through interpretation and anything else that pre-existed it is significant only as a raw datum for the interpretation, but not as self-standing component of the forthcoming interpretive fact. To use an example: we cannot say that a legal obligation X (say to act as good faith requires) can be broken down to distinctive parts, some of them being facts about legislation, others about adjudication, or even about the value of promises. Obligation X exists only after the interpretation has taken place.

[18] See Dworkin, *Law's Empire*, above n 11, 65–68.

refers to the requirement that any interpretation cohere with the institutional pedigree of the practice in question, to the effect that it still constitutes an interpretation of that practice as opposed to any other. Justification, on the other hand, purports to capture the evaluative dimension of the practice. An interpretation will be adequately justified only if it amounts to the morally best reconstruction of the factual components of the practice in the light of the values the practice serves.

What confers its moral quality on an interpretation is a rather obscure matter in Dworkin's theory. Although this is supposed to be judged against the values that together comprise the point of the practice, Dworkin seems to postulate an extra modicum of moral correctness that springs from a standpoint more universal in scope. The latter requires that the interpreter transcend the boundaries of the local values of the practice and refer to a set of moral values or ideals which enjoy a context-independent or universal status.[19] This is, for instance, the case when judges dealing with a hard case need to 'import' into the legal system principles which did not form part of the corpus of legal knowledge up to now.[20] Such principles often are taken to express the content of values that are independent of particular social practices, claiming a validity that is universal in scope. Finally, interpretive judgements do not occur in isolation but usually form part of a wider web of judgements, each of which depicts a distinct interpretative fact that illustrates a different aspect of the overall practice (and, in this manner, enables us to reconstruct the practice as a whole). Consequently, it makes sense to talk of interpretive theories or theory (henceforth, IT) instead of isolated judgements.[21]

With the main parameters of interpretivism in position, it is time to enquire in a more sustained manner about the claims of objectivity IT raises. The topic of objectivity is vast and any attempt to survey the relevant philosophical discussion would, of course, exceed the limits of this chapter.[22] A simple way to capture the

[19] See below n 23.

[20] See the principles stated in *Riggs v Palmer*, above n 14; or in *Donoghue v Stevenson* (discussed in N MacCormick, *Legal Reasoning and Legal Theory* (Oxford, Clarendon Press, 1978)); or the use of the Radbruch formula in several post-war judgments of German courts dealing with issues of legality of provisions passed under national-socialism (discussed in R Alexy, *The Argument from Injustice: A Reply to Legal Positivism*, S L Paulson and B Litschewski Paulson (trans) (Oxford, Clarendon Press, 2002)).

[21] Dworkin argues that the theoretical character of IT derives from the type of disagreement that pertains to interpretive concepts (see *Law's Empire*, above n 11, 4–5). Along these lines, the main feature of theoretical disagreement, and one that distinguishes it from its opposite, empirical disagreement, is that it cannot be settled by reference to empirical facts only, but instead, requires reference to evaluations. The distinction is somewhat arbitrary, for a lot of philosophers would nowadays argue that disagreement about empirical concepts in science requires as much reference to evaluations (hence, is theoretical in Dworkin's sense). It seems more coherent to say that the theoretical character of IT derives from its forming a network of judgements which demarcates a domain of knowledge and raises claims to consistency and coherence.

[22] For a discussion of objectivity, *cf* Chapter 1. For more detailed accounts, see R Nozick, *Invariances* (Cambridge Mass, Harvard University Press, 2001); and in the domain of law, see the seminal work of N Stavropoulos, *Objectivity in Law*, above n 8; also his more recent paper

central intuition behind objectivity is to make room for a gap between what we think to be the case and what actually is the case. This gap is supposed to take into account the finiteness and imperfection of our cognitive capacities which make it possible that, although most of the time we do get things right, there are cases in which we fail to do so. The likelihood of error suggests the existence of objective standards which inform the content of our mental states and allow us to ascribe error to or affirm the truth of what we (or others) think and say. Insofar as those standards determine the correctness not only of our mental states but also of the language we use and the thoughts we think, the issue of objectivity seems to touch upon more than one domain: our mental lives, perceptive powers, the language we use, the external world, as well as the relations between and among all of the above. It is not out of place, therefore, to employ the vocabulary of *propositions* as a means of capturing the complexity of the demands of objectivity.[23]

Speaking generally, propositions are the 'objective' counterparts of sentences that enable communication between speakers independently of the subjective features of speakers' utterances (such features include the particular language an utterance is made in). Given the function they fulfil, propositions are equipped with a hybrid nature that places them at the interface of language, mind and world. Leaving out a lot of detail, one of the most controversial issues regarding propositions concerns their individuation—or their existence. Contested as it may be, the issue of individuation is crucial as regards the degree and the foundations of objectivity a philosophical theory aspires to. As regards this matter, philosophical theories are traditionally classified in two large groups: on the one hand we have those theories that are *realist in nature*: here criteria of individuation are fully located outside our practices of communication. The attractiveness of such a strong degree of objectivity notwithstanding, realist philosophies are vulnerable to sceptical arguments that call into question our ability to acquire the degree of certainty that realism requires. On the other hand there are theories, call them in contradistinction *non-realist*, which suggest that propositions with respect to any domain be individuated intra-linguistically, that is, within the structures of sentences and the communicative practices of a linguistic community. Although such theories lack the objectivist force of the

'Objectivity' in M Golding and W Edmundson (eds), *The Blackwell Guide to the Philosophy of Law and Legal Theory* (Oxford, Blackwell, 2005) 315–23. See also my discussion of objectivity with respect to legal knowledge in my 'Normative Knowledge and the Nature of Law' in S Coyle and G Pavlakos (eds), *Jurisprudence or Legal Science?* (Oxford and Portland, Hart Publishing, 2005) 89–125.

[23] I should guard against a possible misunderstanding that was drawn to my attention by Carsten Heidemann: Talk of propositions usually evokes the suspicion of Platonism (ie the view that there is a realm comprising entities that are simultaneously non-physical and mind-independent). However, for the suspicion of Platonism to be substantiated propositions need to be combined with a strong objectivist theory like the one I ascribe to Dworkin in this chapter. Conversely, if propositions are made entirely dependent upon linguistic usage, as I believe they are within a rationalist programme, they are disarmed of their 'explosive' metaphysical load and may serve as useful means for addressing the complex nature of objectivity as suggested above. See section 1.2.

realist ones, they may well turn out to be far more enduring against sceptical attacks, for they depart from modest claims that are more difficult to undermine.

Against the canvas of those remarks, it is possible to distinguish between two alternative understandings of IT as regards grounds of individuation for legal propositions (hence, the disposition of the bedrock of legal practice).[24] In advancing those understandings one should bear in mind that interpretivist grounds of individuation ultimately rest on the (moral) values which shape the point of any legal practice. Thus, any understanding of the grounds of individuation is linked to an attempt to specify the nature of those values.[25] The importance of this point can hardly be overstated, for Dworkin takes such values to exist independently of the interpretative practice of any particular community,[26] despite the constitutive role they play as regards interpretive accounts of law. Consequently, an explication of their character is essential for specifying the type and degree of objectivity advocated by interpretivism, as well as its compatibility with the condition of intelligibility imposed by the idea of a grammar of cognition.

The first understanding, the weaker of the two, argues that grounds of individuation are determined internally to some[27] practice the members of a legal community engage in, pretty much along the lines proponents of philosophical

[24] Two seemingly appealing answers to the problem of individuation need to be summarily rebutted here: it will not help to tackle individuation through either interpretive facts or claims of fit and justification. Instead of determining the issue of individuation, these items depend themselves on a prior settlement of it. The answer to what is an interpretive fact can turn out in a number of ways, depending on how we identify the grounds of legal propositions. The same applies to fit and justification. Which interpretation strikes the right balance between fit with past instances, on the one hand, and justification within the scheme of principle of a practice, on the other, presupposes that we have an answer with respect to the issue of individuation. It follows that an explanation of the issue of individuation of interpretive propositions which rests on either interpretive facts or claims of fit and justification will be circular.

[25] Even if one argues that such values are not the only individuating grounds, the problem still persists: owing to their centrality in Dworkin's account, the interpretivist needs to offer a plausible explanation of their nature.

[26] In *Law's Empire*, above n 11, 424–25, Dworkin argues that conceptions of justice transcend the boundaries of particular social practices and can serve as the basis for criticising other peoples' practices of justice; elsewhere he states that justice has a latent global reach which exempts it from having to fit the practice of any particular community, see *Law's Empire*, 425 and 'What Justice Isn't' in R Dworkin, *A Matter of Principle* (Oxford, Clarendon Press, 1986) 214–20 (at 219); also the exchange between Dworkin and Walzer through the pages of the *New York Review of Books* (*NYRB*, 14 April 1983) where Dworkin rejects Walzer's suggestion that justice be explained along the lines of an interpretive account. On these points see also the discussion in G Sreenivasan, 'Interpretation and Reason' (1998) 27 *Philosophy and Public Affairs* 142, who attempts to extend the interpretive account to moral and ethical concepts.

[27] I say 'some' because Dworkin seems prima facie to reject the dependence of moral values on any communal practice, although he still wants to conceive of moral concepts as interpretive (above n 23). Clearly it is not possible to have interpretive concepts without any practice of interpretation, and to that extent Dworkin's strategy of postulating practice-independent values, which he insists are interpretive, is incoherent. In order to relax the tension between the two statements, one really has to choose between a strong realist conception of values and a weaker rationalist explication thereof. This chapter has set out to outline the conditions of the rationalist explication while showing that Dworkin's own theory follows rather the route of moral realism. The next chapter outlines the

rationalism subscribe to. Rationalism can, for present purposes, be summed up by the idea that knowledge of any domain depends on a conceptual scheme which underwrites our cognitive practices and determines the correctness of the judgements which are advanced within the practice.[28] What is of key importance as regards this tenet, is that the practice is not exhausted by any random moves (and utterances) of the participants but possesses a deeper rationale which normatively constrains the practice. This idea, far from being hostile to a semantic explication of (legal) content, relies on it, for it assumes that every cognitive practice is a practice of judging which is linguistically structured. In that respect, semantic analysis, instead of obscuring the rationale of cognition, constitutes the means for gaining access to it. The interdependence between practice and language requires that, in order to arrive at an understanding of the deep rationale of the practice, one stay within the practice and engage in sustained inquiry beneath its surface, into the conditions of judging. When measured against this conception of objectivity, Hart's method of conceptual analysis appears merely insufficient as opposed to wrongheaded, for despite having identified a correct diagnosis of the problem of legal content, it fails to implement it: instead of accounting for the salient norms at the bedrock of legal practice, it ends up picking a class of normatively inert behavioural facts which are situated at the surface of the practice. It turns out, then, that if the rationalist explication were compatible with Dworkin's idea of objectivity, it would merely bring Dworkin only a step ahead of Hart, rather than cancelling altogether Hart's intuitions.

Contrapositively, the second, the strong explication of objectivity, argues that IT needs to discover some set of moral values which transcend the practices of particular (legal) communities and form the ultimate test for the truth of legal propositions. In this case, and despite the fact that legal propositions are considered to rest on additional considerations of fit, moral values play the decisive role, for it is they that carry the full burden of justification. The idea of objectivity implied in this context is a strong one and requires commitment to some version of moral realism or, roughly put, the view that there exist evaluative entities in the environment which are causally efficacious, having the capacity to render our evaluative sentences true.[29] In effect, interpretive practices with respect to law, are reduced to simple heuristic devices, given that what matters are the practice-independent (or -transcendent) moral values which perform a full justification of legal propositions. Dworkin's preference for a strong conception

conditions of a universal practice of content formation as one that underpins the idea of a grammar of cognition, thus fleshing out the rationalist conception of objectivity and content formation.

[28] For a reliable summary of rationalist programmes with respect to meaning and conceptual content, see T Burge, 'Frege on Sense and Linguistic Meaning' reprinted in *idem, Truth, Thought Reason: Essays on Frege* (Oxford, Clarendon Press, 2005) 242–69; in the same vein, see S Schiffer, *The Things We Mean* (Oxford, Clarendon Press, 2003) especially chs 1 and 2.

[29] For a reliable overview of contemporary moral realism, see R Shafer-Landau, *Moral Realism* (Oxford, Clarendon Press, 2003).

of objectivity is suggested by his attacks on Hart's semantic account of law. In rejecting the semantic account of legal content, Dworkin parts with the view that what matters for conceptual content is the deep structure of a practice of judging (with respect to law) and, in its place, substitutes the position that content is causally determined by an (evaluative) reality which exists independently of any cognitive practice. This view reverses the priority of judgement over non-propositional/non-conceptual content for it contemplates the possibility of entities which may exist beyond our ability to think of them. Such elusive items, however, far from offering a strong ground of objectivity, against which the correctness of our thoughts is to be measured, open up the possibility of radical scepticism along the lines explained in earlier chapters.[30] Thus, to the extent that interpretivism subscribes to a strong understanding of objectivity, it parts with Hart's rationalist intuitions and runs the danger of falling short of satisfying the condition of intelligibility grammar imposes on our cognitive practices.[31]

Next, I turn to explore in more depth the two possible understandings of the objectivity involved in interpretivist propositions.

6.3 Rationalist Objectivity

Is it possible to explicate interpretivism in a manner that would make it compatible with the philosophy of pragmatic rationalism, as this was put forward in Chapter 4? This would require that interpretivism share the notion of objectivity pragmatic rationalism solicits. In a nutshell, this idea of objectivity makes truth (and, as a result, knowledge) dependent on a practice of cognition, for there is no such thing as a pure or unadulterated reality, which could render our thoughts true by impinging upon our minds in some immediate or direct sense.[32] As much as the centrality of practice goes, the two theories seem to be in agreement at least with respect to the vocabulary they employ. This is partly the result of the widespread influence of the so-called pragmatic turn in philosophy, which was initiated by the later work of Wittgenstein and furnished later by a line of philosophers who drew upon the rich tradition of American pragmatism.[33] But rationalism, as argued earlier, goes a step further: lest pragmatism deteriorate into mind-world dualism and scepticism, rationalism requires that the grounds (or reasons), which lead to the truth of propositions, remain at all times practice-immanent. At the same time, it postulates a rich notion of criteria by declaring that those amount to more than just the mere fact of acceptance on

[30] See Chapters 1 and 2.

[31] *Cf* Wittgenstein's slogan in section 1.4.

[32] These are the lines along which Chapters 1 and 2 have argued.

[33] For an excellent discussion of the tradition of pragmatism and its impact on the analytical philosophy of language, see H Putnam, *Words and Life*, J Conant (ed) (Cambridge Mass, Harvard University Press), part III (151 *ff*). Putnam is, of course, himself the foremost example of a philosopher working in both traditions.

behalf of those who partake of a cognitive practice (a requirement that was summarised as ratification-independence). We may say that those two conditions, practice-immanence and ratification-independence, are the core features of rationalism. They capture the rationalist intuition about standards of knowledge such that, in arising within a conceptual scheme, to which we can have access via our thinking, they can claim objectivity. Although interpretivism seems to be in line with the condition of ratification-independence there is less there to ascertain that it sits well with the requirement of practice-immanence. The issue ramifies, for if one rejects the component of practice-immanence, then ratification-independence as regards grounds for knowledge is also deeply affected; indeed, so much so that it threatens with a collapse of certainty and knowledge and a new exposure to scepticism and its undesirable consequences. Conversely, it is the powerful combination of ratification-independence and practice-immanence that offers rationalism its anti-sceptical and objectivist stance.[34]

In light of this combination, rationalism can, on the one hand, explain cognitive practices as having a foundation that is salient to understanding concepts, which is deeper than what contingently happens to be the behaviour of the participants of the practice. Transcribed into the vocabulary of the linguistic turn, this thesis amounts to the claim that the foundation of cognition lies deeper than the conventions of a linguistic community. The key idea is, here, that mastery of concepts is a normative operation, which obeys to standards that are not immediately or directly available to participants. Such standards were shown to comprise the rules of a grammar that regulate the structure of sentences as well as the inferential relations that hold between them. In that respect the idea of ratification-independence, pertinent to rationalism, is linked to the grammatical structure of the activity of judging. As a result of this move, sentences, rather than isolated concepts or predicates, need to be placed at the centre of our activity of judging.[35] On the other hand, rationalism demonstrates mastery of the deeper rationale of the practice as enabling an insight into ontology. Thus, it is through the rationale or the structure of judging we 'come to know' what kinds of objects there are: the more we grasp the conceptual conditions (grammar) of judging, the more we understand the structure of the environment and the clearer a view we gain of the objects and properties that put it together. Here, the priority of practice renders all standards of cognition practice-immanent. When combined with the condition of a deep structure of judging, one that remains ratification-independent, practice-immanence underpins a powerful conception of knowledge which proves particularly enduring against sceptical attacks.

Well before turning to the idea of interpretation, Dworkin had proposed an account of constraints of legal practice which seemed to echo a great deal of the

[34] Of course rationalism should further be supplemented by pragmatism; however the latter, as noted, is not contested by interpretivism.

[35] See, for a detailed discussion of the grammar of judging, Chapter 2.

rationalist idea of practice-immanence. His proposal relates to an early passage of *Taking Rights Seriously* dealing with two philosophical models (natural and constructivist) as possible candidates for interpreting Rawls' reflective equilibrium. In arguing for the advantages of the constructivist model, he points out the following characteristics[36]: (a) *Theory dependence*: the constructivist model understands principles of political morality as being dependent on judgements that arise in the context of a theory which departs from existing moral convictions that enjoy a high degree of plausibility, as opposed to arising from observations of a robust moral reality; (b) *Truth-minimalism*: what makes theoretical judgements true is their ability to cohere with the overall body of judgements of the theory. Thus, the question whether there actually exist moral properties, which function as truth-makers for our judgements, loses its edge. Even if such properties existed, their degree of importance would be low from the point of view of the constructive model, for what matters for truth is coherence between judgements rather than correspondence with something in the environment; (c) *Practice-dependence*: in putting the emphasis on theoretical judgements, constructivism departs from a strong individualistic model which focusses on the perceptual input of individuals, and moves on to a public model which takes judgement construction to be a collective exercise; (d) *Falsifiability*: no judgement is final but needs to be asserted within the theory. As the theory evolves, with new judgements joining it and others being revised or even discarded, no judgement remains impervious. The deep reason for this is the irrelevance of any perceptual hard evidence about a moral reality and, instead, the importance of the connections between the various judgements of the theory.

Those requirements come as close as it gets to the conception of objectivity and knowledge which is to be found in the philosophy of pragmatic rationalism, and the conception of constraints of practice the latter solicits.[37] To redeem those requirements we need to think of legal practice as a cognitive activity with a deep structure, on whose basis we can depict grounds for propositions of law. Dworkin never managed to further develop his early insights in order to flesh out an adequate notion of structure, which would allow depicting grounds in a manner compatible with rationalist knowledge. In the last chapter of the book I shall put forward such an account which contrasts itself strongly with the Dworkinian account in that it takes constraints of legal practice to spring out from the practice itself. While Dworkin takes the grounds of legal propositions to be values that are conceptually prior to legal practice, the proposed account takes those grounds to fall within the domain of legal practice itself. Most notably, I shall argue that what renders true propositions of law are legal norms. What explains the existence of legal norms is a semantic conception of the norm, which

[36] *Taking Rights Seriously*, above n 14, 160–68.

[37] *Cf* the conditions the constraints have to meet in section 4.2.2. Those comprise: independent identifiability; direct readability; and fallibility; *cf* P Pettit, *The Common Mind: An Essay in Psychology, Society and Politics* (Oxford, Oxford University Press, 1993) 82–83.

understands norms in the framework of true normative sentences along the lines of the semantic exhausts ontology thesis.[38] The semantic conception of the norm will, therefore, become the centrepiece of an account of law that abides by the main lines of pragmatic rationalism.

Next I shall show how, despite early adherence to a constructivist model of ethics, Dworkin's criticisms of legal conventionalism led him to abandon the rationalist spirit involved in his early constructive account and, instead, to embrace a stronger conception of objectivity, one that involves an essentialist understanding of the values which constitute the grounds of legal propositions. This inability can, to a great extent, be attributed to Dworkin's devotion to the dualistic framework of referential realism, in other words the idea that true propositions must refer to something outside themselves. Plausible as it may sound, this idea becomes harmful when it assumes further that there is already a reality, which is structured in objects, properties and events which impinge upon our thoughts, making them true. But this is absurd, because all ontological categories are intrinsically connected with our conceptual scheme and only make sense in the light of the connections between sentences when we employ language as a condition for regarding something as an object (property, and so on).[39] Conversely, the assumption that permeates pragmatic rationalism is that objects are constituted in judgements within a practice of predicating properties of things, a practice that is subject to constraints but which cannot reach outside of itself.

6.4 Anti-rationalism and the Rejection of Grammar

Dworkin's departure from rationalism may be illustrated in two steps: first, the rejection of conventionalism as the quintessentially semantic account of legal content; secondly, the adherence to a model of strong objectivity which presupposes an essentialist account of value.

6.4.1 Rejection of Conventionalism

In taking issue with conventionalist accounts of law, Dworkin assumes that every practice-immanent explication of objectivity is weak and will amount to a

[38] A possible objection to this scheme could be that if legal sentences depict their truth-makers, then all sentences will be automatically true. Well, more or less, this is true, for most of the times we get things right (or at least this is the whole point of pragmatic rationalism). But then there are some higher-order constraints which still allow for error: these are the a priori constraints of grammar, as well as a postulate of coherence between true sentences that arises form the semantic account of truth. As regards the domain of practical reason, there is one additional constraint arising from the substantive notion of autonomy, which springs from the universalisation of practical reasons; this commands, roughly, that all judging subjects as ends-in-themselves. See section 4.4.

[39] *Cf* Chapters 1 and 2.

shallow understanding of legal practice, one that focusses on behavioural facts, thus missing out the normative dimension of legal phenomena. What is less obvious is his belief that every semantic account of legal content must with necessity lead to this debilitating conception of objectivity.

Dworkin takes weak understandings of objectivity to suggest that the grounds of legal propositions be specified internally to the practice of a legal community. This means, roughly, that in order to meet the requirements of fit and justification an interpretive judgement would have to undertake a reconstruction of the evaluative point of a practice through reference to existing, past and present, instances of that practice and not some item that is characterisable independently of the practice. Reconstruction of those instances amounts to stating criteria derivable from the behaviour of the participants of the practice, which are deemed relevant to the individuation of legal propositions. Under Dworkin's influential reading, Hart's analytical jurisprudence has come to be regarded as a paradigm case of this type of analysis. Dworkin's reading of Hartian positivism adds a semantic flavour to it which purports to capture the post-linguistic-turn spirit of Hart's method of analysis. Thus, instead of being concerned about just any practice-dependent criteria of individuation, Hart is alleged to be interested in semantic criteria (hence the characterisation of Hart's theory as semantic).[40] In this case what individuates propositions of law are criteria for the use of legal expressions which are made explicit through a systematic analysis of the linguistic behaviour of the community in question.[41] Through observation of a particular practice the legal theorist can infer 'implicit' rules that determine the use of legal language and specify a number of criteria which may be grouped together into a master definition of the concept 'law' (what Hart calls the rule of recognition of a system). Subsequently, this definition functions as a litmus test for the existence of a proposition of law and the meaningfulness of the sentence it is expressed in. In addition, any violation of the putative criteria by any of the members of the community is to be treated as an instance of misunderstanding rather than an act of meaningful disagreement. Anyone who fails to act upon them will be assumed to have misapprehended the criteria and would have to re-explain their content. On the face of it, by specifying the extension of the concept 'law', semantic analysis undertakes the seminal task of illustrating the kind of phenomenon law is, and demarcating it from other related normative phenomena (ethics, morality and so on).

Famously, Dworkin has criticised these views by putting forward the argument from the *semantic sting* which attacks a conception of legal meaning based on semantic criteria specified by a rule of recognition.[42] What is more, owing to his

[40] See Dworkin, *Law's Empire*, above n 11, chs 1 and 2. Dworkin's claim has been further explored in Stavropoulos' highly incisive 'Hart's Semantics' in J Coleman, *Hart's Postscript: Essays on the Postscript of the Concept of Law* (Oxford, Oxford University Press, 2001) 59–98.

[41] Stavropoulos, above n 40, 69–79.

[42] See Chapter 5.

framing it in semantic terms, the argument has been directed not merely at Hart's theory but, also, at any other semantic account of legal content. Consequently, to the extent that rationalist accounts of legal content tend to be *semantic* in character, the semantic sting seems to leave little space for them.

6.4.1.1 Essentialism

Having rejected conventionalism Dworkin turns, in more recent writings,[43] to offer a strong reading of the dimension of depth of legal practice, one that departs decisively from the practice-immanent logic of the rationalist model and adheres to practice-independent grounds of legal propositions. This account is underpinned by a realist or essentialist theory of value which is in a position to cash in Dworkin's conception of values as practice-independent grounds of legal propositions. There is one more reason to support such a reading: Dworkin's famous allusion to a superhuman judge (judge 'Hercules') who, by relying on his immense intellectual capacities and his thorough knowledge of the law, can give the right answer to every legal problem posed to him. How else, if not by assuming access to a privileged realm of value, one that is not contaminated by the actual practice of a community, could Dworkin make this metaphor work? Although essentialism as regards value is a far more nuanced position than I could ever accommodate in this chapter, two distinct versions of it may be distinguished for present purposes.[44]

In its purest form essentialism in ethics is associated with the philosophy of G E Moore who argued that evaluative concepts are unanalysable because they refer to basic moral universals that can be perceived through intuition. Intuitionism, as Moore's theory came to be known, has been attacked in many occasions for its metaphysical extravagance, the most distinctive attack being the one by John Mackie who famously accused Moore's metaphysics of being queer.[45] Although Dworkin's account does not, outright, rule out an intuitionist explication of values, this path will not be pursued further in this book, for the metaphysical extravagance intuitionism entails would fly in the face of Dworkin's general anti-metaphysical stance.[46] A less rampant formulation of the essentialist view is one adopted by Stavropoulos in his *Objectivity in Law*.[47] Although he too subscribes to the idea of evaluative essences, Stavropoulos adheres to a more contemporary form of essentialism which is compatible with semantic analysis.[48]

[43] See especially R Dworkin, 'Objectivity and Truth: You'd Better Believe it' (1996) 25 *Philosophy and Public Affairs* 87; and his more recent, 'Hart's Postscript and the Character of Political Philosophy' (2004) 24 *Oxford Journal of Legal Studies* 1.

[44] See, for a review of different essentialist strategies, Shafer-Landau, above n 29.

[45] See G E Moore, *Principia Ethica*, revised edn (Cambridge, Cambridge University Press, 1993); and J Mackie, *Ethics: Inventing Right and Wrong* (Hamondsworth, Penguin Press, 1977).

[46] For these metaphysical extravagances see Mackie, above n 45, 30–42; and G Oddie, *Value, Reality and Desire* (Oxford, Clarendon Press, 2005) ch 6; also Shafer-Landau, above n 29, chs 1 and 2.

[47] Stavropoulos, above n 8.

[48] *Ibid* ch 2.

Owing to its ability to steer clear of metaphysical extravagances, the semantic version of essentialism will be assumed to capture the content of Dworkin's essentialist explication of objectivity in an ideal way.[49]

Dworkin's criticisms of conventionalism range over conceptions of objectivity which exhaust themselves in criteria that are immanent to legal practice. Conversely, the argument from the semantic sting shows that the source of objectivity regarding legal judgements must extend beyond the practice of any legal community. In particular, the argument from the semantic sting must be understood as arguing that, unless one exempts from the grinding mill of interpretive practice, those values Dworkin takes to constitute the grounds of legal propositions,[50] one will fail to explain communication between lawyers. For, even though Dworkin rejects semantic criteria, the idea of meaningful disagreement still requires that some amount of agreement prevail between disagreeing parties.[51] Such agreement, however, cannot rest on semantic criteria but, instead, needs to hook up directly on the essence of some practice-independent values, as opposed to any semantic criteria of a linguistic nature. What strong objectivity requires, in other words, is agreement in essence (ie the essence of those values that constitute the grounds of legal propositions).[52]

Agreement in essence presupposes that it be possible to settle semantic issues, including those of agreement and disagreement, by linking up legal language with law's essential characteristics, those that are assumed to be non-linguistic, hence independent of the practice of communication. This possibility becomes available only if the bearers of legal meaning, ie propositions of law, are individuated through direct reference to law's extra-linguistic nature. A theoretical model that allows for individuation along these lines can be traced back to recent work in the philosophy of mind and language.[53] In the late 1970s and early 1980s, a group of philosophers, in particular Hilary Putnam and Saul Kripke, forcefully argued that the meanings of our words are 'not in our heads' but in the

[49] What is more, Dworkin himself seems to subscribe to the philosophical subtlety of Stavropoulos' explication. See *idem* 'Objectivity and Truth: You'd Better Believe it', above n 43; and 'Hart's Postscript and the Character of Political Philosophy', above n 43.

[50] See above n 23.

[51] See Dworkin's discussion of agreement as regards the so-called pre-interpretive stage in Dworkin, *Law's Empire*, above n 11, 46–49 and 65–68; also the discussion in Kress, 'The Interpretive Turn' (1987) 97 *Ethics* 834 (at 854–56).

[52] Kress (*ibid*) has suggested this option as a version of semantic theory that escapes Dworkin's attack on criterial theories and, also, resolves some of the problems that relate to Dworkin's explanation of a necessary amount of agreement through reference to the pre-interpretive stage. I shall assume, henceforth, that this kind of essentialist semantics, which Kress suggested in 1987 as a middle solution, was taken up later by Stavropoulos and made an integral part of Dworkinian interpretivism (Stavropoulos, *Objectivity in Law*, above n 8). A question lingers as to whether this kind of essentialist semantics really differs from the (merely verbally) more robust version of moral essentialism endorsed by Michael Moore (*cf* his *Educating Oneself in Public* (Oxford, Oxford University Press, 2000)). To the extent it does not my criticism applies to both.

[53] One may even speak here of a semantic theory, albeit one of a very different kind than those we have been discussing so far. This shows that Dworkin's real target are not semantic theories *tout court*, but only a particular kind thereof: those resting on criteria that are internal to a linguistic practice.

environment. Their argument was chiefly directed against internalist theories of meaning, then dominant in the philosophical landscape. Those theories took concepts to refer to whatever was stipulated by appropriate definitions that contained necessary and sufficient conditions and could be arrived at independently of the environment. It is not difficult to see some form of radical scepticism associated with such an idea: should meaning be rooted in speakers' heads, one would end up believing in the existence of a well-defined conceptual universe that has no relevance whatsoever with the actual environment.[54] Putnam and Kripke set out to undermine this particular understanding of meaning by demonstrating that the meaning of natural kind and name concepts is causally determined by the actual properties of the entities referred to, rather than any properties of our mental states.[55] On the face of it, the importance allocated to the *intension* (conventions of use or definitions) and the *extension* (actual referents) of (natural kind) concepts is being reversed: conventions and definitions are rendered subordinate to actual referents. Moreover, conventions and definitions may retain their value as guidelines for speakers only to the extent that they remain open to revision in the light of new (empirical) discoveries vis-à-vis the environment. Thus, our language and the ways we employ it ceases to be constitutive in our understanding of the environment and instead the latter becomes the measure for a successful employment of language that leads to communication. This new explication of meaning makes it possible for a speaker correctly to employ a concept (say 'water') without having a complete understanding of the conventions or the definitions that determine its use within a linguistic community, for stability in communication relies on the properties of the actual referent (the fact that it is H_2O) rather than any facts about the linguistic practice.

This notion of a standard of meaning that lies outside our practices opens up a gap between the practice and its referent, a gap that makes room for the

[54] This should be the case if the meaning of, say, 'water' should be determined by a linguistic convention as opposed to the actual stuff it refers to (H_2O). This is not an extravagant thought: just think of speakers in classical Athens using 'water' without knowing much about its actual chemical composition. In their case it would be very easy to confuse water with some other stuff that superficially resembles it.

[55] Roughly speaking, Putnam's argument runs as follows: suppose there are two parallel universes: Earth and Twin-Earth. Two-thirds of Earth's surface is covered by some colourless and odourless liquid stuff whose chemical composition is H_2O. Equally, Twin-Earth is covered for two-thirds of its surface by some superficially identical stuff, whose chemical composition is XYZ. Now the inhabitants of earth use 'water' to depict H_2O whereas the inhabitants of Twin-Earth use 'water' to depict XYZ. Suppose also that both groups of speakers refer to the same definition or conventional rule when they use 'water' (that is, there is an identity of *intension*). Be that as it may, 'water' as employed by Earthians has a different reference (or *extension*) than 'water' as employed by Twin-Earthians. It follows that the difference in extension must cause some difference in meaning. Hence 'water' has a different meaning in each case, one that is determined by the actual stuff the concept depicts. See Hilary Putnam, 'The Meaning of "Meaning"' in *idem, Mind, Language and Reality* (Cambridge, Cambridge University Press 1975) 215–71 and his more concise 'Meaning and Reference' reprinted in A W Moore (ed), *Meaning and Reference* (Oxford, Oxford University Press 1993) 150–61.

possibility of error and, hence, the idea of objectivity. Objectivity is intertwined with the possibility that we might be wrong in our understanding of the world precisely because the world may actually be different than what we take it to be. To put it in a different way, what determines how the world is, is the world itself rather than our linguistic practices.

It is not difficult to see why moral and legal philosophers were mesmerised by those ideas.[56] Considering that problems of scepticism and relativism are much more intense in the domain of evaluative (moral, legal or ethical) language, these philosophers were very happy to be given a new theory that set meaning free from conventions and definitions, the latter two being particularly prone in substantiating the suspicion of relativism. In contrast, the new theory would allow an explication of normative meaning as depending on the actual properties of normative (moral, ethical or legal) kinds, properties that exist independently of a community's linguistic practices and the conventions they give rise to.

Tempting as the analogy with natural and name kinds may sound, it is in fact unworkable, the main reason concerning the different nature of the kinds depicted in each case. Normative kinds (rights, contracts, norms and so on) lack the essential underlying microstructural property[57] of natural kinds that allowed Putnam and Kripke to develop their theory of meaning.[58] The microstructural property of natural kinds (which, incidentally, can be discovered by science) is responsible for causally determining meaning from the outside, ie independently of any convention or definition and irrespective of our knowledge of the microstructural property itself. This is not the case with normative kinds. Unless one postulates something like an *underlying microstructural property* for normative kinds, the option of causal determination of normative meaning from the outside is not available. In other words, there is nothing in the environment that is essentially normative and is capable of causally determining the reference of our normative expressions irrespective of our knowledge of it. Be that as it may, Dworkin's theory (and other similar theories from the field of moral philosophy) seems to rely on such a microstructure and to look for entities of the appropriate kind. To that extent, and despite declaring the opposite, Dworkin sets out to discover *sui generis* or, to echo Mackie, *queer* evaluative particles[59] that (causally?)

[56] The way to such work in the area of normative philosophy was paved by the writings of Tyler Burge who developed a sophisticated externalist theory of meaning for concepts that denote 'social' and 'artefact' kinds (eg 'arthritis' and 'sofa' respectively). See Tyler Burge, 'Intellectual Norms and the Foundations of Mind' (1986) 83 *Journal of Philosophy* 697. And for an explicit reliance on Burge's work see Stavropoulos, *Objectivity in Law*, above n 8, especially chs 2 and 6.

[57] The term connotes the fact that such kinds exist *qua* the elementary particles of matter (atoms and electrons).

[58] Similar criticism has been developed with respect to Tyler Burge's externalist theory of meaning for artefact kind concepts. See the recent discussions of Jessica Brown, 'Critical Reasoning, Understanding and Self-Knowledge' (2000) LXI *Philosophy and Phenomenological Research* 659; Åsa Maria Wikforss, 'Externalism and Incomplete Understanding' (2004) 54 *Philosophical Quarterly* 287.

[59] In the twentieth century, the first to postulate such entities was the Cambridge philosopher G E Moore, who argued that evaluative concepts are unanalysable because they refer to basic moral

determine the meaning of legal expressions.[60] How these properties are individuated and by what means we access them cognitively, must remain a mystery.[61] As a result, essentialism requires that there exist a causally efficacious reality which is independent of any judgements we form in the context of our cognitive practices. This requirement renders interpretivism radically incompatible with the (rationalist) idea of a deep rationale which lies at the bedrock of any cognitive practice, and can be disclosed through careful reflection on the conditions of the practice. While both accounts allow for objective grounds which lie beyond the ephemeral behaviour of the participants of the practice, essentialism locates them outside the practice altogether, while rationalism argues that such grounds must be always accessible from within the practice (adding that grasping them might involve a great deal more than a mere description of the participants' behaviour).[62]

What is more, the essentialist underpinning of objectivity entails a picture of legal meaning which fails on an additional ground. This takes on board the issue of normativity of meaning and is discussed by Wittgenstein in his *Philosophical Investigations* under the rubric of rule-following.[63] Leaving aside the plethora of interpretations that have been offered as regards Wittgenstein's views, his remarks bear a high degree of relevance to the present discussion of objectivity, for Wittgenstein discusses rule-following with respect to standards that may effect a match between mind, language and world. On his view, anything that purports to determine conceptual content in a conclusive way, by forming something like an ultra-criterion, is doomed to fail, for it will itself be in need of further criteria of application and so on until a hopeless regress of interpretations arises.[64] The deep

universals that can be perceived through intuition. Intuitionism, as Moore's theory came to be known, has been attacked on many occasions for its metaphysical extravagance, the most distinctive attack being the one by John Mackie who famously accused Moore's metaphysics of being queer. See Mackie, above n 45.

[60] Many philosophers evoke the notion of supervenience in an attempt to avoid both the reduction of evaluative properties to physical properties, and the idea of some robust evaluative realm that is non-physical and whose perception would require that agents be equipped with some kind of sixth sense; *cf* the discussion on reductionism and physicalism below.

[61] See Mackie's accusation of queerness in Mackie, above n 45.

[62] For that reason I do not think rationalism can be combined with essentialist metaphysics as Stavropoulos attempts to do in *Objectivity in Law*, above n 8. The contradiction inherent in such a project becomes especially apparent when he interprets the rationalist philosophies of Davidson and McDowell as sitting comfortably next to Kripke's semantic programme. To put it in a nutshell: while McDowell and Davidson are committed to the key, for rationalism, idea that anything that exists is thinkable, Kripke's realism would comfortably allow for entities that are in principle unthinkable (elusive entities). For a illuminating discussion of the idea of elusiveness as marking the opposition between rationalism and realism, see T Williamson, 'Past the Linguistic Turn?' in B Leiter (ed), *The Future for Philosophy* (Oxford, Clarendon Press, 2004) 106–28 (at 106–12). And for a similar view on the incompatibility between rationalism and realism see G Curie, 'Interpretation and Objectivity' (1993) 102 *Mind* 413 (at 418). Of a different opinion is Shafer-Landau in *Moral Realism*, above n 29, ch 8, who thinks that the two are compatible.

[63] See L Wittgenstein, *Philosophical Investigations*, 3rd edn (Oxford, Blackwell, 2001) para 134-242.

[64] *Ibid*; see also the discussion in S Kripke, *Wittgenstein: On Rules and Private Language* (Oxford, Blackwell, 1982) 7–54.

reason for this is that ultra-criteria tend to highlight one particular aspect or moment of a broader practice of rule-following, cutting it off from the rest of the practice and freezing it into some kind of guideline that purports to determine conclusively the propositions we form as a result of our participation in that practice. This amounts to a rather *static* picture which cannot explain how and why a practice manages to be normative, in the sense of being capable of showing past and future instances thereof to fall under the same scheme of conduct. Conversely, the normative element behind any practice that is responsible for its continuity requires a dynamic reading of criteria, one that prevents them from becoming privileged points of reference and, instead, shows them to be continuously amenable to the pattern of conduct the practice realises. It would not be an exaggeration to say that through the prism of Wittgenstein's thoughts, essentialist as well as semantic criteria, akin to those Dworkin takes Hart to employ, present us equally with a static conception which falls short of supporting a viable notion of objectivity. In fact, it is this *staticity* rather than the semantic or practice-dependent character of criteria which actually bears on the issue of objectivity.

A theme emerging from the discussion of the reasons for rejecting interpretivism, is that an account of law involves two levels of normativity: on the one hand, the normativity of conceptual content; this is the normativity of judging simpliciter and concerns the structure of judgements (propositional, non-propositional); the grounds of truth of propositions; as well as issues relating to the ontology of the relevant domain of knowledge. On the other hand, there is the normativity which is pertinent to legal obligations. This relates to the nature of legal obligations and their relations to other types of obligation: are they commands (expressions of a will) or are they objective meaning contents (as in Kelsen)? Do they overlap with moral obligations or are they of a different character? Do they exist in a peculiarly legal manner (legal validity) or does their existence depend on them being properly justified (say, by moral reasons)? In addition, there is a whole set of questions arising with respect to the interaction between the two levels of normativity. Prima facie it seems reasonable to suggest that issues of conceptual content must assume priority over substantive matters relating to legal obligations, for the activity of thinking and judging is more fundamental than that of law. From this it would follow that the normativity of content may be used in order to constrain or delimit our answers as regards the normativity of legal obligations. That said, issues of conceptual content alone cannot bring us too far either; if, indeed, legal practice is a cognitive practice, then our cognitive judgements with respect to law will have to take into account the substantive normativity of the practice they are inscribed in. To slightly sharpen the same point: if cognition is embedded in concrete practices giving rise to substantive obligations (be they legal, moral or other) how is it possible for cognition to remain impermeable by them?

Before turning to a first treatment of these questions, one that purports to prepare the ground for the concluding chapter of the book, one quick word on an alternative route which is available to the interpretivist for rebutting the objections raised against essentialist metaphysics.

6.4.1.2 Ethical Naturalism

A common strategy for escaping the cul-de-sac involved in the essentialist account of value is ethical naturalism (EN). EN enables the essentialist to retain a strong understanding of objectivity without endorsing a *sui generis* evaluative reality, by allowing evaluative facts to integrate with the natural environment. Succinctly put, naturalism is the thesis that a complete description of the facts of the environment exhausts the question 'what is right to do'. The assumption here is that normative language depicts descriptive properties and to that extent normative knowledge can be reported by descriptive language.[65] From a systematic standpoint EN is a highly successful move vis-à-vis the accusation of metaphysical queerness of normative discourse. To that accusation EN replies that no metaphysically queer entities need to be presupposed because the totality of our normative judgements applies to one kind of thing only: the entities that constitute our natural environment. Furthermore these entities are what they are in virtue of their descriptive properties. It follows that normative properties exist *qua* descriptive properties. One should distinguish between two, at least, directions into which EN could be further developed. The first is the *eliminativist* direction: as normative properties do not, strictly speaking, exist we would be much better off to altogether forget about them (eliminate them) and stick to those properties that actually do exist. In doing so it would make more sense to favour descriptive language over normative, as the latter might give rise to confusions and support metaphysical illusions. Given interpretivism's interest in defending the autonomy of normative discourse, this line of thought seems to be of little help. Besides, the fact that normative disagreement outlasts any description of the environment agreed upon by all parties shows that the level of normativity cannot be eliminated without causing serious misrepresentations of the way we talk and act.

Conversely, the second strategy, instead of eliminating normative properties, takes them to be distinct properties that sit on top or *supervene* upon descriptive properties. Leaving aside the theoretical complexities pertaining to the notion of supervenience,[66] the basic idea here is that normative properties do not exist independently of descriptive properties (or the way objects are) but are still discernible as distinct properties by perceivers. Usually an analogy between normative properties and secondary qualities of objects (colour, smell, sound, etc) is evoked in this context: the property of being violet (melodic, smelly, etc)

[65] This is the view associated with moral theories that aim to provide a naturalistic explication of normative judgements by relating their truth to the *empirical* circumstances of particular situations (moral particularism). For an overview of particularist views see B Hooker and M Little (eds), *Moral Particularism* (Oxford, Clarendon Press, 2000). See also Pavlakos, above n 16.

[66] For the notion of supervenience in general see above n 15.

exists as an experience-dependent property that, however, is a genuine property of objects that look violet. As such, secondary properties have two aspects: a *subjective/perspectival* aspect (they depend upon human perception); and an *objective* aspect (they are perceived according to how objects actually are, where the latter is determined by the primary qualities of objects). On this account, normative properties, like secondary qualities, are intrinsically phenomenal *and* genuine properties of objects.[67] The variant of supervenience is perfectly compatible with interpretivism, for it enables the latter to utilise a strong notion of objectivity without being saddled with the usual problems linked to it in the context of essentialism.[68] However, an elaboration of EN on the basis of supervenience gives rise to two, at least, objections, that render it futile: the *objection of subjectivism* and the *objection of justification.*

The objection of subjectivism rests on the fact that normative judgements are true only relative to perceivers. It is possible, the objection submits, that this fact outbalances any objective aspect of normative properties with the effect that normative qualities will always be relative to the perceiver's viewpoint. However, unlike secondary qualities, in the case of normative qualities the viewpoint will depend on the perceivers' attitudes as they are shaped by the social and historical context in which perceivers are embedded. Accordingly, depending on the viewpoint, the judgement that 'slavery is wrong' could be equally deemed false (classical Greece) or true (modern constitutional democracies). On the other hand, the objection of justification[69] says that, unlike judgements on colour (descriptive properties), evaluative judgements are usually underpinned by reasons. Indeed, it is the case that when we make evaluative judgements we tend to support them with reasons, aiming thus to produce *justifications* rather that merely give *evidence* for them. To that extent the analogy with secondary qualities, which underpins supervenience, breaks.

6.5 Normativity of Practice

The discussion of this chapter offers the opportunity to address a more salient problem which will assume a more central role in the next chapter. This is the issue of interaction between two distinct levels of normativity: on the one hand, this of the normativity of content; on the other, that of the normativity of action or agency (part of what law is about). Norms of action (legal, moral or other), to the extent that can form the content of our thoughts, are also objects of cognition. Thus, any theory that strives to understand normative requirements of action (be they legal, moral or other) is still confined by the requirements of

[67] *Cf* P Benn, *Ethics* (London, UCL Press, 1998) 42–43.

[68] For this compatibility see Dworkin, 'On Gaps', above n 12; and more generally, *idem*, *Law's Empire*, above n 11, chs 1 and 2; and Stavropoulos, *Objectivity in Law*, above n 8, chs 3 and 4.

[69] See also Benn, above n 67, 45.

content formation. It follows that any adequate understanding/explanation of action-guiding entities (norms, be they legal, moral or other) must still observe the normative conditions of content formation, those laid down by the rules that govern judgement formation (rules of grammar). Thus norms of action must cohere with the conditions of their knowledge. But here we have the following odd phenomenon: any time the content of our thoughts is about action-guiding items (norms) we are faced with an interaction between two levels of normativity: on the one hand, the more basic normativity of content formation; on the other, the more substantive normativity of action. Connectedly, one may pose the justified question: to what extent do the two levels of normativity interact? So far we have encountered two opposing ways for understanding conditions of content formation; for simplicity, call them the criterial and the rationalist conceptions of practice respectively. As a result an answer to the above question must draw on the different nuances of the two accounts.

The criterial conception of practice enables a separation of the two levels of normativity. Once the content of judgements is imposed from the outside, by reference to criteria that are independent of the very practice of content formation (because it is the criteria and not the practice that counts) it is possible to imagine various standards that may function as criteria of correctness for what belongs to the practice of law (for here there is no normativity at the basic level of content formation to constrain the 'subject matter' of the practice). This is the strategy endorsed by both legal conventionalism and interpretivism: criteria of correctness remain, here, external to the practice. In the case of conventionalism, they are perceptible tokens of behaviour of officials; in the case of interpretivism, evaluative essences that pertain to naturalistically conceived states of affairs (supervenience). Thus, the criterial conception keeps the content of substantive action-guiding norms separate from the conditions of their cognition. Of course, there is an important difference between conventionalism and interpretivism: in the former, legal norms are being reduced to behavioural facts about those who partake of the practice of law. In the latter, legal norms refer to moral commands that do not depend on the practice of law but, conversely, are called upon to 'shape' or 'guide' the cognition this practice effects. This difference brings about different types of failure. In the case of conventionalism, the result is indeterminacy and loss of normativity; essentialism, on the other hand, fosters scepticism and loss of objectivity. Such differences notwithstanding, both failures have one in common: they fail to account for our knowledge of the law.

Conversely, the rationalist explication of grammar (one that pertains to the philosophy of pragmatic rationalism), allows for integration between the two levels of normativity: that of content formation (judging) and that of action. This follows from the fact that every action-guiding practice, as well as being a practice for a particular type of obligation, is a practice of content formation, ie a cognitive activity regarding the domain it covers (law, morality, a game, etc). This makes it possible to individuate reasons for action as grounds for knowledge internally to the domain. Being so individuated, such reasons avoid degenerating into indeterminate criteria or sceptical standards, which allows them to account in a robust manner for the normativity of the domain they belong to. In addition, their upgrading into grounds for knowing entails that such reasons partake of the broader normativity of judging, one that was earlier found to bestow autonomy on judging subjects.[70]

Developing such an account for law, which may deliver the unity between grounds of knowledge and reasons for action, will be the aim of the Practice Theory of Law, to which I now turn in the last chapter of the book.

[70] *Cf* section 4.4.

7

The Practice Theory of Law

7.1 Introduction

The analysis of Chapters 5 and 6 yields the conclusion that both conventionalism and interpretivism must be set aside, for they fail to account for the depth of legal practice.[1] Conventionalism fails because it breaks down practice to components that are inert of normativity, while interpretivism, in conceiving of normative standards independently of legal practice, faces the insurmountable difficulty of explaining how those standards can ever make contact with the practice they purport to regulate. Most notably the criteria stipulated in either of those cases fail to develop a normative role vis-à-vis the practice, because they give rise to an array of unconstrained interpretations and the hopeless regress yielded by them (section 7.2). Unconstrained interpretations, however, fall short of supporting knowledge, because the latter requires that practices be constrained in such a manner that would allow distinguishing good cases of knowledge from other unsuccessful cognitive moves.

Conversely in this, the final chapter I shall propose a fresh account of law, one I shall label the Practice Theory of Law, for short PTL (sections 7.3 to 7.5). The practice theory argues that the concept of law is a constraint-generating concept, in other words one that can support claims of knowledge. Seminal in rendering law a constraint-generating concept is a particular conception of legal practice, which is where the practice theory derives its name from. This particular conception of practice involves the idea—one propounded by pragmatic rationalism in Chapter 4—that any normative understanding of practice presupposes that it be conceived as a reflexive activity that is responsive to reasons (section

[1] For a *sui generis* view combining elements of conventionalism and interpretivism, see N MacCormick, *Institutions of Law* (Oxford, Oxford University Press, 2007), especially ch 16. In that book MacCormick undertakes a restatement of his institutional theory of law, arguing that legal phenomena can be explained as institutional arrangements that 'sit on top' of some more fundamental practices of rule-following, such that express particular values, in whose light law should be interpreted. This account is extremely appealing, although not necessarily of an interpretivist disposition. Truth be told, the issue of the nature of value in *Institutions of Law*, is not clarified further. That said, in light of the essentialist explication of value interpretivism solicits (as Chapter 6 has argued), MacCormick's account seems to sit much better with an anti-essentialist metaphysics of value, like the one advanced in this chapter.

7.3). Such reasons, far from either dissolving into pure behaviour or instantiating independently of practice, may be conceived of as being both internal to the practice (as an antidote to mind-world dualism) and ratification-independent, ie not reducible to the pure fact of acceptance by the participants of the practice. It is on this condition only that a cognitivist account of law may flourish.

Working out a normative conception of legal practice involves showing that this is only an instantiation of the activity of forming judgements in general (section 7.4). The more basic activity of judging (judging simpliciter) is a reflexive activity, which is subject to general structural constraints in the form of a fundamental grammar of thought.[2] In the light of those constraints, legal practice reappears as a normative instance of judging in the domain of law. Here it is possible to depict legal norms within judgements that are subjected to the general constraints of the grammar of judging (section 7.4). The process of depicting legal norms within an overarching activity of judging, by subjecting legal practice to the general constraints of judging, renders it a reflexive activity that is responsive to reasons. To that extent the reflexivity of judging simpliciter permeates legal practice and 'shapes' the various instances of the construction of legal norms. Although the normative constraints of legal practice, those that in the end correspond to the characteristics of law, are domain specific (ie legal), they remain through and through linked with an overall scheme of cognition, which is generated by the activity of judging.

Most notably the link with the overall scheme of cognition effects a communication between the various types of practical reasoning, as a result of which law becomes a (special) case of practical reason (section 7.5). What renders possible the communication between the various domains of the practical is the concept of the person, which, as Chapter 4 has argued, is incorporated by the general activity of judging as one aiming to connect predicates to subjects with a claim to universalisation. The concept of the person effects a communication between legal and moral reasons at the stage of judging, such that the legal norms depicted by the relevant judgements have already incorporated moral reasons. With this an old controversy about the connection between law and morality becomes a little easier to resolve. Far from leading to confusion between legal and moral domain, the concept of the person demonstrates in its full range the depth of legal practice, ie the ability to refer to normative reasons that are both practice immanent and ratification-independent, thus being capable of grounding legal knowledge on a solid ground.

One final note as regards the content of the argument: throughout the demonstration of the depth of legal practice, I shall borrow elements from the discourse theory of law, as the one theory that has attempted to work out

[2] For the idea of a grammar of thought, see Chapter 2.

normative constraints of legal practice that respect both the conditions of practice-immanence and ratification-independence, with a view to effecting a cognitivist account of law.[3]

7.2 Failure of Conventionalism and Interpretivism

The failure of conventionalist and interpretivist theories of law to account for the depth of legal practice is rooted in a failure to work out a normative conception of practice. Normativity, in the sense required for present purposes, has to do with the ability to reconstruct legal practice as a coherent activity that is responsive to standards that spring from a reflexive attitude vis-à-vis the practice. Such standards become evident when agents (the participants of the practice) can adduce reasons in whose light their behaviour within the practice makes sense as a rule-governed, as opposed to random, activity.[4] It is only then, as the account of pragmatic rationalism has illustrated,[5] that we can steer clear of scepticism and the attendant loss of meaning, not just with regard to law, but also every other domain of human activity.

7.2.1 Conventionalism and its Discontents

The loss of normativity conventionalism effects is not peculiar to law but pertains to every explication of practice that attempts to ground normativity in the convergence of behaviour between members of a collective. To that extent the failure of the conventionalist account goes back to the same reasons that were adduced earlier for the failure of a conventionalist explication of meaning by S

[3] In doing so I am not endorsing any of the existing versions of discourse theory. In particular, I would like to explicitly distance the present project from either consensus-based and realist interpretations of discourse theory. The former, notably propounded by the early Habermas, in soliciting a consensus theory of truth, runs the danger of slipping into a conventionalist explication of practice and should be rejected. The latter, increasingly featuring in recent writings of Habermas and in the work of Christina Lafont, resembles strongly the interpretivist project, and must be abandoned for the very same reasons the latter was turned down. Contrapositively, the version of discourse theory I am soliciting remains faithful to the Kantian ideal that reality is constituted in an objective way through a mind-dependent activity of judging, which effects a synthesis of empirical input and rational form. For the consensual variant of discourse theory see J Habermas, 'Diskursethik – Notizen zu einem Begründungsprogramm' in *idem*, *Moralbewußtsein und kommukatives Handeln* (Frankfurt am Main, Suhrkamp, 1983) 53–125; and in English translation 'Discourse Ethics: Notes on a Program of Philosophical Justification' in *idem*, *Moral Consciousness and Communicative Action*, C Lenhardt and S Weber Nicholsen (trans) (Cambridge Mass, MIT Press, 1992) 79n. For the realist variant, see J Habermas, *Truth and Justification* (Oxford, Polity, 2002); also C Lafont, *The Linguistic Turn in Hermeneutic Philosophy* (Cambridge Mass, MIT, 1999) and more recently, C Lafont, 'Realismus und Konstruktivismus in der kantianischen Moralphilosophie – das Beispiel der Diskursethik' in (2002) 50 *Deutsche Zeitschrift für Philosophie* 39.

[4] In light of the overall spirit of the present work, such activity comprises both conceptual activity (judging) and intentional action. See also the discussion in section 7.3.

[5] See section 4.5.

Kripke and C Wright.[6] As regards the domain of law, the conventionalist account commits a similar error in conceiving of the legal practice at a fundamental level as an unprincipled convergence of behaviour amongst the members of a collective.[7] The course of action on which participants in the practice converge is taken to constitute a complex social rule which operates as a general formula, identifying a number of criteria for the validity of legal norms. In other words, nothing may count as a legal norm unless it satisfies the test of validity specified by the master rule of the system. Typically, amongst the criteria of validity count acts of officials, procedures of Parliament and the case law of particular courts.

Hart famously contrasted the conventionalist account to a predictive model of law propounded by the school of Legal Realism.[8] For the latter, a legal precept is whatever we can predict the judge will treat as a reason for deliberation and action. The dimension of prediction is supposed to be providing for a regularity which aims to redeem the normative content of legal norms.[9] Obviously such a contention must be defective as long as it is not supplemented with a sufficient criterion of prediction: if the criterion is the norm itself then the argument is circular. If, on the other hand, the criterion of prediction can be set apart from the norm predicted in virtue of its standing on a distinct, non-normative level, then it may relate, at most, in a causal manner to the norm. But proclaiming a non-normative basis for a legal norm will effect a slip into the sub-normative level and an attendant loss of meaning.

Its higher degree of sophistication notwithstanding, the validity account does not manage to steer clear of the pitfalls of the predictive model, for in the end, it too, ends up reducing law to facts that are normatively inert.[10] The validity conception assumes norms to be generated at a very basic level from the fact that a collective endorses them. In being basic, this act of acceptance/endorsement is a non-analysable feature of normativity, or of what renders legal norms standards for action and deliberation. However, such a view is problematic insofar as it makes norms dependent upon what the community happens to think or do at a given time; which in a sense implies that the community can never be in error. But such a statement would most definitely run against our intuition that legal norms possess a degree of stability and externality that raises them above the most particular of contexts. So where to look for a more firm foundation of

[6] Compare the discussion in section 3.3.2.

[7] Although I have in mind H L A Hart's version of positivism, I take his analysis to be representative, *mutatis mutandis*, of most contemporary forms of legal positivism. As regards Hart's analysis the most pertinent work is still his *The Concept of Law*, 2nd edn (Oxford, Clarendon Press, 1994), especially chs 5 and 6. See also the account in Chapter 3.

[8] *Ibid* 136–41.

[9] For a succinct, albeit subtle, presentation of the main tenets of legal realism, see B Leiter, 'American Legal Realism' in M Golding and W Edmundson (eds), *The Blackwell Guide to the Philosophy of Law and Legal Theory*, 50–66.

[10] Both the predictive and conventionalist accounts amount to reductionism. For a detailed discussion of reductionism in legal theory compare G Pavlakos, *Rechtsontologie und praktische Vernunft* (Baden-Baden, Nomos, 2007) ch 2.

norms? Unless a retreat to private mental states or practice independent criteria were to obtain,[11] the next possible point of reference is the set of conditions that bring about membership in the legal community. Such conditions have the obvious advantage of affording for a high degree of determinability, owing to their descriptive character. By confining ourselves to criteria of membership, the validity conception is able to identify with certainty the space of legal norms: ie the practice of the community those criteria circumscribe. What is more, one need not go in detail into an analysis of why and how a legal community validates norms. It suffices that it does so. Another advantage of this view is that it makes norms extremely flexible, for it allows them to adjust to the ways the community adapts to new situations. To put it in a nutshell, the validity conception explains away normativity by delegating it to a membership formula that is descriptive in its essence.

The problem with any such formulas is that, inasmuch as they are disjoined from the reasons the community accepts as valid standards for action and deliberation, they fail to underpin constraints for the use of legal concepts. Such constraints, however, are precisely what a normative understanding of legal practice requires. Instead, validity formulas end up representing a random collection of facts which is unable to support the idea of normativity and justification required by thinking and acting for a reason. Notably, the most common symptom of this pathology are so-called hard cases[12]: these are cases where the legal community is at odds about the content of some legal reason, as a result of the unprincipled understanding of the process of validation. Suppose, for instance, that I am pondering on my legal duties as a parent. On the validity model, I would have to specify the meaning of 'parenthood' along the lines of a formal test of validity. This test would seek to identify criteria for 'parenthood' by looking into the convergent behaviour of the members of the relevant community of lawyers. The next step would proceed to check whether my case can be subsumed under the stipulated criteria (say, degree of relationship, biological links, and so on). In this context a hard case would arise if the formula of validity excluded same-sex couples while the issue at hand was about the right of parents to adopt children. As long as this right is considered on a validity basis, it would be hard to arrive at a principled solution, other than quoting or repeating the criteria that determine the law-giving community, whose behaviour is salient for who counts as a 'parent'. But would our so doing constitute a genuine instance of deliberation/action? In this and similar cases, the difference between acting/thinking for a reason and acting/thinking for no reason (which equals to no

[11] See section 7.1.

[12] *Locus classicus* for a discussion of hard cases is R Dworkin, *Taking Rights Seriously* (Cambridge Mass, Harvard University Press, 1977) cs 2–4; for a reiteration with new examples, see *idem*, *Justice in Robes* (Cambridge Mass, Belknap Press, 2006), Introduction and ch 6.

acting/thinking at all!) is not that clear. Orienting oneself to validity might make one aware that there is nothing left which one can align one's reasoning and acting with.

7.2.2 Interpretivism and its Discontents

Interpretivism is not in a much better position to generate any constrained conception of legal practice either. In postulating practice-independent essences it commits no smaller a fallacy than falling within the second of the horns of a sceptical dilemma Wittgenstein identified with respect to general meaning.[13] Such essences open up a gap between legal practice and the grounds or reasons that underpin the truth of propositions of law, one that may prove impossible to bridge.[14] It should be reiterated that interpretivism succumbs to this hazard, despite Dworkin's recent denials of essentialism. In particular Dworkin, in an effort to distance himself from essentialism, has recently rejected the interpretation of his theory as one that conceives law as a natural kind.[15] However, in order for his defence to amount to anything more than wishful thinking, Dworkin would have to offer a plausible (and more detailed) explanation of interpretivist grounds, ie grounds that lend themselves to the truth of legal propositions. In simply propounding that such grounds do not attach to any natural kinds, while maintaining his old position about them not being exhausted by the actual practice of a legal community,[16] he only complicates things further. For those two premisses are mutually incompatible and at least one of them would have to be dropped.

In being committed to grounds of practice that can be individuated independently of the latter, Dworkin seems to be echoing the *realism fallacy* that was elsewhere associated with the work of a number of prominent defenders of a pragmatic reading of practice.[17] To repeat succinctly, the motivation for this fallacy is the fear that any prioritisation of practice may lead to idealism and from there back to dualism. With an eye to avoiding such detrimental effect, those philosophers attempt to identify grounds for practice that are conceptually independent and prior to the practice. Although this conceptualisation does not entail epistemic priority (ie practice may still be deemed necessary in order to access such grounds, a claim that is perfectly compatible with interpretivism) it fosters belief in a (legal) realm that is prior to the practice purporting to disclose it. Conceiving the legal realm thus, however, is bound to lead to an understanding of the grounds of legal propositions as super-facts that determine the normativity

[13] See section 3.2.1.
[14] See Chapter 6.
[15] See Dworkin, above n 12, ch 6, reprinted from (2004) 24 *Oxford Journal of Legal Studies* 1.
[16] This has been a standard thesis of Dworkin since the early days of *Taking Rights Seriously*, above n 12.
[17] See section 3.6.1.

of practice, sparking off the bad effects of scepticism. This, then, should be the task for defenders of interpretivism: to convince us that the grounds of legal practice they propound are not conceptually prior to or independent from practice. Absent such a demonstration, the accusation of essentialism will continue, with right, to stand.

7.2.3 Common Failures

In a nutshell, both interpretivism and conventionalism fail as a result of fostering a dichotomy between legal practice and the reasons that guide it. One way to conceive of the dichotomy is as distance between two domains: the domain where reasons are cognised and the domain in which reasons are applied. On this reading, while reasons (be they mental constructs,[18] conventionalist formulas or essentialist properties) can be cognised with reference to a distinct realm, their application requires a separate intellectual process, consisting in the matching of cognised reasons with actual situations that stand in need of regulation.[19] Such a picture is doomed to failure, for any standards that are conceived of outside the domain they purport to regulate are bound to lead to radical indeterminacy and eventual breakdown of the purported regulation. This is the result attached to almost any effort to restore a link between standards conceived of independently of a domain and that domain.[20] Wittgenstein has, famously, located this difficulty in the effort to generate additional criteria or standards which are themselves not open to ambiguity and, as a result, capable of pulling off the trick of connecting the original criteria with the domain they purport to regulate. He argued that any such effort is bound to lead to a regress of interpretations, for there are no self-interpreting standards, hence each time a need for new criteria arises, thereby representing an external ground for making the required connection.[21] This impasse pertains to conventionalist as much as essentialist reasons, for in both cases reasons are incapable of interpreting themselves, therefore they stand in need of linkage with further criteria of determination.

[18] In legal theory cases of mental constructs would include: (1) utilitarian accounts, purporting to individuate grounds of legal propositions by means of a hedonistic calculus (for a discussion of such efforts with respect to rights-norms, see A S Laden, 'Evaluating Social Reasons: Hobbes versus Hegel' (2005) 102 *Journal of Philosophy* 327); (2) any other theory attempting to work out exhaustive definitions of legal concepts along the lines of Austinian Positivism or the movement of Conceptual Jurisprudence (*Begriffsjurisprudenz*) in nineteenth-century Germany.

[19] Here regulation has a broader meaning that also encompasses conceptual regulation, ie one aiming at understanding.

[20] One can imagine various degrees of complexity depending on the ontology of the stipulated criteria: if, for instance, those are mental states, such as individual or collective interests, then they need, first, to be communicated to other agents and, secondly, to be connected to the case at hand.

[21] The same problem has arisen at the most abstract level of the problem of connecting universals and particulars: this is what Plato first identified as the third man argument: this seeks to specify in virtue of what do properties (universals) connect with the particular objects that have them. For a superb analysis and a most illuminating survey of the problem in the history of ideas, see D Davidson, *Truth and Predication* (Cambridge Mass, Belknap Press, 2005), chs 4 and 6.

7.3 Law as a Constraint-generating Concept

In contradistinction to both interpretivism and the conventionalist account of law, the Practice Theory of Law (PTL) argues that law is a *constraint-generating concept*. PTL seeks to demonstrate this claim by illustrating the reflexive character of legal practice as consequential upon its responsiveness to reasons (legal reasons). As a result the most important task of PTL is to develop a working conception of legal reasons such as can underpin the claim for the reflexive character of legal practice. In doing so it must defend the normative character of legal reasons against the pitfalls of both the interpretivist and the conventionalist accounts of law with an eye to avoiding losing hold of the reflexivity of legal practice. Before looking closer into the details of PTL, some introductory remarks are owed for the sake of clarity and good navigation.

First of all, for the purposes of the exposition that follows, norms alone will be considered as legal reasons. For the sake of simplicity, and in order to avoid unnecessary ontological debates, I shall assume that what primarily constrains legal practice are norms rather than properties (eg 'being insolvent') or objects (eg the *contract* between A and B).[22] The main reason that may be adduced for this choice, and I will leave the matter here, is that norms, in having a complete sentential structure, are, in the domain of obligation, the ontological analogue of facts.[23] As the reader may recall from Chapter 2, facts were deemed there to be ontologically primitive in working out all other ontological categories, owing to the primacy sentences enjoy over other semantic units in the context of the semantics exhausts ontology thesis.[24]

Secondly, norms are reasons for action within legal practice in a twofold sense: they are reasons as regards the activity of judging; and they are reasons for acting legally, so to speak. While the activity of judging involves making existential judgements with respect to which norms are valid, 'acting legally' involves engaging in intentional action with a view to bringing about what a norm commands (arresting someone, imposing a fine, granting a right, or paying back a debt). The distinction can be illustrated clearly with an example. Take judgement <J>: 'it is true, that "thieves ought to be punished"'. This judgement depicts norm N: 'thieves out to be punished'. What grounds this judgement (in the sense of making it true) is the norm 'thieves ought to be punished'. At the same time, N is normative in a further sense: it obligates someone (one or many officials) to

[22] Properties and objects are further possible candidates for reasons or constraints of judging. See the discussion in section 4.2.1. There I offer a more detailed justification for the priority of facts over properties and objects.

[23] For a more detailed justification for preferring facts over properties and objects, in the spirit of the semantics exhausts ontology thesis, see section 4.2.1. Also, for a strategy of individuating legal objects and properties parasitically to norms, see section 7.4.

[24] A key component of this thesis is the so-called *context principle*; this says that ontological categories are individuated by the role semantic units play in the context of the sentence. For a detailed discussion of this claim, see section 2.3.1.

impose a penalty on thieves; this time the action prescribed is not an instance of judging but an instance of bringing about a change in the environment.

In view of the above, a key contention of PTL is that the two levels of normativity are intertwined.[25] In particular a norm N becomes normatively efficacious for action only if it has been depicted validly within a reflexive activity of judging (ie if it has already been normatively efficacious for judging[26]). At the same time what can be depicted validly/truly in judgments are not any but only such norms that may function as obligating reasons within legal practice. To that extent, the normativity of judging must make contact with the normativity of action. How are the two levels of normativity related to one another? PTL argues for a unified conception of normativity which takes the activity of judging to determine the overall nature of normativity. This last point needs further explanation: the fact that N is a normative reason for judging 'that N' is more basic than the fact that N is a normative reason for doing what N says one should do. For the role of N as a constraint of a practice of judging relates to the possibility of conceiving of N in the first place. If a norm N is conceived in any manner other than its being a normative constraint in a reflexive activity of judging then it must fail to be depicted (and consequently known), for, in that case, the cognitive act of judging 'that N' will have been left exposed to the indeterminacy pertaining to essentialist or conventionalist explications of practice.

This brings me to the last of the preparatory remarks: it must be shown that legal reasons (norms) retain their normative, practice-constraining role only if, according to the earlier insights of pragmatic rationalism, they can be depicted within a fundamental practice of judging which requires reference to reasons. As far as this goes, the practice of judging enables the normativity of legal norms with respect to their judgement-guiding role. However, this requirement is not without consequences for the action-guiding content of a norm. In fact, as will be shown, the capacity to function as a reason in a reflexive cognitive practice makes legal norms receptive to reasons stemming from other practical domains (ie moral, ethical and so on), with the result that law becomes one amongst other cases of practical reason. No sooner, however, has law been 'infected' by other practical domains than the content of legal norms ceases to be specifically legal in an exclusive manner. For, in that case, what may be depicted as a legal reason will have already been balanced against other practical (moral and ethical) reasons.

[25] A link between those two levels of normativity is also latent in Neil MacCormick's recent restatement of his institutional theory of law (above n 1). In ch 16 of his book, MacCormick takes implicit and explicit forms of rule-following to constitute the evaluative background on which institutional legal facts rest. One can only assume that, save for an undesirable fallback to essentialism, the same rule-following that engages action is also responsible for the cognition of legal norms (*cf* in particular sections 2 and 3 of ch 16 of the same book).

[26] Of course there is a certain degree of circularity here, to the extent that judging is itself a practice and indeed one that is not disconnected from the various domain practices (in this case the practice of law).

The commutability between law and the other domains of practical reason is illustrated through Robert Alexy's special case thesis, while it is further underpinned by the conception of the person enshrined in the normative understanding of the activity of judging, the one which was advanced in the context of pragmatic rationalism.[27] This conception on the one hand imposes some outer boundaries on what can become the action-guiding content of any norm; on the other, it undermines the insularity of the various domains of practical reason, for it belongs to the very essence of any practical domain to compete for the best understanding of agency and personhood.

The analysis of conditions of normativity of legal reasons that follows will point towards the need to conceive legal practice as an instance of a unified practice of judging with respect to the domain of law. In this respect the first requirement is the availability of a structure/grammar of judging which enables the depiction of legal norms. Following that, I shall look into the further substantial constraints that grammar imposes upon legal reasons, along the lines of the thesis that law is a special case of practical reason.

7.4 Conditions of Normativity

There are two conditions for a legal reason to be normative: motivational relevance and objectivity.[28] Motivational relevance refers to the claim agents raise that reasons constitute correct or justified standards for action.[29] Objectivity, on the other hand,[30] ensures that reasons are cognitively available to agents in a manner that renders them impervious to particular conceptual schemes, mental states, definitional formulas or other standards that are unfathomable (because radically inaccessible) to agents—call all of the above 'sceptical facts'.[31] Let me ponder on each of the two conditions in turn.

[27] See Chapter 4.

[28] These apply, of course, to all kinds of reasons, not just legal ones. C Korsgaard makes a related distinction between an explanatory and a justificatory aspect of reasons. While the former requires an internal link between reasons and agents, in the sense that agents think of those as justified standards for action, the explanatory aspect addresses the problem of how reasons interact causally with the psychophysical make-up of agents. The distinction proposed here should be understood as a further distinction inside C Korsgaard's justificatory aspect of reasons. See the first lecture in C Korsgaard, *The Sources of Normativity*, O O'Neill (ed) (Cambridge, Cambridge University Press, 1996) 7–21.

[29] *Cf* the discussion on the conditions of normativity for reasons in general in section 4.2.2. There, motivational relevance was explained as the result of the universality of reasons. Reasons were deemed universal in the sense that they command to be applied in a uniform way in all similar situations. With respect to obligating reasons, or reasons for action, universality as consistency implies further that the reason is a correct one.

[30] *Cf* the discussion in section 4.2.2, on conditions of normativity of reasons in general.

[31] Let 'sceptical facts' comprise anything that purports to function as a self-interpreting entity or ultra-interpretation, as those were labelled elsewhere (Chapter 3). In the case of law, such entities

First, a few words on motivational force. This pertains mainly to reasons' capacity to bring about action. For any reason to develop a regulatory capacity over action, it is essential that the agent it addresses claims that it is a correct standard of action. To that extent, motivational relevance constitutes the substantive aspect of normativity, one that requires that legal reasons be justified reasons for action from the first person point of view of the agent who employs them. As such, reasons must be capable of transcending particular agents and contexts of application. The condition of context-transcendence may be further illustrated through stability and externality: reasons must remain stable when they retain their content across a number of situations and contexts. At the same time, externality commands that reasons retain a relative distance vis-à-vis the various contexts of action. Such distance is valuable in allowing agents to criticise, improve or even revise those contexts. Considering that these are, usually, taken to be the typical marks of the one or the other conception of critical morality (one conceived of *sub specie aeternitatis*), some connection between legal reasons and the reasons of such a morality is sought in this context. All in all, the motivational aspect of normativity seems to be addressing the aspect of legal reasons as reasons for action.

On the other hand, the requirement of independence from 'sceptical' facts, encapsulated by objectivity, purports to block the eventuality of indeterminacy connected to such facts, with a view to grounding knowledge. Objectivity, in this context, requires that agents have access to reasons in a manner that allows them to determine what standards of action they should abide by. This entails that reasons should neither be located in any realm that is inaccessible to agents' cognitive capacities (interpretivism), nor consist in facts that fail to provide determinate grounds for judging that some reason R is the case (conventionalism); nor be incommunicable to other agents (cases of privileged mental states as some hedonistic/utilitarian legal theory might have it). At the same time, objectivity need not be conceived of in rigid terms either. It is not required, in other words, either that reasons remain unchangeable or that they be a priori, as in independent of any context of application. Extreme rigidity is detrimental because it renders reasons unworkable as normative guidelines. This is common to all rigid standards, for such standards fail to live up to the dynamism of actual contexts of practical action and deliberation and, as a result, break down.[32] Standards which break down, however, are prone to invite indeterminacy and scepticism as regards the domain they are employed in. Other than in the case of motivational relevance, the condition of objectivity relates more to the aspect of legal reasons as grounds for judging.

comprise utilitarian or hedonistic facts about the psychological make-up of persons; validity-formulas along positivist lines; or essentialist facts in the spirit of interpretivism. Sceptical facts are blocked when legal reasons are independently identifiable; directly readable; and fallible; see the discussion in section 4.2.2.

[32] See the criticism of Logical Positivism's effort to list sets of exhaustive criteria in section 2.6.

PTL aims to live up to the challenge of both the above conditions by conceiving legal practice as a public practice of deliberation and action. In this manner, legal practice preserves objectivity because it avoids the indeterminacy inherent in interpretivist and conventionalist understandings of reasons. On the other hand, reasons preserve their motivational relevance for, in contrast to validity-based and interpretivist theories of law, legal practice allows for the depiction of legal reasons that are sufficiently linked to a wider scheme of practical reasons, which permeates law *qua* reflexive activity of judging.

7.4.1 Legal Practice and Objectivity

First some remarks on the ability of legal practice, conceived as public practice, to guarantee objectivity. This ability springs out from a decisive rejection of dualism between judging and the grounds of judging. Contrapositively, practice is in a position to dispose of a dualist understanding of reasons, albeit without discarding the notion of reasons as normative standards capable of generating objective (or interpersonal) judgements, about what the law really requires. This is rendered possible by the fact that the space of legal reasons becomes public in a constitutive manner. What is meant by this is that nothing agents perceive as a ground for judging can be so perceived independently of a public practice of judging. An alternative way to make the same point is to say that legal reasons do not any longer require a matching of any privileged facts or ultra-interpretations, as these were coined elsewhere,[33] with the public space of communication and action, for their appreciation already implies participation in a public space which is shared between the members of a legal community.[34]

Two consequences are worth mentioning in this context: first that the content of our reason-relating mental states (beliefs, memories, desires, etc) cannot be conceived of independently of practices. My belief in reason R, far from arising from the matching of a super-fact or formula with the world, is shaped as a result of my partaking of a public practice of depicting reasons of the relevant kind. Linked to it is the further consequence that there is no Archimedean or final point of view (be it internal or external to minds) for validating reasons outside the practice that depicts them. Far form leading to circularity, this point brings home a new kind of objectivity: as the locus of reasons' authority shifts from minds and formulas to the public space of practices, the possibility of error, criticism, improvement and correction is preserved in the space that separates

[33] See Chapter 3 and above n 31.

[34] This rests on the philosophical view that mental states (beliefs, etc) acquire their contents as a result of a practice of rule-following. Traditionally this view is associated with the later work of L Wittgenstein; see G P Baker and P M S Hacker, *Wittgenstein: Rules, Grammar and Necessity*, vol 2 of an Analytical Commentary on the Philosophical Interpretations (Oxford, Blackwell, 1988); S L Hurley, *Consciousness in Action* (Cambridge, Mass., Harvard University Press, 1998); J McDowell, 'Wittgenstein on Following a Rule', reprinted in A Miller and C Wright (eds), *Rule-Following and Meaning* (Chesham, Acumen, 2002) 45–80. Also compare with the more detailed discussion in Chapter 4.

less good from better understandings of the practice at hand. This space can be represented through the dimension of 'depth' as one that pertains to practices: in being deep, legal practices are not readily fathomable by the subjects who partake of them[35]; in other words it will always be possible upon careful reflection to 'discover' that what someone (or even the community as a whole) perceived all along as a valid legal reason might turn out not to be one, or to be one in need of revision/improvement.[36]

7.4.2 Legal Practice and Motivational Relevance

Most notably, the rejection of dualism and the indeterminacy attendant on it, leads to a fresh understanding of legal practice, one that avoids interpretations which fall below the threshold of normativity into the sub-normative level of description and prediction. No sooner are reasons plugged into the public space of practices than it transpires that what is basic, hence, unanalysable in respect of legal practice are not facts of validation or other essentialist data but, more interestingly so, the ability of agents to respond to reasons. On this understanding, practice rises to a reflexive activity which requires agents to adduce reasons for the justification of their thoughts and actions. Any other analysis of practice (as recognition, convention, response to essences and so on) fails to preserve reflexivity as a result of its need to appeal to bridging criteria such as purport to connect agents with practice. Such criteria, however, are doomed to lead to a regress of interpretations that would undermine the reflexive (or normative) character of practice. This radicalisation of the normative character of legal reasons goes a fair way towards establishing a link between legal reasons and those of a critical or universal morality, for the same activity that enables the normative status of legal reasons, namely reflexive judging, also empowers a concept of the person which functions as a yardstick for what may be depicted as a valid legal reason within legal practice.[37]

In the following two sections, I shall demonstrate in more detail how the two aspects of the normativity of legal reasons—objectivity and motivational relevance—are satisfied in PTL. First of all, I shall illustrate the objectivity of legal reasons as the ability to depict legal norms within the structure of a public

[35] This does not yet imply that the full depth of a practice is beyond the capacity of knowledge of the agents that partake of the practice. Such a view would entail that practices are (at some level at least) hopelessly elusive, a claim that would, further, lead head on to radical indeterminacy and scepticism. See the section on pragmatic rationalism in Chapter 4.

[36] For this 'rationalist' view of objectivity (one soliciting the possibility to reconstruct criteria of correctness without leaving the particular context of their application) see the early work of R Dworkin in *Taking Rights Seriously*, above n 12, 160–68; also for an excellent philosophical discussion T Burge, 'Frege on Sense and Linguistic Meaning' in *idem*, *Truth, Thought, Reason: Essays on Frege* (Oxford, Clarendon Press, 2005) 242–69.

[37] For the relation between the activity of judging and the concept of the person, see section 4.4.4. See also the more detailed analysis in section 7.6.

practice of judging. On this level I shall use the philosophical insights of discourse theory with an eye to capturing best the character of legal practice as an instance of a public practice of judging in the domain of law. Following this demonstration, I shall take up the substantive aspect of the justification of legal reasons. There I shall argue that the explication of legal practice as an instance of judging in a domain[38] lends itself to a substantive justification of legal norms as correct standards for action. Robert Alexy's claim that law is a special case of practical reason will be employed in order to establish a link between legal reasons and general practical reason. Elaborating on Alexy's argument, I shall argue that the special case thesis should be best understood as a corollary of the reflexive character of judging and the concept of the person that springs from it and permeates the various domains of judging.

7.5 Depicting Legal Norms I: the General Rules of Discourse

The condition of objectivity requires demonstrating that legal practice has the resources to depict legal norms in a manner that renders them objective constraints of practice. Such resources become available when the practice of law is reconstructed as an instance of judging along the lines pragmatic rationalism requires.[39] As a consequence, legal practice must be shown to possess a grammatical structure, one that demonstrates such inferential relations between judgements as can underpin a semantic account of legal norms as reasons that constrain legal practice.[40] To that extent, the semantic conception of the norm becomes central to the project of PTL, for this alone amongst possible explications of norms complies with the key requirement of pragmatic rationalism for grounds of knowledge, namely, being both practice-immanent and independent of some conventional configuration of practice.

Next I shall employ the so-called discourse theory of law in order to underpin the postulated grammatical structure and the semantic conception of the norm attendant to it. The notion of discourse, which this theory advances, ideally combines the intuition of a general practice of judging with the ability to identify objective conditions for the truth of legal propositions. As such, the category of discourse redeems the reflexive character of legal practice by making possible the

[38] For the distinction between judging simpliciter (JS) and judging in a domain (JD) see Chapter 4.

[39] The main tenets of pragmatic rationalism are discussed in Chapter 4.

[40] For conditions of individuation for norms, via the inferential relations between sentences and the semantic theory of truth those underpin, see Chapter 2.

depiction of legal norms within the grammar of a practice that is argumentative in nature. To that extent, the practice of judging in the domain of law may be coined as a discourse.[41]

7.5.1 Judging as Discourse

In an early work from the 1970s, Alexy elaborated a system of rules (discourse rules) which constitute a formal structure that spells out criteria of validity for any normative proposition (discursive grammar).[42] Alexy, along with Apel and Habermas,[43] argues that every instance of evaluative or prescriptive speech which aims at communication must possess an argumentative or discursive structure along the lines prescribed by the rules of discourse. The necessity of the communicative aspect is demonstrated against the background of a transcendental argument[44] whose task is to make explicit the rules which make up the discursive structure. These rules spell out a series of standards which regulate the happy employment of prescriptive utterances and ultimately effect the elevation of prescriptive speech to discourse. Failing to live up to these requirements, a normative utterance will either fall short of qualifying as a norm or will be deemed faulty. Somewhat simplifying Alexy's own classification, one may distinguish between three kinds of rules of discursive grammar: rules of logic; rules of rationality; finally, pragmatic rules for the utterance of normative sentences. Whereas rules of the first and second categories address largely the level of semantics, those of the third category refer to the pragmatic relation between subjects who engage in normative communication.

In view of the two requirements for the normativity of reasons that were identified earlier, the rules of discourse can be grouped together in two large categories. On the one hand, the semantic rules of discourse can be viewed as addressing the aspect of objectivity, in other words the property of legal reasons

[41] In claiming this I am not alone. In a series of highly incisive papers S Bertea has recently argued for the argumentative or discursive nature of law by identifying the activity of legal reasoning as the centrepiece of legal practice. See S Bertea, 'Certainty, Reasonableness and Argumentation in Law' (2004) 18 *Argumentation* 465; *idem*, 'On Law's Claim to Authority' (2004) 55 *Northern Ireland Legal Quarterly* 396; *idem*, 'Contemporary Legal Theory towards a Non-Objectualist Paradigm: the Contribution of Neil MacCormick' in A Soeteman (ed), *Pluralism and Law* (Stuttgart, Franz Steiner, 2004) 119 n.

[42] I am referring in particular to transcendental-pragmatic reasoning and the long list of discourse rules Robert Alexy identified as early as in his PhD thesis, *Theorie der juristischen Argumentation* (Frankfurt, Suhrkamp, 1978) and in English translation *A Theory of Legal Argumentation: the Theory of Rational Discourse as Theory of Legal Argumentation*, R Adler and N MacCormick (trans) (Oxford, Clarendon Press, 1989); see also G Pavlakos, 'The Special Case Thesis: An Assessment of R Alexy's Discursive Theory of Law' (1998) 12 *Ratio Juris* 126; and C Roversi, 'Constitutionalism and Transcendental Arguments' (2007) 58 *Northern Ireland Legal Quarterly* (forthcoming).

[43] See K-O Apel, 'Das Apriori der Kommunikationsgemeinschaft und die Grundlagen der Ethik' in *idem, Transformation der Philosophie*, vol 2, *Das Apriori der Kommunikationsgemeinschaft* (Frankfurt Main, Suhrkamp, 1976) 358–435; Habermas, above n 3.

[44] For the details of this argument refer below to section 7.6.1.

to be normative for judging. Here, discursive grammar corresponds, roughly, to a set of logical rules of syntax which, in making it possible to depict legal norms within sentential structures, demonstrate the reflexive character of legal discourse. The depiction of legal norms is effected by no other method than the one familiar from the semantics exhausts ontology thesis.[45] On this method, a norm is depicted when it is embedded in a true (normative) sentence, whose truth conditions are accounted for within a semantic theory of truth. Semantic accounts of truth explicate truth conditions of sentences as a result of the combinatorial structure of sentences, one that is illustrated by an analysis of the semantic relations that pertain between sentences, when those are embedded in valid inferences.[46] This account firmly underpins a semantic conception of the (legal) norm.[47]

On the other hand, the pragmatic rules of discourse lend themselves to fleshing out the second requirement for the normativity of reasons: motivational relevance. In particular, in spelling out a fundamental interest in correctness, which is enshrined in discursive argumentation, pragmatic rules of discourse generate a concept of the person, capable of effecting a link between law and the other species of practical reasons. Through this link, discourse theory redeems the context-transcendent or universal character of legal reasons which is a condition for bestowing on them motivational relevance. Taken together, the two aspects of discursive grammar, the semantic and the pragmatic, make it possible to recast legal practice as a discourse, in the sense stated earlier. Recast as such,

[45] This is the philosophical thesis that ontological categories can be fully demonstrated (ie are exhausted) by the semantic structure of language, ie its grammar. This, in other words, is the thesis that we do not have direct access to anything such as the *Ding an sich*, but only to such things that fall under the ontological categories of our most universal scheme of thinking and communication (ie language). For a thorough discussion of the semantics exhausts ontology thesis, see Chapter 2. For the idea that language constitutes the most universal scheme of thinking, one that underpins claims of objectivity and knowledge, see the classic text by D Davidson, 'On the Very Idea of a Conceptual Scheme' in idem, *Inquiries into Truth and Interpretation* (Oxford, Clarendon Press, 1984) 183 n.

[46] See section 2.5.2.2.

[47] See R Alexy's brief attempt to flesh out a semantic conception of constitutional rights norms in his *Theorie der Grundrechte* (Frankfurt am Main, Suhrkamp, 1985) and in English translation by J Rivers, *A Theory of Constitutional Rights* (Oxford, Oxford University Press, 2002) 21–25. Alexy bases his conception on the difference between norm-text and norm: the semantic understanding should amount to an explication of the norm, such that it renders it independent from the particular text. Although Alexy is right in arguing that the norm should enjoy a relative independence from the norm-text, this should not mislead us into thinking that norms could be (ontologically) individuated independently of a semantic account of legal sentences. In addition the semantic concept of the norm is most apposite for an explication of norms as institutional facts, along the lines of N MacCormick's institutional theory of law (see N MacCormick and O Weinberger, *An Institutional Theory of Law: New Approaches to Legal Positivism* (Dordrecht, Reidel, 1986), especially ch II). See also the fresh restatement of the institutional theory in MacCormick, *Institutions of Law*, above n 1, where he takes a more 'value-laden' approach on legal institutional facts. Given that the institutional theory does not contain a detailed semantic account of norms, the present account could be used to supplement it. In this direction argues G Pavlakos, 'Normativity versus Ontology: Law, Facts and Practical Reason' (2003) 34 *Rechtstheorie* 393.

legal practice may empower an understanding of law as a constraint-generating concept that may underpin claims of knowledge and objectivity.

Before turning to demonstrate how legal norms are depicted within legal discourse, it is appropriate to offer a brief reminder on the notion of grammar. The idea of grammar has been employed many a time in the twentieth century in order to offer an objective account with respect to knowledge and meaning.[48] Roughly speaking, grammar-based accounts of propositional content identify some 'objective' logico-syntactical structure of sentences on the basis of which it is possible to reconstruct the world within language. The advantage of grammar is that it allows for the possibility to individuate concepts and propositions in a language-immanent way, albeit without succumbing to psychologism or scepticism. Connectedly, the idea of grammar is receptive to an account of normative content without succumbing to the sceptical objections raising from realist or conventionalist explications of practice (as above with interpretivism and the validity-conception of legal practice). Having said that, the notion of grammar is not sufficient on its own for substantiating a deep conception of practice for, as has been the case in the past, philosophers of grammar have taken rules of grammar to be dependent on some privileged segment of the environment that functions as an ultra-determinant.[49] Despite good intentions, such conceptions cancel what is most appealing in the project of a philosophical grammar, for they allow a gap to open between the rules of grammar and the criteria for their application, a gap that invites scepticism and indeterminacy along the lines explained earlier. Discourse ethics must avoid such pitfalls or backlashes by ensuring that (legal) discourse is conceived of as a reflexive practice of judging, within which reasons are strictly conceived of in connection to their applications.[50]

7.5.2 The Semantic Conception of the Norm

It is time to unpack the semantic conception of the norm. First a clarification is owed: why do norms acquire primacy over other legal entities? Why, in other words, isn't the focus placed on legal properties (such as 'being insolvent') or legal

[48] Among the philosophers who employed it are the logical positivists and the early Wittgenstein. For an account of grammar in the context of legal and more general philosophical positivism see section 2.6.

[49] For instance Wittgenstein's picture theory of meaning in his early work; or the logical positivists' idea that all rules of grammar must be reducible to some simple propositions which make direct contact with elementary sensorial input from the environment (Otto Neurath's notorious *Protokollsätze*). See section 2.6.

[50] It should be remarked that not all interpretations or versions of discourse-ethics take a clear stance in this matter: in particular such versions that encourage realist or consensus-based conceptions of truth are doomed to fall back into the objections raised earlier against realism and conventionalism. For representatives of such defective views see above n 3. It is hoped that a more detailed defence of the proposed understanding of discourse theory will be taken up on a future occasion.

objects (the contract between A and B)? To prevent any misunderstanding, it is not a contention of PTL that such entities do not exist or that they are not important. What is claimed, rather, is that the category of the norm occupies the most fundamental place in an account of law. This may be argued on two grounds: first, it has been a central claim of the semantic account of ontology[51] that ontological categories can be disclosed within the environment of the (assertive) sentence. Focussing on the role sentences play within a semantic account of truth it is possible to offer a semantic account of the referents of sub-sentential units (names and predicates). In this account whole sentences correspond to facts, while sub-sentential units correspond to other ontological categories (roughly speaking, names correspond to objects while predicates to properties). As a result, speaking ontologically, facts are more basic than objects and properties. Now, norms, to the extent they are embedded in whole sentences, are the corollary of facts in the normative domain, hence, more basic than other legal entities. Secondly, it is norms which principally guarantee the irreducibility of the legal domain, by blocking any reduction of legal practice to conventional or predictive facts. That is, even if it were possible to reduce legal properties (like 'being insolvent') to some non-normative (conventional, predictive and so on) properties, this is never an option as regards norms, for norms precisely demonstrate the reason-responsive character of legal practice, where responsiveness to reasons is the essence of normativity. Conversely, any reduction of legal properties must presuppose the existence of some legal norm in order to be able to make sense of the reducing properties, for it is in the environment of normative assertions that isolated normative terms develop referential function.[52] It follows that legal norms may safely be placed at the *bedrock* of legal practice. Having clarified the central role of norms for legal practice, we may move on with the analysis.

The possibility of denoting legal objects is fundamental for our ability to acquire legal knowledge. What performs the function of denoting are *linguistic* entities, in particular expressions and sentences; what is denoted are *non-linguistic* entities, in particular norms and other legal entities. The things denoted are the objects of legal cognition. It follows that an account of the ontology of norms and other legal entities is central for legal knowledge.

An expression refers to a legal object if it functions as a singular term[53] within the context of a true sentence. Normally, on the supposition of a semantic theory of truth, a sentence will be true when there is a fact that makes it true. This fact will be stated in the right-hand side of a clause of the form *'S' is true iff S*. When this is the case the relevant expression will also refer according to the clause: *'F' refers to F*. The formal condition for that will be given through an affirmative

[51] See Chapter 2. For a succinct statement, see also Pavlakos, above n 47.

[52] For a full discussion of this point see G Pavlakos, *Rechtsontologie und praktische Vernunft* (Baden-Baden, Nomos, 2007) ch II.

[53] See section 2.3.2.

existential sentence of the form: (∃x)(Fx). Take for instance the sentence 'the contract between X and Y is valid'. In the correct use of this sentence, that is if the sentence is true according to the schema *'S' is true iff S*, the existence of the object contract will be granted. It will be possible, in other words, to create the affirmative existential sentence: 'there is something that is a contract'. This will be *mutatis mutandis* the case for all legal expressions that denote (abstract) legal objects.

Things are more complicated for norms. Norms are embedded in whole sentences, and sentences do not refer to objects the way singular terms do. Thus the problem of objectifying norms will relate largely to the problem of objectifying whole sentences. This is where the account should begin[54].

Sentences set out the environment within which object-terms refer; moreover, they are the environment in which the existence of objects is articulated: an object exists in the correct use of an assertive sentence. This is granted through the correct use of an assertive sentence which entails the possibility of its restatement as an affirmative existential sentence. But can a whole sentence be considered as being an object in itself, according to the same method? Does, in other words, an objectivation take place if we insert some sentence into another sentence in a manner that the former occupies the role of the object-term? Take, for instance, sentence (1): 'the contract between X and Y is valid'. The correct use of sentence (1) establishes the existence of the object contract. Now let us insert sentence (1) in the following sentence (2) of a meta-language:

Sentence (2): '"the contract between X and Y is valid" is true iff the contract between X and Y is valid'.

At first blush, sentence (1) might be taken to function as an object-term within sentence (2): in this case, the object denoted is the contract between X and Y. However, this solution seems to give rise to a discrepancy that is not easy to dispense with: if we take the contract between X and Y to be the object denoted by the objectivation of sentence (1), then how does it differ from the object denoted by the actual object-term 'the contract between X and Y' in the correct use of sentence (1)? In other words, it cannot be the case that both the term 'the contract' and the objectivation of sentence (1) refer to the same thing. Moreover, to say that sentence (1), a whole sentence, refers to the object contract is not very convincing. The problem emerges from the fact that sentences do not refer like object-terms but are merely used in a referential way, namely as providing the appropriate environment for singular terms to refer.

Heidemann[55] suggests an alternative way for arriving at a nominalisation of an assertive sentence that allows it to be treated as a singular term: this involves restating it as a 'that-clause'. In our example this would amount to the sentence

[54] The discussion follows C Heidemann, *die Norm als Tatsache* (Baden-Baden, Nomos, 1997) 320 n.

[55] *Ibid* 309–36; also C Heidemann, 'Hans Kelsen and the Transcendental Method' (2004) 55 *Northern Ireland Legal Quarterly* 358.

'that the contract between X and Y is valid'. This nominalised sentence can easily be inserted within a reference schema of the form *'S' refers to S*:

'that the contract … is valid' refers to (the fact) that the contract … is valid

The role of the 'that-clause' in this schema is not merely to refer to a linguistic entity, ie sentence S, by constituting nothing more than the name of that sentence. Rather, it should be considered as referring to a non-linguistic entity or object. This becomes clearer if we employ a sentence on a meta-level, say, the sentence: 'I am glad that the contract …is valid'. Here my being glad cannot really be associated with the linguistic entity 'that the contract …', but should be associated with some non-linguistic entity denoted by the 'that-clause'. In fact, the 'that-clause' can be taken to denote the same entity denoted by the noun 'validity (of the contract)'. This entity is the fact that the contract …is valid. Thus my being glad is associated with the fact that a particular contract is valid. Put in more general terms, any entity denoted by nominalisations of assertive sentences in the form of 'that-clauses' may be called a *fact*.[56]

This analysis elucidates adequately the way facts are disclosed in the use of assertive sentences. Insofar as those assertions are about legal entities, we are entitled to talk about legal sentences and legal facts respectively. Now, norms present us with a further peculiarity: besides being embedded in legal sentences they further express the modality of 'ought'. Heidemann suggests that any normative sentence can be reconstructed as a second order sentence in which the modality of 'ought' is related to some fact expressed in terms of a 'that-clause', akin to the modalities of possibility and necessity. Accordingly any normative sentence can be rephrased as:

(NS): It is required that x.

The second part of NS is a that-clause which depicts a fact. To that extent NS can be understood as being already a *second order sentence* which states a *modal meta-fact*. A modal meta-fact consists in the fact that the relevant modality (here the modality of 'ought'), is related in a specific way to a fact which is named by the 'that-clause'. More specifically, to the degree that normative sentences were taken to correspond to norms, it can be argued that norms are modal meta-facts which consist in the fact that a first order fact is placed under the modality of 'ought'.[57]

To sum up: the semantic conception of the norm explains legal norms as constituting higher-order abstract entities or *facts* which are available to lawyers' cognitive powers. Constituted thus, norms function as ontologically basic entities which demarcate the legal realm and enjoy priority over other legal entities (eg contracts, wills, testators, claimants and so on). In this manner, legal norms may

[56] In his recent *Things We Mean* (Oxford, Clarendon Press, 2003) 71–88, S Schiffer attempts to offer a similar account of propositions through 'that clauses' as pleonastic entities, meaning entities that are individuated linguistically, albeit denoting extra-linguistic aspects of the environment.

[57] *Cf* Heidemann, above n 54, 309 n.

function as reasons within a legal discourse, capable of underpinning claims of objectivity and knowledge with respect to the legal domain.

7.6 Depicting Legal Norms II: Law as a Special Case of Morality

Having explored in some detail the first condition of normativity, that of the possibility of depicting legal norms in a knowledge-generating manner, within a reflexive practice of judging (discourse), I shall now turn to shed light on the second, more complex condition of normativity, the one requiring that legal norms be capable of supporting action as justified reasons of agency. This, the motivational aspect of reasons, completes the effort to work out effective legal reasons, which can ground the reflexivity of legal practice.

Most pertinent to such an exploration are, as already indicated, the pragmatic rules of legal discourse. Alexy employs what he takes to be the most fundamental such rules with an eye to constructing an argument for the connection between law and the substantive norms of obligation residing in the other domains of practical reasons (in particular those of critical or universalistic morality). After presenting his seminal argument about legal discourse being a special case of practical discourse, I shall attempt to show that this is merely a corollary of the fundamental thesis of pragmatic rationalism that any form of judging is an instance of universalisation, in whose light judging subjects acquire the status of persons.[58]

7.6.1 The Claim to Correctness: the Core of Discursive Rationality

Alexy has advanced a transcendental argument for grounding the claim to correctness regarding legal propositions.[59] The argument's scope refers to legal sentences but can *mutatis mutandis* apply to any normative sentence. Alexy's argument for the claim to correctness is a type of the more general argument that the act of uttering a normative proposition (Np) presupposes a series of pragmatic rules which render Np intelligible. Since, de facto, we utter normative propositions in our every day communicative practice, the conclusion to be

[58] This was the conclusion of Chapter 4.

[59] See R Alexy, *Begriff und Geltung des Rechts* (Freiburg und München, Alber, 1994) 64–70, and in English translation by B Litschewski Paulson and S L Paulson, *The Argument from Injustice: A Reply to Legal Positivism* (Oxford, Clarendon Press, 2002) 35–40. And for a succinct formulation R Alexy, 'On Necessary Relations Between Law and Morality' (1989) 2 *Ratio Juris* 167 (at 177–83). It should be noted here that there are several authors who accept the conception of legal discourse as a rational argumentation without explicitly referring to the claim to correctness and the connection between rationality and practical reason that is inherent in the work of Habermas and Alexy. For instance see M Atienza, 'For a Theory of Legal Argumentation' (1990) 4 *Rechtstheorie* 393.

drawn is that those pragmatic rules ought to be necessarily valid. To the extent that this argument purports to disclose the pragmatic conditions that can universally guarantee the happy employment of a particular speech act, it can be labelled *transcendental-pragmatic*.[60]

Alexy, like many other proponents of discourse theory, employs the apparatus of the *performative contradiction* in order to show that the connection between a pragmatic rule R and the meaning of a normative proposition Np is compelling: according to it, any Np that does not respect the content of a valid pragmatic rule R entails a contradiction of the form $\Box\neg p$.[61] The contradiction is, further, performative—or pragmatic—because rule R is evoked through the uttering of Np. Let me specify the transcendental construction in relation to the claim to correctness.

7.6.1.1 A Transcendental Argument

A transcendental argument concerning the claim to correctness has, roughly, the following form:

P1: We employ legal propositions (statements).

P2: The act of uttering them necessarily presupposes the rule R: 'normative propositions raise a claim to correctness'.

C: Necessarily rule R is valid (or, 'necessarily normative propositions raise a claim to correctness').

Or

P1: Np

P2: $Np \rightarrow \Box R$

C: $\Box R$

Clearly P2 introduces too much content in what can be taken to be a contestable way; this is where the device of the performative contradiction is employed. This develops its justificatory power by exploiting the feeling of absurdity or inconsistency, as it were, that we experience whenever we explicitly deny the pragmatic rule R, which is implied through the act of uttering Np. Thus, the counterintuitive effect of any normative proposition of the form 'Φ ought to be done, though Φ is wrong', functions as an indication or proof for the fact that the act of uttering a normative proposition entails the pragmatic rule R: 'normative propositions raise a claim to correctness'.[62]

[60] See Apel, above n 43, at 405 *ff*; also section 4.4.1.

[61] This reads: 'necessarily not p'.

[62] As Neil MacCormick has repeatedly pointed out to me, it is not the proposition itself, but the act of uttering it which raises the claim (see for a recent statement of this objection his 'Why Law Makes No Claims' in G Pavlakos (ed), *Law, Rights and Discourse: Themes from the Legal Philosophy of Robert Alexy* (Oxford and Portland, Hart Publishing, 2007)). Provided one doesn't lose sight of this caveat, I still think that the shortcut to propositions is legitimate. In this I fully concur with Robert Alexy, who first used the device of performative contradiction in the area of law; see his 'My Philosophy of Law' in L Wintgens (ed), *The Law in Philosophical Perspectives* (Dordrecht, Kluwer, 1999) 23–45 (at 24).

In particular in the context of legal discourse, a pragmatic contradiction would be instigated if a legislator were to pronounce the constitutional norm[63]:

(1) 'X is a sovereign, federal and unjust state'

Or if a judge were to issue the decision[64]:

(2) 'The defendant is—wrongly, because the valid law was interpreted incorrectly—sentenced to life imprisonment'.

Both these propositions imply a performative contradiction to the extent that their content contravenes the claim that is raised through the act of their pronouncement.[65] The contradiction establishes, indirectly, the necessary validity of the claim to correctness in relation to any legal proposition. This conclusion is used in order to support the further thesis that legal propositions are practical to the extent that they raise a claim to correctness. This thesis is put forward as the *Richtigkeitsargument* (rightness argument). It is based on the following implicit syllogism:

a. a proposition is practical if and only if it raises a claim to correctness[66]
b. legal propositions necessarily raise a claim to correctness
c. legal propositions are necessarily practical

Hence the fact that the claim to correctness is a necessary condition for legal propositions makes them a species of practical propositions. Accordingly the pragmatic rule of correctness constitutes something like the formal aspect of the rightness argument, as it prescribes that legal propositions ought to raise a claim to correctness.[67] On this level the content or the standards of correctness are not further specified.

[63] See Alexy, *Argument*, above n 59, 36. Also his 'On Necessary Relations', above n 59, 167–83 (at 178).

[64] Alexy, 'On Necessary Relations', above n 59, 179.

[65] It should be noted that in the second case, that of the judicial decision, the contradiction needs to be more than a legal contradiction, ie of wrongly applying a statue contrary to the requirements of a legal system. This can be granted if we assume that, despite proclaiming so, the judge erroneously believes that he or she misapplied the statute, where actually the case is that the interpretation was legally correct. Only in this case (2) entails more than a contradiction within the scope of a legal system, one that can be taken to constitute a performative contradiction. See Alexy, 'On Necessary Relations', above n 59, 179–80.

[66] Of course the point of discourse theory is to establish that the claim to correctness is entailed by the act of uttering both theoretical and practical propositions. Interpreted this way, the stated argument is rather trivial. It merely says that a sub-class of propositions raises a claim that, in any case, all propositions do! Accordingly the conclusion should just be that 'all legal propositions are propositions' or that 'all legal propositions are either theoretical or practical'. However, I prefer to associate with practical propositions a more comprehensive notion of correctness than the one referring to theoretical propositions. In doing so I abide by Alexy's suggestion that correctness in the realm of practical reasoning is connected with the idea of a body of substantive criteria for action (the idea of a right morality). In the PTL this substantive notion is cashed in by the concept of the person, see section 7.6.3.

[67] For a thoughtful criticism, forcefully stated, see J Raz, 'The Argument from Justice, or How not to Reply to Legal Positivism' in G Pavlakos (ed), *Law, Rights and Discourse: The Legal Philosophy of Robert Alexy* (Oxford and Portland, Hart Publishing, 2007) and the reply by Alexy, 'An Answer to Joseph Raz', printed in the same volume.

7.6.1.2 The Morality Thesis

The formal aspect of the rightness argument is supplemented by a second substantive aspect which is advanced as the *morality thesis* [*Moralthese*].[68] According to this thesis, the correctness of normative (legal) propositions is measured against the idea of a *right morality*. In advancing the *Moralthese* Alexy adheres to the idea that correctness regarding standards for action (normative utterances) cannot but itself refer to action and hence to designate material criteria for acting correctly. Contrary to what one would expect, the idea of a right morality is elaborated as a *procedural notion*; Alexy seems to designate it as a *justified morality*.[69] This justification takes place within rational discourses, which operate according to certain pragmatic rules which, along with the rule of correctness, are conceived as necessary presuppositions of the act of uttering practical propositions. Those rules are not yet themselves action-guiding standards, in the sense of providing reasons for action, but constitute the pragmatic presuppositions of the discursive procedure, whose outcomes are justified (moral) action-guiding norms. This conception yields a picture of the right morality as the outcome of procedural rightness.[70]

The rightness argument—in both its formal and substantive aspect—supports the broader claim that the legal argumentation or discourse is a *special case* or *Sonderfall* of the general practical argumentation or discourse, the so-called *Sonderfallthese* (henceforth SFT).[71]

7.6.2 The Special Case Thesis

SFT contains the claim that legal or juridical discourse is a special case of general practical discourse, namely the discourse concerning the existence and the validity of normative propositions and/or the conditions under which an action of a rational agent is valid/right. The claim of SFT refers to all types of legal discourse, institutionalised or not: the plaintiff's argumentation in the courtroom, the law professor's opinion delivered at his lectures, the lawyer's advice, the

[68] Alexy, *Argument*, above n 59, 74–76.

[69] *Ibid* 80.

[70] See R Alexy, 'Nachwort' in *idem*, *Theorie der juristischen Argumentation*, 3rd edn (Frankfurt am Main, Suhrkamp, 1996) 410 n.; see also R Alexy, 'Discurstheorie und Menschenrechte' in *idem*, *Recht, Vernnft, Diskurs* (Frankfurt Main, Suhrkamp, 1995) 127–64.

[71] See Alexy, *Theorie*, above n 70, 263–72, 349–59. *Idem*, *Argument*, above n 59, 74–81; *idem*, 'The Special Case Thesis' (1999) 12 *Ratio Juris* 374. For criticisms of the *Sonderfallthese* see instead of others A Engländer, 'Zur begrifflichen Möglichkeit des Rechtspositivismus. Eine Kritik des Richtigkeitsarguments von Robert Alexy' (1997) 28 *Rechtstheorie* 437. Part of the criticism of SFT originates from inside the camp of discourse theory, despite the fact that its authors appear to endorse the claim to correctness. See J Habermas, *Faktizität und Geltung. Beiträge zur Diskurstheorie des Rechts und des demokratischen Rechtsstaats*, 2nd edn (Frankfurt am Main, Suhrkamp, 1992) 283–91. Also K Günther, *Der Sinn für Angemessenheit. Anwendungsdiskurse in Moral und Recht* (Frankfurt am Main, Suhrkamp, 1988); and for a summary of his criticism in English refer to his 'Critical Remarks on Robert Alexy's "Special-Case Thesis"' (1993) 6 *Ratio Juris* 143.

legislative debate in the Parliament, even the journalist's comment on a court's decision stated in the morning paper's legal column.[72] The common denominator in all these types of discourse is their reference to valid positive law, a feature which at the same time distinguishes legal discourse from other types of practical argumentation. SFT has three components: (1) legal questions are practical insofar as they ask what must/is allowed to be done/omitted.[73] This is further supported by the claim that answering legal questions, like answering all other practical questions, raises a claim to correctness (2), which has already been discussed.[74] Finally, SFT is supplemented by a restrictive argument which defines legal discourse merely as a special case of general practical discourse: legal discourse is a special case of general practical discourse due to its being bound by a series of restrictions. These include the positive law, the judicial precedents, the legal dogmatic and the procedural law's provisions[75] (3).

SFT, via the claim to correctness, associates the validity claims of legal normative propositions with the claims of the normative propositions of morality and, broader, general practical reason. Legal norms and moral norms rest, on the supposition of SFT, on a common pragmatic-normative bedrock which must be presupposed in order to render those norms correct or valid. This bedrock contains a set of meta-norms that, like the norm postulating the claim to correctness, can be backed by the method of transcendental deduction. The task of grounding and finally spelling out the content of those meta-norms is undertaken by the discourse theory of law (regarding legal argumentation) and, broader, the general discourse theory which in regard to moral or general practical argumentation is usually referred to as discourse-ethics. Discourse-ethics takes the level of the pragmatic meta-norms to consist in procedural rules or rules for the regulation of argumentative procedures. These rules are procedural in the sense that they 'accomplish' or better respond to the claim of correctness by organising argumentative procedures which can result in justified (right) normative propositions, moral or legal according to the case. These rules regulate the argumentative procedure by dividing burdens and rights among speakers and providing criteria for the validity of the various argumentative speech acts through which the speakers agree about the valid (action-guiding) norms, moral or legal, that will regulate their everyday lives. In this sense the rules of the argumentation are merely rules for the speech and not action-guiding norms, as are the practical norms grounded through the discourse. This is further the reason why the rules of the argumentation cannot directly provide substantive criteria (in the sense of criteria for action) for the grounding of the moral or legal norms that constitute the object of the discourse. Thus discourse-ethics is alleged to constitute a modern, *post-conventional* —as Habermas likes to call

[72] Alexy, *Theorie*, above n 70, 17–49.
[73] *Ibid* 263.
[74] See section 7.6.1.
[75] Alexy, *Theorie*, above n 70, 34, 263 *ff*.

it—ethical theory that puts the emphasis on a procedural framework of norm-grounding that guarantees practical rightness. Framed in this way discourse-ethics is alleged to avoid absurd moral ontology while guaranteeing a *discursive* (as opposed to *monological*) grounding of normative propositions that realises in the best way the universalisation principle (which is taken to be the condition for the validity of every practical norm).

7.6.3 Judging and Autonomy

The claim to correctness and the attendant SFT demonstrate the substantive component that is required by the motivational aspect of the normativity of reasons. When combined with the formal aspect of objectivity, the one illustrated by the semantic conception of the norm, it leads to a full explication of the reflexive character of legal practice. In this context, SFT can be linked with the idea of autonomy that is enshrined in the normativity of cognition *qua* action. The link arises from the fact that SFT and the claim to correctness may demonstrate successfully the substantive meaning of autonomy that has been located in the concept of universalisation as a key component of the capacity to judge.[76] This is how an argument to this end might get off the ground:

In Chapter 4 I demonstrated how reflexive judging may be represented as involving an activity of universalisation of reasons, where universalisation safeguards the strict normativity of judging, by striking out any sceptical entities purporting to function as reasons for judging. As a result, agents capable of engaging in reflexive reasoning were shown to be capable of engaging in universalisation as a prerequisite of the normativity of reasons. In the light of the ability to handle *proper* (ie *universalised*) reasons, agents make sense as beings that demonstrate a normative attitude. A normative attitude bestows on its possessor (actual and potential) autonomy, for, when one is called to apply a normative standard, one is granted a certain leeway of appreciation with respect to the application of the standard.[77] This leeway consists in the freedom to choose amongst plural applications of the standard at hand; this, in turn, implies a certain sense of responsibility for the choice made, in the light of the standard applied. Autonomy, in this case, is the outcome of the interplay between freedom and responsibility.

Although in the domain of theoretical judging the meaning of autonomy is exhausted by the sheer ability to appreciate reasons, the domain of obligating or practical reasons lends itself to a much richer understanding of autonomy. This rich meaning of autonomy springs out from the application of the principle of universalisation on practical contexts. In the light of their ability to universalise

[76] See Chapter 4.
[77] For a detailed exposition of these claims, see Chapter 4.

practical judgements, ie judgements foundational of obligation, agents are rendered the sole and ultimate source of value, for it is only through such judgements that value can be distributed into the world. In an argument borrowed from recent work by Christine Korsgaard, this capacity was deemed[78] to render agents persons who are valuable-in-themselves, in line with one of Kant's alternative formulations of the supreme principle of morality (the formula of humanity as end-in-itself).[79]

The proposition that agents are persons goes a long way in the direction of the unity of practical reasons, as indicated elsewhere.[80] Personhood becomes the focus or the locus where practical reasons compete with an eye to specifying the precise content of personhood. Although this endeavour is bound to remain an ongoing process, on pain of degenerating into rigid definitions and other ultra-interpretations, it may remain focussed enough so as to generate a unified account of personhood. Here, the unifying principle derives from the premiss, demonstrated in Korsgaard's argument, that all those who can partake of practical judgement are valuable-in-themselves: it follows that all competing criteria or interpretations stemming from the various competing practical reasons—be they moral, legal, or ethical—may only amount to such formulations of the person as respect the capacity of agents to be the authors of all practical judgements (which is precisely what makes them valuable-in-themselves).[81]

The claim to correctness fits neatly into this picture for it precisely undertakes to demonstrate the link between legal and other reasons by pointing out the common substratum of universalisation that underlies practical judgements of any sort. Although an explicit reference to the concept of the person is missing from the discursive account of law, something of the sort must be assumed. Here the PTL may supplement the claim to correctness in pointing in the direction of the substantive notion of autonomy that was supplied by pragmatic rationalism.

With these remarks, a connection between the discursive account of law and PTL has been demonstrated.

7.6.4 Law's Autonomy

Before rounding up, a short comment on a concern whose substance is certainly less than meets the eye. This is the concern: if everything is part of the same discourse, how do we come to distinguish law from other practical domains? The

78 See section 4.3.

79 Kant's formulation derives from the *Groundwork of the Metaphysics of Morals*, T E Hill Jr and A Zweig (eds) (Oxford, Oxford University Press, 2002) 4:429; *cf* 4:436). See also the discussion in section 4.4.3.

80 Chapter 4.

81 In the context of the discourse theory of law, this constraint is illustrated through the category of discursive impossibility. Discursively impossible is a norm that can never, on the face of its content, be validated by an unfettered practical discourse. See Alexy, *Theorie*, above n 70.

initial claim of this book was to defend the possibility of legal knowledge and, yet, one could object, by the end of the discussion there is nothing that has advanced this possibility: true enough, it has more or less been shown how to acquire normative knowledge in general, however all the complex distinctions put forward and the talk of grammar and pragmatic rationalism rather suggest that there is little hope for a clear-cut distinction between law on the one hand, and other domains of the practical, on the other. Were this the case, however, any knowledge we thought we acquired with respect to the law would simply evaporate into some general normative knowledge, one of little or no help to lawyers or anyone else dealing with the law. So on this reading we have only come full circle: in purporting to defend legal knowledge, in rejecting the view that no special legal knowledge is possible, we ended up losing hold of legal knowledge for the sake of a robust account of normative knowledge.

Indeed, this suspicion is not just fanciful talk. And yet, one is tempted to ask, 'why should that be a problem?' In fact, as the whole analysis of rule-following has demonstrated, perhaps it should be so. It should be the case, in other words, that law is not (at least) prima facie distinct from morality or ethics.[82] Take for instance the account of meaning put forward in the context of pragmatic rationalism. The gist of that account was that if we want to save meaning we have to conceive it in a strict normative manner, as amounting from a reflexive practice of judging. If, however, meaning in general should be connected with the normativity of judging, what reasons do we have to exempt legal meaning from it?

Secondly, it is not true that PTL does not allow for a distinction between legal and other types of obligation. There will always be a manner to draw such a distinction. It is only that, to the extent that such a distinction purports to remain meaningful (ie normative), it will have to also remain connected with the normativity of judging, as a practice that is constrained by reasons. Depicting such reasons is precisely a sign for the normativity of judging, hence for its capacity to generate meaning. Transfer this to the realm of law and you realise that being normative there means simply being autonomous in a strong sense. In this case, the meaning of autonomy ceases to be a 'legal' matter. Conversely, what is law becomes a matter for autonomy. In other words, to the extent that the distinction between law and non-law remains meaningful, it has to be treated as a normative question, which in this case means a question about the autonomy of persons.[83] Law, however, is too ill-equipped to answer this question by itself.

[82] I say prima facie, because if it were definitively undistinguishable, there would be no valid use for such words as 'law', 'legal' and so on, which is, to say the least, counterintuitive. In any case this is not a claim advanced in the context of PTL as argued next.

[83] This view is not peculiar to PTL. Ronald Dworkin, amongst prominent contemporary legal theorists, seems to share it, or something close to it, when he argues that the conceptual boundaries of law (ie rule of recognition) are not fixed but are constantly subject to interpretation in the light of the best possible moral theory. For a recent statement of his views, see Dworkin, above n 12.

Concluding Remarks

The Practice Theory of Law in a Nutshell

The Practice Theory of Law (PTL) offers a fresh look into the possibility of legal knowledge, by enabling the depiction of legal norms in a practice that combines the two levels of thought and action. This possibility opens up when we move beyond the two currently dominant legal theories concerning the possibility of legal knowledge, namely conventionalism and essentialism. This move requires that one leave behind the philosophical assumptions that underpin these two theories and advance a new account of knowledge, one that connects it with the idea of a practice of judging which is normatively constrained by reasons or, to say the same thing in different terms, reflexive. Pragmatic rationalism, the new account that has been put forward in the book, argues that nothing can be known unless it can function as a reason or a constraint within such a practice. Unless, for instance, a norm imposing penalties for tax evasion can function as a constraint for a judgement purporting to determine fines within a legal system, that norm cannot be known. As a result, reflexivity, or the ability of agents to think on reasons, becomes a key concept for knowledge.[1]

Granted the importance of reflexivity, pragmatic rationalism proceeded to specify its structure. What in other words makes it possible for facts in general to assume the role of reasons? After rejecting conventionalist and essentialist explications, on the grounds that they generate indeterminacy and scepticism, the reflexive structure was explained through the linguistic structure (grammar) that pertains to the activity of thought-formation, or else judging. Judging is neither just acting nor merely thinking, for otherwise thoughts would anew become either indeterminate or unintelligible. Instead it is an integrated instance of thinking and acting, or a practice, which asks for justifying reasons with respect to any cognitive move performed within it. Against this background, something can be depicted (and known) as a fact only if it can function as a reason for backing a cognitive move, ie a judgement, in the practice.

[1] Only during the last stages of writing I came across to a book by Andrea Kern, which puts forward related ideas with respect to knowledge in making central to any account of knowledge the notion of reason and reflexivity. See A Kern, *Quellen des Wissens* (Frankfurt am Main, Suhrkamp, 2006), especially chs 6–8.

In a further step, the reflexive structure of practice was elaborated with regard to law as being argumentative or discursive in nature. Lest it be conceived of as a random sequence of accidental movements or sounds, the creation and application of law has to be deemed susceptible to claims of justification and correctness. Such claims can be organised into a network of speech acts which is dialogical or discursive in essence, as a result of which agents can reflect upon the purposes of legal instruments and institutions and engage in corrective moves aimed at improving the practice, enforcing rules, protecting rights and interests, criticising others, and so on. As a result, it was argued, law becomes a constraint-generating concept, one that cannot be determined arbitrarily but, instead, needs to be specified according to criteria that are intersubjectively valid (in other words, criteria that can be known). In addition, the discursive character of law disclosed a fundamental practical commitment of legal practice: in being a practice of judging, legal practice must respect a certain amount of autonomy of agents, which is enshrined in the activity of reflexive judging. Although in other domains of judging this autonomy is of thin or minimal importance, in the case of practical reason—ie in law, morality and ethics—it assumes a substantive dimension, as a result of the intrinsic relevance those domains bear to the subject matter of autonomy. In other words, while physical or chemical knowledge might not itself say anything about the capacity of physicists and scientists to engage in the reflexive practice of physics and chemistry respectively, legal (or moral, or ethical) knowledge is bound to have direct bearing on the capacity of agents to judge autonomously. There are two important consequences of this: first, owing to the overlap between the general capacity to judge and the domains of law, morality and ethics, the capacity to judge imposes general limitations on what can be validly depicted as a legal or other practical norm. Secondly, the fact of a common reference to the autonomy of judging requires that the particular practical domains compare their views on autonomy and align themselves with one another. Here moral, ethical and legal norms stand in a complementary relation, to the extent that the general capacity to judge requires that valid norms exhibit the form of universality as a condition for being valid reasons for judging. In this context law becomes one amongst many cases of practical reason.

Explicating law as a constraint-generating concept with a discursive/argumentative structure brings about a number of important consequences for its form and substance. I can only offer what is a very cursory discussion of the most notable of them and only hope to be given the chance to develop them further on some future occasion.

Outcomes and Some Applications

With a view to structuring the discussion, I shall distinguish between three categories of outcomes.

Critical Dimension

The argumentative structure of law makes it possible to refer to normative standards that constrain legal practice. Reference to such standards bestows on legal practice a critical-reflexive dimension, through which the participants can reflexively interact with the practice with an eye to assessing it, reconstructing its meaning or, even, giving it a new direction by replacing any obsolete components thereof with fresh insights. In that respect PTL moves legal analysis, aimed as it is at an explanation of law's nature, a step beyond the two traditions that currently dominate legal theory, the conceptual and the sociological.

Conceptual analysis[2] purports, by taking a detached point of view, to work out criteria for the identification of legal materials. Such criteria arise from the meaning competent speakers intuitively associate with the relevant legal concepts. Far from constituting rigid definitions, such criteria are supposed to be reflecting the nature of legal phenomena. But here comes the sociological method[3] with some bad news : what the conceptual method assumed all along to be true depictions of legal phenomena are simply the intellectual fictions of speakers, for in reality any criteria they associate with legal concepts rarely fit the actual way those concepts function. By debunking detached conceptual analysis as covering up the real causes of legal phenomena, sociological analysis urges us to look into such causes. These are to be found in an empirical analysis of class, gender, race, ethnicity and so on. It is factors like these that determine the course of legal practice and bring about legal meaning, rather than the beliefs competent speakers intuitively associate with legal language. However, the sociological analysis is doomed to become indeterminate or, even, uncritical, if it constrains itself to the task of deconstruction: indeterminate because, unless it identifies certain normative constraints, in whose light the practice can be interpreted consistently, the practice is inevitably reduced to a mere collection of random events, which will expose it to a regress of interpretations. Secondly, it will remain uncritical, because any lack of normative standards amounts to an inability to critically reflect on the existing practice and propose alternatives and modifications, such as can improve existing social conditions, uproot long-standing exploitative relations, reverse practices of inequality and disrespect or put in place institutions aimed at long-term improvements in society.

The valuable role of the critical dimension was redeemed in the context of PTL. This took place in two moves. To begin with it was shown that legal practice is a reflexive practice of judging which, to speak with Robert Alexy, underpins legal propositions with a claim to correctness. This claim makes available the critical perspective by prescribing that any assertion of a legal standard needs to

[2] See section 5.2.

[3] For basic claims and methodological trends of sociological jurisprudence see instead of others P Leith and J Morison, 'Can Jurisprudence Without Empiricism Ever be a Science?' in S Coyle and G Pavlakos (eds), *Jurisprudence or Legal Science?* (Oxford and Portland, Hart Publishing, 2005) 147.

be justified. To the postulate of justification corresponds a basic capacity of the participants of the practice to be rational, in the sense of being capable of backing their judgements with justificatory reasons. This basic capacity of rationality was deemed to bestow judging subjects with a minimum amount of autonomy. At another level, PTL prescribes that the capacity of judging be connected with a more substantive meaning of autonomy, one that relates to the universalisation of normative (as in action-guiding) propositions: here, the capacity to adduce justificatory reasons was connected with the claim that judging subjects possess absolute value, for, in being the authors of every justified normative proposition they are also the ultimate source of all value (granted, of course, something like the Kantian thesis that values exist only through norms).

When compared with the interpretivist project of Ronald Dworkin, PTL's seminal difference lies in its capacity to deliver legal knowledge as a result of the metaphysical modesty it solicits. Whereas Dworkin's theory takes as its starting point a realm of value that is conceptually prior to and independent of legal practice—for, in his project, it is perfectly conceivable that the two may come apart—PTL insists on an explanation of the constraints of legal practice as normative facts that are practice-immanent and ratification-independent. This amounts to a further difference of utmost importance between the two accounts: granted the practice-independent character of value in his account, Dworkin is happy to concede that all it takes to acquire legal knowledge is a Herculean judge, who, by putting his immense intellectual capacities at work, arrives at a complete account of the values and principles underpinning the legal system. One does not need to stretch one's imagination too far to understand that what guarantees epistemic access in this context is some kind of intuition that hooks on to the relevant values and principles, intuition that can operate independently of any instance of argumentation and justification. Even if this is not what Dworkin had in mind, when setting out the main ideas of interpretivism, there is nothing in his account to decisively block such a possibility. This model contrasts sharply with the argumentative epistemology of PTL: given the practice-immanent character of the constraints of legal practice, it is impossible to postulate any knowledge thereof outside the interaction of the participants of the legal practice in their exchange of arguments aimed at the best justification of the norms proposed. While the interpretivist model must face anew the accusation of scepticism and the attendant loss of intelligibility,[4] PTL's account is likely to accomplish the difficult task of grounding legal knowledge. In placing law's argumentative nature in the centre of a cognitivist account of law, PTL aligns itself with a long and prominent tradition in legal theory, which focusses on the argumentative nature of legal practice: from Perelman's *New Rhetoric* to Alexy's *Theory of Legal*

[4] See Chapter 6.

Argumentation[5] and MacCormick's *Legal Reasoning and Legal Theory*,[6] but also some other more recent important accounts[7]; legal practice has been, with success, explained as an argumentative activity, which is aimed at the justification of legal norms through the best possible argument.

Finally, the critical dimension or argumentative character of law is likely to underpin the demand for more democracy and rights within legal institutions both at the national and international levels.[8] To the extent that the reflexive structure of law is intrinsically connected with the possibility of legal knowledge, democratic arrangements—such as fostering discourse and the exchange of argument—as well as rule of law institutions may come to stand under a normative postulate. Were this claim to be developed in more depth, it could lead to significant insights with respect to a number of hotly contested topics drawn from the practice of nation-states and the international community. Although this is not the place to take up such an endeavour, its significance for a proper understanding of legal institutions in a rapidly developing world cannot be overstated.

Methodological Holism

PTL encourages methodological openness by adhering to a version of holism with respect to the understanding of legal phenomena. Methodological holism allows for a synergy and mutual benefit between methods that usually are presented as antithetical by those schools of thought that dominate current legal theory. Typical examples in this context are the sociological and the analytical method, which were referred to earlier. The sociological method, hailed by the so-called socio-legal jurisprudence to be the foremost method for the study of law, focusses on the actual ways law functions in human societies. In revealing the actual uses of legal concepts this method aims at a clarification of the real meaning of legal language and the actual impact it inflicts on society and its institutions. This is largely an explanatory project aimed at illustrating how the workings of law and legal vocabulary are causally determined by an array of non-legal social facts and institutions. By contrast, the so-called analytical school

[5] See R Alexy, *Theorie der juristischen Argumentation* (Frankfurt, Suhrkamp, 1978) and in English translation *A Theory of Legal Argumentation: the Theory of Rational Discourse as Theory of Legal Argumentation*, R Adler and N MacCormick (trans) (Oxford, Clarendon Press, 1989).

[6] N MacCormick, *Legal Reasoning and Legal Theory* (Oxford, Clarendon Press, 1976); and his most recent restatement of the theory in *idem*, *Rhetoric and the Rule of Law* (Oxford, Oxford University Press, 2006).

[7] See in particular S Bertea, 'Certainty, Reasonableness and Argumentation in Law' (2004) 18 *Argumentation* 465; and with regard to MacCormick's theory *idem*, 'Law and Legal Reasoning' (2008) 59 *Northern Ireland Legal Quarterly* (forthcoming).

[8] For the connection of discourse and democracy see J Habermas, *Between Facts and Norms* (Oxford, Polity Press, 1996) ch 7; also R Alexy, 'Balancing, Constitutional Review, and Representation' (2005) 3 *International Journal of Constitutional Law* 572, where he uses the term 'argumentative representation' to indicate the discursive character of representative institutions.

of jurisprudence adheres to some version of conceptual analysis, which looks for the meaning of legal concepts by focusing on the conceptual rules that underpin the use of legal language, rules that can be extracted from the (linguistic) behaviour of competent speakers of the language. Each of the two schools remains convinced of the exclusive nature of its own views and is hardly prepared to learn anything from the other. What is more, the hostile nature of the debate between the two schools, in the few occasions it takes place, reinforces the appearance that the two methods they represent are incompatible.

In dispelling the appearance, PTL aims to illustrate the complementary nature of the two methods of analysis, with an eye to enriching the methodological debate and sharpening the explanatory tools of legal theory. A decisive step in this direction is the demonstration that both conceptual and sociological analyses aim to each capture one aspect only of a broader phenomenon, which is not exhausted by any one of its distinct aspects. This phenomenon can be best described in terms of a practice. Legal practice is the overarching process within which sociological fact and conceptual articulation go hand in hand, on pain of an incomplete understanding of all things legal. The point is not difficult to demonstrate, if we consider that, for it to materialise, a legal practice needs both of the above aspects. It would be ludicrous to suppose that a practice can be conceptually articulated without having any objective existence, without really happening in the world. On the other hand, it would be almost as incredible to argue that something happening in the world cannot be thought of or articulated conceptually, in the sense of being depicted in a language that is used according to such guidelines and criteria as those competent speakers abide by. Why then does current jurisprudential thinking present those aspects as being antagonistic with one another? The answer has to do with the fact that neither of the two aspects, of fact and of criteria of usage, can indicate by itself the complementary relation with the other. Or, which is to say the same, neither can, on its own, demonstrate the need to view legal practice as a continuous phenomenon. This impossibility becomes the more probable when the theorist is firmly located in either of the two approaches and looks from a distance at the other. PTL resolves this conundrum, by putting forward reasons for the continuity of legal practice. In PTL the continuity of practice derives from a third element that is never made explicit by either of the two other methodological approaches: the normativity of practice. Rather than being random in the fashion of facts or criteria, legal practice is conceived of as a reflexive activity which amounts from a response to reasons. In the light of such reasons the factual as well as the conceptual elements of practice make sense as distinct aspects of the same phenomenon.

Equipped with the normative or reflexive dimension, the legal theorist can make good sense of all three levels or dimensions of legal practice: the conceptual, the factual and the normative. In the light of the normative level a case for the continuity of all three levels can be made, albeit without ranking the normative level higher or the two others as redundant, considering that a complete explanation of legal phenomena requires that use be made of insights stemming from all three levels.[9] To that extent, PTL solicits less of a methodological syncretism and much more of a methodological holism. As such, it is particularly well placed in taking contemporary debates in legal theory beyond their current state of stagnation into a dialogue that may benefit all sides.

Form Pluralism in a Globalised World

Finally, PTL encourages a shift from the formal to the substantive features of law. Owing to the opening up of legal phenomena to the argumentative practice that underpins them, legal form may be explained as depending on the concrete substantive principles that are at work with respect to particular situations. In this context, form loses its 'uniqueness', for it becomes possible to identify more than one formal or institutional arrangement as suitable for serving the same underlying principle or cluster of principles. Flexibility of form resists formalistic analyses of legal phenomena, especially those that attempt to specify exhaustive sets of criteria for the validity or legal rules, usually by offering a complete list of legal sources within a legal system. In addition, the mistrust of formal analysis extends into the level of the application and interpretation of legal rules. With respect to those, PTL encourages forms of legal reasoning which are susceptible to substantive argument and context-dependent considerations. The two main options here are balancing and defeasible reasoning.[10] Both aim at relaxing the more rigid logical form of deduction, which fosters the formalisation of rules and situations into definitions and criteria.

The opening up to substance endows PTL with increased explanatory power, especially in contexts where legal regulation becomes diffuse as a result of the competition it faces by new codes or sources of social normativity. Notable examples here are the recent phenomena of globalisation. More than any other current family of phenomena, those have persistently challenged traditional perceptions of law, pressing for new understandings and explanations. The transformations effected by globalisation are mostly manifested along the two axes of public-private and national-international. In the former case, non-state forms of social normativity permeate the law; in the latter, non-governmental forms of regulation acquire priority over state law. Things become even more complex as the two axes cut across each other: often the private demonstrates abilities of an international standing, while the public remains confined within

[9] See for a similar project of analysis that integrates the three levels of the conceptual, the empirical and the normative the excellent paper by S Haslanger, 'What Good are our Intuitions' (2006) LXXX *Aristotelian Society Supplementary Volume* 89.

[10] For present purposes it is not necessary to take a stance on the issue whether balancing and defeasible reasoning are compatible or antithetical to one another. As regards theories of balancing the most sophisticated account to date is to be found in R Alexy, *Theorie der Grundrechte* (Frankfurt am Main, Suhrkamp, 1985) and in English translation by J Rivers, *A Theory of Constitutional Rights* (Oxford, Oxford University Press, 2002) ch 3 and 'Postscript'.

national boundaries. As a result, legal *form* undergoes a radical change, as a plethora of effective new sources of regulation end up determining its shape.[11]

PTL meets the explanatory challenge posed by those changes through the thesis of the relativity of legal form: as long as the salient substantive principle which constraints the practice is realised, the forms that effect its realisation are not rigid. In such cases it is possible to free our thinking from the rigidity or the necessity of a particular form and accept or adopt new forms that may realise as efficiently the substantive issue involved. On the other hand, PTL resists a full surrender to simple-minded explanations that simply carry the fashionable label of globalisation. This it does, by pointing out what is so important about such formal arrangements that we connect intuitively with the idea of law. Why should there be no crime without statute? Or why should everyone enjoy formal equality before the law? Or, even, why should we think that it is better to have our laws voted in Parliament rather than be decided with the toss of a coin? All these formal constraints, which seem to belong to the core of legal systems, can be justified on the basis of the substantive principles that permeate the idea of law, as the thesis about the discursive character of law has demonstrated. Each time such 'formal' principles or characteristics are at stake, the form that accompanies them needs to be protected vis-à-vis claims of flexibility and modernisation/liberalisation. It is only then that the critical reflexive aspect of the law, one that PLT has shown to belong to the core characteristics of law's normativity, may be upheld. This is a key point of PTL, and one that can be demonstrated against the background of a number of topics, which are hotly debated in the literature of globalisation. Here is a sketchy selection of such topics, indicative of the complexity of the issues, but also the versatility of PTL.

International trade has, in recent decades, followed paths of regulation that are at odds with classical legal forms. Most notable amongst them is private arbitration, which is more and more employed by the major actors in international trade. From the point of view of a substantive legal theory, such as PTL, the crucial question is about the material reasons that can be adduced for the legitimacy of those arrangements. On the one hand, there are reasons of efficiency, technical expertise and the facilitation of international trade which can legitimise those arbitration arrangements.[12] On the other hand, there are reasons from human rights, social justice and democratic accountability, which may run

[11] For recent efforts to ground a legal theory of pluralism that steers clear of the reductionist claims of classical Legal Realism, see B Z Tamanaha, *A General Jurisprudence of Law and Society* (Oxford, Oxford University Press, 2001) especially ch 7.

[12] Analogous thoughts apply in the case of regulation of uniform technical standards in the context of the European Union. There, manufacturers have set up 'private' standard-setting bodies (such as the CEN and CENELEC) which the European Court of Justice has accepted as producing standards that are legally valid. The problem of legitimacy is, also in this case, clear. For a thorough discussion, see M Egan, *Constructing a European Market: Standards, Regulation, and Governance* (Oxford, Oxford University Press, 2001). I owe many thanks to Koen de Feyter and Panos Koutrakos for drawing my attention to this debate.

in the opposite direction. PTL in principle requires the widest possible forum of deliberation in order to resolve such problems. When questions of accountability arise (and they are bound to arise more often than not in the framework of the PTL), the importance of the public sphere becomes salient, owing to its privileged role as a source of legitimacy. However, the judgement about what is part of the public sphere is more subtle from the point of view of PTL. In the light of the source pluralism PTL upholds, the classical distinction between public and private collapses. Consequently, despite the fact that the national level remains pertinent as a source of regulation, it may be the civil society (eg consumer organisations) that actually becomes the source of regulation.

Similar thinking pertains to other topics such as the *environment* or issues of *social justice.* In both these cases civil society can play a decisive regulatory role, for it seems to possess the justificatory basis for developing the substantive principles that are at stake. In this context, as in the context of trade, what is highlighted as global is, in fact, a particular problem that cannot be confined within the limits of a polity, traditionally conceived, but ranges in its impact and effects over many states and territories. In this as in previous cases, however, the most appropriate regulation of the problem may still lie within the boundaries of the territorial state, even though it springs from areas that are not traditionally conceived of as falling within the public domain. Also, in this case PTL interprets the global in the light of substantive principles which empower sources of regulation that traditionally would fall within the domain of the national or the private.

The above substantive topics point towards a wider problem that pertains to the logic of globalisation: this is the problem of *regulation.* In other words, at what level should legal regulation take place? Shall it remain at the national or the international level? Or shall it be undertaken by private initiative, as the case of arbitration has suggested? This question has wide implications also for our understanding of the role of the various legal disciplines (do we need international law; can we uphold the distinction between national/international law; or between public/private law?). There are, obviously, no a priori answers to be given here. In the context of PTL the flexibility of the form and the encouragement for pluralism of sources opens up a large leeway for setting up mechanisms of regulation at various levels. What is important is that the level of regulation should secure the necessary degree of legitimacy. And if it does not, then there is no reason to 'respect' formal arrangements in an absolute way: the sooner they are replaced the better. Take, for instance, the case of the prosecution of war crimes in a post-conflict situation.[13] Which one is the best arrangement: to set up criminal courts locally? To use international structures (ICC)? Or to install a mixed system of regulation (hybrid courts)? PTL may offer a structure of

[13] I am indebted to Estelle Zinsstag for stimulating discussion that led me to work out these potential connections between PTL and international criminal justice.

reasoning by placing the emphasis on the salient factors that need to be balanced and, in any case, by sharpening our critical angle in arguing that the best solution is the one that can best be justified in the light of some overarching values, those that can recommend the solution offered to those involved as a justified reason to act upon. If, in this context, a local tribunal proves to be too close to the context of the conflict then some of its jurisdiction will be displaced to a more international context—say, by setting up a hybrid court. To remove, however, the full jurisdiction of such courts out of the local context would probably require too strong reasons to justify.

The question of regulation has, finally, a further dimension, as regards actors that are not states but claim legitimacy (on the basis of something akin to prima facie sovereignty). One could name here the Taliban (or even Al Qaeda) in Afghanistan; or the Hezbollah in Lebanon. Such organisations need to be dealt with beyond the traditional understanding of sovereignty. PTL will again point at the issue of substantive rationality: what counts in this case is whether accepting such formations corresponds to the critical/discursive structure of legal regulation and the idea of democratic legitimacy the latter incorporates. In all those cases, what should and what should not be included within the legal realm must be carefully considered in the light of the rights and interests of the individuals and groups living under those regimes. In addition, such decisions should aim to secure the widest possible consensus in the international community, in order to generate sufficient legitimacy. What is certain, however, is that there are better and worse decisions, for in the light of PTL's principled understanding of law, 'not anything goes'.

Bibliography

ALEXY, R, *Theorie der juristischen Argumentation. Die Theorie des rationalen Diskurses als Theorie der juristischen Begründung*, 1st edn (Frankfurt, Suhrkamp, 1978) and in English translation by R Adler and N MacCormick, *A Theory of Legal Argumentation: The Theory of Rational Discourse as Theory of Legal Argumentation* (Oxford, Clarendon Press, 1989)

____, *Theorie der Grundrechte* (Frankfurt am Main, Suhrkamp, 1985) and in English translation by J Rivers, *A Theory of Constitutional Rights* (Oxford, Oxford University Press, 2002)

____, *Theorie der juristischen Argumentation. Die Theorie des rationalen Diskurses als Theorie der juristischen Begründung*, 2nd edn (Frankfurt am Main, Suhrkamp, 1986)

____, 'On Necessary Relations Between Law and Morality' (1989) 2 *Ratio Juris* 167

____, *Begriff und Geltung des Rechts* (Freiburg and München, Alber, 1992) and in English translation by S L Paulson and B Litschewski Paulson, *The Argument from Injustice* (Oxford, Clarendon Press, 2002)

____, *Recht, Vernunft, Diskurs. Studien zur Rechtsphilosophie* (Frankfurt am Main, Suhrkamp, 1995)

____, 'Diskurstheorie und Menschenrechte' in *idem*, *Recht, Vernnft, Diskurs. Studien zur Rechtsphilosophie* (Frankfurt Main, Suhrkamp, 1995)

____, 'My Philosophy of Law' in L Wintgens (ed), *The Law in Philosophical Perspectives* (Dordrecht, Kluwer, 1999)

____, 'The Special Case Thesis' (1999) 12 *Ratio Juris* 374

____, 'Balancing, Constitutional Review, and Representation' (2005) 3 *International Journal of Constitutional Law* 572

ALEXY, R, 'An Answer to Joseph Raz' in G Pavlakos (ed), *Law, Rights and Discourse: The Legal Philosophy of Robert Alexy* (Oxford and Portland, Hart Publishing, 2007)

ALEXY, R *et al* (eds), *Neukantianismus und Rechtsphilosophie* (Baden-Baden, Nomos Verlag, 2002)

AMSELEK, P and N MACCORMICK (eds), *Controversies about Law's Ontology* (Edinburgh, Edinburgh University Press, 1991)

APEL, K-O, *Transformation der Philosophie, vol 2: Das Apriori der Kommunikationsgemeinschaft* (Frankfurt am Main, Suhrkamp, 1973) and in English

translation by G Adey and D Frisby as *Towards a Transformation of Philosophy* (London, Routledge & Kegan Paul, 1980)
____, *From a Transcendental-Semiotic Point of View*, M Papastephanou (ed) (Manchester and New York, Manchester University Press, 1998)
ATIENZA, M, 'For a Theory of Legal Argumentation' (1990) 4 *Rechtstheorie* 393
AYER, A J, (ed), *Logical Positivism* (New York, Free Press, 1959)
BAKER, G P and P M S HACKER, *Wittgenstein: Rules, Grammar and Necessity*, vol 2 of an Analytical Commentary on the Philosophical Interpretations (Oxford, Blackwell, 1988)
BANKOWSKI, Z and J MACLEAN (eds), *The Universal and the Particular in Legal Reasoning* (Aldershot, Ashgate, 2006)
BEANEY, M (ed), *The Frege Reader* (Oxford, Blackwell, 1997)
BENN, P, *Ethics* (London, UCL Press, 1998)
BERTEA, S, 'Remarks on a Legal Positivist Misuse of Wittgenstein's Later Philosophy' (2003) 22 *Law and Philosophy* 513
____, 'Certainty, Reasonableness and Argumentation in Law' (2004) 18 *Argumentation* 465
____, 'Contemporary Legal Theory towards a Non-Objectualist Paradigm: the Contribution of Neil MacCormick' in A Soeteman (ed), *Pluralism and Law* (Stuttgart, Franz Steiner, 2004)
____, 'On Law's Claim to Authority' (2004) 55 *Northern Ireland Legal Quarterly* 396
____, 'The Arguments from Coherence: Analysis and Evaluation' (2005) 25 *Oxford Journal of Legal Studies* 369
____, 'Law and Legal Reasoning' (2008) 59 *Northern Ireland Legal Quarterly*, forthcoming
BILETZKI, A and A MATAR 'Ludwig Wittgenstein' in E Zalta (ed), *The Stanford Encyclopaedia of Philosophy*, Summer 2005 edn, available at <http://plato.stanford.edu/archives/sum2005/entries/wittgenstein/>
BIX, B, (ed), *Analysing Law: New Essays in Legal Theory* (Oxford, Clarendon Press, 1998)
BLACKBURN, S, *Spreading the World* (Oxford, Clarendon Press, 1984)
BLACKBURN, S and K SIMMONS (eds), *Truth* (Oxford, Oxford University Press, 1999)
BONGIOVANNI, G, A Rotolo and C Roversi, 'The Claim to Correctness' in G Pavlakos (ed), *Law, Rights and Discourse: The Legal Philosophy of Robert Alexy* (Oxford and Portland, Hart Publishing, 2007)
BRACKER, S, *Kohärenz und juristische Interpretation*, Studien zur Rechtsphilosophie und Rechtstheorie vol 27 (Baden-Baden, Nomos, 2000)
BRANDOM, R, *Making it Explicit* (Cambridge Mass, Harvard University Press, 1994)
____, *Articulating Reasons* (Cambridge Mass, Harvard University Press, 2000)
BROWN, J, 'Critical Reasoning, Understanding and Self-Knowledge' (2000) LXI *Philosophy and Phenomenological Research* 659

BROZEK, B, *Defeasibility of Legal Reasoning* (Zakamyce, Kantor, 2004)
BURGE, T, 'Intellectual Norms and the Foundations of Mind' (1986) 83 *Journal of Philosophy* 697
____, 'Frege on Sense and Linguistic Meaning', reprinted in T Burge, *Truth, Thought, Reason* (Oxford, Clarendon Press, 2006)
____, *Truth, Thought, Reason* (Oxford, Clarendon Press, 2006)
CARNAP, R, 'The Old and the New Logic' in A J Ayer (ed), *Logical Positivism* (New York, Free Press, 1959)
____, *Der Logische Aufbau der Welt* (Hamburg, Meiner, 1961)
COFFA, A, *The Semantic Tradition from Kant to Carnap* (Cambridge, Cambridge University Press, 1993)
COLEMAN, J (ed), *Hart's Postscript: Essays on the Postscript to the 'Concept of Law'* (Oxford, Oxford University Press, 2001)
COYLE, S, 'On the Foundations of Legal Reasoning in International Law' (unpublished doctoral thesis, University of Glasgow, 1998)
____, 'Positivism, Idealism and the Rule of Law' (2006) 26 *Oxford Journal of Legal Studies* 257
COYLE, S and G PAVLAKOS (eds), *Jurisprudence or Legal Science?* (Oxford and Portland, Hart Publishing, 2005)
CURIE, G, 'Interpretation and Objectivity' (1993) 102 *Mind* 413
DAVIDSON, D, *Inquiries into Truth and Interpretation* (Oxford, Clarendon Press, 1984)
____, 'On the Very Idea of a Conceptual Scheme' in D Davidson, *Inquiries into Truth and Interpretation* (Oxford, Clarendon Press, 1984)
____, 'The Structure and Content of Truth' (1990) 87 *Journal of Philosophy* 279
________, 'Seeing through Language' in J Preston (ed), *Thought and Language* (Cambridge, Cambridge University Press, 1998)
____, *Subjective, Intersubjective, Objective* (Oxford, Clarendon Press, 2001)
____, 'Knowing One's Own Mind' in *idem, Subjective, Intersubjective, Objective* (Oxford, Clarendon Press, 2001)
____, *Truth and Predication* (Cambridge Mass, Belknap Press, 2005)
DAVIDSON, D and G HARMAN (eds), *Semantics of Natural Language*, 2nd edn (Dordrecht and Boston, D Reidel, 1972)
DUMMETT, M, *Truth and Other Enigmas* (London, Duckworth, 1978)
____, *The Logical Basis of Metaphysics* (London, Duckworth, 1991)
____, *The Seas of Language*, softcover edn (Oxford, Clarendon Press, 1996)
DWORKIN, R, *Taking Rights Seriously* (London, Duckworth, 1977)
____, *Law's Em*pire (London, Fontana Press 1986)
____, *A Matter of Principle* (Oxford, Clarendon Press, 1986)
____, 'What Justice Isn't' in *idem, A Matter of Principle* (Oxford, Clarendon Press, 1986)
____, 'On Gaps in the Law' in P Amselek and N MacCormick (eds), *Controversies about Law's Ontology* (Edinburgh, Edinburgh University Press, 1991)

——, 'Objectivity and Truth: You'd Better Believe It' (1996) 25 *Philosophy and Public* Affairs 87
——, 'Hart's Postscript and the Character of Political Philosophy' (2004) 24 *Oxford Journal of Legal Studies* 1
——, *Justice in Robes* (Cambridge Mass, Belknap Press, 2006)
EGAN, M, *Constructing a European Market: Standards, Regulation, and Governance* (Oxford, Oxford University Press, 2001)
ENGLÄNDER, A, 'Zur begrifflichen Möglichkeit des Rechtspositivismus. Eine Kritik des Richtigkeitsarguments von Robert Alexy' (1997) 28 *Rechtstheorie* 437
EVANS, G, 'The Causal Theory of Names' (1973) 47 *Aristotelian Society Supplementary Volume* 187
FINNIS, J M, *Natural Law and Natural Rights* (Oxford, Clarendon Press, 1980)
FITZPATRICK, W J, 'The Practical Turn in Ethical Theory: Koorsgaard's Constructivism, Realism and the Nature of Normativity' (2005) 115 *Ethics* 651
FREGE, G, 'Über Sinn und Bedeutung' in *idem*, *Kleine Schriften*, I Angelelli (ed) (Hildesheim, Georg Olms, 1967)
——, *Logische Untersuchungen*, 4th edn, G Patzig (ed) (Göttingen, Vandenhoeck & Ruprecht, 1993)
——, 'Der Gedanke. Eine Logische Untersuchung' in *idem*, *Logische Untersuchungen*, 4th edn, G Patzig (ed), and in English translation as 'Thought' in M Beaney (ed), *The Frege Reader* (Oxford, Blackwell, 1997)
——, 'Logik in der Mathematik' in *idem*, *Schriften zur Logik und Sprachphilosophie. Aus dem Nachlaß*, G Gabriel (ed) (Hamburg, Felix Meiner, 2001)
——, *Schriften zur Logik und Sprachphilosophie. Aus dem Nachlaß*, G Gabriel (ed) (Hamburg, Felix Meiner, 2001)
FRIEDMAN, M, *Reconsidering Logical Positivism* (Cambridge, Cambridge University Press, 1999)
GETTIER, E, 'Is Justified True Belief Knowledge?' (1963) 23 *Analysis* 121
GOLDING, M and W EDMUNDSON (eds), *The Blackwell Guide to the Philosophy of Law and Legal Theory* (Oxford, Blackwell, 2005)
GÜNTHER, K, *Der Sinn für Angemessenheit. Anwendungsdiskurse in Moral und Recht* (Frankfurt am Main, Suhrkamp, 1988)
——, 'Critical Remarks on Robert Alexy's "Special-Case Thesis"' (1993) 6 *Ratio Juris* 143
GUYER, P, *The Cambridge Companion to Kant and Modern Philosophy* (Cambridge, Cambridge University Press, 2006)
——, *Kant* (London and New York, Routledge, 2006)
HAAPARANTA, L and J HINTIKKA (eds), *Frege Synthesized*, Synthese Library, vol 181 (Dordrecht, Reidel, 1986)
HAGE, J, *Studies in Legal Logic* (Dordrecht, Springer, 2005)
HALE, B, *Abstract Objects*, Philosophical Theory Series (Oxford, Blackwell, 1987)
HALE, B and C WRIGHT (eds), *A Companion to the Philosophy of Language* (Oxford, Blackwell, 1999)

HABERMAS, J, 'Diskursethik – Notizen zu einem Begründungsprogramm' in *idem*, *Moralbewußtsein und kommukatives Handeln*, 5th edn (Frankfurt am Main, Suhrkamp, 1992)

____, *Faktizität und Geltung. Beiträge zur Diskurstheorie des Rechts und des demokratischen Rechtsstaats*, 2nd edn (Frankfurt am Main, Suhrkamp, 1992); and in English translation, *Between Facts and Norms* (Oxford, Polity Press, 1996)

____, *Moralbewußtsein und kommunikatives Handeln*, 5th edn (Frankfurt am Main, Suhrkamp, 1992); and in English translation by C Lenhardt and S Weber Nicholsen, 'Discourse Ethics: Notes on a Program of Philosophical Justification' in *idem*, *Moral Consciousness and Communicative Action* (Cambridge Mass, MIT Press, 1992)

____, *Truth and Justification* (Oxford, Polity, 2002)

HANNA, P and B HARRISON, *Word and World: Practice and the Foundations of Language* (Cambridge, Cambridge University Press, 2004)

HARE, R M, *The Language of Morals* (Oxford, Clarendon Press 1952)

___, *Freedom and Reason* (Oxford, Clarendon Press 1962)

HART, H L A, *Essays in Jurisprudence and Philosophy* (Oxford, Clarendon Press, 1983)

____, 'Jhering's Heaven of Concepts and Modern Analytical Jurisprudence' in *idem*, *Essays in Jurisprudence and Philosophy* (Oxford, Clarendon Press, 1983)

____, 'Positivism and the Separation of Law and Morals' in *Essays in Jurisprudence and Philosophy* (Oxford, Clarendon Press, 1983)

____, *The Concept of Law*, 2nd edn with a postscript edited by P A Bulloch and J Raz (Oxford, Clarendon Press, 1994)

HASLANGER, S, 'What Good are our Intuitions' (2006) LXXX *Aristotelian Society Supplementary Volume* 89

HEIDEMANN, C, *die Norm als Tatsache. Zur Normentheorie Hans Kelsens*, Studien zur Rechtsphilosophie und Rechtstheorie vol 13 (Baden-Baden, Nomos, 1997)

____, 'Hans Kelsen and the Transcendental Method' (2004) 55 *Northern Ireland Legal Quarterly* 358

HERSHOVITZ, S, 'Wittgenstein On Rules: The Phantom Menace' (2002) 22 *Oxford Journal of Legal Studies* 619

HONNETH, A *et al* (eds), *Zwischenbetrachtungen im Prozeß der Aufklärung* (Frankfurt am Main, Suhrkamp, 1989)

HOOKER, B and M LITTLE (eds), *Moral Particularism* (Oxford, Clarendon Press, 2000)

HORWICH, P, *Meaning* (Oxford, Clarendon Press, 1998)

HURLEY, S L, *Natural Reasons: Personality and Polity* (New York and Oxford, Oxford University Press, 1989)

____, *Consciousness in Action* (Cambridge Mass, Harvard University Press, 1998)

JABLONER, C and F STADLER (eds), *Logischer Empirismus und Reine Rechtslehre* (Wien and New York, Springer, 2001)
JACKSON, F, *From Metaphysics to Ethics* (Oxford, Clarendon Press, 1998)
____, *Mind, Method and Conditionals*, International Library of Philosophy (London, Routledge, 1998)
____, 'Epiphenomenal Qualia' in *idem, Mind, Method and Conditionals*, International Library of Philosophy (London, Routledge, 1998)
____, 'What Mary Didn't Know' in *idem, Mind, Method and Conditionals*, International Library of Philosophy (London, Routledge, 1998)
KANT, I, *Groundwork for the Metaphysics of Morals*, T E Hill Jr and A Zweig (ed) (Oxford, Oxford University Press, 2002)
KELSEN, H, *Reine Rechtslehre*, 2nd edn (Vienna, Franz Deuticke, 1960)
KERN, A, *Quellen des Wissens* (Frankfurt am Main, Suhrkamp, 2006)
KERSTEIN, S J, *Kant's Search for the Supreme Principle of Morality* (Cambridge, Cambridge University Press, 2002)
KIM, J, *Supervenience and Mind: Selected Philosophical Essays* (Cambridge, Cambridge University Press, 1993)
KLATT, M, *Theorie der Wortlautgrenze*, Studien zur Rechtsphilosophie und Rechtstheorie vol 38 (Baden Baden, Nomos, 2004)
KORSGAARD, C, *The Sources of Normativity*, O O'Neill (ed) (Cambridge, Cambridge University Press, 1996)
KREMER, M, 'Wilson on Kripke's Wittgenstein' (2000) 85 *Philosophy and Phenomenological Research* 571
KRIPKE, S, 'Naming and Necessity' in D Davidson and G Harman (eds), *Semantics of Natural Language*, 2nd edn (Dordrecht and Boston, D Reidel, 1972); published separately as *Naming and Necessity* (Oxford, Blackwell, 1980)
____, *Wittgenstein on Rules and Private Language* (Oxford, Blackwell, 1984)
LADEN, A S, 'Evaluating Social Reasons: Hobbes versus Hegel' (2005) 102 *Journal of Philosophy* 327
LAFONT, C, *The Linguistic Turn in Hermeneutic Philosophy* (Cambridge Mass, MIT, 1999)
____, 'Realismus und Konstruktivismus in der kantianischen Moralphilosophie – das Beispiel der Diskursethik' (2002) 50 *Deutsche Zeitschrift für Philosophie* 39
LANGTON, R, *Kantian Humility: Our Ignorance of Things in Themselves* (Oxford, Clarendon Press, 1998)
LEITER, B (ed), *The Future for Philosophy* (Oxford, Clarendon Press, 2004)
____, 'American Legal Realism' in M Golding and W Edmundson (eds), *The Blackwell Guide to the Philosophy of Law and Legal Theory* (Oxford, Blackwell, 2005)
LEITH P and J MORISON, 'Can Jurisprudence Without Empiricism Ever be a Science?' in S Coyle and G Pavlakos (eds), *Jurisprudence or Legal Science?* (Oxford and Portland, Hart Publishing, 2005)

LEPORE, E and B SMITH (eds), *The Oxford Handbook of Philosophy of Language* (Oxford, Clarendon Press, 2006)

LUNTLEY, M, *Contemporary Philosophy of Thought and Language* (Oxford, Blackwell, 1998)

MACCORMICK, N, *Legal Reasoning and Legal Theory* (Oxford, Clarendon Press, 1978)

____, *Rhetoric and the Rule of Law* (Oxford, Oxford University Press, 2006)

____, *Institutions of Law* (Oxford, Oxford University Press, 2007)

____, 'Why Law Makes No Claims' in G Pavlakos (ed), *Law, Rights and Discourse: The Legal Philosophy of Robert Alexy* (Oxford and Portland, Hart Publishing, 2007)

MACCORMICK, N D and O WEINBERGER, *An Institutional Theory of Law: New Approaches to Legal Positivism*, Law and Philosophy Library vol 3 (Dordrecht, Reidel, 1986)

MACKIE, J, *Ethics: Inventing Right and Wrong* (Harmondsworth, Penguin Books, 1990)

MARMOR, A, 'An Essay on the Objectivity of Law' in B Bix (ed), *Analysing Law: New Essays in Legal Theory* (Oxford, Clarendon Press, 1998)

____, *Interpretation and Legal Theory*, revised 2nd edn (Oxford and Portland, Hart Publishing, 2005)

MCCULLOCH, G, *The Mind and its World* (London, Routledge, 1995)

MCDOWELL, J, *Mind and World* (Cambridge Mass, Harvard University Press, 1994)

____, 'Meaning and Intentionality in Wittgenstein's Later Philosophy' in *idem, Mind, Value and Reality* (Cambridge, Mass, Harvard University Press, 1998)

____, *Mind, Value and Reality* (Cambridge, Mass, Harvard University Press, 1998)

____, 'Wittgenstein on Following a Rule', reprinted in A Miller and C Wright (eds), *Rule-Following and Meaning* (Chesham, Acumen, 2002)

MELLOR, D H, 'Natural Kinds' (1977) 28 *British Journal for the Philosophy of Science* 219

MILLER, A, and C Wright (eds), *Rule-Following and Meaning* (Chesham, Acumen, 2002)

MOORE, A W (ed), *Meaning and Reference* (Oxford, Oxford University Press, 1993)

MOORE, G E, *Principia Ethica*, revised edn (Cambridge, Cambridge University Press, 1993)

MOORE, M, *Educating Oneself in Public* (Oxford, Oxford University Press, 2000)

MURPHY, T, *Western Jurisprudence* (Dublin, Round Hall, 2004)

NEURATH, O, 'Protocol Sentences' in A J Ayer (ed), *Logical Positivism* (New York, Free Press, 1959)

NOZICK, R, *Invariances* (Cambridge Mass, Harvard University Press, 2001)

ODDIE, G, *Value, Reality and Desire* (Oxford, Clarendon Press, 2005)

PAULSON, S L, 'On Transcendental Arguments, their Recasting in Terms of Belief, and the Ensuing Transformation of Kelsen's Pure Theory of Law' (2000) 75 *Notre Dame Law Review* 1775

____, 'Zwei Wiener Welten und ein Anknüpfugspunkt' in C Jabloner and F Stadler (eds), *Logischer Empirismus und Reine Rechtslehre* (Wien and New York, Springer, 2001)

____, 'Faktum/Wert-Distinktion, Zwei-Welten-Lehre und immanenter Sinn. Hans Kelsen als Neukantianer' in R Alexy *et al* (eds), *Neukantianismus und Rechtsphilosophie* (Baden-Baden, Nomos Verlag, 2002)

____, 'Der Normativismus Hans Kelsens' (2006) 11 *Juristenzeitung* 529

PAVLAKOS, G, 'The Special Case Thesis: An Assessment of R. Alexy's Discursive Theory of Law' (1998) 12 *Ratio Juris* 126

____, 'Persons and Norms: On the Normative Groundwork of Discourse-Ethics' (1999) 85 *Archiv für Rechts und Sozial Philosophie* 7

________, 'Normativity versus Ontology: Law, Facts and Practical Reason' (2003) 34 *Rechtstheorie* 393

________, 'Law as Recognition: H L A Hart and Analytical Positivism' in T Murphy (ed), *Western Jurisprudence* (Dublin, Round Hall, 2004)

____, 'Normative Knowledge and the Nature of Law' in S Coyle and G Pavlakos (eds), *Jurisprudence or Legal Science?* (Oxford and Portland, Hart Publishing, 2005)

____, 'Two Conceptions of Universalisation' in Z Bankowski and J Maclean (eds), *The Universal and the Particular in Legal Reasoning* (Aldershot, Ashgate, 2006)

____ (ed), *Law, Rights and Discourse: The Legal Philosophy of Robert Alexy* (Oxford and Portland, Hart Publishing, 2007)

____, *Rechtsontologie und praktische Vernunft*, Studien zur Rechtsphilosophie und Rechtstheorie (Baden-Baden, Nomos, 2007)

PETTIT, P, *The Common Mind: An Essay in Psychology, Society and Politics*, 2nd edn (New York and Oxford, Oxford University Press, 1996)

PRESTON, J (ed), *Thought and Language* (Cambridge, Cambridge University Press, 1998)

PUTNAM, H, *Mind, Language and Reality*, Philosophical Papers vol 2, softcover edn (Cambridge, Cambridge University Press, 1979)

PUTNAM, H, 'The Meaning of "Meaning"' in *idem*, *Mind, Language and Reality*, Philosophical Papers vol 2, softcover edn (Cambridge, Cambridge University Press, 1979)

____, 'Meaning and Reference' reprinted in A W Moore (ed), *Meaning and Reference* (Oxford, Oxford University Press, 1993)

____, *Words and Life*, J Conant (ed) (Cambridge Mass, Harvard University Press, 1995)

QUINE, W V O, 'Speaking of Objects' in *idem*, *Ontological Relativity and Other Essays* (New York, Columbia University Press, 1977)

J RAZ, 'Dworkin: A New Link in the Chain' (1986) 74 *California Law Review* 1103

____, 'The Truth in Particularism' in B Hooker and M Little (eds), *Moral Particularism* (Oxford, Clarendon Press, 2000)

____, 'The Argument from Justice, or How not to Reply to Legal Positivism' in G Pavlakos (ed), *Law, Rights and Discourse: The Legal Philosophy of Robert Alexy* (Oxford and Portland, Hart Publishing, 2007)

RICKETTS, T, 'Objectivity and Objecthood: Frege's Metaphysics of Judgement' in L Haaparanta and J Hintikka (eds), *Frege Synthesized*, Synthese Library, vol 181 (Dordrecht, Reidel, 1986)

____, 'Logic and Truth in Frege' (1996) LXX *Aristotelian Society Supplementary Volume* 121

RODRIGUEZ-BLANCO, V, 'A Defence of Hart's Semantics as Nonambitious Conceptual Analysis' (2003) 9 *Legal Theory* 99

ROVERSI, C, 'Constitutionalism and Transcendental Arguments' (2008) 59 *Northern Ireland Legal Quarterly*, forthcoming

RUSSELL, B, *Our Knowledge of the External World* (London, Allen & Unwin, 1972)

SAINSBURY, R M, 'The Essence of Reference' in E Lepore and B Smith (eds), *The Oxford Handbook of Philosophy of Language* (Oxford, Clarendon Press, 2006)

SAVELLOS, E E and Ü D Yalçin (eds), *Supervenience: New Essays* (Cambridge, Cambridge University Press, 1995)

SCHIFFER, S, *The Things We Mean* (Oxford, Clarendon Press, 2003)

SELLARS, W, *Empiricism and the Philosophy of Mind* (Cambridge, Mass, Harvard University Press, 1997)

SHAFER-LANDAU, R, *Moral R*ealism (Oxford, Clarendon Press, 2003)

SKORUPSKI, J, 'Meaning, Use, Verification' in B Hale and C Wright (eds), *A Companion to the Philosophy of Language* (Oxford, Blackwell, 1999)

SOAMES, S, *Understanding Truth* (New York and Oxford, Oxford University Press, 1999)

SREENIVASAN, G, 'Interpretation and Reason' (1998) 27 *Philosophy and Public Affairs* 142

STAVROPOULOS, N, *Objectivity in Law* (Oxford, Clarendon Press, 1996)

____, 'Hart's Semantics' in J Coleman, *Hart's Postscript: Essays on the Postscript of the Concept of Law* (Oxford, Oxford University Press, 2001)

____, 'Interpretivist Theories of Law' in N Zalta (ed), *The Stanford Encyclopedia of Philosophy*, Winter 2003 edn, available at http://plato.stanford.edu/archives/win2003/entries/law-interpretivist/

____, 'Objectivity' in M Golding and W Edmundson (eds), *The Blackwell Guide to the Philosophy of Law and Legal Theory* (Oxford, Blackwell, 2005)

STELMACH, J and B BROZEK, *Methods of Legal Reasoning* (Berlin and New York, Springer, 2006)

STERN, R, *Transcendental Arguments and Scepticism* (Oxford, Clarendon Press, 2000)

STRAWSON, P F, *Individuals: an Essay in Descriptive Metaphysics* (London, Methuen, 1959)

____, *The Bounds of Sense: an Essay on Kant's Critique of Pure Reason* (London, Methuen, 1966)

____, *Scepticism and Naturalism* (London, Routledge, 1985)

STROUD, B, *Understanding Human Knowledge* (Oxford, Oxford University Press, 2000)

____, 'Transcendental Arguments' (1968) 65 *Journal of Philosophy* 241, reprinted in *idem, Understanding Human Knowledge* (Oxford, Oxford University Press, 2000)

TAMANAHA, B Z, *A General Jurisprudence of Law and Society* (Oxford, Oxford University Press, 2001)

TARSKI, A, 'The Semantic Conception of Truth and the Foundations of Semantics' repr. in S Blackburn and K Simmons (eds), *Truth* (Oxford, Oxford University Press, 1999) 115-143

TAYLOR, K, *Truth and Meaning* (Oxford, Blackwell, 1998)

TUGENDHAT, E, 'Überlegungen zur Methode der Philosophie aus analytischer Sicht' in A Honneth *et al* (eds), *Zwischenbetrachtungen im Prozeß der Aufklärung* (Frankfurt am Main, Suhrkamp, 1989)

TYE, M, *Consciousness, Colour, and Content* (Cambridge Mass, MIT Press, 2000)

VON MIES, R, *Positivism* (Cambridge Mass, Harvard University Press, 1951)

WALDRON, J, *The Dignity of Legislation* (Cambridge, Cambridge University Press, 1999)

WIKFORSS, Å M, 'Externalism and Incomplete Understanding' (2004) 54 *Philosophical Quarterly* 287

WILLIAMSON, T, 'Past the Linguistic Turn?' in B Leiter (ed), *The Future for Philosophy* (Oxford, Clarendon Press, 2004)

WILSON, B, *Wittgenstein's 'Philosophical Investigations'* (Edinburgh, Edinburgh University Press, 1998)

WILSON, G, 'Semantic Realism and Kripke's Wittgenstein' (1998) 83 *Philosophy and Phenomenological Research* 99

WITTGENSTEIN, L, *The Blue and Brown Books* (Oxford, Blackwell, 1974)

____, *On Certainty*, G E M Anscombe, G H v Wright and P Denis (eds) (Oxford, Blackwell, 1975)

____, *Philosophical Investigations*, E Anscombe (trans), 3rd rev edn (Oxford, Blackwell, 2001)

____, *Tractatus Logico-Philosophicus* (Frankfurt, Suhrkamp, 2003) and in English translation by D F Pears and B F McGuinness (London, Routledge and Kegan Paul, 1961)

WOOD, A W, 'The Supreme Principle of Morality' in P Guyer (ed), *The Cambridge Companion to Kant and Modern Philosophy* (Cambridge, Cambridge University Press, 2006)

WRIGHT, C, *Truth and Objectivity* (Cambridge Mass, Harvard University Press, 1992)

____, *Saving the Differences* (Cambridge Mass, Harvard University Press, 2003)

Index

www.ingramcontent.com/pod-product-compliance
Ingram Content Group UK Ltd.
Pitfield, Milton Keynes, MK11 3LW, UK
UKHW020832290926
15470UKWH00009B/1856/J

9 781841 135038